THE LIVING HISTORY OF PAKISTAN

Judges & Generals in Pakistan

Volume-II

by

INAM R SEHRI

CONTEMPORARY HISTORY IS NOT
THAT WHAT HAS BEEN HAPPENING AROUND?
IT IS THE STATEMENT OF FACTS
ABOUT WHAT THE PEOPLE
CONSIDERED SIGNIFICANT

Grosvenor House
Publishing Limited

This book is published by
P H P Grosvenor House Publishing Ltd
28-30 High Street, Guildford, Surrey, GU1 3EL.
www.grosvenorhousepublishing.co.uk

A CIP record for this book
is available from the British Library

[All page with usual statements ending with]

ISBN 978-1-78148-760-0

For

FATIMA
MAIRA
AND
DAAUD

My younger partners & friends

(.... A fresh source of inspiration for me)

Other Books from

INAM R SEHRI

KHUDKUSHI
(on Suicide) [in Urdu]   (1983)
{Details of historical perspective of 'Suicide' in various societies; &
investigation techniques differentiating in Murder & Suicides}

WARDI KAY ANDAR AADMI
(Man in uniform) [in Urdu]   (1984)
{Collection of short stories keeping a sensitive policeman in focus}

AURAT JARAIM KI DALDAL MEIN
(on Female Criminality) [in Urdu]   (1985)
{Describing various theories and cultural taboos concerning Female
Criminal Behaviour}

POLICE AWAM RABTAY
(on Police Public relationship) [in Urdu]   (1986)
{Essays describing importance of mutual relationships}

DEHSHAT GARDI
(on Terrorism) [in Urdu]   (1987)
{Various theories and essays differentiating between Freedom
Fighting & Terrorism in Middle Eastern perspective}

QATL
(on Murder) [in Urdu]   (1988)
{The first book written for Police students & Lawyers to explain
techniques of investigation of (difficult) Murder cases}

SERVICE POLICING IN PAKISTAN
[in English]   (1990)
{A dissertation type book on which basis the PM Benazir Bhutto, in
1990, had okayed the Commissionerate System of Policing in Pakistan.
Taking Karachi as the pilot project, later, it was levied for all major cities
and still going on as such}

SHADI

(on Marriages) [in Urdu]   (1998)

{A detailed exposition of Marriage explained in various religions, cultures, countries and special groups; much applauded & commented upon on PTV in 1998-99}

All the above books were published by Pakistan's number one publisher

SANG E MEEL PUBLICATIONS,
25 - The Lower Mall LAHORE, Pakistan

And are normally available with them in latest re-prints.

Judges & Generals in Pakistan VOL-1

[in English]   (Jan 2012)

{Collection of essays mostly published; dealing with Pakistan's chequered history of army rule and higher judiciary's gimmicks during 1971 to 1999; the military & judiciary's nexus made the politicians more corrupt.}

Published by

**Grosvenor House Publishing Ltd
28-30 High Street, Guildford
SURREY UK GU1 3HY**

It's me; my Lord!

INAM R SEHRI

- Born in Lyallpur (Pakistan) in April 1948

- First Degree from Government College Lyallpur (1969)

- Studied at Government College Lahore & got first Master's Degree from Punjab University Lahore (1971);

- Attachment with AJK Education Service (1973-1976)

- Central Superior Services (CSS) Exam passed (batch 1975)

- Civil Service Academy Lahore (joined 1976)

- National Police Academy Islamabad (joined 1977)

- LLB from BUZ University Multan (1981)

- Master's Degree from Exeter University of UK (1990)

- Regular Police Service: District Admin, Police College, National Police Academy, the Intelligence Bureau (IB), Federal Investigation Agency (FIA) [1977-1998] then migrated to the UK permanently.

A part-script copied from the earlier volumes:

Just spent a normal routine life; with hundreds of mentionable memoirs allegedly of bravery & glamour as every uniformed officer keeps, some times to smile at and next moment to repent upon but taking it just normal except one or two spills.

During my tenure at IB HQ Islamabad I got chance to peep into the elite civil and military leadership of Pakistan [then] existing in governmental dossiers and database.

During my stay at FIA I was assigned to conduct special enquiries & investigations into some acutely sensitive matters like Motorway Scandal, sudden expansion and build-up of Sharif family's industrial empire, Sharif's accounts in foreign countries; Alleged Financial Corruptions in Pakistan's Embassies in Far-Eastern Countries; Shahnawaz Bhutto's murder in Cannes (France); Land Scandals of CDA's Estate Directorate; Ittefaq Foundry's 'custom duty on scrap' scam, Hudaibya Engineering & Hudaibya Paper Mills enquiries, Bhindara's Murree Brewery and tens more cases like that.

[Through these words I want to keep it on record that during the course of the above mentioned, (and also which cannot be mentioned due to space limits) investigations or enquiries, the then Prime Minister Benazir Bhutto, or [late] Gen Naseerullah Babar the then Federal Interior Minister, had never ever issued direct instructions or implicit directions or wished me to distort facts or to go malafide for orchestrating a political edge or other intangible gains or hidden benefits.]

Hats off to both of them!

I should feel proud that veracity and truthfulness of none of my enquiry or investigation could be challenged or proved false in NAB or Special Courts; yes, most of them were used to avail political compromises by Gen Musharraf's government.

That's enough, my dear countrymen.

Contents

My Apologies Again:

This volume-II points towards more facts of unlawful compromises and concessions unmasking the actual faces of Pakistani rulers.

Some people are living in that part of the world called Pakistan:

- Where the ruling political party {the PPP} does not opt to complete investigation concerning Ms Benazir Bhutto who was murdered three (3) years earlier but takes pride in reopening of the case of Mr Bhutto who was (judicially) murdered thirty (30) years ago. [*See the Reference no: 1 of 2011 of the SC*]

- Where a sitting prime minister {Mr Gilani} appeared in person before the SC [in January 2012] in contempt of court charges and shown respect for the apex court but his Parliament never explored the possibility of re-considering those laws under which certain military officers could be taken through due process in courts who were guilty of keeping the Chief Justice and seven judges of the SC in 'illegal confinement' [in Nov 2007] for days & weeks.

- Where 103 journalists were killed in 2011; 44 in 2010 and 110 were slaughtered in 2009, making it the 4th dangerous country in the world to work for the media. Not even a single case worked out yet. [*Referred to Vienna-based press watchdog IPI's press briefing dated 5th January 2012*]

- Where the ISI & MI admitted before the SC that four out of eleven prisoners they had taken out from Adiala Jail for interrogation had died in their custody; five were in hospital. Then what; in Pakistan even SC cannot take action against any army officer in any context. [*Referred to SC proceedings dated 30th January 2012*]

- Where a Federal Minister raises demand in a press conference that '*all groups: Sindhi, Pakhtun, Baloch, Seraiki and Punjabi, should get an equal share in corruption.*' [Referring to Abdul Qayyum Jatoi's press conference in Quetta on 26th September 2010]

- Where more than one third of cabinet ministers pay no taxes whatsoever and that Prime Minister Gillani had not paid tax for any of the three years covered by the disclosure. [*Referring to GEO TV dated 27th September 2010*]

It had continuously been debated through the whole decade that whether the 'War on Terror' propelled into the South Asian region after 9/11 was of America or Pakistan's own. Long ago, the question had lost its utility. When the fire engines are busy in showering fountains over the burning fields, no body ponders that which non-smoker was having lighter in his pocket. This question is always left for insurers to dig out but till then everything goes in ashes. In Pakistan, nothing is insured; neither the people, nor their future, nor their dreams, nor the governance patterns and not even the governments in succession.

Referring to the daily *'Jang' of 27th May 2009* [Dr Shahid's opinion]:

'The last decade of battles & wars spread over the territories of Iraq, Lebanon, Palestine and Afghanistan had made it clear that to start a war you may not need permission from any but to win the same you definitely need assistance of all.'

True, the peace palaces cannot be built on foundations and drenches which are filled with skulls and bones; not at all. It also questions a common perception that *'is the majority always right; not at all'.*

We are all intellectually dishonest [purposefully word 'corrupt' is avoided], probably the whole crowd of 187 million. Only one person is needed, one more Qaid e Azam, one Ahmedi Nejad like of Iran, one Mohatir Mohammad like of Malaysia.

Lt Gen K M Arif once himself narrated Pakistan's 'glorious past': the Chief Justice of Pakistan Anwarul Haq was attending a state dinner when Sharifuddin Pirzada [then military government's lawyer to contest the validity of Martial Law of July 1977] conveyed him a message of Gen Ziaul Haq. The CJP left the dinner in between, reached home and made changes under his own hand in the typed manuscript of the judgment to be announced next day; the CJP had allowed Gen Ziaul Haq to make changes in the Pakistan's Constitution of 1973 *(PLD 1977 SC 639)*.

By virtue of that judgment, the General made major amendments in the 1973 Constitution *interalia* to oust the jurisdiction of the superior courts to review the orders passed by the Martial Law authorities and to remove 'honourable justices' who were not acceptable to the 'establishment'. The judiciary had cut its own hands with the CJP's 'sharp edged' judgment.

Similar nice treat was given to the next military monarch in year 2000 by another CJP Irshad Hasan Khan who had not only once more validated the military coup but also allowed Gen Musharraf to avail another three years in his office as ruler & dictator; a relief which was not even prayed from the court.

In *ARY's live TV program of 30th January 2012,* Hassan Nisar had rightly pointed out that Pakistan is being governed by mafias since its birth [forget mafias of Italy and Sicily which only deal in drugs]. It started from PM Liaqat Ali Khan's announcement that *'if you are not in possession of your degree, never mind; give an affidavit, the government would believe you.'* Result was that the librarians of undivided India got Vice Chancellor's slots in universities of newly born Pakistan.

Consider it further; then 'Claim Mafia' surfaced; the tenants and sharecroppers claimed lands in thousands of acres; the labourers claimed factories & mills. Then 'Syed Mafia' cropped up; once there were more *Syeds & Shah jees* in Pakistan than the whole population of Saudi Arabia from where they originated.

During Gen Ayub Khan's rule, an 'industrialist mafia' was purposefully sponsored and backed by the government which had only 22 families as members virtually controlling 85% of the whole Pakistan's wealth. Zulfikar Ali Bhutto developed his own 'jiala mafia'; creating Iftikhar Taris and Manzoor Mohals like parliamentarians who used to enter the DC's offices by banging their doors with their foot-kicks. Gen Ziaul Haq gave birth to 'Kalashnikov & drug mafia' which had joined hands with *Mujahideens* to betray the police and courts but contrarily introduced 'Akhtar Brother's Dynasty of industrialists' to the nation.

The next decade was of 'politician mafias' of Sharifs and Zardaris under the banners of PML and PPP which befooled their innocent public turn by turn by building up their foreign accounts in Dubai, London and Geneva and expanding their industrial and real estate empires un-proportionately. Under their auspices, small mafias continued to prosper but remained subservient to their political bosses at all times.

In metropolises, especially in Islamabad, Lahore and Karachi, land & *Qabza* (occupation by force) mafias, *bhatta* (cash money extortions) mafias, *chanda* (donations) mafias; sugar and textile quota mafias (nexus between high stake hoarding politicians) and Bank Loan Eaters are operating since three decades. In all these fields the ruling regimes issue SROs, circulars and notifications to favour their party members to provide them extra financial gains and legal protections. *Above all there exists a 'target killer mafia' to serve all the above groups to provide 'an adequate answer' if someone questions their authority.*

The last decade was of 'Chaudhrys & [some] Generals' in which era the mafias of two newly elite allegedly brewed maximum advantage from Gen Musharraf's lust to remain in power. Elahis and Hussains were comparatively new in the field and in-experienced so were un-necessarily dragged in mud by the 'links & ties' of Sharifs & some judges in the name of 'independent judiciary'; ultimately forced to join the PPP to save their skins.

Since about three decades, the parliamentarians, both at provincial and federal level, are mostly related with mafias mentioned in above paragraphs, generously termed as 'elite classes'. One needs quarter a million Pounds to buy major party's ticket for provincial assembly; about half a million Pounds to have major party's ticket for National Assembly and a million pounds are needed for a Senate seat; but all feel pleasure to 'invest' [in the name of 'party fund'] for their bright future.

After general elections, when Z A Bhutto's dubious National Assembly met in Islamabad on 28th March 1977, only the PPP members had shown up. He offered to enter into a dialogue with the opposition thinking that it would settle for increased representation in the Assembly's session but miserably failed. Afterwards Mr Bhutto declared a national emergency and used *'Defence of Pakistan Rules'* under which all the opposition leaders were arrested. He called for his political opponents to negotiate a solution but they did not trust Bhutto and the demonstrations continued throughout April till June [1977].

Tired of the strikes and agitations, once Mr Bhutto called an emergency meeting, where Gen Ziaul Haq and Gen F A Chishti were also present amongst other key persons, and said: *'Gentlemen, I've decided to resign; brother Ziaul Haq would take over.'*

In the meeting, Gen Chishti had the courage to say: *'Sir, I'm personally your humble servant but cannot guarantee the behaviour of jawans who believe that the elections were vastly rigged.'*

But Gen Ziaul Haq stood up with his right hand on the left part of his chest, little bowed down and said that *'Sir, Army is with you; you are Fakhr e Asia, have been the Chairman Islamic Summit Conference; you will not resign whatsoever.'*

The irony of fate: Mr Bhutto was confident that with the allegiance of the Army under Gen Ziaul Haq he would be able to control the situation, but he could not. The result was that, after the military coup of 5th July 1977, Mr Bhutto was first sent to jails and then to gallows. Pakistan's stalwart PM of today, Syed Yousaf Raza Gilani, was the right hand man of Gen Ziaul Haq then.

Referring to *pages 245-246 of Qayyum Nizami's book* [*Jo Dekha; Jo Suna*]: a veteran columnist, late Irshad Haqqani was once called by Malik Meraj Khalid, Prime Minister in the interim government of 1996 and told him while on the breakfast table that the then CJP Sajjad Ali Shah had met him [the interim PM] and told: *'most of the judges on the SC bench hearing Benazir Bhutto's petition were holding opinion of re-instating her government back in line with Justice Nasim Hassan Shah's judgment in Nawaz Sharif's case of 1993.'*

President Farooq Leghari had also got air of that development. Mr Leghari had also known about one Kh Tariq Rahim who had tried to convince the judges that the army wanted BB's re-instatement. Due to Leghari's timely handling, the 'agencies' had conveniently managed to convey to the judges of the bench that *'the army is not interested in the come back of Ms Bhutto.'* Democracy was upheld again.

One can imagine the bravery of our superior judiciary that even in the 'top democratic era' of 1990s, the judges were always found ready to play at the tunes of their army counterparts and the agencies were playing the 'ruling games' at their whims and wishes.

Since the last coup in 1999 the military has lost a lot of power and influence inside Pakistan. The Internet, and more media outlets in Pakistan, has made it impossible for a government to control the news. Evil acts of some short sighted officers in the ISI or the military now get publicized immediately resulting in much reduced popular support for military coups. More and more journalism is coming from unidentified amateurs. The warrior groups and the military both resorted to raise their death squads hunting down journalists who were seen as 'unhelpful'.

A total 103 journalists were killed in 2011, with Mexico as the most dangerous and Pakistan as fourth dangerous place to work for the media; Vienna-based press watchdog IPI told on 5th January 2012. This was the second highest toll on record after 2009, when 110 journalists were killed. Cases of Wali Khan Babar and Saleem Shahzad went hot in media; although no cogent results but intelligence agencies went naked in public. Alarming to note was that 55 journalists were killed in 2001.

Coming back:

Again submitted; these are mostly my published articles and live TV discussions, so chapters may not be inter-related. Each chapter is a different scenario.

Judges & Generals in Pakistan' is a collection of essays, may be irritating for some; explaining diverse scenarios. This book evaluates some varying news, editorials, opinions and criticisms on historical issues.

No misleading intelligence story, no distracting investigative report, no concocted interview and no feed from the 'concerned ones' yet everything seems innovative; no fiction in this book but simple narration of facts.

> *'It is the collection of tragedies and misgivings which are deliberately buried in suspicious darkness since decades. I've simply dig them out, collated and placed together for those who want to keep a track of their past.'*

I want to end this chapter of apologies with a special note of thanks for Umezahra for all material assistance concerning language and references.

(Inam R Sehri)
Manchester UK
March 2012

Scenario 32

HISTORY OF JUDICIAL PAKISTAN:

Draconian 'Doctrine of Necessity'

Earlier history of Pakistan's Judiciary, as owned by the Supreme Court of Pakistan itself through one of its judgments made in 2002, gives an interesting account of intrigues amongst the then state institutions.

From 1947 till 1954 the Constituent Assembly, which was also the legislature of the country, failed to give a Constitution to the nation. Nothing was done beyond the passing of the Objectives Resolution by it. Failure to give a Constitution to the nation coupled with in-palace intrigues and the musical chair game for power and with a view to having absolute powers Governor General Ghulam Muhammad dissolved the Constituent Assembly. This act of the Governor General was challenged by Moulvi Tamizuddin Khan, President of the Assembly, in the Chief Court of Sindh.

The Sindh Chief Court allowed the petition and declared the dissolution of the Assembly as illegal. The judgment of the Sindh Chief Court was challenged in the Federal Court and by virtue of the judgment reported as *Federation of Pakistan* v. *Moulvi Tamizudding Khan* (**PLD 1955 FC 240**), the Federal Court reversed the judgment of the Sindh Chief Court and held that assent of the Governor General was necessary to all the laws and the amendments made in the Government of India Act 1935, which was the interim Constitution. According to the Court, section 223-A conferring power on the High Courts to issue writs had not received assent of the Governor General and the Chief Court could not have issued writ holding the act of the Governor General as invalid.

Therefore, by means of the Emergency Powers Ordinance 1955 (Ordinance No: IX of 1955) issued under section 42 of the Government of India Act 1935 the Governor General sought to validate such Acts by indicating his assent with retrospective operation. The Federal Court in *Usif Patel's case* (**PLD 1955 FC 387**), however, declared that the Acts mentioned in the Schedule to the aforesaid Ordinance could not be validated under Section 42 of the Government of India Act 1935, nor could retrospective effect be given to them.

A noteworthy fact was that the Constituent Assembly had ceased to function, having been already dissolved by the Governor General by a

Proclamation on 24th October 1954 and no Legislature competent to validate these Acts was in existence.

The Governor General made a Reference to the Federal Court under section 213 of the Government of India Act 1935 asking for the Court's opinion on the question whether there was any provision in the Constitution or any rule of law applicable to the situation by which the Governor General could, by order or otherwise, declare that all orders made, decisions taken, and other acts done under those laws, should be valid and enforceable and those laws, which could not without danger to the State be removed from the existing legal system, should be treated as part of the law of the land until the question of their validation was determined by the new Constituent Convention.

The answer returned by majority judges of the Federal Court to the *Reference by The Governor General* (**PLD 1955 FC 435**) was that '*in the situation presented by the Reference, the Governor General has, during the interim period, the power under the common law of civil or state necessity of retrospectively validating the laws listed in the Schedule to the Emergency Powers Ordinance 1955*'. The Constituent Assembly, reconstituted as per the guidelines given by the Federal Court, with great efforts and pains, framed the 1956 Constitution wherein Pakistan was declared an Islamic Republic.

Unfortunately, the political stability could not be achieved and frequent changes of the government, apathy on the part of the legislators to the problems of the country, killing of the Deputy Speaker of the East Pakistan Assembly, beating up of the Speaker and desecration of national flag in Dacca led to the abrogation of the 1956 Constitution and imposition of first Martial Law in the country in October 1958.

The central and provincial governments were dismissed, the national and provincial assemblies were dissolved, the political parties were abolished and Gen Muhammad Ayub Khan, the Commander-in-Chief of the Army, took reigns of the country as the Chief Martial Law Administrator, who later became the Field Marshal. It was declared that a Constitution more suitable to the genius of the Muslim people would be devised.

On 10th October 1958, President Iskandar Mirza promulgated the Laws (Continuance in Force) Order 1958 wherein it was, interalia, provided that notwithstanding the abrogation of the Constitution, Pakistan shall be governed, as nearly as may be, in accordance with the 1956 Constitution, all Courts in existence immediately before the Proclamation shall continue in being, the law declared by the Supreme Court shall be binding on all Courts in Pakistan, the Supreme Court and the High Courts shall have power to issue the writs of *habeas corpus, mandamus, prohibition, quo warranto* and *certiorari*, etc.

Under Clause (7) of Article 2 of the Laws (Continuance in Force) Order 1958, all writ petitions pending in the High Courts seeking enforcement of Fundamental Rights stood abated. Interpretation of the said clause [no: (7) of Article 2] was debated in the Supreme Court and in the famous case reported as *State v. Dosso* (**PLD 1958 SC 533**) the Supreme Court held that if the Constitution was destroyed by a successful revolution, the validity of the prevalent laws depended upon the will of the new law-creating organ. Therefore, if the new legal order preserved any one or more laws of the old legal order, then a writ would lie for violation.

As regards pending applications for writs or writs already issued but which were either *subjudice* before the Supreme Court or required enforcement, the Court in the light of the Laws (Continuance in Force) Order 1958 held that no writ or order for a writ issued or made after the Proclamation shall have any legal effect unless the writ was issued on the ground that any one or more of the laws mentioned in Article 4 or any other right kept alive by the new order had been contravened.

To sum up, the Supreme Court, on the basis of the theory propounded by Hans Kelsen, accorded legitimacy to the assumption of power by Gen Muhammad Ayub Khan holding that *coup d'etat* was a legitimate means to bring about change in the government and particularly so when the new order brought about by the change was accepted by the people.

In 1959 the Basic Democracies Order was promulgated and 40,000 basic democrats from each province, i.e. the West Pakistan and the East Pakistan were elected, who formed the Electoral College for election to the office of the President. Gen M Ayub Khan sought referendum and more than 94-95 percent of the basic democrats voted in his favour and thus he assumed the office of the President of Pakistan. The basic democrats were then entrusted with the task of electing national and provincial assemblies ultimately leading to the framing and promulgation of the 1962 Constitution.

War between India and Pakistan in 1965, the Tashkent Declaration of 1966, dissatisfaction over the tremendous Presidential powers as against the helplessness of the National Assembly and screams and shouts for restoration of the Parliamentary system in which the Government was controlled by the Legislature and answerable to it, gave rise to agitations by the political leaders in both wings of the country. As a result, Field

Marshal Ayub Khan had to descend from power. However, instead of transferring power to the Speaker of the National Assembly in accordance with the 1962 Constitution, he called upon Gen Agha Yahya Khan to take control of the affairs of the country that abrogated the said constitution and another phase of military rule commenced in Pakistan.

Gen Yahya Khan dissolved the National and the Provincial Assemblies, imposed Martial law and promulgated Legal Framework Order 1970. In addition thereto one unit in the West Pakistan was dissolved, the old four provinces were restored and general election to the Constituent Assembly / National Assembly under the Legal Framework Order was announced and held in 1970.

Unfortunately, the members returned to the Assemblies could not see eye to eye with each other and no compromise formula could be arrived at. The Awami League led by Sh Mujeebur Rehman was the majority party in the East Pakistan while the Pakistan Peoples Party (PPP), led by Mr Zulfiqar Ali Bhutto, was the majority party in two provinces namely Punjab and Sindh. The session of the Assembly, which had to take place immediately after elections, was postponed, dragged up to March 1971 to be held at Dacca which never assumed.

The Awami League of the East Pakistan led by Sh Mujeebur Rehman had returned with a thumping majority on the basis of 6-point political programme announced by it. The postponement of the Assembly session infuriated the Awami League and the public in East Pakistan and thus a revolt took place there. To cut the long story short, ultimately the separation movement in the East Pakistan succeeded and that province became Bangladesh; a separate independent country. In the remaining Pakistan, Zulfiqar Ali Bhutto of PPP, the leader of the majority party in two provinces, became the President of Pakistan and the CMLA on the eve of transfer of power to him by Gen Yahya Khan.

1973's CONSTITUTION HELD IN ABEYANCE:

The Interim constitution of 1972 was promulgated and then by consensus of all, the 1973 Constitution was framed which came into force on 14th August 1973. Zulfiqar Ali Bhutto became the Prime Minister under the said Constitution. However, the country could not be brought on path of development and in 1977 elections were announced which was allegedly rigged leading to countrywide agitation against the PPP; the Pakistan Army intervened and Martial law was imposed by Gen Ziaul Haq on 5th July 1977.

The Constitution was not abrogated but was put in abeyance and the National as well as the Provincial Assemblies were dissolved. After the general elections of 1985, which was held on non-party basis, Gen Ziaul Haq nominated Muhammad Khan Junejo as the Prime Minister of Pakistan. A row between the two erupted and continued to prosper. However, ultimately the National and Provincial Assemblies were dissolved on 29th May 1988 by Gen Ziaul Haq.

Gen Ziaul Haq had publicly announced that the next elections would also be held on non-party basis. Before Gen Ziaul Haq could do so, he died in an air crash on 17th August 1988 at Bahawalpur and Ghulam Ishaq Khan, Chairman of the Senate became the President of Pakistan who announced that elections would be held in November 1988.

In the meantime, Benazir Bhutto filed a petition in the Supreme Court praying that the soul of parliamentary democracy, which was the hallmark of the 1973 Constitution, required that the election be held on party basis. The apex Court allowed the said petition through the judgment reported as *Benazir Bhutto's case* (**PLD 1988 SC 416**) and it was directed that the elections would be held on party basis.

The elections were held on party basis and Benazir Bhutto formed the government at the centre and two Provinces [Sindh and NWFP] while Pakistan Muslim League (PML) which was the rival political party, formed government in the Punjab with Nawaz Sharif as the Chief Minister. Simultaneously, an unfortunate period of confrontation between the two rival parties and their leaders started. The two leaders were at daggers drawn with each other, the history witnessed.

Hardly any tolerance was shown and instead of solving the problems of the country and the people they were trying to malign and humiliate each other. Attempts for vote of no confidence in the centre against Benazir Bhutto were made in ending 1989. The members of the National Assembly of both the factions were taken to different places by the leaders, kept them hidden under duress and a new era of *'lotacracy'* started in the history of Pakistan. The stories of corruption, mal-administration, nepotism, favouritism, etc were rampant both in the Punjab and at Federation level.

PARLIAMENT DISSOLVED IN 1990:

In this background, on 6th August 1990 Ghulam Ishaq Khan under Article 58(2)(b) of the Constitution dissolved the National and the Provincial Assemblies on the following grounds:

'The President having considered the situation in the country, the events that have taken place and the circumstances, and among others for the reasons mentioned below is of the opinion that the Government of the Federation cannot be carried on in accordance with the provisions of the Constitution and an appeal to the electorate is necessary:-

(a) The utility and efficacy of the National Assembly as a representative institution elected by the people under the Constitution, and its mandate, is defeated by internal dissensions and frictions persistent and scandalous 'horse-trading' for political gain and furtherance of personal interests, corrupt practices and inducement, in contravention of the Constitution and the law, and by failure to discharge substantive legislative functions other than the adoption of the Finance Bill, and further the National Assembly have lost the confidence of the people.

(b) The Constitution envisages the Federation and the Provinces working within the spheres respectively assigned to them with clearly delineated executive and legislative authority, and with a view to safeguarding the structure of the Federation also contains special provisions of mandatory nature to ensure and protect the authority granted to provinces, by creating the specific constitutional institutions consisting of Federal and Provincial representatives, but the Government of the Federation has wilfully undermined and impaired the working of the constitutional arrangements and usurped the authority of the Provinces and of such institutions, resulting in discord, confrontation and deadlock, adversely affecting the integrity, solidarity and well-being of Pakistan, in that, *interalia*:

(i) The Council of Common Interests under Article 153, which is responsible only to Parliament, has not been allowed to discharge its Constitutional functions and exercise its powers despite persistent demands of the Provinces, and Parliament has also not been allowed to function in this regard as required by Articles 153 and 154, and in relation to Articles 155 and 161.

(ii) The National Finance Commission under Article 160 has never been called to meet and allowed to function, thus blocking mandatory constitutional process in the matter of allocation of shares of revenues to the Provinces despite their persistent demands.

(iii) Constitutional powers and functions of the Provinces have been deliberately frustrated and extension of executive authority of the

Federation to the Provinces in violation of Art 97 and by manner of implementation of the Peoples' Program.

(iv) The Senate, which is representative of the Federating Units under Article 59 and is an integral part of Parliament, has been ridiculed and its Constitutional role eroded.'

Next general elections were held in November 1990 and at that point of time, an alliance of certain political parties known as *Islami Jamhuri Ittehad* (IJI) was formed which won the majority seats and Pakistan Muslim League (PML) formed the government headed by Nawaz Sharif and the PPP went in opposition. Personal hostility between the leaders of the two factions continued as before.

PARLIAMENT DISSOLVED AGAIN IN 1993:

On account of this acute confrontation, absence of attempt on the part of the leaders to arrive at a consensus and to solve the problems of the country, failure to improve the quality of human life and the deteriorating economy of the country again led President GIK to dissolve the National Assembly in April 1993. In the dissolution order, the President gave the following grounds:

'The President having considered the situation in the country, the events that have taken place and the circumstances, the contents and consequences of the Prime Minster's speech on 17th April 1993 and among others for the reasons mentioned below is of the opinion that the Government of the Federation cannot be carried on in accordance with the provisions of the constitution and an appeal to the electorate is necessary: -

(a) The mass resignation of the members of the Opposition and of considerable number from the Treasury Benches, including several Ministers, *interalia*, showing their desire to seek fresh mandate from the people have resulted in the Government of the Federation and the National Assembly losing confidence of the people; that the dissent therein, has nullified its mandate.

(b) The Prime Minster held meetings with the President in March and April and the last on 14th April 1993 when the President urged him to take positive steps to resolve the grave internal and international problems confronting the country and the nation was anxiously looking forward to the announcement of concrete measures by the Government to improve the situation.

Instead, the Prime Minster in his speech on 17th April 1993 chose to divert the people's attention by making false and malicious allegations against the President of Pakistan who is Head of State and represents the unity of the Republic.

The tenor of the speech was that the Government could not be carried on in accordance with the provisions of the Constitution and he advanced his own reasons and theory for the same which reasons and theory, in fact, are unwarranted and misleading. The Prime Minister tried to cover up the failures and defaults of the Government although he was repeatedly apprised of the real reasons in this behalf, which he even accepted and agreed to rectify by specific measures on urgent basis.

Further, the Prime Minster's speech is tantamount to a call for agitation and in any case the speech and his conduct amounts to subversions of the Constitution.

(c) Under the Constitution the Federation and the Provinces are required to exercise their executive and legislative authority as demarcated and defined and there are specific provisions and institutions to ensure its working in the interests of the integrity, sovereignty, solidarity and well-being of the Federation and to protect the autonomy granted to the Provinces by creating specific Constitutional institutions consisting of Federal and Provincial representatives, but the Government of the Federation has failed to uphold and protect these, as required, *interalia*:

　(i) The Council of Common Interests under Articles 153 which is responsible only to Parliament has not discharged its Constitutional functions to exercise its powers as required by Articles 153 and 154, and in relation to Articles 161, and particularly in the context of privatization of industries in relation to item 3 of Part II of the Federal Legislative List and item 34 of the Concurrent Legislative List.

　(ii) The National Economic Council under Article 156, and its Executive Committee, has been largely bypassed in the formulation of plans in respect of financial, commercial, social and economic policies.

　(iii) Constitutional powers, rights and functions of the Provinces have been usurped, frustrated and interfered with in violation of Article 97.

(d) Mal-administration, corruption and nepotism have reached such proportions in the Federal Government, its various bodies, authorities and other corporations including banks supervised and controlled by the Federal

Government, the lack of transparency in the process of privatization and in the disposal of public properties, that they violate the requirements of the Oath(s) of the Public representative together with the Prime Minister, the Federal Ministers and Ministers of State prescribed in the Constitution and prevent the Government from functioning in accordance with the provisions of the Constitution.

(e) The functionaries, authorities and agencies of the Government under the direction, control, collaboration and patronage of the Prime Minster and Ministers have unleashed a reign of terror against the opponents of the Government including political and personal rivals & relatives, and media-men, thus creating a situation wherein the Government cannot be carried on in accordance with the provisions of the Constitution and the law.

(f) In violation of the provisions of the Constitution:

(i) The Cabinet has not been taken into confidence or decided upon numerous Ordinances and matters of policy.

(ii) Federal Ministers have, for a period, been called upon not to see the President.

(iii) Resources and agencies of the Government of the Federation, including statutory corporations, authorities and banks, have been misused for political ends and purposes and for personal gain.

(iv) There has been massive wastage and dissipation of public funds and assets at the cost of the national exchequer without legal or valid justification resulting in increased deficit financing and indebtedness, both domestic and international, and adversely affecting the national interest including defence.

(v) Articles 240 and 242 have been disregarded in respect of the Civil Services of Pakistan.

(g) The serious allegations made by Begum Nuzhat Asif Nawaz as to the high-handed treatment meted out to her husband, the late Army Chief of Staff, and the further allegations as to the circumstances culminating in his death indicate that the highest functionaries of the Federal Government have been subverting the authority of the Armed Forces and the machinery of the Government and the Constitution itself.

(h) The Government of the Federation for the above reasons, *interalia*, is not in a position to meet properly and positively the threat to the security and integrity of Pakistan and the grave economic situation confronting the country, necessitating the requirement of a fresh mandate from the people of Pakistan.'

Although the Supreme Court in the judgment reported as *Mian Nawaz Sharif's case* (**PLD 1993 SC 473**) restored the Assembly but the system did not work and the Prime Minister had to advise dissolution of the Assemblies.

BENAZIR BHUTTO SENT HOME AGAIN 1996:

Thereafter the government of Benazir Bhutto formed as a result of the 1993 election; but was dismissed by the then President Farooq Ahmed Leghari in November 1996 on the following grounds: -

• "And whereas on 20th September 1996 Mir Murtaza Bhutto, the brother of the Prime Minister, was killed at Karachi along with seven of his companions including the brother-in-law of a former Prime Minister, ostensibly in an encounter with the Karachi Police.

The Prime Minister and her Government claim that Mir Mutaza Bhutto has been murdered as a part of conspiracy. Within days of Mir Murtaza Bhutto's death the Prime Minister appeared on television insinuating that the Presidency and other agencies of State were involved in this conspiracy.

These malicious insinuations, which were repeated on different occasions, were made without any factual basis whatsoever. Although the Prime Minister subsequently denied that the Presidency or the Armed Forces were involved, the institution of the Presidency, which represents the unity of the republic, was undermined and damage caused to the reputation of the agencies entrusted with the sacred duty of defending Pakistan.

In the events that have followed, the widow of Mir Murtaza Bhutto and the friends and supporters of the deceased have accused Ministers of the Government, including the spouse of the Prime Minister [Mr Asif Ali Zardari], the Chief Minister of Sindh, the Director of the Intelligence Bureau and other high officials of involvement in the conspiracy which, the Prime Minister herself alleged led to Murtaza Bhutto's murder.

A situation has thus arisen in which justice, which is a fundamental requirement of our Islamic Society, cannot be ensured because powerful members of the Federal and Provincial Government who are themselves accused of the crime, influence and control the law-enforcing agencies entrusted with the duty of investigating the offences and brining to book the conspirators.

- And whereas, on 20th March 1996, the Supreme Court of Pakistan delivered its judgment in popularly known as the *'Appointment of Judges Case'*; the Prime Minister ridiculed this judgment in a speech before the National Assembly, which was shown more than once on nationwide television. The implementation of the judgment was resisted and deliberately delayed in violation of the Constitutional mandate that all executive and judicial authorities throughout Pakistan shall act in aid of the Supreme Court.

The directions of the Supreme Court with regard to regularization and removal of Judges of the High Courts were finally implemented on 30th September 1996 with a deliberate delay of six months and ten days and only after the President informed the Prime Minister that if advice was not submitted in accordance with the judgment by end (of) September 1996 then the President would himself proceed further in this matter to fulfil the Constitutional requirements.

The Government has, in this manner, not only violated Article 190 of the Constitution but also sought to undermine the independence of the judiciary guaranteed by Article 2A of the Constitution read with the Objectives Resolution. And whereas the sustained assault on the judicial organ of State has continued under the garb of a Bill moved in Parliament for prevention of corrupt practices. This Bill was approved by the Cabinet and introduced in the National Assembly without informing the President as required under Article 46(c) of the Constitution.

The said Bill proposes that on a motion moved by fifteen per cent of the total membership of the National Assembly, that is any thirty two members, a Judge of the Supreme Court or High Court can be sent on forced leave. Thereafter, if on reference made by the proposed special committee, the Special Prosecutor appointed by such Committee, forms the opinion that the Judge is prima facie guilty of criminal misconduct, the special committee is to refer this opinion to the National Assembly which can, by passing a vote of no confidence, remove the Judge from office.

The decision of the Cabinet is evidently an attempt to destroy the independence of the judiciary guaranteed by Article 2A of the Constitution and the Objectives Resolution.

Further, as the Government does not have a two-third majority in Parliament and as the Opposition Parties have openly and vehemently opposed the Bill approved by the Cabinet, the Government's persistence with the Bill is designed not only to embarrass and humiliate the superior judiciary but also to frustrate and set a naught all efforts made, including the initiative taken by the President, to combat corruption and to commence the accountability process.

- And whereas the judiciary has till not been fully separated from the executive in violation of the provisions of Article 175(3) of the Constitution and the dead-line for such separation fixed by the Supreme Court of Pakistan.

- And whereas the Prime Minister and her Government have deliberately violated, on a massive scale, the fundamental right of privacy guaranteed by Article 14 of the Constitution. This has been done through illegal phone-tapping and eaves-dropping techniques. The phones which have been tapped and the conversations that have been monitored in this unconstitutional manner include the phones and conversations of Judges of the Superior Courts, leaders of political parties and high-ranking military and civil officers.

- And whereas corruption, nepotism and violation of rules in the administration of the affairs of the Government and its various bodies, authorities and corporations has become so extensive and widespread that the orderly functioning of Government in accordance of the provisions of the Constitution and the law has become impossible and in some cases, national security has been endangered. Public faith in the integrity and honesty of the Government has disappeared.

Members of the Government and the ruling parties are either directly or indirectly involved in such corruption, nepotism and rule violations.

Innumerable appointments have been made at the instance of members of the National Assembly in violation of the law declared by the Supreme Court that allocation of quotas to MsNA and MsPA for recruitment to various posts was offensive to the Constitution and the law and that all appointments were to be made on merit, honestly and objectively and in the public interest.

The transfers and postings of Government servants have similarly been made, in equally large numbers, at the behest of members of National Assembly and other members of the ruling parties.

The members have violated their oaths of office and the Government has not for three years taken any effective steps to ensure that the legislators do not interfere in the orderly executive functioning of the Government.

- And whereas the Constitutional requirement that the Cabinet together with the Ministers of State shall be collectively responsible to the National Assembly has been violated by the induction of a Minister against whom criminal cases are pending which the Interior Minister has refused to withdraw.

In fact, at an earlier stage, the Interior Minister had announced his intention to resign if the former was inducted into the Cabinet. A Cabinet in which one Minister is responsible for the prosecution of a cabinet colleague cannot be collectively responsible in any matter whatsoever.

- And whereas in the matter of the sale of Burmah Castrol Shares in PPL and BONE / PPL shares in Qadirpur Gas Field involving national asset valued in several billions of rupees, the President required the Prime Minister to place the matter before the Cabinet for consideration & re-consideration of the decisions taken in this matter by the ECC. This has still not been done, despite lapse of over four months, in violation of the provisions of Article 46 and 48 of the Constitution.

- And whereas for the foregoing reasons, taken individually and collectively, I am satisfied that a situation has arisen in which the Government of the Federation cannot be carried on in accordance with the provisions of the Constitution and an appeal to the electorate is necessary."

It may be stated here that on both occasions when the governments of Ms Benazir Bhutto were dismissed, the dissolutions were challenged and the Supreme Court in the judgments reported as **PLD 1992 SC 646** and **PLD 1998 SC 388** upheld the dissolution orders and the grounds on which the Assemblies were dissolved.

In the 1997 general elections, PML again returned to power with a thumping majority in the Assemblies and by means of the 13th Amendment, Article 58(2)(b) of the Constitution was omitted and the

President Leghari's power to dissolve the National Assembly was taken away. In the meanwhile, a tug of war started between PM Nawaz Sharif and the CJP Sajjad Ali Shah. The Prime Minister introduced the 14th Amendment to the Constitution as a result of which the persons elected on the ticket of a particular party were debarred from speaking against the policies of the party concerned at the floor of the house or outside.

A petition was moved challenging the 14th Amendment on the ground that it infringed the fundamental right of freedom of speech and the then Chief Justice of Pakistan suspended the operation of the 14th Amendment which was resented by the party in power. The justification advanced by the party in power [PML] to introduce 14th Amendment was that they were trying to bring an end to the floor crossing.

The suspension of the operation of the 14th Amendment made the Prime Minister and others to ridicule the Chief Justice and certain derogatory remarks were made against the Supreme Court, which led to initiation of Contempt of Court proceedings against the Prime Minister and others.

Although the Prime Minister appeared in Court but as expected the apex Court desired to proceed further in the matter which again infuriated the PML and thus through a concerted effort the Supreme Court was attacked by an unruly mob to deter the Court from hearing the contempt case as a result of which the Chief Justice of Pakistan and other Judges had to leave the Courtroom. Crocodile tears were shed by the party in power over the incident. The mob which attacked this Court included one MNA and two MsPA with other PML formation commanders.

[*It was another tragic part of Pakistan's history that the said MNA & the 2 MsPA and leading political figures all were made free despite verbal, written and electronic media-evidence on record by the Supreme Court but numerous police officers were punished taking them as escape goats.*]

Later, the Chief of Army Staff Gen Jehangir Karamat delivered a speech in the Pakistan Naval War College and while commenting upon the prevalent circumstances in the country he suggested that a National Security Council should be formed to advise the Prime Minister so that appropriate measures be taken to reform the administration in running the affairs of the country. This speech was disapproved by the Prime Minister and consequently Gen Jehangir Karamat was sent home.

NAWAZ SHARIF SENT HOME AGAIN 1999:

Such like circumstances ultimately precipitated the military coup by Gen Musharraf and his colleague Generals on 12th October 1999, reinforced by Proclamation of Emergency of 14th October 1999, which was validated by the Supreme Court in *Syed Zafar Ali Shah's case* on the basis of doctrine of state necessity in year 2000.

It is pertinent to mention that the personal hostility between the two leaders [Benazir Bhutto & Nawaz Sharif] and the confrontation between them never ceased. Both of them on coming to power tried to involve each other in criminal cases. The government of Nawaz Sharif filed references against Benazir Bhutto, her husband and others and similar course of action was followed by Benazir Bhutto when she was in power. On a reference about the receipt of kickbacks in SGS case Benazir Bhutto was convicted in 1998 but on appeal the conviction was set aside and the case was remanded for fresh trial in 2001.

When Gen Musharraf took over the reins of power, there was a sigh of relief because the people were fed up with the confrontation and lack of understanding between the two leaders and their followers. The apex Court's decision in the above referred *Syed Zafar Ali Shah's case,* three years' period was also given to the Gen Musharraf to achieve his declared objectives; reproduced hereunder: -

• Rebuild national confidence and morale;

• Strengthen federation, remove inter-provincial disharmony and restore national cohesion;

• Revive the economy and restore investor confidence;

• Ensure law and order and dispense speedy justice;

• Depoliticize state institutions;

• Devolution of power to the grass roots level; and

• Ensure swift and across the board accountability.

The Supreme Court had held that:

> *'Changes in the social, political and economic fields are not brought about at once with a magic wand but involve a journey of thousands miles, which requires a start with the first step. In our view, the*

Election Order deserves approval being the first step aimed at bringing about a change in the political culture, which has been described in the **International Encyclopedia of the Social Sciences** *by David L. Sills,* **Volume 12, page 218** *as under:*

- *[Political culture is the set of attitudes, beliefs, and sentiments which give order and meaning to a political process and which provide the underlying assumptions and rules that govern behaviour in the political system. It encompasses both the political ideals and the operating norms of a polity. Political culture is thus the manifestation in aggregate form of the psychological and subjective dimensions of politics. A political culture is the product of both the collective history of a political system and the life histories of the members of that system, and thus it is rooted equally in public events and private experiences.]'*

Once it was argued before the Supreme Court that *'the imposition of educational qualification would not bring about any change because the kith and kin of the old politicians would reach the Assemblies.'* But the Court held that for the making of new laws in the light of the changing circumstances and social and political values the public representatives should be well versed with the modern trends, changing social order and the events on the international scene.

No doubt wisdom is not related with degrees but this is an exception to the rule. Education certainly broadens the vision, adds to knowledge, brings about maturity and enlightenment, promotes tolerance and peaceful coexistence and eliminates parochialism. The apex court was convinced that the educational qualification prescribed for membership of Assemblies would raise their level of competence; bring change in the political culture and would also be an incentive to education.

Hence petitions praying for relief against education qualifications were dismissed but subsequently, the political nexus amongst various clans got this barrier removed through the parliamentary benches.

Scenario 33

DECLINE IN JUDICIAL VALUES:

At the outset one can say that major causes of decline in judicial respect have been the personal rifts and aversions among the judges coupled with tendencies of staying in judiciary for long times. External factors were never been as responsible as widely pre-empted.

If one can afford to sit in any High Court Bar for instance, he would find tens of remarks emanating from all the corners describing alleged stories about corrupt judges. They themselves feel embarrassed some times when a nexus between a particular judge and a specific law chamber is openly discussed, may not be true, but at least speaks about minds of the bar members. Those bar members are mostly the perspective candidates for being a judge of the same high court in near future.

Political affiliations of bar members are always open and make their way to the possible slots in higher judiciary when their parties come in power but seldom they discuss about the positive virtues their colleagues possess being the bar members; the stories, however, travel along.

Due to political affiliations referred above, the petitions and cases carrying political issues decided in the superior courts have always been considered controversial because the opponent bar members normally do not accept the judgments whole heartedly. A case about a judge's alleged corruption can be referred to the Supreme Judicial Council but till today only four cases could be sent there; one against J Fazal Ghani of Peshawar High Court; one against J Shaukat Ali of Lahore HC and the other two against J Ghulam Safdar & J Iftikhar M Chaudhry were referred to on political grounds.

It has been a topic of high debate that if a senior civil servant can be tried for 'living beyond means' then why a judge or General cannot be taken through the same mill on same like charges.

In the past, the practical way of appointment of judges remained varied and above the provisions given in the framework of Judge's Decision of 1996 or a change adopted in SC's decision of 2002. Most of the times the heads of political parties especially the Pakistan Peoples Party (PPP) and both Pakistan Muslim Leagues, [PML(N) & PML(Q)], whenever they came in power, tried to bring their own party supporters belonging to the lawyer community as judges of higher courts. [*When these key parties were out of government, the military rulers also did the same.*] They used to bribe, pay back or compensate their associated party workers and on the other side, mostly jeopardized and compromised with the demands of justice by showing their sympathies with the political parties they belong secretly and sometimes quite openly.

In Pakistan, whenever the political governments changed hands, the Governors of the provinces made out a list of perspective judges and handed over to their respective chief justices for inclusion in their lists. The chief justices used to express a little say in acceptance of those names. What happened; we all got a corps of political judges.

Whenever a military dictator took over, he never bothered to get any list from their governors even. The ISI and MI made lists for them and the only quality considered was their 'loyalty to the army' and the presence of germs of 'PCOship behaviour' in the candidates. In our country, it was because after taking oath, those judges had to complete uphill tasks of issuing green slips to the CMLAs cum Presidents for acceptance, their nominated Prime Ministers and their teams in corruption cases placed before them. Our history is jam-packed of tens of such examples if we start counting.

For instance; the name of Maulvi Mushtaq Hussain cannot be scrapped from the judicial history of Pakistan for being accused of 'judicial murder' of PPP's founder Z A Bhutto. The grudge was that during Z A Bhutto's rule, he was not considered for the slot of Chief Justice Lahore High Court due to certain reasons. When Gen Ziaul Haq took over in July 1977 he picked him as his main representative in Judiciary by awarding him the top slot in the name of compensation. Mr Maulvi repatriated the blessings of Gen Ziaul Haq by taking his 'rival' through a shabby judicial process putting all judicial norms at stake.

The next stage of Bhutto's case was in the Supreme Court. J Yaqub Ali was the Chief Justice of Pakistan since 1st November 1975, He was a great believer in democracy and the then military dictator Gen Ziaul Haq knew it well. Thus the CJP Yaqoob Ali was forced to retire by the General on 22nd July 1977. Justice Yaqub Ali had held a previous martial law by a usurping General *ultra-vires* to the Constitution of Pakistan declaring that *'martial law undermines concept of the rule of law which is the basis for a Constitution'*.

The usurping Gen Ziaul Haq had realised that his illegal actions would be overturned in the superior court of law headed by a Judge who believed in democracy so he proposed certain amendments to force the Chief Justice of the Supreme Court to retire. In fact, Gen Ziaul Haq did not just stop there but went further on to remove his like minded judges, too.

Gen Ziaul Haq then brought Justice Anwarul Haq as the CJP who later headed a bench to hear the appeal of Z A Bhutto. One Justice Nasim Hassan Shah was a member of that bench of seven judges who had upheld the decision of Bhutto's death sentence. When Justice Shah became Chief justice, his favourable tilt towards Nawaz Sharif's Muslim League and his antipathy towards Pakistan Peoples Party (PPP) were well known. He had exchanged harsh words with his CJ Afzal Zullah when the later had once received Benazir Bhutto at a function being an opposition leader. J Nasim Hassan Shah had headed the bench which restored Nawaz Sharif's government in May 1993.

Why Justice Nasim Hassan Shah was against the PPP could be traced back; he had been humiliated during Benazir Bhutto's first tenure when she had refused to sit on the same table with him. The reason was that Nasim H Shah was one of the justices who had upheld the death sentence of Benazir's father Zulfiqar Ali Bhutto in 1979. Benazir Bhutto could be condoned for being in her very young age dominated by her father's tragic treatment at the hands of judiciary whereas J Nasim Hassan was a mature member of the superior court; should have been above bias and prejudices.

Thus the military guided judicial process which was given start by Maulvi Mushtaq, CJ of the Lahore High Court and upheld by another stooge CJP Anwarul Haq ended at gallows of Rawalpindi Central Jail. However, the history remembers all the three characters with different connotations. The echo will continue to sound all the hails & praises for Z A Bhutto and curses for the two judges for all times to come.

Going deep into the decline of judicial values, one can say that first visible dent was seen on 5th July 1977 when Gen Ziaul Haq had toppled Mr Bhutto's government. *Justice Fakhruddin Ebrahim* told during an interview, published in daily *'Jang' of 16th May 1999,* that:

> *'Immediately after promulgation of Martial Law, Gen Ziaul Haq got worried about the possible reaction of judiciary. At 3 AM Gen Ziaul Haq got the then Federal Law Secretary, Abdul Haye Qureshi, on phone line and asked him that how the judiciary would react as he was going to abrogate the Constitution. Gen Zia also told Mr Qureshi that*

he wanted to elevate all the four chief justices as governors of the
respective provinces. At about 5.30 AM, Mr Qureshi had confirmed
back to Gen Ziaul Haq that all the four CJs had agreed to go for
Acting Governors – well done, the General had replied.'

Thus when the custodians of law had become Acting Governors, who
was there to take care of the Constitution of 1973 under which a General
could be challenged.

In early 1993, relations between Prime Minister Nawaz Sharif and
president Ghulam Ishaq Khan deteriorated quite rapidly and Khan was
planning to ouster Sharif. Some statements attributed to the then CJP
Afzal Zullah indicated that judiciary may act to counter president's
move. President waited till 18th April 1993; the day of retirement of the
chief justice. In a very curious development, chief justice on the very day
of his retirement was on a plane heading out of the country. Justice
Nasim Hassan Shah was sworn in as Acting CJP; the President took
decision at the same moment sending Nawaz Sharif home & ordering the
National Assembly to pack up and to vacate the chambers.

The judicial crisis of 1997 severely damaged country's image and
judiciary's reputation. A reckless civilian prime minister and his cronies
clashed head on with an equally reckless chief justice of the Supreme
Court. The trouble between judges of the Supreme Court had been
brewing over a long time. The enmity had taken start in 1993, when
Justice Sajjad Ali Shah had given the lone dissenting opinion in the
judgment in which the Supreme Court had restored Sharif's government
by a majority decision. Two judges; Muhammad Rafiq Tarar and
Saeeduzzaman Siddiqui had asked the Chief Justice Nasim Hassan Shah
to take disciplinary action against J Sajjad Ali Shah for the language he
used in his dissenting note.

Referring to *'Judicial Jitters in Pakistan' by Hamid Hussain* published in
the **Defence Journal of June 2007** issue; the row between the Chief
Justice Sajjad Ali Shah and Justice Saeeduzaman Siddiqui [*for calling the*
Supreme Court proceedings in all its registries to halt on the point that
the CJP had gone abroad and there was no Acting CJ in the country] was
quite an odd instance and uncalled for. The event has been mentioned in
detail earlier which nurtured a rift between the two judges for a long time
because on his return from foreign tour the CJP Sajjad Ali Shah had
conveyed his disapproval in writing. The same Justice Saeeduzzaman
Siddiqui became the champion of democracy when in 2000 he was not
called to take oath as Chief Justice of Pakistan or he had declined to take
oath under Gen Musharraf's PCO; the result was the same – going home.

It had been a tradition in the Supreme Court that whenever there was some internal problem or grave disagreement, the court used to call a full court meeting to find out solution. In those days the CJP Sajjad Ali Shah had developed a habit of issuing press statements, holding media meetings and seeing the senior executives wherever he went. When in Lahore, the CJP Sajjad Ali Shah used to have dinner with the Chief Minister Shahbaz Sharif and paying visit to Raiwind Palace to see (late) Mian Sharif but those dinners could not save him from disaster of November 1997 when the Supreme Court was attacked and he was sent home in an un-ceremonial way.

Similarly the CJP Sajjad Ali Shah used to keep constant liaison with Mr Jatoi and Gaus Ali Shah etc when on Sindh or Karachi's tour, whereas all the other judges were upset. The judges wanted to call a meeting for discussion on such issues. The CJP Sajjad Ali Shah never called or encouraged any such meeting because of expected humiliation on account of lack of support.

When in 1997, the Chief Justice Sajjad Ali Shah had gone to Saudi Arabia for *Umra* and J Saeeduzzaman was in London, Justice Ajmal Mian being the senior most in country had called that full court meeting. The CJP Shah came to know of it in Saudia, he immediately rushed back without performing *Umra*.

During the same days, when the CJP had developed some differences with the Chief Justice Lahore HC Sh Riaz Ahmed, he simply promoted him to join the Supreme Court where he had to work as a junior judge.

It is on record also that CJP Sajjad Ali Shah had moved for change in his date of birth when he was just near retirement. Later it transpired that the 'date of birth issue' was only orchestrated to keep the official residence of the CJP in Rawalpindi under use which otherwise should have been vacated within three months. What a way to earn respect from the junior colleague judges.

Sometimes people occupying high offices act in a childish manner embarrassing not only the high office but also the country. In August 1997, the CJP Sajjad Ali Shah recommended elevation of five judges to the Supreme Court without consulting with the executive. Nawaz Sharif's government in return issued an order duly signed by the President of Pakistan reducing the strength of the Supreme Court from seventeen to twelve. Few days later the Chief Justice, while presiding a three member's bench, had suspended the notification and the government withdrew the same.

Once the Supreme Court's judges, rather than brainstorming about legal issues, were found clashing with each other about the colour of the Supreme Court flag. One Chief Justice had arranged for the inauguration of the incomplete building of the new Supreme Court because he wanted to be in the limelight before his retirement.

J BHAGWANDAS CALLED IN DOCK:

Sometimes the judges themselves have provided good material to the general populace for stunning jokes. Even if their appointments were made on merits but they were not ready to tolerate each other. One episode from the judicial history of Pakistan was the appointment of Rana Bhagwandas, a judge of the Sindh High Court, which has another kind of story behind it. A petition was filed before a Division Bench of the Sindh High Court challenging an order of the Income Tax Appellate Tribunal in Karachi. The Division Bench which heard the case was presided over by Justice Rana Bhagwandas and Justice Sabihuddin Ahmed, and the appeal was dismissed.

The petitioner then filed a constitutional petition (No: 1069/1999) against the Government of Pakistan to declare the bench unconstitutional as Justice Bhagwandas was Hindu and only Muslims could be appointed to the superior judiciary. On 1st September 1999, the Chief Justice of the Sindh High Court ordered a full bench to hear that petition challenging the appointment of a non-Muslim judge. The bench, comprising Justice Dr Ghous Mohammad, Justice Abdul Hameed Dogar and Justice Roshan Essani, on the first instance, directed the petitioner to amend the title of the petition by incorporating the name of Justice Rana Bhagwandas as another respondent. It was because the petitioner, Shafi Mohammadi, himself a former judge of the Sindh High Court and Federal Shariat Court, had made the state, through secretary of Ministry of Law and Parliamentary Affairs, the sole respondent.

The petitioner, interalia, had also prayed to the court to restrain Rana Bhagwandas from working as a judge of the high court till disposal of the case. He had also prayed to the court to hold back the then high court judge, Justice Ms Majida Rizvi, from sitting over the cases involving Hudood and Qisas matters because she was a lady.

United Nation's representative on human rights in Pakistan Asma Jehangir regretted the petition against appointment of Justice Bhagwandas on account of his faith. In a Press statement, she said religion and patriotism had time and again been used to advance mischief in the country. She said Sindh High Court's decision to issue a notice to the sitting judge had eroded the image of Pakistani judiciary. The decision to constitute a full Bench to determine the constitutionality of the judge's appointment on the basis of his belief or religion was unwise as it had implications for the independence of judiciary and the rights of minorities. She was hailed for pointing out the mischief caused to Pakistan in the name of faith.

Challenging Justice Bhagwandas's appointment was another step towards intimidating individuals and institutions into subjugation. Religious minorities and women's rights groups had much to lose from such acts. The case was heard on 22nd September then on 19th October 1999 but the irony of fate was that the judgment was kept reserved till the judge Bhagwandas, who was in fact next in line to be the chief justice of that High Court, was transferred to the Supreme Court.

SC JUDGE'S SENIORITY ISSUE:

Second episode came in the first week of February 2002, when the Pakistan media published reports regarding a dispute over seniority, which had arisen among the Supreme Court judges. Justice Iftikhar M Chaudhry had questioned the seniority of Justice Nazim Hussain Siddiqui in writing. Justice Chaudhry, who expected to become Chief Justice of Pakistan from July 2005 for about eight years, had made a representation to the CJP asking him to correct the seniority list.

According to his viewpoint, Justice Chaudhry would have assumed the charge two years earlier, from July 2003, and his tenure would end on 12th December 2013. The compulsory retirement of Justice Rashid Aziz Khan had given rise to that seniority dispute. Had Justice Aziz remained on the bench, Justice Nazim Siddiqui had no chance to become the chief justice. Justice Siddiqui was part of the seven-member bench which declared Justice Rashid Aziz Khan and Justice Malik Qayyum biased against former Prime Minister Benazir Bhutto in famous Cotecna case in which *Saif ur Rehman Ehtesab* used to convey them explicit directions.

Un-ceremonial removal of Justice Rashid Aziz had paved the way for Justice Siddiqui to become aspiring expectant for the post of chief justice. He had contended that he and Justice Chaudhry were elevated as SC judges on 4th February 2000. Their date of appointment as chief justices of Sindh and Balochistan high courts respectively was the same, 22nd April 1999. Justice Chaudhry was of the view that under Section 8(4) of the Civil Servants Act 1974, seniority had to be reckoned from the date of elevation as judges in the respective high courts.

Justice Chaudhry contended that Justice Siddiqui was junior to him, as he {J Iftikhar Chaudhry} was elevated as Balochistan High Court judge on 6th November 1990, whereas Justice Siddiqui was elevated as Sindh High Court judge on 22nd March 1992. After two years as ad hoc judge, Justice Siddiqui was not confirmed. However, after the lapse of two months, Justice Siddiqui was reappointed as SHC judge on 5th June 1994. Justice Chaudhry contended that Justice Siddiqui was elevated as judge of SHC on 5th June 1994, and was junior to him. Justice Chaudhry had also cited certain case laws on the subject to support his contention that seniority in such situations would be determined on the basis of original date of induction in service.

As a result, Justice Iftikhar Chaudhry got his seniority as he deserved.

Another row for CJP's slot: Justice Falak Sher was appointed a judge of Lahore High Court on 11th March 1987 and elevated to Supreme Court on 6th July 2002. After retirement of Chief Justice Nazim Hussain Siddiqui, by virtue of being the **longest serving justice on the Supreme Court bench** at the time, Justice Iftikhar M Chaudhry was appointed as next Chief Justice. Justice Iftikhar was appointed a justice of Balochistan High Court in 1999 and was elevated to Supreme Court on 4th February 2000.

Justice Falak Sher maintained that he was senior to Justice Chaudhry based on their respective elevation to High Courts and should be appointed as Chief Justice of Pakistan. On appointment of Justice Chaudhry as Chief Justice, he petitioned the President of Pakistan on that account for which no decision was made.

During the hearing of the Presidential reference against Justice Iftikhar M Chaudhry in March 2007, Justice Falak Sher declined to sit on the full bench hearing the case. He stated that *'on account of seniority and being the senior-most judge in the country, it would be improper for me to hear a case in which the chief justice is a party, who like other judges of the Supreme Court is junior to me from four to nine years'*.

Another fact from the recent history of Pakistan's judiciary: A constitutional petition was moved by Sindh High Court Bar Association (SHCBA) against the appointment of judges on permanent basis and extension of their tenures by terming that the said order was issued without consulting the Chief Justice of Sindh HC. The notification was issued for converting appointment of Justice Bin Yameen to permanent basis on his post as Justice of Sindh High Court, and the extension of the tenures of Justice Arshad Noor Khan and Justice Peer Ali Shah for further six months.

While expressing his satisfaction over such order, President of Sindh High Court Bar Association Rasheed A Rizvi, told the media representatives that after the success of lawyer's movement, they would not fight on roads for the independence of judiciary, however, if the state challenges the Sindh HC order in Supreme Court, they will go against them. The decision was given on the basis that in respect of three alleged justices there was no disagreement of opinion.

Old stories lost with the time. After reinstatement of CJ Iftikhar Chaudhry and his colleague judges on 16th March 2009, the situation changed suddenly. The first instance came up in the first week of May 2009, when a petition against Justice Arshad Noor Khan of the Sindh High Court was dismissed by a full bench comprising of Justice Khilji Arif Hussain, Justice Maqbool Baqar, Justice Gulzar Ahmed and Justice Fasial Arab.

But these are the tales from most of the third world countries. Take an example from India where on 28th November 2009, the Supreme Court of India, stayed the Central Information Commission's (CIC) direction asking it to make public an information pertaining to appointment of three junior judges to the apex court by superseding senior judges.

Not only this, in a separate petition the Indian Supreme Court also issued a stay in another CIC's order which had directed disclosure of a talk between the Chief Justice of India and Justice R Raghupathy of Madras High Court (MHC) on an alleged interference by a union minister in a subjudice matter. Interestingly, deviating from the normal practice which was adopted by the SC in an earlier case on the assets declaration issue, the apex court this time reflected differently sidelining the Delhi High Court where appeals against the CIC's order were filed.

The background was that on 25th November 2009 the CIC had said that appointment of judges is a 'public activity' which cannot be withheld from disclosure and asked the apex court registry to make public the records relating to appointment of three apex court judges who had superseded their seniors. CIC had passed these orders on Subhash Chandra Agrawal's petition seeking complete correspondence between authorities concerned relating to appointment of Justices H L Dattu, A K Ganguly and R M Lodha superseding seniority of Judges A P Shah,

A K Patnaik and V K Gupta. The petition had said that the whole process was allegedly objected to by the Prime Minister's Office.

[*It is on record that one Justice Raghupathy of MHC, a few weeks back, had alleged in an open court that a Union Minister's lawyer spoke to him on telephone seeking favours in a case being probed by CBI. The CIC in a separate order had directed the apex court to reveal the name of that Union Minister and secondly, the complete correspondence with Chief Justice of India concerning that issue.*] (Ref: **Indian Express dated 4th December 2009**)

Coming back to Pakistan; the sitting CJP Iftikhar M Chaudhry when rejoined the Supreme Court in March 2009, started with good intentions with all his colleague chief justices in provinces. Soon he felt that his name sake CJ LHC Ch Iftikhar Hussain was not giving him 'due respect' whereas the CJ LHC held opinion that the CJP Iftikhar M Chaudhry had allegedly 'interfered' in LHC's affairs.

[*The CJ LHC Ch Iftikhar Hussain had somewhere negatively mentioned about the protocol issue which was interalia included in the judicial reference made to the Supreme Judicial Council by Gen Musharraf against the CJP Iftikhar M Chaudhry in March 2007*]

CJP Iftikhar M Chaudhry was also blamed for rejecting some names of would be judges recommended by the CJ LHC. The cold war between the two CJs went so high that once the CJP had to summon two judges of the LHC named Justice Akhtar Shabbir and Justice Sh Rasheed and asked them to show 'judge like' behaviour. That was the breaking point after which the two CJs did not like to communicate each other directly.

The same kind of cold relationship was also seen between CJP Iftikhar M Chaudhry and the CJ Baluchistan High Court (BHC) Justice Amanullah Yaseenzai because the later had manoeuvred to call the examination papers of CJP's son Arsalan Iftikhar against an alleged complaint.

Justice Jehanzeb Rahim of Peshawar High Court was also angry with the CJP Iftikhar M Chaudhry because the later had once given a verdict against Justice Jehanzeb Rahim in a case in which he had row with his own mother in connection with their ancestral property.

All these judges were approached by Gen Musharraf's secret team to bring and manage their complaints against the CJP Iftikhar M

Chaudhry; that was why Justice Jehanzeb Rahim's name was also mentioned in Gen Musharraf's reference of 9th March 2007 against the CJP.

During hearing of the same judicial reference of March 2007, affidavits submitted by Gen Hamid and Gen Nadeem Ejaz of MI had categorically mentioned that *'the CJP wanted certain judges of LHC and Sindh HC to be sent home'*; but not considered worth by the SJC being without any mention of evidence.

It was also mentioned in affidavits that the CJP Iftikhar M Chaudhry used to get secret reports about their colleague judges through the civil and military intelligence agencies; also given therein that the CJP was fond of protocol of high stature. He always expected to be received by the SP / SSP of each district at the boundary of his jurisdiction if and when the CJP travelled. Practically it was not possible nor it is anywhere written in the 'blue book of protocol' under which the SP / SSP sets his protocol plans.

There were many more flimsy charges like above in the reference sent by Gen Musharraf to the SJC; nothing was believed or taken seriously but the whole game was being supervised to create rift amongst the judges of the superior judiciary, to which extent they went successful.

Scenario 34

PAN-ISLAMISM IN PAK ARMY:

BRIG ALI'S STORY:

In Pakistan, Brig Ali Khan's arrest on 6th May 2011 under specific approval of COAS Gen Ashfaq Kayani speaks the deep roots of *'fundamentalism'* still having confused and turbulent trends in the Pakistan Army. The officer was posted in the GHQ Rawalpindi since two years. He was arrested on the allegations of keeping contacts with *Hizbut Tehreer* (HT) which is allegedly known for having discrete links with MI5, an official intelligence unit of the United Kingdom. When HT was contacted by the media for comments they said that:

> *"Our policy is not to confirm or deny such news and expect material support from sincere officers to establish Khalafah".*

Asif Salahuddin, spokesman for HT told the media that:

> *'We normally don't react on such stories and this is the only reaction which can clear our position in regards to Brigadier Ali Khan. Further reaction would be released with the developments. We are organizing a meeting in London on 26th June 2011 and invite all sincere and dedicated Muslims to join us'.*

Brig Ali's wife told the media that: *"Allegations are fabricated, every General knows my husband. He was arrested to gratify America and was to retire next month".*

The Pakistan Army's spokesman Maj Gen Athar Abbas had also told that following the arrest of Brig Ali Khan, four army majors were questioned in the said context. Gen Athar, the Chief of the ISPR, had categorically narrated before the media that Brig Ali Khan had never been associated with Al Qaeda or Taliban or any other *Mujahideen* type group. However, he remained under surveillance of the ISI and Military Intelligence (MI) for about six months and in their joint operation he was finally picked up from outside his residence. The intelligence agencies of army reportedly launched a check on him after some suspicious people were found frequently visiting his home. The call records of his mobile phone had confirmed the said suspicions and the officer was found linked to a contingent of militants having direct ties with the American

CIA, most probably through HT allegedly a front organization of MI5 of England.

HT is active in many Muslim countries and in Britain. The organization was extremely critical of former military ruler Gen Musharraf and his pro-American policies so he had banned it in Pakistan in 2003. Gen Musharraf might have banned it to please Israel with whom he was then trying to 'normalize' diplomatic relations.

HT is strongly anti-Zionist and calls Israel an 'illegal entity'. Some observers believe that HT is the victim of false allegations of connections to terrorism whereas it explicitly commits itself to non-violence. Perhaps, that is why despite ban in Pakistan, it hardly faces any difficulty in disseminating its message to the public through posters, seminars, literature and even rallies. Allegedly a letter, designed by the HT in 2010 had urged the members of the Pakistan's armed forces to revolt against their top civilian and military leadership for their alliance with the United States. The said four officers were only questioned in that context, not detained.

The arrest of these high ranking officers raised fears about growth of a group which aspired to make Pakistan a base for the establishment of an Islamic Caliphate. The army had taken links of serving officers with HT as an illegal activity and against Army discipline. On the other hand Brig Ali dismissed reports that his companion soldiers were in contact with militants or had links with banned organisations like HT.

However, the ISPR contained that in big institutions like army, presence of such individuals could not be immediately dismissed. Efforts were at hand to trace other members of HT in Pakistan Army who had contacts with Brig Ali; showing zero tolerance policy of such activities within the military organization of Pakistan.

Contrarily a general image of Brig Ali khan had been prevailing that:

> '... He might have contacts with the banned group but he was not involved in any type of conspiracy. His father was a junior officer in army. His sons and son in law and younger brothers are also serving there. Every Generals know Brig Ali Khan.
>
> Even Gen Kayani knows him; they (the whole family) can never think of betraying the army or this country. He was an intellectual, an

honest, patriotic and ideological person. It's a fashion here that whosoever offers prayers and practices religion is dubbed as Taliban or militant. Just to please America and to fool the Pakistani people, such allegations have been levelled against him.'

However, one could find a sure fact available on his record that he had been piling up enormous pressure on the top brass to stop extending any moral or intelligence help to the US forces on or around Pak-Afghan borders. Brig Ali had joined army in 1979, went up like a normal career officer but stumbled down when he once openly criticized Gen Musharraf during his visit to the Quetta Staff College.

During his staff course at Quetta Military Staff College, Brig Ali Khan had asked Gen Musharraf, in an open question-answer session, about the contents of key-agreement between the US and Pakistan. Brig Ali had also asked to define the 'limits' of co-operation with US on 'the war on terror'. His questions were never answered but Gen Musharraf was not happy over this unexpected encounter.

After the course, when the next army promotion board was held in GHQ with Gen Musharraf in chair as the Army Chief, Brig Ali was superseded on the same account. Subsequent promotion boards had also rejected him while his colleagues and subordinates continued to rise up the promotion ladder and went senior to him. He should have gone for early retirement but he opted to continue with the same rank and pay. For some he was serving for a 'better' cause. He had developed a habit of writing letters to high-rank Generals who were his colleagues or juniors, with suggestions on how to expel America from his native soils.

Brig Ali had made it as mission to appraise his seniors including Gen Kayani that Pakistan's "unconditional" support to the Americans was causing resentment in the lower ranks of the army. In his opinion the growing American involvement and influence in Pakistan's military affairs was negatively affecting the morale of the army. No senior wanted such advisory notes, he was told to shun this practice, but Brig Ali continued with it taking it as his sacred duty *'to save the prestigious institution he was serving'.*

Once he had addressed a personal letter to President Zardari suggesting him *'to make Pakistan economically self-reliant by freeing the country of American aid and stopping perks and privileges given to senior civil and military officials'.* The said letter was sent back to Gen Kayani for comments and necessary action. Most people understand the meaning of such necessary action in disciplined forces so Brig Ali was earmarked for a cogent tutorial lesson on discipline.

On 5th May 2011, in a meeting at GHQ Rawalpindi, Brig Ali Khan had spoken out before the presiding officer Lt Gen Javed Iqbal over 2nd May's episode of killing Osama. He opined that:

"The culprits who had hidden Bin Laden' and allowed the Americans to get away with breaching Pakistan's sovereignty were to be found within the army."

When he went in details all the officers attending that meeting, except two, were found supporting him. Lt Gen Javed Iqbal was furious and the proceedings were reported to the Army Chief Gen Kayani instantly. Next day a special meeting of Corps Commanders were called, Osama's killing discussed and the same evening Brig Ali was arrested. The problem was that his anti-US views and opinions on self reliance were getting popularity among army ranks at all levels.

Subsequently Brig Ali faced the army's Court Marshal.

GEN ZIA'S RADICALIZATION:

Referring to a recent article from **Sana Ahmed of BBC Urdu;** during Gen Ziaul Haq's regime the *'molvi'* [bearded religious person] had acquisitioned more importance in day to day life of a soldier. Sometimes there were objections on wearing shorts during 'exercise' classes and sometimes on viewing television in common room. Every officer or *jawan* [soldier] was allowed to avail short or long leave on the pretext of going on *tableegh* [preaching Islam] and could be called for explanation for not offering prayer during duty hours at least.

Decidedly, during the last four decades the professional expertise of Pakistan army has been affected but the commentators offer different reasons for that. Its real appreciation depends upon the fact that from whom this question is being asked and how he defines or understands pan-Islamism in contemporary context over Pakistan's Army.

Most people like to debate that Gen Ziaul Haq was the founder or propagator of *'Radicalization in Pakistan Army'*. Some opine that this phenomenon had taken start in late Z A Bhutto's regime. Prof Khurshid Ahmed of *Jamat e Islami* (JI) place all the responsibility of this radicalization on Bhutto's shoulders saying that *'Eemaan, Ittehad aur*

Jehad' slogan was coined by the Pakistan Army during his rule. The fact remains that by urging so Prof Khurshid is trying to dissociate his JI from Gen Ziaul Haq's blessings. No doubt the above slogan was introduced in the army in Bhutto's regime but it was actually the brainchild of Gen Ziaul Haq who was the Army Chief (COAS) those days.

It is an interesting treatise to go into details that how ranks in Pakistan Army got inclined towards pan-Islamic values pushing back the nationalism, which is normally considered a cause of prime honour for and core asset of all armies world over. It was Gen Ziaul Haq who had started making the Pakistan Army a true Islamic *Jehadi Force* (religious fighters) when he assumed the office of the Army Chief in 1976.

However, it also remains a fact that Gen Ziaul Haq himself ruled Pakistan for eleven years in the name of Islam but he never tolerated any other officer taking the flag of Islam in his hand to lead the army or the nation in that direction. See the next few paragraphs.

When Gen Ziaul Haq's name was announced as the new Chief of Army Staff towards the end of February 1976, it came as a very big surprise throughout the country. He was the junior most Corps Commander and had not shown any extraordinary brilliance either in peace or in war. In fact, his past was quite obscure and not many people in the Army had known him. On the other hand most of his seniors who were superseded had distinguished service records. Even Lt Gen Sharif, though promoted to the rank of a General and made Chief of Joint Staff, was in a way superseded because that post carried almost the same constitutional powers as late Chaudhry Fazal Elahi had as President during Mr Bhutto's regime.

Just after three weeks as being the Army Chief, on 24th March 1976, Gen Ziaul Haq announced his team of five new Corps Commanders on the radio. Some very junior Major Generals named M Iqbal, Sawar Khan, Faiz Ali Chishti, Ghulam Hassan and Jahanzeb Arbab were promoted as Lt Generals. The big names Division Commanders Maj Gen Tajammul Hussain, Maj Gen Akhtar Abdur Rehman, Maj Gen Fazal e Raziq, Maj Gen Mateen, Maj Gen Ch Abdur Rehman, Maj Gen Jamal Said Mian, Maj Gen Amir Hamza (DG Civil Armed Forces), Maj Gen Wajahat Hussain (Commandant Staff College) were all superseded.

After the appointment of Gen Ziaul Haq as Chief of Army Staff, about a month earlier, this was the second big jolt in the Army. Except for Jahanzeb Arbab, who had been superseded earlier because of having been found guilty of embezzlement of huge amount of money while in East Pakistan by a Court of Inquiry, headed by Major Gen M H Ansari but continued to remain in an officiating Command of a Division with the rank of a Brigadier for nearly two years up to as late as February 1976 when he was promoted to the rank of a Major General, all others were those who were on staff in GHQ.

GEN TAJAMMUL SACKED:

On 25th March 1976, Major Gen Tajammul called Col Aslam Zuberi to his office to tell that:

> 'I had dedicated my life for the cause of Islam and that I had no desire for the accumulation of wealth and property or even for higher promotion except with the ultimate aim of establishing a truly Islamic State on the pattern of Khulfai Rashideen.'

Major Gen Tajammul had asked him if he could provide him necessary information on the communication set up in the country. His Colonel Staff betrayed him. The same evening he [Col Aslam Zuberi] went to Rawalpindi and reported to his Corps Commander and then perhaps to Chief of Army Staff, Gen Ziaul Haq portraying that Major Gen Tajammul was planning to overthrow the Government.

Next morning major Gen Tajammul was told to attend a conference at GHQ on 28th March. He was briefed about his intentions and also that disciplinary proceedings had been initiated against him. The inquiry launched on him lasted for five days. On 3rd April 1976 he was told to attend the Chief of Army Staff's office. As he entered that office Gen Ziaul Haq, flanked by four Lt Generals, Sawar Khan, Ghulam Hassan, Faiz Ali Chishti and Ghulam Jilani were all sitting for his trial. After some questions Gen Ziaul Haq told him about his retirement being a 'fanatic' which was no more needed in Pakistan Army.

Some young army officers of 3rd Baloch Battalion were inspired by Major Gen Tajammul Hussain who had attempted coup of 23rd March 1980 and was subsequently court martialled. Gen Mirza Aslam Beg immediately restored Major Gen Tajammul's complete military honours and privileges when he assumed the office of the Army Chief after Gen Zia's air crash. Gen Tajammul was serving a sentence of 14 years RI for planning to liquidate all army Generals and Gen Ziaul Haq's government. Both were contesting for the Islamic way of governance in Pakistan but being opposite to each other.

Major Gen Tajammul once commented that:

'I had not intimately known Gen Zia before he became the Chief of the Army Staff but from his conduct during the Divisional Commanders Conferences; he appeared to me an incompetent and low grade officer. In one of the promotion conferences, I even saw him sleeping with his mouth open. He surpassed all limits of sycophancy when meeting the Prime Minister Zulfikar Ali Bhutto. While in uniform, he used to bow when shaking hands with Zulfikar Ali Bhutto.

I remember that Brigadier Hayat, with whom I served as his Brigade Major, once told me that he had written in Major Ziaul Haq's ACR when he served under his command, 'Not fit to go beyond the rank of a Major'. It is an irony of fate that a person of such calibre had ruled Pakistan for a long period of eleven years till he was finally killed in an air crash.'

Coming back; this concept of Islamic values in army was developed further when Gen Ziaul Haq became Chief Martial Law Administrator (CMLA) and the President of Pakistan after military coup of 5th July 1977. Mosques were already there in all the field and staff units of army but got re-built, expanded and decorated with special grants of budget under his directions.

The Commanding officers, even of the highest ranks of Generals, started offering prayers in the front lawns of their offices extending invitations to all around including their security and communication staff. Special supply orders were placed for *lotay*, caps, *chappals,* mats, *tasbeehs* and Maulana Modoodi's books for all mosques of army units everywhere.

In the same Ziaul Haq era, all unit *Imams* were given free summer and winter uniforms comprising of white *Qameez Shalwars, Chappals*, black jackets, black *Sherwani* and *Jinnah* Caps. They were made part of a new army unit of *Khateebs* starting from the basic rank of *Naib Khateeb* with an equivalent rank of Junior Commissioned Officer (JCO).

JCOs were promoted to higher ranks at par with other army ranks as *Khateebs* and *Khateeb e Aala* etc. Orders were conveyed to convene regular competitions for *Na'at Khawni* at all levels. At all formation headquarters a regular post of 'GSO grade II' was sanctioned with necessary staff and budget to handle those religious affairs.

The *Khateebs* had to be 'having beard' and expert in delivering sentimental Islamic sermons. Likewise, at Corp Headquarters there was given a sanctioned post of 'GSO grade I' and those General Staff Officers were to be in army uniforms like other army ranks. In GHQ Rawalpindi a new Directorate of Religious Affairs was established under control of an officer with brigadier rank. This Directorate still convenes annual competitions of Na'at Khawni at the highest level, gives away prizes and trophies to the top winners. Free *hajj* for selected officers and men every year is also arranged, funded and controlled by the same directorate.

In good old days a 'Services Book Club' was established in army for providing books to all army members to enhance their professional knowledge. It was a compulsory membership, a nominal subscription was contributed by all, four books were usually delivered to them yearly but mostly on selected topics of military history or tactics etc. In Gen Ziaul Haq's rule the selection of books was confined to religious subjects starting from '*Tafseer ul Qura'an by Maulana Modoodi*' in six parts. Some of the dissenting voices were also there from officers and men from other sects of Islam but in disciplined forces like army the volume of agitation remained confined to the low tone thus ignored.

The history of Pakistan Army tells that the Islamic values always existed in the institution, as it ought to be, but no General ever interfered in the performance of rituals through any means. Tolerance prevailed and individuality always respected. Discussions on religion and women were already forbidden in army messes and meetings. Gen Ziaul Haq brought the Islamic traditions in, generally guided by JI which created an opponent class within ranks based on sectarian beliefs.

On the other side an altogether new group emerged in the army declaring themselves the flag bearers of Islamic *Jihad*. This phenomenon gave birth to another wave of pan-Islamic ideology meaning thereby that Pakistan Army would look after the whole Islamic world at the cost of its own borders and nationalism. Thus the professionalism moved away from ranks and '*Islamization*' filled the vacuum till Pakistanis entered the Afghan War, the most controversial move in the history of Pakistan army, in 1980s. Gen Ziaul Haq had started that war but still the whole Pakistani nation and the generations thereof are suffering it.

Gen Ziaul Haq's era of *Islamization* of Pakistan Army pushed the country in Afghan Jihad which by and by took away tolerance, nationalism and professionalism from this institution. American dollars had fascinated the then COAS to the extent that he raised slogan of *Jihad* against Russian intruders in Afghanistan. After some years Pakistan was able to expel Russians away from Afghanistan but inadvertently opened tribal borders for Uzbek, Chechnyan and dissident Arabian & Afghan criminals to settle down in Pakistan.

Americans had taken away Gen Ziaul Haq in August 1988's crash, immediately after their mission and his role in the region were accomplished. However, while leaving Pakistan in distress, the US agencies made sure that the above mentioned foreign *jihadists* should stay here, marry the local girls, give birth to another generation of martyrs, train them and bring affront to the same Pakistan Army who had once brought them here in the name of 'greater Islamic cause'.

GEN ASLAM BEG'S REVERSE GEAR:

Undoubtedly, it was COAS Gen Mirza Aslam Beg who became pioneer to mellow down that *jehadi* process in army by getting distributed a published booklet in the whole army declaring that:

- The Army *Khateebs* should have Bachelor's Degree as minimum qualification in any discipline or subjects.

- They would not be able to declare them as member of any sect whatsoever; neither verbally nor by practice.

- They would only be able to deliver certain agreed *'khutbas'* given in that book; approved for all and common in all sects.

- The army officers and *jawans* were able to offer prayers at times convenient to them. Compulsory time observing was abolished.

The *tableegh* holiday trends in officers and *jawans* were discouraged. It created good normalizing effects but it was too late till then to start with. Due to general atmosphere in the country the whole society moved towards conservatism and the same inclinations were reflected in the army for the then developing generation. Subsequent army chiefs could not dare to take away those 'Islamic reforms' from the institution so the suffering continued.

In short, during Gen Ziaul Haq rule, Islam was made an identity for Pakistanis at the cost of nationalism. When *Islamiat* was made an integral part of national syllabus the state media played a vital role for its propagation. In all competitive examinations like PCS, CSS, NIPA, Defence College courses and tens others it was made obligatory to study it and pass through. JI was heading this movement with utmost zeal and vigour because first time with Gen Zia's sanction the JI followers were allowed to enter in command and control of Pakistan's Army.

Interestingly, during Gen Ayub Khan's governance, attachment with JI was banned in the army. A member, *rafique* or associate of JI was normally considered as un-told 'security risk' in Gen Ayub's government and pre-entry intelligence reports of all civil and military gazetted officers had to confirm that the candidate was 'clean' in that respect.

Shiraz Paracha in his article titled 'Time to change: *Imaan, Taqwa, & Jihad* (as cited in *www. Pakspectator. com dated 3rd July 2011)* opines that:

> '...... *(Gen) Ziaul Haq institutionalized religion in the armed forces of Pakistan; during the 1980s practice of religious rituals became common in the Pakistani military so was corruption and incompetence. Some commanders were accused of being involved in criminal activities including drug trafficking and arms sales.*
>
> *Generals turned into wheelers and dealers and receiving kickbacks in military deals touched new heights. The experience of the last 21 years proves that exporting and using militancy as a foreign policy tool has failed miserably. Such policies have backfired causing death and destructions in Pakistan and elsewhere....'*

Another cogent view associated with above lines was also expressed saying that:

> '.....*Gen Musharraf hated religious people so much so he only promoted his breed of liberals and enforced a westernized culture in the forces. The divisions in the army are a natural reaction. All those people who are in bed with CIA should be kicked out as well. Why the double standards .....?'*

Gen Ziaul Haq, while serving as Brigadier and posted in Jordan (1967-1970), was instrumental in killing thousands of Muslim Palestinians and the event is known in history as **'Black September'**. Later he fooled PM Z A Bhutto by giving him a tank uniform in Multan. On 1st March 1976, Mr Bhutto approved Gen Ziaul Haq as the Army Chief, ahead of a number of officers senior to him as stated earlier.

At the time of Gen Ziaul Haq's nomination as COAS, the officers in order of seniority were Muhammad Shariff, Muhammed Akbar Khan,

Aftab Ahmed Khan, Azmat Baksh Awan, Agha Ibrahim Akram, Abdul Majeed Malik and Ghulam Jilani Khan. Mr Bhutto had chosen the most junior, superseding seven Generals senior to Ziaul Haq but he overthrew Bhutto by using the Supreme Court of Pakistan which gave the world a new legitimacy for Military rule under the "doctrine of necessity".

Gen Ziaul Haq had killed Bhutto under the orders of America's Henry Kissinger who had once vowed to show the extreme fate on both Bhutto and Indira Gandhi for their nuclear programs. Mr Bhutto knew it. It is on record that during the PNA movement of 1977, once Mr Bhutto had said in an open gathering in Raja Bazaar Rawalpindi that:

> 'Listen Mr Ambassador (pointing towards America) despite your conspiracy I'm here; my party is here; PPP is here; it is not dead; we are not dead ...'.

Though the protests were being staged by the PNA but Mr Bhutto did not mention PNA rather he had acumen of understanding his background opponents.

One Nazia opined on the above cited internet site that:

> '..... From above discussion it appears that it was just a game of Dollarism and Islam's name was highly misused in Pakistan army and its political structure. Where the Islam goes when they take on defence deals and plans with America. All Generals from Auyb till today who followed US programs are now running billion rupees franchises or own such amount assets. Their Islam hides when matter of national interest comes. Today army management does not need any kind of professionalism in the line of duty but they have different agenda coming from US embassy. Wikileaks have just hinted all this.'

Within the Pakistan Army, once in 1995, Maj Gen Zaheerul Islam Abbasi was arrested and court martially punished on the charges of 'mutiny in the name of Islam' in the army. He was allegedly trying to take over the government using the name of *Islam* by killing the then PM Benazir Bhutto, the then COAS Gen Waheed Kakar and some senior officers of army establishment. Lt Gen Jehangir Karamat had captured those characters headed by Maj Gen Abbasi who were sentenced for seven years after due process. It was the first danger alarm heard and felt in the Pakistan Army. The higher echelons have been trying to encounter that danger since then.

Later, on 4th May 2009, the eagles of Pakistan Army had arrested one Col Shahid Bashir, the commanding officer of Shamsi Airbase [in Balochistan] and his two aides, a former Sq Leader of PAF named Nadeem Ahmed Shah, and a US green-card holder & mechanical engineer name Owais Ahmed Shah. They were charge sheeted for providing secret and sensitive information about the Shamsi Airbase and its strategic location, till recently [precisely till 11th November 2011] being used by the US forces to launch drone attacks on Pakistan's tribal belt. His two civilian companions were hatching terrorist attack on the airbase on the basis of the information provided by Col Shahid. The final outcome of the said trial is not known yet.

Coming back and leaving aside the army, Gen Ziaul Haq, because he was the president of the country too, made '*Islamiat*' a compulsory subject in all school and colleges in which more emphasis was laid on known Islamic historical battles. Thus the fresh crop of entrants in civil and military departments were adequately equipped with the concepts of Jihad, aged old war techniques and sectarian differences rather than contributions of Muslims in science, medicine and technology, open-mindedness, patience and brotherhood. How army as an institution suffered from this theory, one can look into details of our failures in Siachin, Kargil, FATA, Kashmir, Karachi and Peshawar as well as at diplomatic missions in foreign countries.

Allegedly, Pakistan is moving towards a 'failing state' day by day since Gen Ziaul Haq's days. Call it back, if possible.

Scenario 35

PAKISTAN'S JUDICIARY IN 2001:

5th January 2001: President of the Supreme Court Bar Association (SCBA) told the media that *'Nawaz Sharif's Exile has brought [Pakistani] judiciary's credibility at stake'*.

29th January 2001: Abdul Rahim, one former deputy director of Intelligence Bureau Pakistan, wrote a letter to the President of Pakistan alleging that Justice Malik Qayyum had been taking direct orders from Khalid Anwar and Saifur Rehman, both federal ministers of Nawaz Sharif's regime, to convict Ms Benazir Bhutto. A copy of the said letter is pasted below *verbatim*:

TOP SECRET

INTELLIGENCE BUREAU
GOVERNMENT OF PAKISTAN
94-UPPER MALL, LAHORE

No. ARV/2001/01 Dated 29-1-2001

The President,
Islamic Republic of Pakistan,
ISLAMABAD   *THROUGH PROPER CHANNEL*

SUBJ: *SHEER ABUSE OF POWER/ABUSE OF JUDICIARY*

Respected Sir,

I would like to bring it to your kind notice that I am an officer of Intelligence Bureau cadre and have been raised to the rank of Deputy Director out of my sheer hard work. I have always worked honestly, professionally and with full devotions. All my seniors will endorse the high level of my efficiency, professionalism and integrity. I have always pointed out any wrong doings irrespective of any pressure of my seniors. I have no political affiliations, whatsoever.

I, being a conscientious officer, would like to state that an extra-ordinary situation has compelled me to address you directly as I feel that this very sensitive and important matter, which may have very deep impact on the future and present functioning of the judiciary and politics of Pakistan, needs to be dealt at your level. I am constrained to inform you that during my long service career in a very sensitive organisation I have never come across of any such occasion where I was a witness to sheer abuse of state institutions including judiciary of Pakistan by any Chief Executive of the country for the mere satisfaction of his/her personal ego and vendetta. In the instant case, some important dignitaries of the past and the present are involved who have not only violated the Constitution of Pakistan but also crossed other human and legal limits. They have also violated the provisions of their oath, which they took while taking-over their high offices. They have committed such a crime, which no nation on the earth would ever tolerate.

The highly undesirable incident, which I am going to narrate below, in fact, relates to the trial of the Opposition Leader and former Prime Minister of Pakistan Ms. Benazir Bhutto and her spouse conducted by the Accountability Court headed by Mr. Justice Malik Abdul Qayyum of the Lahore High Court. The events which have really shaken my conscious and will also shake you and the whole nation are being summarised below.

With the start of the trial of Ms. Benazir Bhutto and her spouse in SGS Reference in the Accountability Court headed by Mr. Justice Malik Abdul Qayyum, the then Government ordered the Intelligence Sub-Bureau, Lahore for the monitoring of all the office, home and mobile telephones of Mr. Justice Malik Abdul Qayyum in order to keep him under constant observation. Accordingly, I, being the head of the section responsible for the observation / bugging of the telephones, started tapping the telephones of Mr. Justice Malik Abdul Qayyum.

First of all Mr. Khalid Anwar called Mr. Justice Malik Qayyum and told that "Somebody is unhappy over the delay of hearing of this case. He has complained about the case to Saif that nothing has been done so far and why has it not been concluded." He informed the judge that "the gentleman [Mian Nawaz Sharif] was very unhappy" and asked the judge that "Now I am thinking if you could reach the final result within the outside limit of two weeks" and "So get it done on Monday". In response, Mr. Justice Malik Qayyum informed the Minister that "It is being done on Monday. After this we have to give them some time for defence evidence and then the matter will be closed."

During his first conversation with Mr. Justice Malik Qayyum, Mr. Saif-ur-Rehman directed him that "Kindly don't do one thing. Please don't give any further date." to which the judge promised that "Now we are not going to give dates. We are going to finish it by the Grace of God. You don't worry." In a conversation with his wife, Mr. Justice Malik Qayyum told her that "They have said, remove him" and on a further explanation by her wife, the judge stated that Nawaz Sharif has ordered for his removal because "They [Mian Nawaz Sharif] say that he has changed his loyalty." When on his advice the wife of Mr. Justice Malik Qayyum informed Malik Pervez (brother of Justice Malik Qayyum) of this development, he remarked that "But this is Blackmailing" and while agreeing with him, the wife of Mr. Justice Malik Qayyum concluded that "Yes you are right; this is the limit that justice should not be done and only what they want should be done".

In a subsequent conversation with Malik Pervez, Mr. Justice Malik Qayyum informed him that "Regarding the matter of judgement which you know, your friend the biggest boss (Nawaz Sharif) is specially sending two men, one Mehdi and other Pappu (Saif)" to the Chief Justice to ensure "that it should be done with in two days".

In a separate conversation with Mr. Saif-ur-Rehman asked Mr. Justice Malik Qayyum "... we need a place when our man can sit. Kindly permit our man to sit in the room next to your room" to which the judge told him that he "would tell Khawar Sahib". Mr. Saif-ur-Rehman then told the judge that "Then I am going to depute the man Feroz shah who will contact Khawar". When the Judge discusses this development / requirement with the Chief Justice, the Chief Justice remarked that "If we avoid it, it is better for us otherwise the noose will be around our neck if this thing is exposed". Mr. Justice Malik Qayyum in reply told him that "Khawar says that we can place the machine in the Registrar's room" like "when you did it, it was also like this".

Mr. Saif-ur-Rehman, in a separate conversation conveyed the directions of the Prime Minister to Mr. Justice Malik Qayyum and told him that "He [Mian Nawaz Sharif] has asked me to tell you for Monday" and asked him "Whatever you told me before, do exactly like that". Mr. Justice replied that "I am trying my best. You don't worry. You know how sincerely we are trying".

Besides external / political pressure, Mr. Justice Rashid Aziz, the then Chief Justice of Lahore High Court was also used to pressurize Mr. Justice Malik Qayyum. In a telephonic conversation, Mr. Justice Rashid Aziz informed Mr. Justice Malik Qayyum that "Yesterday when I went there, Mr. Yasir Arafat had come. He was busy with him in a meeting. He [Mian Nawaz Sharif] said just wait for ten minutes, twenty minutes, and half an hour. We will talk after lunch" and told Mr. Justice Malik Qayyum that "He [Nawaz Sharif] is a bastard". When Mr. Justice Malik Qayyum enquired about the conversation, Mr. Justice Rashid Aziz told him that "he [Nawaz Sharif] says it has to be tomorrow" and enquired from Mr. Justice Malik Qayyum "Is everything ready?" When Mr. Justice Malik Qayyum asked the Chief Justice that "You should have told him that it would finish only after they finish (defence evidence)" the Chief Justice told him that "He was saying that just do it".

When Mr. Justice Malik Qayyum could not announce the judgement on the pre-determined day Mr. Saif-ur-Rehman called him and asked that "You were supposed to do it today". Mr. Justice Malik Qayyum replied to him that "For your sake I had to beg her lawyer. I told him that I have to go abroad, I am not feeling well but I have to finish it first". When Mr. Saif-ur-Rehman expressed displeasure over delay Mr. Justice Malik Qayyum asked him to "handle him [Mian Nawaz Sharif] and stated that "By the grace of God, this will be done and then both of us will go to him [Mian Nawaz Sharif] and seek forgiveness". Mr. Saif-ur-Rehman asked the same judge to "Give me 100% confirmation that it will be done tomorrow". In the same conversation Mr. Justice Malik Qayyum asked him about the punishment required to be awarded to which Mr. Saif-ur-Rehman told him that "whatever you have been told by him [Mian Nawaz Sharif]" i.e. "Not less than 7 years". Mr. Justice Malik Qayyum suggested to him that the maximum punishment is not appropriate as "Seven is the maximum punishment and no body awards maximum" and requested Mr. Saif to ask him [Mian Nawaz Sharif] to which he promised to let him (Mr. Justice Malik Qayyum) know. In the same conversation Mr. Justice Malik Qayyum informed Mr. Saif that "I have already done about the fine and confiscation of the properties" and "their disqualification also". Mr. Saif-ur-Rehman informed him that "Now more important is the state of madness in which he [Mian Nawaz Sharif] is" to which Justice Malik Qayyum requested him to "Beg forgiveness on my behalf". Mr. Justice Malik Qayyum assured him that "Under all circumstances it will be done tomorrow. We are going to announce the judgement".

In a separate conversation, Mr. Rashid Aziz described the madness of the Prime Minister to Mr. Justice Malik Qayyum and told him that "You can't understand. Do you know what he [Mian Nawaz Sharif] is going to say? He is going to issue warrants for both of us. He has specially called me and told to advice you that what are you doing?" In reply Mr. Justice Malik Qayyum informed the Chief Justice that "90% I will try my best to finish it tomorrow". Mr. Justice Malik Qayyum went on assuring the Chief Justice in the words "OK. Tomorrow I will, even if have to push it". The Chief Justice told the judge that he has told him [Nawaz Sharif] that "It is already written and lying with us. He can sign it for you on it and you can keep it with you".

In another conversation with Mr. Justice Malik Qayyum, Mr. Saif-ur-Rehman told the judge that he had asked him [Mian Nawaz Sharif] about the punishment to which he had directed to tell you that "Give them full dose". Mr. Saif-ur-Rehman also informed the judge that "When I inquired about five or seven, he said I should ask you why you would not like to give them full dose". Explaining the strategy for the next day (the day of the announcement of the judgement) Mr. Justice Malik Qayyum informed Mr. Saif that "Whole day will be given. After eleven (11:00 AM) we would tell him to finish. After the interval at 11:00 AM, even if they disagree, we will not care" and "We will tell them, say whatever they want to say in their defence. It (order) is already prepared in written". The judge went on explaining and stated that "So after half an hour, we will come back and announce it". Mr. Saif-ur-Rehman then suggested to him that "Give the brief tomorrow but try to cover the maximum the brief the judgement".

When the trial of Ms. Benazir Bhutto was over, Mr. Shahbaz Sharif, the then Chief Minister of Punjab rang up the judge and told that "I made a request to you" to which the judge replied that "Sir, I did finish that". Mr. Shahbaz Sharif then informed him that "thank you very much. The matter regarding Ch. Sarwar [MNA], my elder brother has asked me to tell you that Sarwar should be favoured [in his disqualification case]" to which Mr. Justice Malik Qayyum promised that "It's done, as desired by Mian sahib. As per his desire the matter is finished".

During this process of close day to day observation of his phones, I was astonished to note that the judge was being dictated to obtain a judgement of their choice against Ms. Benazir Bhutto and Mr. Asif Ali Zardari by the then Federal Law Minister Mr. Khalid Anwar, Chairman Accountability Bureau, Mr. Saif-ur-Rehman and the then Chief Justice of Lahore High Court, Mr. Justice Rashid Aziz, under the orders of from then Prime Minister of Pakistan Mian Muhammad Nawaz Sharif, to hastily conclude the trial, announce conviction of Ms. Benazir Bhutto and her spouse with maximum punishment or seven years and forfeiture of her entire property. The Honourable Judge was pressurized to the extent that once he was called by the then Chief Justice of Lahore High Court at his residence to convey that Mr. Nawaz Sharif has asked to remove him (Mr. Justice. Malik

Abdul Qayyum) as he (Mian Nawaz Sharif) has become doubtful of his loyalties. The Honourable Judge ultimately succumbed to the pressure and announced pre-written judgement against Ms. Benazir Bhutto and her husband by violating all norms of Justice, provisions of the Constitution of Pakistan and fair-play.

The whole conversation of these important Cabinet Ministers and the judges was part of the official record of the Intelligence Sub-Bureau, Lahore. I am also enclosing my affidavit along with 60-minutes recorded tape and its transcription with the view to assist your kind honour to proceed against two sitting judges, one of the Supreme Court of Pakistan and the other of Lahore High Court, respectively, former Prime Minister of Pakistan Mian Muhammad Nawaz Sharif, Chairman Accountability Bureau Mr. Saif-ur-Rehman and the then Federal Law Minister Mr. Khalid Anwar.

I would also like to state that I have taken on against the most powerful group of politicians, two corrupt and immoral judges and hence I apprehend that I along with my family members are going to be harassed and victimized besides a serious danger to my life too. I also fear that the authorities in the Intelligence Bureau may try to terminate my services on false grounds but fact remains that I am just doing my duty by exposing to you bad elements in our judiciary. I, therefore, appeal to your honour to provide me protection and security against all such dangers. The aforementioned corrupt characters have not only brought bad name to the judiciary itself but also the image of our great nation. I would also like to make it clear that I have no motives whatsoever but I just want you to know as to what kind of havoc is being played by such people who had made mockery of justice without fear of the Almighty Allah.

In the light of the above facts, I would request: to your honour to kindly take necessary and appropriate action into the matter.

In the end I would once again like to reiterate the fact that I have no motives whatsoever in exposing these bad elements as I, being a civil servant, was duty bound to bring the wrong-doings of such like undesirable characters to the notice of such authorities which I am confident would take necessary action. I would also request you to kindly keep this summary confidential till you have taken a final action against them.

Thanking you in anticipation and I am confident that your kind honour, being the custodian of the Constitution of Pakistan and a former judge of the apex court of the country, would definitely proceed in the matter in accordance with the law.

Yours obediently,

[Signature] (A. RAHIM)

Deputy Director / IB

Encl:

1. Copy of the transcript 2. 65 Minutes recorded tape 3. Affidavit cc:
1. Gen. Pervez Musharraf, The Chief Executive of Pakistan, Islamabad.
2. Honourable Chief Justice of Pakistan, Islamabad.
3. Maj. Gen. Rafi-ullah Khan Niiazi, Director General, Intelligence Bureau, Islamabad.
4. Mr. Jehangir Mirza, Joint Director General, PPHQ-IB Lahore.

Sd/- (A. RAHIM)

Deputy Director/IB

[*100 Rupee Certificate*]

AFFIDAVIT

[Stamped by Advocate Notary Public.]

I, A. RAHIM S/o Mr. NAZIR AHMED, do hereby solemnly declare and affirm as under.

1. That I was working in the Intelligence Bureau directorate, Lahore since 1997. Further, I worked in other positions in I.B.

2. That according to the instructions of the Government, the residential, office and mobile numbers of Justice Malik Adbul Qayyum were placed under observation during the trial of former Prime Minister and Opposition Leader Ms. Benazir Bhutto.

3. The Mr. Nawaz Sharif and his associate wanted to know Justice Malik Qayyum's day to day engagements, and contacts. In fact, they wanted to ensure that Justice Malik Qayyum was following the advice

of Accountability Bureau and the Federal Law Minister to implement the pre-determined conviction of Ms. Benazir Bhutto.

4. that the Prime Minister wanted the proof that instructions given by him to Justice Malik Qayyum through Chief Justice Rashid Aziz of Lahore High Court, Mr. Saif-ur-Rehman, Chairman Accountability Bureau and the Federal Law Minister Khalid Anwar were being followed.

5. That accordingly all incoming and outgoing calls in his office, home and mobile were monitored and regular record of day to day conversation started building. I was shocked to find that the concerned judge is being ordered to convict Mr. Benazir Bhutto and Asif Ali Zardari by Saif-ur-Rehman, Chief Justice and Law Minister by hastily concluding the trial at the earliest and announcing the conviction of Ms. Benazir Bhutto with "full dose" at every cost. I found the Judge to be working as junior to the Accountability Bureau and the Federal Law Minister.

6. My conscience felt bad learning about the gross injustice being done to the defendants through the judge trampling the provisions of the constitution of Pakistan. I, being a civil servant felt duty bound to protect the Constitution and not become party to any such violations. I, therefore, decided to make a duplicate copy of the conversation and a 65-minutes long audio recorded conversation to this effect is enclosed with this affidavit. The entire record of conversation between Premier Sharif's cabinet Ministers, namely Saif-ur-Rehman (who had also investigated the case against Ms. Benazir Bhutto), personal friend of Nawaz Sharif, the then Federal Law Minister Khalid Anwar, and Justice Rashid Aziz, the then Chief Justice of Lahore High Court confirms that a conspiracy was hatched against Ms. Benazir Bhutto for getting her convicted through Justice Malik Qayyum.

7. That the above facts are correct and true to the best of my knowledge and nothing has been concealed or withheld.

DECLARANT

[Signature] A. RAHIM 6-12-2000

4th February 2001: the *'Sunday Times' of London* came out with verbatim taped conversations between Khalid Anwar the Federal Law

Minister, Saif ur Rehman the Ehtesab Chief, Chief Justice of the Lahore High Court (LHC) Rashid Aziz and Justice Malik Qayyum to which Mr Rahim had asked the President to take cognizance. That was the moment when the credibility of whole judicial process in Pakistan was made a laughing stock throughout the world.

The *daily Dawn* of the same day had commented that:

> '..... *Justice Malik Qayyum of Lahore High Court had allegedly announced a pre-written judgment in the case; the Sunday Times story revealed. ..... When approached Justice Qayyum said he could not remember the conversations recorded by the IB. "I don't recall any such calls," he said. "I don't know anything about it."*

12th February 2001: Federal Interior Minister of Nawaz Sharif's regime Chaudhry Shujaat himself disclosed to the media that the bugging of Justice Rashid Aziz and Justice Malik Qayyum's phones was ordered by Saif ur Rehman, the former Accountability Minister. It was done by the Intelligence Bureau Lahore and copies of tapes were also kept at IB (HQ) Islamabad.

An editorial appeared in *Friday Times of 16-22nd February 2001*, under caption: *'Far Reaching Repercussions'* (when the verbatim audio tapes of Justice Malik Qayyum's conversation had appeared in 'The Sunday Times of London') wrote:

> ' ...... *Asif Zardari should be released immediately and arrest warrant against BB should be withdrawn. Supreme Court should punish Nawaz Sharif; present rulers (Gen Musharraf) allowed him Scott free. He took 23 bags of male-ghanimat. A billion rupees of jewellery and millions in foreign currency were discovered in his mother's house with white ants eating all the loot hid in a bag. The bias against Asif Zardari and BB is ridiculous.'*

BB'S TRIAL VITIATED BY THE SC:

6th April 2001: a 7-member Supreme Court Bench, presided over by Justice Bashir Jehangiri, pronounced that *'the trial of Benazir Bhutto and her husband A A Zardari stands vitiated'*. The apex court, therefore, set aside their convictions by the Ehtesab Bench of the LHC and ordered retrial of the case by the court of competent jurisdiction. Detail judgment was written after 15 days.

The apex court's decision had, beyond any doubt, established that Justice Malik Qayyum had acquired personal interest in the case by deriving an out of the way favour of securing diplomatic passports for him and his wife in violation of the rules. Besides, Malik Pervez, real brother of Justice Qayyum was elected unopposed from the seat [of National Assembly] vacated by Nawaz Sharif himself, whose political rivalry with Ms Benazir Bhutto was a matter of common knowledge.

The apex court also noted that Justice Qayyum had exerted influence on the second member of the Ehtesab Bench S Najmul Hasan Kazmi, who being an unconfirmed judge of the LHC was sweating for confirmation. Justice Kazmi was consequently appointed permanent judge on 13th May, a month after the Ehtesab Bench's judgment against the appellants. The Supreme Court had observed that:

'In this scenario, judicial propriety demands that Justice Malik Qayyum should tender his resignation as judge of the Lahore High Court in the interest of judiciary's honour and dignity.'

The Supreme Court's verdict held that:

'The element of bias was floating on the surface of the record.'

The most damaging part of the judgment from Justice Malik Qayyum's point of view was its assertion that he had 'chased' the particular reference against Benazir Bhutto and Zardari because he was keen that it should be heard by a bench headed by him. His aim was to 'impose' himself on the case so that he could *'take it to its end according to his preconceived notions.'* In the opinion of the SC judges, there was 'undisputed' evidence that Justice Malik Qayyum wanted the Nawaz Sharif government to give diplomatic passports to him and his wife, and that he [J Qayyum] had frozen the appellant's assets for getting favours from Benazir Bhutto's political adversary.

The Supreme Court verdict also referred to many other technical mistakes in the case like the variation of versions in the short order and the final judgement (the latter having a reference to the necklace while the former not having it); the **'abuse of section 342 CrPC'** with a view to reaching **'a hasty conclusion,'** and **'the mode and manner'** in which Benazir Bhutto's statement was recorded. Finally, the Supreme Court judgment noted the 'glaring injustice' that was meted out to Mr Zardari when Justice Malik Qayyum refused to recall certain witnesses the counsel for the accused wanted to cross-examine. All this goes to show, the SC judgment said, that there was *'a close liaison'* between Justice Qayyum, Senator Saifur Rahman and the PM Nawaz Sharif.

A little background: In April 1999, Justice Qayyum reportedly found late Benazir Bhutto and her husband, Asif Ali Zardari, guilty of taking a $4.3m commission after awarding a pre-shipment inspection contract to the Swiss firms CoTecna & *Societe Generale de Surveillance*. Both were fined $8.6m and jailed for five years. Mr Zardari was already in jail awaiting trial on other cases; Benazir Bhutto had left Pakistan shortly before the verdict and never returned till October 2007.

Daily Times Monitor of 21st November 2010 described that:

> *'.... The audiotape was provided by Senator Faisal Raza Abdi. The TV channel [ARY: 'program Sawal Yeh Hai' by Dr Danish dated 19th November 2010] also aired a conversation between Pervez Elahi, Shahbaz and Justice Qayyum. Following is the transcript of the conversation. Justice (r) Abdul Qayyum: Your task will be done in a day or two. I had to request an adviser (Peerzada) for you. I told him that I am very ill and I have to leave abroad and I have asked him to end up the matter for my sake. Peerzada has told me that he will do it and it will be done. He told me that he would compensate for all the mistakes I have done; adding that Mian Sahib (Nawaz Sharif) would be happy as well. Audiotape reveals Sharifs manipulated verdict in that Zardari's case.'*

The Supreme Court had, interalia, observed that:

> *'We are convinced that the trial in this case was not fair and on account of bias of the Ehtesab Bench the trial of the appellants stands vitiated'.*

The court found that Justice Qayyum and his wife had applied for diplomatic passports on 17th April 1998 after taking up the case. Diplomatic passports were not to be issued to judges and the foreign ministry had opposed the application but with special instructions of the then PM Nawaz Sharif, the process started as a special case. On 27th April 1999 Justice Qayyum issued an order freezing the properties and assets of Ms Benazir and Mr Zardari. Three days later the diplomatic passports were issued to Justice Malik Qayyum and his wife. It was also held by the Supreme Court that the judge had ignored 10 other accused in the trial and rushed the hearing.

> [*Finally, the Supreme Court noted that the verdict was written and dated on 14th April 1999, one day before the trial actually ended.*]

'Give them full dose;' Ehtesab Chief Saifur Rehman had told Justice Qayyum on phone. Pakistan's hard luck was that Gen Musharraf, the army dictator did not bother to take action against Justice Qayyum for that corrupt practice. Instead he was allowed to start his legal practice in the same higher courts; rather he was made Attorney General of Pakistan later in 2006-07; reasons best known to Gen Musharraf; the successor king of Nawaz Sharif's dynasty.

What matters for the people of Pakistan and for history was the truth it revealed about the judiciary as well as the executive. In a sense, it was an indictment of the kind of politics we had in this country and reflected upon the depths of aberrations to which governments and some judicial misfits and adventurers could descend in pursuit of questionable ends. The Supreme Court sent back the case and ordered retrial of Ms Benazir and Mr Zardari because Justice Qayyum had shown bias towards both of the PPP leaders during her trial in the Lahore High Court.

AYAZ AMIR's HISTORICAL VERDICT:

A paragraph from an essay, written by PML(N)'s own party legislator *Ayaz Amir, published on 20th April 2001* is placed here to reflect the minds of a judge and rulers of those days:

'His Lordship Justice Qayyum of the Lahore High Court was the Sharif family's personal judge, settling matters, both private and state, to their complete satisfaction.

The Sharifs' notions of government were intensely private: which is to say, have your own man at every key post. They began with commissioners and police DIGs, the dregs of both services pandering to their whims and enriching themselves in the process. But when Nawaz Sharif became Prime Minister the second time round the family's sights were set higher.

They had whiz-kid younger brother running Punjab. They had their own man in the presidency. After Sajjad Ali Shah's arranged departure from the Supreme Court, they thought they had the apex court lined up in their favour. In the person of Justice Qayyum at the Lahore High Court they had the closest thing they could get to a personal judge. Division of family assets, balancing of huge bank loans against dummy collateral, tightening the noose around Asif Zardari and Benazir: the only judge who could handle these sensitive matters was Justice Qayyum.

In the Qayyum tapes which detail conversations between Justice Qayyum and Nawaz Sharif's fox-hound, Saifur Rehman, nothing matches the echo of these words uttered by His Lordship: "By the grace of God this will be done (that is, the judgment against Bhutto and Zardari) and then both of us will go to him (Nawaz Sharif) and seek forgiveness." Forgiveness for what? For not being able to wrap up the case against Benazir and husband as quickly as Nawaz Sharif desired.

But Saifur Rehman and his goons in the Accountability Bureau aimed not at justice but victimization. And because their hands were not clean retribution has knocked at their doors. The losers as always are the people of Pakistan. Of what matter to them if one set of looters is embarrassed while another set is distributing sweets over a form of judicial vindication?'

At the same time Ayaz Amir was right to raise questions like: 'Does any newspaper-reading man in Pakistan doubt Benazir's and Asif's guilt? Does anyone think they got no commission from the Swiss firm, SGS-Cotecna? Does anyone doubt the financial acumen of the then ruling couple who turned Islamabad into an open auction mart where every deal, no matter how outrageous, was on offer provided the right palms were greased?'

Certainly not; but it was Saifur Rehman and Justice Qayyum's foolishness which helped Bhuttos and Zardaris to get green labels for them to befool the innocent people again.

[On 26ᵗʰ June 2001, the game was over. Malik Qayyum was asked to resign from his seat as judge of the Lahore High Court and he was un-ceremoniously sent home. On 9ᵗʰ July 2001 Chief Justice of Lahore High Court Rashid Aziz preferred to seek early retirement. A chapter of intellectual and judicial corruption closed.]

20th June 2001: Gen Musharraf, while he was also Chief Executive, took over the office of the President of Pakistan, under the Provisional Constitutional Order (PCO) by removing a dummy Rafiq Tarar before he was allowed to complete his five-year tenure. With immediate effect he dissolved the suspended Senate, National and Provincial Assemblies and dismissed the Chairman of the Senate and the Speaker of the National Assembly. J Irshad Hassan Khan, Chief Justice of Pakistan administered this swearing.

More than fifty years back, Justice Muhammad Munir had strengthened the forces opposed to 'rule of law', legitimizing Mr Ghulam

Mohammad's rule giving an idea of 'legalised illegality' providing a solid foundation for repressive rule over democracy; government of men as opposed to government of laws, 'rule of persons' as opposed to 'rule of law'. It is an old story now where the legislative pillar of the state became a consistent looser. Justice Munir had decided in favour of a wrong person; Justice Anwarul Haq decided in favour of another General and Justice Irshad Hassan Khan decided in favour of a third similar General.

In essence, affirming the 'doctrine of necessity' depends upon the inside strength of sitting judge; see Justice Yaqoob Ali. Such like judges are the light towers in the history of nations. Mostly the politicians provide opportunities to the military dictators to continue in the wake of certain calculated compromises. Example is the circumstances around 2003-04; when all the PML(Q) and MMA parliamentarians opted to twist themselves in favour of uniform, no body raised his hand against the military dictator only to save his seat, then putting the burden of doing wrong on the courts alone do not justify at all. Every one had to play his role judiciously, if they wanted to keep history on their side.

On **21st June 2001**, the very next day, Gen Musharraf's holding of the Office of President was challenged in Sindh High Court and on **31st July 2001** Chief Justice of Sindh High Court, Syed Saeed Ash'had had dismissed petitions against Gen Musharraf challenging him.

6th October 2001: Gen Musharraf himself extended his term as Chief of the Army Staff (COAS) for an indefinite period. The details have already been enumerated in the preceding chapters.

Scenario 36

JUDICIARY'S FACE BLACKENED (2001):

No one would feel pleasure while calling back those dark moments of Pakistan's history when country's senior judges, including Chief Justice (CJ) Lahore High Court (LHC) Justice Rashid Aziz and trial Judge Justice Malik Qayyum had worked out a joint plan to slaughter the prevailing judicial norms. These judges of an Islamic country, sworn to uphold the scales of Justice but degraded themselves and humiliated the Judiciary, just to seek pleasure of some stooge politicians.

The judges and the then Federal Cabinet ministers, in an unholy conspiracy, plotted against former Prime Minister Benazir Bhutto and her husband Asif Ali Zardari, who was behind the bars then. They had frozen their owned and allegedly disputed assets through judicial orders drafted not by them but in concerned minister's chambers. Members of the Cabinet included Federal Law Minister Khalid Anwar and Accountability Minister Senator Saifur Rahman. They liaised with the CJ and the trial Judge to politically eliminate the then Leader of Opposition Ms Bhutto while completing 'a sacred' mission given to them by the then Prime Minister Nawaz Sharif. It was done just to 'politically kill' a former PM, his political opponent.

J MALIK QAYYUM'S TRANSCRIPTS:

The judges on the bench took orders from the above mentioned two federal ministers of Law and Accountability respectively — on *'what sentence to give'*. According to the tapes of conversations, which were placed before the bench of the Supreme Court later as evidence, the Chief of *Ehtesab* (Accountability Minister) had told the trial judge J Qayyum how pleased PM Nawaz Sharif would be *'when Ms. Bhutto's inherited properties are confiscated, she is imprisoned for seven (7) years and disqualified from politics'*.

In selling himself to the regime, Justice Malik Qayyum and other Judges disgraced the high judicial echelons they occupied. There were other judges also who were named in those tapes. The transcripts indicated that a race was going on between the three trial-courts before whom Ms Bhutto was forced to stand trial on an investigation described as 'politically driven' by the World's Human Rights Forum [but facts might be otherwise]. At one stage Accountability Minister taunted Justice

Malik Qayyum that *'Maulvi', (referring to another Accountability Judge named Ehsan ul Haq of the same LHC) would finish the case before Malik Qayyum's decision.'*

Benazir Bhutto was seemingly right to allege that all the three judges conducting the trials were biased. In one case, Justice Nawaz Abbasi gave an *ex parte* judgment freezing her undisputed assets in 1998 on the request of Saifur Rehman and his team. **The *'freeze order'* was announced by the Cabinet Minister several hours before it was actually signed.** Forever, the annals of judicial history will be stained by a judgment written before the trial concluded. A judgment dictated by the Prime Minister's office against the PM's main political foe, the leader of opposition in the Parliament.

For aforesaid act of judicial misdeed, Justice Nawaz Abbasi was rewarded with retrospective seniority putting him in line for the coveted position of Chief Justice of LHC.

Another judge, Justice Najm ul Hassan, was also rewarded after he signed the 'historical' conviction order against Ms Bhutto (he was on the bench with Justice Qayyum). From an acting Judge, he was elevated to a full judge. A layman would be astonished to know the details that how Pakistani Judges once became tennis rackets hitting Ms Bhutto from court room to court room, in city after city and province after province, in a bid to become the first to 'convict' her and reap the bitter harvest of sweet favours from the ruling regime. Shameful it was.

*[Ms Bhutto's judgment was signed on **14th day of April 1999;** sentenced on the charge of influencing a Swiss pre-shipment contract to benefit her husband; Senator Zardari. She denied the charge claiming she was a victim of political enmity {though another debateable issue}. The written order convicting Ms Bhutto & Mr Zardari had already been read before some media men by the Ehtesab Minister on 14th but in the court-room it was announced on **15th April 1999.** The PPP then charged that the order was pre-written but the judge claimed that it was a typing error.]*

It is interesting to note that Generals and Judges have never been tried in Pakistan. Under the provisions of the Army Act, all members of armed, air and naval forces are exempt from any kind of interrogation, investigation, judicial trials and appearance in courts & tribunals. Under this amnesty the army is ruling over Pakistan since 1957 and will continue for ever. Similar is the case of judges. No body can raise finger on them, no paper can publish comments on judges, judiciary or judgments because the law of 'Contempt of Court' is there to give them protection even when documentary evidence exists.

Such was the injustice that it gave birth to the phrase in Pakistan, *'After Justice Qayyum's judgment in Benazir Bhutto's case, one should hire a judge rather than a lawyer'*.

The telephone of Justice Malik Qayyum at his Lahore residence was under surveillance during the period of trial of Ms. Bhutto. The then Chief Justice of LHC Rashid Aziz was also on tape. He was the judge chosen to hear accountability cases against Benazir Bhutto in her first term. Justice Rashid Aziz was afterwards sent to the Supreme Court where Ms Bhutto's appeal was to be heard.

The audio tapes proved beyond doubt that Senator Saifur Rehman had supervised the proceedings by liaising between Justice Qayyum and others. The tapes proved that he took directions personally from the then PM Nawaz Sharif regarding the conduct of the proceedings and the punishment to be awarded to Ms Bhutto and her spouse. The tapes indicated that Chief Justice LHC had met the PM Nawaz Sharif shortly before the judgment. The Chief Justice discussed the judgment with Mr Sharif including the timing of its announcement.

It is also on record that when Justice Qayyum once failed to deliver the judgment on a given 'tomorrow', Senator Saifur Rehman rang up Justice Qayyum from the PM's Office to further pressurize him to announce the judgment *'definitely tomorrow'*; Justice Malik Qayyum had affirmed he would do so.

In the same conversation, Justice Malik Qayyum and an official of the PM Secretariat discussed the quantum of punishment to be given to Ms. Bhutto. Justice Qayyum asked: " ..... *Tell me how much punishment do you want me to give her?" In reply the official told him "what ever you have been told by **him** (PM Nawaz Sharif)" and "not less than seven (7) years (page 29 of transcripts placed before the Supreme Court is referred). Justice Qayyum assured the official that "under all circumstances it will be done tomorrow. We are going to announce the judgment"*.

At the time the judge made this statement, the trial was still proceeding. A Swiss defence witness had arrived to depose in the court. Summing up arguments was still to be made by defence lawyers. In London, Ms Bhutto was at a CNN studio with Riz Khan, an anchor, when she received a call on Mr Wajid's mobile telephone informing by some secret sympathizer that the judgment would come the next day. She rang up defence lawyer Farooq Naek who had replied *'impossible, the trial has not yet concluded'*. However, true to his promise, Justice Qayyum announced judgment the next day.

[By announcing the judgment against Ms Bhutto and Mr Zardari, the Nawaz regime tried to divert attention from a judgment given by a British Court in the Al-Toufiq case against members of Mr Sharif's family amounting to millions of dollars in a hidden offshore account.]

In another conversation, the Prime Minister's official asked the judge to **"give them full dose (with regard to Ms Bhutto and her husband)"** (page no: 36 of transcript is referred). In the same conversation the judge informed the official of his plan and timing to deliver the judgment *'tomorrow'*.

The conversation between CJ Rashid Aziz of LHC and Justice Malik Qayyum had also indicated that the Chief Justice was in possession of the pre-written judgment concerning Ms Bhutto, which Justice Qayyum had to sign (page no: 35 of the transcript is referred). The Chief Justice said *"do you know without asking you it is already written and lying with us. He (Judge) can sign it for you and you can keep it with you"*. *Justice Qayyum replied: "I have already written the short order."*

This conversation took place on 14th April 1999 as it was announced next day. In fact the short order announced by Justice Qayyum on 15th April 1999, winding up the trial midway without examining remaining defence witness, was signed on 14th April 1999, a day before the actual decision. The PPP's lawyers had to point out this discrepancy in dates when filing an appeal. In one conversation, Senator Saifur Rehman had asked Justice Malik Qayyum *"one thing is to be done that is to get their (Bhutto's and Zardari's) video tape... kindly permit our man to sit in the room next to your room"* (Page no: 19 of the transcript is referred).

Justice Qayyum discussed the matter of video tape with the CJ Rashid Aziz. The Chief Justice said: *"It is right. Now also tell them that we are not supposed to know"*.

It cannot be a mere coincidence that **when Nawaz Sharif was sent home in October 1999, he was convicted too by the same Justice Malik Qayyum in chair.** Almighty GOD is there to take account of all (mis)deeds. History often repeats itself. Justice Qayyum's father Justice Malik Akram had sentenced Z A Bhutto to death in 1979 to oblige the then military dictator Gen Ziaul Haq in a controversial judgment. His son Justice Malik Qayyum sentenced Bhutto's daughter, Benazir, to please Gen Zia's political son, Nawaz Sharif.

Justice Qayyum took personal favours from Nawaz Sharif in person including diplomatic passports for him and his wife. The bestowal upon Justice Qayyum of diplomatic passports for himself and his wife, an act that appeared to have been unprecedented, following shortly after his issuance of a ruling against Ms Bhutto, was sufficient proof of the said judge's ill intentions.

It is also on record that once the Pakistani courts had ordered Zardari's release on medical grounds but the PML regime blocked it through a stay order from the Supreme Court in violation of the law of consistency. Nawaz Sharif, while he was in Attock Jail later, wrote a letter to the military authorities seeking medical treatment. Without constituting a medical board and without seeking a court order, a convict was released by Gen Musharraf on medical grounds. In contrast four trial courts and a High Court had ordered the release of Mr Zardari on similar grounds including medical, but the military authorities kept on denying him bail and allegedly demanded medical treatment.

In this context, Justice Qayyum did not hesitate to show his open bias. Even former Attorney General for Pakistan (Senator Syed Iqbal Haider) and former Law Minister (Senator Raza Rabbani) were denied admission to the Court room in which the said trial was proceeding.

Justice Malik Qayyum had imposed himself on this matter despite the Appellant's apprehensions of his bias by the fact that even when the Reference was transferred by the Court from the Principal seat of Lahore High Court to its Rawalpindi Bench, where other learned Judges were available, he took it upon himself to hold dual charge at Lahore and Rawalpindi Bench, just to hear Ms Bhutto's case. This was against the Constitutional provisions and the relevant law, rules and regulations but Justice Malik Qayyum chased the case with ulterior motives perhaps on the instructions of PM Nawaz Sharif and Senator Saif ur Rehman.

Justice Malik Qayyum did not allow sufficient time to Ms Bhutto to engage a counsel in Rawalpindi after the Reference was transferred to Rawalpindi Bench from Lahore. When the appellant had no lawyer, the judge ordered the case to be proceeded and told her that if she did not have a lawyer by the next day, he would not allow her to proceed out of the country to visit her children although court holidays were then beginning. Mention of her children by a judge was shocking to everyone.

Justice Malik Qayyum's brother Pervez Malik was an MNA of PML(N) and PM Nawaz Sharif was also playing pressure through him. During a hearing in Lahore High Court Justice Qayyum had expressed unhappiness over a remark by Ms Bhutto that *'Judges with close links to the regime should not be trying her.'* Justice Qayyum said in open Court:

> *'Had I seen the statement earlier I would not have granted the bail yesterday to Mr Iqbal Tikka, a Provincial Minister belonging to the Appellants party'.*

On 1st March 1999, Justice Malik Qayyum had adjourned the matter to 8th March 1999, but however, he passed the orders for issuance of commission to go to Switzerland to verify the authenticity of the so-called foreign documents produced by Ms Bhutto in the said case. This decision of Justice Qayyum was immediately challenged in the Supreme Court vide CrPLA No: 46/99 & 47/99 and leave to appeal was granted on 12th March 1999 in this regard and it was ordered that the report of the commission be kept in sealed cover till its call later.

Though the appeals no: 46-47/99 mentioned above were pending in the Supreme Court but, on **15th March 1999** Justice Malik Qayyum had closed the defence evidence and refused to summon the witnesses without hearing Ms Bhutto or Asif Ali Zardari's Counsel in the matter. The order was passed in a post haste manner to help the prosecution.

Justice Malik Qayyum asked for argument on the main case without deciding the application under Section 265-K CrPC filed on behalf of Ms Bhutto and Asif Ali Zardari since long rendering the said applications in fructuous. Furthermore as the prosecution had failed to file reply to the said application, Justice Qayyum verbally ordered on **15th March 1999** on the request of Mr Farooq H Naek, the defence counsel, that *'the prosecution's right to reply has been forfeited'* but the same was not incorporated in the order sheet.

Once, during the trial, Justice Malik Qayyum had allowed the pleader of Ms Bhutto & Mr Zardari to call their Swiss expert witness Mr Salvatore Aversano at any time before the prosecution closed its case. When the witness, having travelled overnight from Switzerland and arrived in the court to give his evidence he was neither allowed to give evidence nor allowed to swear an affidavit. This course was deliberately adopted by Justice Qayyum to satisfy his then political masters.

On **27th April 1999**, Justice Malik Qayyum arbitrarily and without giving notice to or hearing Ms Bhutto, ordered to freeze their assets and all accounts as a result of which the appellant could not engage a counsel to defend her [though it was not a plausible excuse]. The court also ignored Ms Bhutto's request that the government be asked to pay for her defence counsel as her assets had been frozen.

Later, the Supreme Court, while deciding Ms Bhutto & Zardari's appeal, had categorically declared that:

> 'Justice Qayyum was naturally and materially affected by his personal bias and prejudice and other judge Justice Najam-ul-Hassan Kazmi was an unconfirmed judge of the Lahore High Court and that too on an extended one year term'.

The Supreme Court of Pakistan held in the said appeal that the proceedings by the trial court (comprising of J Malik Qayyum and J Kazmi) were violative of a basic principle that:

> 'Justice should not only be done but it should also be seen to have been done. This principle was recently upheld by the House of Lords in England in the "Pinochet Case" whereby it historically set aside one of its own judgment on this principle. In that case the "perception" that one of the members of the court might be bias towards one side was sufficient to set aside the order.'

J MALIK QAYYUM'S VIEWPOINT:

However, J Malik Qayyum, in an interview published in daily *'Jang'* **dated 5th February 2006,** had denied the whole set of charges and miss-perceptions referred to his person as judge. The summary of explanations forwarded by him is given below:

- I've not ever heard about those audio tapes, never seen them, don't know from where they had come. The government of Pakistan had denied those tapes ever made or possessed. Those audio tapes were not placed before the court even during appeal of the said Benazir Bhutto's case. No body, even the Supreme Court, had ever asked us to comment if those tapes were concerning us.

- Is there any sane judge existing anywhere who would ask a politician to tell him *'how much punishment should be awarded in a case'*?

- I had not resigned from my position of a HC judge because those audio tapes were correct. I had resigned because the Supreme Court had given verdict against me. I did not want to go in detail nor in controversy so I went side lined.

- The then military government had never exerted any pressure on me to resign, I did it voluntarily. Yes! I myself had felt more pressure from media campaigns against me.

- The Supreme Court had done wrong with us. The apex court had not gone through the judgment I wrote but they went for trial of the judge. The SC did not see what was written in the judgment; it went after the judge who had written it. They should have analyzed the judgment first.

- Regarding resignation of CJ LHC Rashid Aziz, the truth was that the CJP Irshad Hassan Khan went somewhat personal against the former. In a mutual meeting, the CJP had asked J Rashid Aziz that why he was not inclined to tender his resignation. J Rashid Aziz said that because:

'We have not been heard on tapes issue. The decision has been made against judicial spirits. We'll be moving the SC in September, after vacations.'

The CJP Irshad Hassan Khan got furious and asked J Rashid Aziz to move tomorrow and why to wait till September.

'I'll sit in the court tomorrow and turn down your petition or appeal immediately'.

J Rashid Aziz was stunt to hear the mind of a CJP.

- The CJP Irshad Hassan Khan had also threatened CJ LHC Rashid Aziz that he would refer his case to the Supreme Judicial Council if he would not resign. [*It should not be termed as threat. The CJP might have spoken about a possibility.*]

- My relations with Nawaz Sharif were not secret. I heard Benazir Bhutto's cases because the same were not Benazir Bhutto vs Nawaz Sharif.

- Once Benazir Bhutto was present before the court I was presiding. She said that:

'Your father had given verdict against my father Mr Bhutto and you want to punish me. Please do not hear my case.' [The irony of fate was

that even then J Malik Qayyum continued with the trial like J Maulvi Mushtaq Hussain in the past]

I asked her to give me in writing which she never opted to do.

- The red passports were issued to us much earlier than the said decision announced in Benazir Bhutto's cases. [*The Foreign Office holds that the same were issued a week after the judgment.*]

- What to speak about Saifur Rehman. He was a little fry, how could he dare to talk to a judge of High Court on phone. Dictations by him are cooked stories.

- Once, Benazir Bhutto came to see me in my hotel's room I was staying in at Dubai. In those days I had no case against her to hear. She had actually come to see the CJ LHC Rashid Aziz who was staying in the next room to request that her four different cases, being heard by four different judges, should be placed before one judge. Later, she made a written request with that plea to the CJ LHC and specifically mentioned that she had full faith in J Malik Qayyum. The said letter is still available in LHC's record. [*How an accused could demand for a judge of her choice: no tradition, never heard*]

Much water had passed through the bridge of judicial values till then. Still there exists a school of thought who raises questions like:

- If the CJ LHC Rashid Aziz was upright then why he got aback when he was asked to face Supreme Judicial Council, he would have liked so to clear the filth.

- J Malik Qayyum, however, avoided confirming that Nawaz Sharif and Saifur Rehman were taking keen interest in Benazir Bhutto's hearings through him.

- Fact remains that the SC had gone through J Malik Qayyum's judgment first and observed '.... *The bias is seen floating at the surface of the judgment*'.

- The truth lies that it was Nawaz Sharif who had got referred the Benazir Bhutto's cases especially to J Malik Qayyum otherwise there were about thirty more judges in the LHC. J Malik Qayyum should have refused to hear those cases being known that his brother, Pervez Malik, was an MNA of PML got elected virtually unopposed due to Nawaz Sharif's special blessings.

It is an endless debate. Let us hope such episodes do not surface again in Pakistan.

One can, however, aspire that on the similar given lines Mr Z A Bhutto was hanged just because he was allegedly the directing authority in the killing of Nawab Ahmed Qasuri; Nawaz Sharif was also the directing authority of cases against Benazir Bhutto & Mr Zardari. Nawaz Sharif was the actual beneficiary in those trials whereas CJ LHC Rashid Aziz, Justice Malik Qayyum, Saif ur Rehman and Khalid Anwar were the 'obeying ponies' and front actors only. Will ever our judiciary take notice of this bitter fact?

PRESIDENT RAFIQ TARAR SENT HOME:

It is interesting to note that Rafiq Tarar was continuing with his office as the President of Pakistan till 20th June 2001, when Gen Musharraf issued an amendment Order No. 2 of 2001 saying that:

'The person holding the office of the President of the Islamic Republic of Pakistan immediately before the commencement of the Proclamation of Emergency (Amendment) Order 2001, shall cease to hold the office with immediate effect.'

Not only this, under the same order it was declared that:

'The Chairman and Deputy Chairman of the Senate have already ceased to hold office; the Speaker and Deputy Speaker of the National Assembly and the Provincial Assemblies shall also cease to hold office with immediate effect.'

On the same day of 20th June 2001, Gen Musharraf issued another Order No. 3 of 2001 saying that his order of 14th October 1999 would take effect notwithstanding anything contained in the Constitution or any other law and he would take over Office of the President immediately.

Some historians has painted him as a saint saying that *'President Tarar was in deep shock and wholeheartedly upset after hearing the military coup d'état took place to remove the elected prime minister Nawaz Sharif and voluntarily resigned from the presidency in favor of General Pervez Musharraf on June 20, 2001'*, but it was not the whole truth. Tarar chose to remain in office until 2001, at which point Gen Musharraf assumed the presidency in order to restructure Pakistan's model of government. The question arises that if he [Mr Tarar] was so fond of democraccy, he should have left the presidency on 12th October

1999 declaring that *'having a judicial mind he was not in a position of approving the military coup'* but he never did so untill he was kicked out of the presidency by Gen Musharraf in June 2001.

Once in December 1997, the Acting CEC Justice Mukhtar Ahmed Junejo, had found Mr Tarar, a former Supreme Court Judge, guilty of propagating views prejudicial to the integrity and independence of the judiciary at the time of his nomination as a presidential candidate under Article 63(G) of the Constitution and debarred him on 18th December 1997 to contest the presidential elections.

J Rafiq Tarar was found guilty of making derogatory remarks against the apex judiciary. In a seven-page order released later J Junejo had said: *'I am of the view that case of Mr Tarar is covered by sub-clause (g) of clause (1) of Article 63 of the Constitution and since he cannot be elected as member of parliament, hence in terms of Article 41(2) of the Constitution of Pakistan, he cannot be elected as president of Pakistan. I therefore, reject his nomination papers.'* Parliamentary Secretary for Law Syed Zafar Ali Shah, termed the order of the acting CEC unconstitutional and illegal, thus had challenged the said decision.

Now see a script of the *'Dawn' dated 28th February 1998* written by Ardsher Cowasjee:

> *'What was Leghari's successor in office, Rafiq Tarar, doing in Quetta on the day the order suspending Chief Justice Sajjad Ali Shah was handed down by the Quetta Bench of the Supreme Court? Why did Tarar and two others fly to Quetta in a special plane on that disastrous day? Leghari is right. Questions are being asked. Why were the police at the Quetta airport ordered not to manifest his arrival (which instructions they in fact manifested)? Where did Tarar stay on the night of November 26 (his departure on November 27 having been manifested by the airport police)? What reward was he given for his day's efforts? Why, on January 20, was a story leaked by the government to the press about the obstruction of justice early in 1997 in an alleged rape case involving a servant in the then Justice Ajmal Mian's Karachi house when he, as CJ, was presiding over the bench hearing contempt of court cases against Nawaz Sharif and others? Why were stories leaked about the foreign scholarship sponsored by the government to the wife of the good [Justice] Saeeduzzaman Siddiqui?'*

The judicial record would reflect that during the three year's stay in the Supreme Court, J Rafiq Tarar could only author two judgments worth to be mentioned in the PLD including one in the case of the 1993 dissolution of the National Assembly restoring Nawaz Sharif. The second being Criminal Appeal No. 74/SAC/L, decided by J Tarar on 19th February 1994, reported at *1994 SCMR 1466* namely "Muhammad Ashraf and Others vs The State". Muhammad Ashraf, Khalid Javaid and Zafar Ali had been sentenced to have their right hands amputated from the wrist and their left legs from the ankle, to seven years RI, and to a fine of Rs.20,000 each being guilty of theft of Rs.40,000 and of a licensed pistol. Justice Rafiq Tarar had headed the bench comprising members J Afrasiab Khan & J Muhammad Zubair and the judgment concluded with:

> '...... *The only punishment provided by section 17(3) is the amputation of right hand from the wrist and left leg from the ankle which has been imposed by the learned trial Court and we confirm the same.*'

Another interesting case was of 3rd August 1994, heard by J Munir Khan and J Mir Hazar Khan Khoso of the Supreme Court, reported at *PLD 1994 SC 885*. This was an appeal against a 'not reported' judgment of that court dated 14th March 1993, passed in Criminal Appeal 91/SAC/L/92 by the honourable Supreme Appellate Court comprising Justice Tarar.

Supreme Court Judges Munir Khan and Khoso heard the convict's appeal against Justice Tarar's judgment and, interalia, recorded that:

> '...*we are in no manner of doubt that the trial Court and also the learned Appellate Court had no lawful authority / jurisdiction / power whatsoever to convict the petitioner under section 302 PPC or to impose penalty of death on him, and have acted in gross violation of law. The Courts derive authority to punish the accused from the statute. If the statute does not provide death penalty for the offence then obviously the Court would have no jurisdiction to award the same, and, as such, the conviction and sentence of the petitioner recorded under section 302 PPC is coram non judice.*'

It was declared that the error committed by the Courts in convicting the accused / petitioner under section 302 PPC and sentencing him to death was so serious that had the petitioner eventually been hanged to death, it would have amounted to murder through judicial process. The said case was remitted back to the Lahore High Court for a "fresh decision in accordance with law."

Three years later, whilst the Anti-Terrorism Act was being drafted, retired judges but subsequently made Senators, Rafiq Tarar and Afzal Lone [*another benefactor of the Ittefaq empire and later rewarded with Senate seat*], were called in. They recommended what could be termed a parallel judicial system composed of special courts with special judges with special powers to try all those suspected of terrorist acts. Chief Justice of Pakistan Sajjad Ali Shah objected, and proposed that suspects be tried in the normal course by Session Judges (requesting that many more be appointed). To expedite matters, trials could be held in the jails. Those convicted could appeal to the High Court, and then to the Supreme Court. The CJP had assured the prime minister that the entire trial period would be completed within three months. Nawaz Sharif did not want trials held in three stages, so it was finally agreed by all that the Session Court stage would go, that suspects would be tried in the High Courts, and then allowed an appeal to the Supreme Court.

However, much to the CJP's surprise, when the Act was passed by the parliament, the law laid down that a suspect would be tried by a special judge in a special court, that an appeal would lie only before a special tribunal of two specially appointed high court judges, that no bail would be granted, and no appeal to the Supreme Court allowed. It was all as initially recommended by Justice Tarar & Justice Lone on the whims of their PM Nawaz Sharif.

The PML nominated Senator Rafiq Tarar on 15th December 1997 as their presidential candidate [it was *Abbajee's* order: *'Select my friend and legal adviser, Rafiq Tarar, whose wit and wisdom I share, and with whom I often sup late into the night'*]. What was good for the Sharifs, was good for the party, and was good for the nation. Without further argument, without consulting his ruling party members, or the leaders of the coalition parties, Nawaz Sharif nominated Tarar. But on 18th December, the Acting Chief Election Commissioner Mukhtar Junejo rejected his nomination papers under Article 63(g) of the Constitution.

'Can we remove Junejo', was Nawaz Sharif's first aristocratic reaction. **'Risky'**, he was told. Rather than honourably withdrawing from the race, Rafiq Tarar appealed for help to Mian Sharif. Within moments, the prime minister ordered to place an appeal before their family judge Justice Malik Qayyum of the Lahore High Court for an interim stay and appropriate verdict to allow J Tarar to successfully contest the election. On 19th December, Justice Qayyum suspended Junejo's order, allowing Tarar to *'participate in the election provisionally subject to further orders. A larger bench will hear the petition on the 23rd.'* The issue was resolved and Sharif's wish upheld because *'it was in the greater interest of the nation'.*

[*It has already been mentioned elsewhere that Justice Malik Qayyum was sitting on a condolence mat to offer 'Fateha' of a nearby relative when he received Nawaz Sharif's message to issue stay order for J Rafiq Tarar on urgent basis. He immediately left the condolence mat, reached the court and issued orders.*]

Earlier, Senator Justice (Rtd) Rafiq Tarar was despatched to Quetta by his PM Nawaz Sharif in a special flight which landed at Quetta at night. The Quetta airfield was not normally lit up after nightfall as no flights used to land there. The runway was specially lit up for Tarar and the security man on duty had reportedly noted in his log: *'Instructions have been received from Islamabad that the details of the special flight carrying the visiting dignitary, Senator Rafiq Tarar, must be kept confidential and not reported'.*

Referring to 'Laughing at ourselves' by Ardeshir Cowasjee appeared in the *'Dawn' dated 11th November 2000,* it should remain available on the pages of history that Senator Rafiq Tarar had known that the Supreme Court building was going to be attacked on 27th November 1997 of which he had been a part for about three years as Mr Justice. Not only this, the ISI also knew it before hand and the then Incharge ISI, Gen Rana had reported the then COAS, Gen Jehangir Karamat, at the dawning of 27th November, that *'Nawaz's cohorts were to raid the Supreme Court in the morning'.* Even they did not bother to check the raid.

Referring to comments by Kunwar Idris, published in the *'Dawn' of 20th December 1998:*

'Also casting a dark shadow on him [Mr Tarar] is the referendum of December 1984 when, as a member of Zia's Election Commission, he solemnly assured the people that 55 per cent and not just five per cent of the electorate had turned out to confer legitimacy on Zia's dictatorial rule. Mr Tarar also has to dispel the widely insinuated impression that he was involved in the 'Quetta Shuttle' which divided the Supreme Court and wrote the saddest chapter in Pakistan's constitutional history.'

Scenario 37

PAKISTAN'S JUDICIARY IN 2002

On **14th January 2002:** Justice Irshad Hassan Khan was made Chief Election Commissioner of Pakistan.

On **10th February 2002;** in the case of Supreme Court Bar Association through its President Hamid Khan vs the Federation of Pakistan, a five-member bench examined the appointment of judges in the Supreme Court and the issue of seniority in the High Courts for such appointments. Explaining the spirit of the Judges' Case of 1996 and subsequent precedents, the apex Court held:

> *"The contention that the chief justice of a High Court is entitled to be elevated to the Supreme Court due to seniority is misconceived and travels beyond the parameters indicated in the Judges' Case. In our considered view, the scope of seniority and legitimate expectancy enunciated in those cases is restricted to the appointments of the Chief Justice of a High Court and the Chief Justice of Pakistan, and these issues neither apply nor can be extended to the appointment of Judges of the Supreme Court."*

It was categorically stated that there was neither constitutional convention nor past practice to elevate the senior-most judges of a High Court to the Supreme Court. An interesting comparison was also drawn by the Supreme Court between Article 180 of the Constitution of Pakistan, which governs the appointments of acting chief justices of the Supreme Court and where the words "the most senior of the other Judges" are mentioned, and Article 177, which deals with the appointment of a Supreme Court judge and where such language is missing. In the Supreme Court's own words:

> *"The absence of the words 'most senior' in Article 177 for appointment of Judges of the Supreme Court would show that the seniority of a Judge in the High Court is not a sine qua non for his appointment as a Judge of the Supreme Court."*

Gen Musharraf's Referendum:

2nd April 2002: Qazi Hussain Ahmed filed a Constitution Petition No. 15/2002 and a similar Constitution Petition No. 22/2002 was filed by

Syed Zafar Ali Shah before the Supreme Court of Pakistan. It was prayed in both the petitions that:

> 'The Chief Executive (Gen Musharraf) has unlawfully occupied and taken over the position of the President of the Islamic Republic of Pakistan in violation of the judgment of this Court in Syed Zafar Ali Shah's case;

- That Muhammad Rafiq Tarar still continues to be the President notwithstanding the Chief Executive's Order 3 of 2001;

- That writ in the nature of quo warranto be issued against the Chief Executive;

- That the holding of referendum for election to the office of the President be declared illegal, unconstitutional and violative of the judgment of this Court in _Syed Zafar Ali Shah's case._'

On 9th April 2002, Gen Musharraf issued Chief Executive's Order No. 12 of 2002, commonly known as the 'Referendum Order' which provided that the Referendum would be held on 30th April 2002 and meant that:

> 'Notwithstanding anything contained in the Constitution or any law for the time being in force, if the majority of the votes cast in the referendum are in the affirmative, the people of Pakistan shall be deemed to have given the democratic mandate to General Pervez Musharraf to serve the nation as President of Pakistan for a period of five years.

> The period of five years mentioned above would be computed from the first meeting of the Majlis-e-Shoora (Parliament) to be elected as a result of the forthcoming general election to be held in October 2002, in accordance with the Judgment of the apex Court.'

The referendum question was: 'For the survival of the local government system, establishment of democracy, continuity of reforms, end to sectarianism and extremism, and to fulfil the vision of Quaid e Azam [Great leader: Pakistan's late founder, Mohammed Ali Jinnah], would you like to elect President General Pervez Musharraf as president of Pakistan for five years?'

Gen Musharraf wanted to establish his legitimacy. He took power in a military coup on 12th October 1999 that ousted the then Prime Minister

Nawaz Sharif, but promised to be only a caretaker leader until democracy could be restored. The referendum allowed him to be seen to be abiding by democratic ideals.

Pakistani politicians believed the army was denying them power thus termed the referendum as unconstitutional. Under the constitution, the president should be chosen not on a direct vote of the people, but by the elected members of the National Assembly, Provincial Assemblies and the Senate. Many had hoped that the general elections which were due in October that year could be followed by the picking of a new president.

Earlier in January 2002, Gen Musharraf had delivered a speech advocating reform and calling for Pakistan to return to the values upon which it was founded. He urged to stay in power to counter unnamed destabilising influences. The referendum was preceded by a month-long campaign by Gen Musharraf, while a ban on public rallies prevented political parties from campaigning against the referendum. The Governor Punjab, Gen Khalid Maqbool, during a pro-referendum rally, had warned that journalists could face revenge from the public if they did not cease their 'misreporting'.

The referendum, however, took place. The government said that with most of the votes counted [turnout was around 70%] around 98% backed Gen Musharraf continuing in office. It was hotly disputed by the opposition, which called for a boycott of the vote. It said little more than 5% of the electorate bothered to vote, illustrating that Gen Musharraf did not have popular support.

Pakistan's Human Rights Commission told there were flagrant abuses with instances of multiple voting and pressure on state employees to vote. They had also found evidence of widespread fraud and coerced voting. Electoral rolls and national identification cards were dispensed with, ballots were routinely stamped in the presence of, or even by, polling officials, and observers reported cases of repeat voting. Gen Musharraf pointed to the result as a popular endorsement of his rule, and also hoped that it reinforced him in the eyes of the rest of the world. He had largely escaped the diplomatic isolation and foreign condemnation followed by his armed, though bloodless, coup of 1999.

The CNN dated 27th April 2002 had argued: the Pakistan's Supreme Court had ruled that Gen Musharraf's planned referendum to extend his term of office was legal. That the order issued by the president on holding a referendum was valid as upheld by the nine-member bench of the apex court, in a unanimous decision, reached after days of deliberations and hearing arguments. CNN had observed that:

'Gen Musharraf's critics had gone to the Supreme Court to try to block the move ahead of the vote on Tuesday [30th April 2002; the Referendum Day]. A declaration issued by the so-called "All Parties Conference" in Lahore appealed to Pakistani people not to vote in referendum and to the international community to support them in its bid for a restoration of democracy.

Farooq Hassan, a prominent lawyer representing referendum opponents, called the decision "a sad day in the history of Pakistan." However, Sharifuddin Pirzada, a constitutional expert and legal adviser to Musharraf, hailed the ruling as one that "will help restore democracy."

The General argues the constitution allows him to hold a referendum on "important national issues." Musharraf, who toppled the previous elected government on charges of corruption and misrule, was given three years by the Supreme Court to curb corruption, introduce reforms and return the country to democracy. The Supreme Court deadline ends this October [2002], but Musharraf says his task is not yet finished.

So far none of Musharraf's opponents have been able to mobilise a popular movement against the plebiscite. On Saturday, his opponents were holding a counter rally in Lahore, where the police arrested 14 activists a day earlier for distributing anti-referendum leaflets.'

Evidently, the critics had held that the referendum was illegal under the constitution because the president should have been elected by the parliament and the four provincial assemblies. A declaration issued by the 'All Parties Conference' in Lahore had appealed to Pakistani people not to vote in the referendum but the response of the people was not so encouraging.

As Gen Musharraf's Referendum Order was challenged through the two Constitution Petitions Nos. 15/2002 filed by Qazi Hussain Ahmed of JI and 22/2002 from Zafar Ali Shah of the PML [mentioned earlier], it was thought that the people would like to take it as a revolt against the military regime and formal political activities were likely to initiate in the masses. Gen Musharraf took these petitions seriously and hired, of course on the expense of poor people of Pakistan, the top law experts to defend him and his intentions before the Supreme Court.

Syed Sharifuddin Pirzada, Mr Abdul Hafeez Pirzada and Syed Iftikhar Hussain Gillani, appeared on behalf of the Federation and Mr Makhdoom Ali Khan, Attorney General of Pakistan appeared on Court's notice and urged that the petitions be looked into while keeping in mind the ground realities prevailing in the country in the aftermath of the events of 12th October 1999. Moreover, the general elections fixed in October 2002 would also help the required transition process towards democracy. The highly paid counsels had also informed the Apex Court that:

> 'Gen Musharraf, ever since the assumption of power, has been performing his functions and duties in accordance with the mandate given to him by this Court in Syed Zafar Ali Shah's case and has been striving to transform the Army rule into a democratic set up as envisaged in the aforesaid case.'

They also guided the Court that Gen Musharraf's Referendum Order was not aimed at converting the parliamentary system envisaged under the Constitution into presidential form of government.

Some members of the intelligentsia kept the opinion that challenging the 2002 referendum in the Supreme Court was a conspiracy launched by Gen Musharraf's legal team. To legalize the referendum, the military's old buddies from Jama'at e Islami were brought forward and Qazi Hussain Ahmed was there to file the petition in the apex court. All of them knew that historically the Supreme Court has always been in the military pocket. Filled with frustration and despair the people of Pakistan had no alternative except to put a light of hope and test the Supreme judiciary of Pakistan.

By the way; at the instance of making a mention of the Election Commission, one should not forget the brave and truthful judges, though very few in Pakistan's history, who had taken bold stand for their cause. A letter written on 17th April 2002, by Fauzia Wahab of the Pakistan Peoples Party (PPP), to Mrs Robinson of a UN body, speaks of the event itself:

> 'Justice Tariq Mahmood of the Balochistan High Court has finally resigned from his office. During the last five days, since he resigned from the membership of the Election Commission he was subjected to harassment and intimidation by the military regime. Ever since this news leaked out that a senior member of the Election Commission had resigned, this move was expected any time.

Justice Tariq Mahmood faced the wrath of the junta when he took a principle stand that holding referendum to extend the tenure of president-ship for five years was not a mandate of the Election Commission. In his resignation letter he wrote that "the issuance of ballot paper for the referendum and the Referendum Order were unconstitutional and it is not the mandate of the Election Commission to conduct such an exercise." The resignation was tendered on the 6th April, a day after the announcement for referendum was made. The disclosure, however, was made five days later.

Justice Tariq Mahmood was "pressurized by the [then military] government to repudiate the reasons that appeared in the press regarding his resignation, but he refused to change his stand after which he was told that if he did not deny his statement, the Election Commission would issue a statement on the subject."

In his press statement the judge has said that 'There is no justification to hold the office of a judge while telling lies. The government left me no option, but to resign.'

For the democratic forces, the truthful stand taken by a member of the judiciary has illuminated a small ray of hope in a dark world where human rights are blatantly trampled and laws are encouraged for violation.

The Human Rights Cell of the Pakistan Peoples Party hails Justice Tariq Mahmood's courageous step for not bowing to the dictates of the government and upholding the principles of justice and fair-play before one's self. The resignation also vindicates our stand that referendum is unconstitutional and can carry grave implication for the country and the federal forces.'

(17th April 2002: Daily 'Dawn' & 'the News')

In nut shell, the independence of judiciary was put on trial in **April 2002** when Gen Musharraf sought to stay in office for five years through a referendum; was challenged as being a violation of the Constitution stipulating a definite procedure for the election of the President and which was being circumvented through the device of referendum. The *'Dawn'*, a leading newspaper of Pakistan, quoted an extract that: *'the Supreme Court's validation of various actions of Gen Musharraf after seizing power in a military coup was aimed at enslaving the constitution and the people's will'.*

Simultaneously, despite all the exercises by the Bar Council in August 2002, the Legal Framework Order, issued by the military rulers, extended the age of retirement of the superior judiciary by three years.

On **27th April 2002**, these fragile hopes were dashed and once again the judiciary had taken stand by the General in power. The Judges went by their tradition again. It was too much to expect from the honourable judges to have shot themselves in their foot.

One Shehla Butt from *'Media Monitors'* had opined that:

> *'By legalizing a referendum, behind which was overtly malicious intents of a military usurper, Chief Justice of Pakistan Sheikh Riaz Ahmed and company has precipitously lowered their stature. Justice Irshad Hassan, a fresh retiree from the apex of judicial structure of Pakistan and currently heading the Election Commission, went a step further. He left us aghast by announcing that the most fraudulent electoral exercise in the history of Pakistan was free, fair and transparent. This was a monumental lie which not only blighted Justice Irshad's credibility but blackened the face of the institution that he belongs.'*

There were many question marks over the integrity and truthfulness of these statements before the SC. Over the questions of occupancy of the President's Office, the apex Court was apprised that no relief should be made available to Rafiq Tarar because:

- The outgoing President continued in office under the PCO 1 of 1999 and was part of the present government for nearly less than two years;

- He had been performing the functions and duties of the office of President on and in accordance with the advice of the Chief Executive of Pakistan under the new dispensation and was a party to various legislative and executive actions of the present government;

- He did not launch any protest when he ceased to hold office;

- After he ceased to hold the office of President, he accepted the retirement benefits of that office and thus acquiesced in his ceasing to hold the office;

- The petition suffers from *laches* inasmuch as the former President left the office on 20th June 2001 whereas Qazi Hussain Ahmed filed

Constitution Petition No. 15/2002 in this Court on 2nd April 2002, i.e. after a lapse of about 10 months;

* The issuance of writ of *quo warranto* is discretionary in nature and as held in *Sabir Ali Shah's case* (**PLD 1994 SC 738**), such a writ cannot be issued in collateral proceedings.

On 27th April 2002, the Supreme Court's bench, under the chair of the then Chief Justice Sh Riaz Ahmed announced judgment in respect of the above mentioned two petitions and also giving consideration to a Civil Petition for Leave to Appeal No. 512/2002.

Sh Riaz Ahmed, CJP passed the order that on account of an extraordinary situation, which prevailed on 12th October 1999, Gen Musharraf, the then CAOS through an extra constitutional measure took over the government and the affairs of the country. On 14th October 1999, Proclamation of Emergency was issued, which had to take effect from 12th October 1999. The Court had considered it appropriate to go through these petitions in the light of their earlier decisions in that respect. The judgment held that:

> 'We have heard the learned counsel for the parties at great length. In view of the peculiar facts and circumstances of the present case, we are not persuaded to hold that a case for issuing the writ of quo warranto prayed for in Constitution Petitions No. 15 and 22 of 2002 has been made out.

> We, therefore, hold that the Chief Executive's Orders No. 2 and 3 of 2001 have been validly issued by the Chief Executive of Pakistan in exercise of his powers under the Proclamation of Emergency of the 14th day of October 1999 and the Provisional Constitution Order No. 1 of 1999 as validated by this Court in Syed Zafar Ali Shah's case. Consequently, these petitions [praying for the issuance of writ of quo warranto] are dismissed.'

Deciding the legal status of the Referendum Order, the Court held that *'it has been issued by the Chief Executive and the President in a legal way duly authorized by this Court through an earlier decision on record'.*

It was further held by the apex Court that the Referendum Order was not intended to amend the Constitution of Pakistan and the questions regarding its consequences were declared as purely academic, hypothetical and presumptive in nature, therefore, being left to be determined at a proper forum at the appropriate time. No relief was given and the said Constitution Petitions were disposed of being premature. Further, the apex Court had not felt the necessity of passing any order in Civil Petition for Leave to Appeal No. 512/2002 in the light of above decision.

The subsequent days proved that, like Gen Ziaul Haq's notorious referendum of 1984, Gen Musharraf also behaved in the same manner. After the general elections of October 2002, he got passed 17th Amendment from his stooge Parliament practically distorting and negatively affecting the Constitution of Pakistan while defying all his promises before the Supreme Court and the people of Pakistan.

LEGISLATORS SHOULD BE GRADUATE:

11th July 2002, the Supreme Court, after hearing in detail, had dismissed all the five petitions in which it was prayed that the *condition of being a graduate for the candidates* of National and Provincial Assemblies be declared unconstitutional.

The background was that in the General Election Order of 2002, Gen Musharraf had prescribed a minimum qualification of being a degree holder for the candidates of National and Provincial Assemblies. The order was that:

> 'Notwithstanding anything contained in the Constitution of the Islamic Republic of Pakistan, 1973, the Senate (Election) Act, 1975 (LI of 1975), the Representation of People Act, 1976 (LXXXV of 1976), or any other law for the time being in force, a person shall not be qualified to be elected or chosen as a member of Majlis e Shoora (Parliament) or a Provincial Assembly unless he is at least a graduate possessing a bachelor degree in any discipline or any degree recognized as equivalent by the University Grants Commission.'

Pakistan Muslim League (Q), Jamhoori Watan Party, Awami National Party and some others had moved the Supreme Court to get remedy that this order should be declared null and void and against the fundamental rights given in the Constitution. The condition was upheld.

August 23, 2002: Gen Musharraf unilaterally redressed the country's constitution, imposing 29 amendments that expanded his control of the country he took over by coup in 1999 - changes that undermined coming parliamentary elections meant to return the nation to democracy. The new measures stated that *'he may make further constitutional amendments at will and allow him to dissolve the elected parliament and to appoint the country's military chiefs and Supreme Court judges'*.

24th August 2002: Chief Executive Gen Musharraf formally issued the Legal Framework Order 2002, announcing general elections for the National and Provincial Assemblies to be held in October 2002. Its details are given on separate pages in next chapters.

Scenario 38

LEGAL FRAMEWORK ORDER (2002)-I:

24th August 2002: Chief Executive [& 'PCOed' President of Pakistan] General Musharraf issued the Legal Framework Order (LFO) 2002, announcing general elections for the National and Provincial Assemblies to be held in October 2002. Constitutional Provisions were amended for smooth and orderly transition of power from the Chief Executive to the newly elected Prime Minister after the elections.

The **main text** of the L. F. O. 2002 stated as follows:

.... It will come into force henceforth and in the first meetings of National Assembly, Senate and Provincial Assemblies and that if any necessity arises for any further amendment of the Constitution or there is any difficulty in giving effect to any of the provisions of this Order, the Chief Executive will have the discretionary power to make provisions and pass orders for amending the Constitution or for removing any difficulty. It has been further asserted that *the validity of any provision made, or orders passed, under clauses (1) and (2) shall not be called in question in any court on any ground whatsoever.* The main points of LFO 2002 may be summed up as below:

i) Every political party shall, subject to law, hold intra-party elections to elect its office-bearers and party leaders.

ii) Having received the democratic mandate to serve the nation as President of Pakistan for a period of five years, the Chief Executive on relinquishing the office of the CE, shall assume the office of President of Pakistan forthwith and hold office for a term of five years under the Constitution, and Article 44 and other provisions of the Constitution shall apply accordingly.

iii) There shall be 342 seats of the members in the National Assembly, including seats reserved for women and non-Muslims.

iv) The seats in the National Assembly are allocated to each Province, the Federally Administered Tribal Areas and the Federal Capital as under:

- Balochistan:	General 14, Women 3, Total 17
- N. W. F. P:	General 35, Women 8, Total 43
- Punjab:	General 148, Women 35, Total 183
- Sindh:	General 61, Women 14, Total 75
- F. A. T. A:	General 12, Women 0, Total 12
- Federal Capital:	General 2, Women 0, Total 2
- **Total:**	General 272, Women 60, Total 332

v) In addition to the number of seats referred to in clause (iv), there shall be, in the National Assembly, ten seats reserved for non-Muslims.

vi) Members to the seats reserved for non-Muslims shall be elected in accordance with law through proportional representation system of political parties' lists of candidates on the basis of total number of general seats won by each political party in the National Assembly. A political party securing less than five per centum of the total number of seats in the National Assembly shall not be entitled to any seat reserved for women or non-Muslims.

vii) If any question arises whether a member of the Parliament is disqualified from being a member, the Speaker or, as the case may be, the Chairman Senate shall, within 30 days, refer the question to the Chief Election Commissioner who shall give his decision thereon not later than three months from its receipt by the Chief Election Commissioner.

viii) If a member of a Parliamentary Party resigns from membership of his political party or joins another; or votes or abstains from voting in the House contrary to any direction issued by the Parliamentary Party to which he belongs concerning election of the Prime Minister or the Chief Minister; a vote of confidence or no-confidence; or a Money Bill, he may be declared in writing by the Head of the Parliamentary Party to have defected from the political party. The Head of the Parliamentary Party shall forward a copy of the declaration to the Presiding Officer, and a copy thereof to the member concerned.

ix) A member of a House shall be deemed to be a member of a Parliamentary Party if he having been elected as a candidate or nominee of a political party constituting the Parliamentary Party in the House or, having been elected otherwise than as a candidate or nominee of a political party, has become a member of such Parliamentary Party after such election by means of a declaration in writing.

x) With an addition of "a situation has arisen in which the Government of the Federation cannot be carried on in accordance with the provisions of the Constitution and an appeal to the electorate is necessary", the clause 58 is revived.

xi) Where a Bill is referred to the Mediation Committee, it shall, within 90 days, formulate an agreed Bill likely to be passed by both Houses of the Parliament and place the agreed Bill separately before each House. If both the Houses pass the Bill, it shall be presented to the President for assent.

xii) All decisions of the Mediation Committee shall be made by a majority of the total number of members of each House in the Committee.

xiii) The President may, in consultation with the Speaker of the National Assembly and Chairman of the Senate, make rules for conduct of business of the Mediation Committee.

xiv) With an insertion of a new article 152A, there shall be a National Security Council (NSC) whose chairman shall be the President in order to serve as a forum for consultation on strategic matters pertaining to the sovereignty, integrity and security of the State, and the matters relating to democracy, governance and inter-provincial harmony. Other members of NSC shall be the Prime Minister, the Chairman of the Senate, the Speaker of the National Assembly, the Leader of the Opposition in the National Assembly, the Chief Ministers of the Provinces, the Chairman Joint Chiefs of Staff Committee, and the Chiefs of Staff of the Pakistan Army, Pakistan Navy and Pakistan Air Force. Meetings of the NSC may be convened by the President either in his discretion, or on the advice of the Prime Minister, or when requested by any other of its members, within the time frame indicated by him.

xv) On dissolution of an Assembly under article 58(2)(b) or, on completion of its term, the President, in his discretion, or, as the case may be, the Governor, in his discretion but with the previous approval of the President, shall appoint a caretaker Cabinet. When a caretaker Cabinet is appointed, on dissolution of the National Assembly under Article 58 or a Provincial Assembly under Article 112, or on dissolution of any such Assembly on completion of its term, the Prime Minister or, as the case may be, the Chief Minister of the caretaker Cabinet shall not be eligible to contest the immediately following election of such Assembly.

xvi) The Proclamation of Emergency of the 14th October 1999, all President's Orders, Ordinances, Chief Executive's Orders, including the PCO No: 1 of 1999, the Oath of Office (Judges) Order 2000, the Referendum Order 2002 (Chief Executive's Order No: 12 of 2002), and all other laws made between the October 12, 1999 and the date on which this Article comes into force, are hereby affirmed, adopted and declared notwithstanding any judgment of any court, to have been validly made by competent authority and notwithstanding anything contained in the Constitution shall not be called in question in any court on any ground whatsoever.

xvii) All Proclamations, President's Orders, Ordinances, Chief Executive's Orders, laws, regulations, enactments, notifications, rules, orders or bye-laws in force immediately before the date on which this Article comes into force shall continue in force until altered, repealed or amended by competent authority.

Through LFO 2002, the President and Chief Executive revived the Constitution of Pakistan, except a few articles pertaining to the Provincial Governments and the Senate of Pakistan etc, with effect from 16th November 2002. Those parts of the Constitution which were restored immediately included 'Preamble, Article 1 to 58 (both inclusive), Article 64 to 100 (both inclusive), Annex, insertion of Article 152A and the schedule to the Constitution'.

Some of the immediate implications of the L. F. O. 2002 were:

A) LFO 2002 was sanctified by postulating that no body could challenge it in any court of law 'on any ground whatsoever.'

b) It was then assumed to be an integral part of the Constitution and there was no imperative left for the newly and duly elected National Assembly but to accept it willingly or unwillingly. The Parliament was quite unable to reverse or do away with any of the Amendments, especially the one relating to the National Security Council. The Prime Minister and the whole Parliament were at the will of the President for their survival.

c) Many believed that the LFO 2002 was enforced without any regard for the Constitutional and democratic norms and proprieties. By terminating the 13th Amendment that was not passed by two-third majority but a unanimous vote of the Parliament, the President was again authorized to enjoy the powers of dismissing the Prime Minister along with his Cabinet and the Parliament.

d) With the adoption of the Legal Framework Order 2002, Pakistan was virtually advanced from the parliamentary form of government to the presidential system. The Article 58(2)(b) clause was revived and an insertion of the new clause 152A was introduced which created the National Security Council (NSC).

e) Though the function of NSC and the clause 58(2)(b) was to provide a system of checks & balances, there were some more issues to be considered. In case of a confrontation between the President and the Prime Minister, the majority of votes in the NSC would automatically go in favour of the President who could thus easily remove the Prime Minister, putting the Parliamentary form of government once again in jeopardy as has been happening in 1990s.

f) With a radically altered Constitutional Framework, in whose making the people of Pakistan had no say, the sovereignty of the Parliament was severely crippled.

g) Although the Article 58(2)(b) did not specifically mention the President as having the power to sack the Prime Minister, the dissolution of the Assembly would automatically make the Prime Minister go. During 1988-96, this clause was misused by three Presidents to remove Prime Ministers for purely political reasons, even though the Constitution authorized the President to take such a drastic step only after it had become clear that.

'A situation has arisen in which the government of the federation cannot be carried on in accordance with the provisions of the Constitution.'

There is no doubt that every future Prime Minister would prefer to work under the constraints of 58(2)(b) at all times.

The only way to constitutionally amend the Constitution was through the Article 239, which lays down the following procedure:

"A bill to amend the Constitution may originate in either House (National Assembly or the Senate) and, when the bill is passed by the votes of not less than two-thirds of the total membership of the House, it shall be transmitted to the other House."

In the given circumstances, it was considered by the Constitutional experts that Gen Musharraf would require two-thirds majority to have his Constitutional Amendments or LFO 2002 validated. In addition, the legal position of Gen Musharraf was also not in accordance with the Constitution of Pakistan for it does not recognize a uniformed Army Chief as the Head of State. Under the Constitution of 1973, only a majority vote in National Assembly, Senate, and four Provincial Assemblies could elect a President.

One *Naeem Shakir Advocate* had rightly pointed out that the LFO remained under fire inside and outside Pakistan for the changes it brought in 2002 to our original Constitution, although it was just the latest in a seemingly endless series of challenges and changes to the constitution. In fact Gen Musharraf took powers in 1999 from an elected government that alone had affected 29 constitutional amendments.

17th CONSTITUTIONAL AMENDMENT:

The Legal Framework Order 2002 was promulgated and was passed into the constitution, by way of the **17th Amendment 2003**, which went through parliament on 31st December 2003. This constitutional amendment had validated all the regulations established, appointments made and other steps taken by Gen Musharraf and his government under the LFO, and protected it from legal action against persons who would have it otherwise.

The history would remember that the legal authority that the military commander had exercised to effect those constitutional amendments had taken birth from a Supreme Court order in the case of *Zafar Ali Shah v. Pervez Musharraf* (**PLD 2000 SC 869**). As the Supreme Court had conferred vast powers on the military government, it became extremely difficult to challenge its legal legitimacy. However, some jurists held that the Supreme Court was not authorised to confer such powers on an individual, as only the chosen representatives of the people could exercise them. Some powerful voices were also raised that the superior courts should have exercised their powers to judicially review the actions of the armed forces, including the proclamation of emergency, as deemed necessary.

How the outer world had seen that 17th Amendment, one can see 'Reforming the Judiciary in Pakistan' *Asia Report N°160 released on 16th October 2008* which says:

> *'Like Zia's Eighth Amendment, Musharraf's 17th Amendment, passed by a rubber-stamp parliament in December 2003, enshrined all executive orders and changes made under military rule. The 17th Amendment gave the president, the titular head of state, the power to*

dismiss elected governments and parliament and also transferred from the prime minister, the head of government, key appointment powers to the president including appointments of governors, the three service chiefs and the chief justice of the Supreme Court. Gen Musharraf's constitutional distortions weakened civilian institutions. By sidelining secular democratic forces, the military government also enabled right-wing religious parties to fill the vacuum. In dismissing legal challenges to 17th Amendment, the Supreme Court shirked its responsibility to protect constitutional rule.

Some courageous judges, such as Justices Dorab Patel and Fakhruddin G. Ibrahim, had refused to sanctify authoritarian interventions, and preferred to resign rather than undermine constitutionalism and the rule of law. By legitimising military rule and intervention, most have, however, abdicated their duty to uphold the law.

After the PCO of year 2000, the reconstituted Supreme Court was composed of judges who willingly accepted the military's directions. They included Iftikhar Chaudhry, who was on the bench which had upheld the legality of Musharraf's coup under the doctrine of state necessity. The Supreme Court also authorised the army chief to amend the constitution. It was Gen Musharraf who had elevated Justice Iftikhar M Chaudhry to the slot of the Chief Justice of Pakistan in 2005.'

Thus the Supreme Court had allowed the same person to hold the office of the President and Commander of the armed forces, despite the fact that this had contravened the spirit of 1973's Constitution. It was undemocratic for the same person to hold these two offices, as one was a position of public service whereas the other was a public office to represent the people.

Inevitably, this subject also came before the Supreme Court in the case of *Qazi Hussain Ahmed v. Gen Pervez Musharraf (**PLD 2002 SC 853**)*. In this instance, lawyers asserted that the 1973 Constitution was the supreme law of the land and Gen Musharraf's powers were strictly circumscribed as per Supreme Court's judgement in Zafar Ali Shah's Case. However, the court again refused to take on the military ruler, by deciding that the relevant provisions of the constitution were still being held in abeyance.

It may not be out of context to recall some background to explain the real intent of the LFO with regards to the judiciary, as judges were retained or dismissed by the military ruler on the basis of their political allegiance. Superior court judges have from the beginning been obliged to take an oath of the office to uphold the constitution. However, the relevant provisions of the Provisional Constitution Order 1 of 1999, introduced by Gen Musharraf, remained in vogue till then. Recall that PCO:

> 'No Court, tribunal or other authority shall call in question the Proclamation of Emergency of 14th day of October 1999 or any other Order made in pursuance thereof. No judgement, decree, writ, order or process whatsoever shall be made or issued by any court or tribunal against the Chief Executive or any other authority designated by the Chief Executive.
>
> All persons who, immediately before the commencement of this Order, were in service of Pakistan as defined in Article 260 of the Constitution and those who immediately before such commencement were in office as Judge of the Supreme Court, the Federal Shariat Court or a High Court or Auditor General or Ombudsman and Chief Ehtesab Commissioner, shall continue in the said service on the same terms and conditions and shall enjoy the same privileges, if any.'

10th October 2002: Article 179 of the Constitution was amended through the Legal Framework Order (LFO) under which the retirement age of SC Judges was enhanced from 65 to 68 years. Due to reasons best known to Gen Musharraf or his military or legal advisors, the amendment was not enforced on the same date. The new seniority list of the 37 Lahore High Court judges was issued on 2nd January 2003, confirming enforcement of amendment to Article 195 of the Constitution governing the retirement age of High Court judges.

Following enforcement of the amendment, Chief Justice Sheikh Riaz Ahmad, who was to attain the age of retirement on 8th March 2003, under the previous law was to retire in 2006. Two other SC judges - Justice Munir A Sheikh and Justice Qazi Mohammad Farooq – were scheduled to retire on 1st July and 5th January 2006 respectively.

Urging the legislature to abrogate this amendment, the Supreme Court Bar Association President, Hamid Khan, had raised his voice that the government had enforced it to prolong the tenure of judges whose oath was administered under the PCO. The Bar Association had held that enforcement of the amendment was a clear violation of the Constitution since the Supreme Court, while deciding the Zafar Ali Shah case in May 2000, had observed that the then chief executive could not make any amendment regarding affairs of judiciary.

31st October 2002: Taking serious exception to Supreme Court Bar Association's charge that it had "ceased to be independent", the Supreme Court reminded the body that it was due to its judgement that Gen Musharraf had held the general elections [of October 2002] to hand over power to an elected government. It was reacting to the SCBA statement that arguing a case before the present judiciary was a futile exercise "as it had ceased to be independent", due to the oath taken by the judges under the Provisional Constitutional Order (PCO), promulgated by the Gen Musharraf regime.

23rd November 2002: Gen Musharraf administered oath of office to Faisal Saleh Hayat, Aftab Ahmed Sherpao and Nilofar Bakhtiar. All the three were allegedly involved in corruption cases prepared by the 'Accountability Bureau' while the later two politicians were formally convicted by Accountability Courts.

EX ISI CHIEF AGITATES LHC:

27th December 2002: The former chief of the ISI, Lt Gen Javed Nasir (Retd), filed a petition before Lahore Anti-Terrorist Court seeking the death sentence for four top journalists responsible for a report accusing him of embezzling Rs:3 billion. Gen Nasir, perhaps for the first time before the Pakistani courts, had confirmed the ISI's 'worldly criticized role' in Afghanistan and Bosnia, true or false.

The petition, published in *the South Asia Tribune*, claimed that the ISI under him [Lt Gen Javed Nasir] had decided to curb the 'free hand' acquired by RAW since 1948 in the "manipulation and control of Sikh *yatris*" travelling to Pakistan to attend religious functions. He had set up the Pakistan Sikh *Gurdwara Prabandhak* Committee to snatch control from the Indian intelligence agency and had succeeded in gaining control over the management of the festivals within a year. This matter had incensed the Indian government so much that Prime Minister Atal Behari Vajpayee preferred to raise the issue with the then Prime Minister Nawaz Sharif during their one-on-one meeting during the famous Lahore *yatra* in February 1999.

Lt Gen Javed Nasir further said that the Punjab chief minister had accompanied Mr Vajpayee and that eventually the Pakistan government ensured that the Indian plan to regain control was "aborted." Gen Nasir had cited this to substantiate a claim that RAW, along with the CIA, was behind the effort to discredit him through the newsmedia.

Lt Gen Javed Nasir had also disclosed in the petition that:

'*Despite the UN ban on supply of arms to the besieged Bosnians, he successfully airlifted sophisticated anti-tank guided missiles which turned the tide in favour of Bosnian Muslims and forced the Serbs to lift the siege, much to the annoyance of the US government. He thus became the target of US, Indian and secular minded lobbies both inside and outside Pakistan.*

Having failed to buy him, the US government started a fabricated and mendaciously false propaganda against him and demanded his removal as ISI chief, failing which Pakistan would be declared a terrorist state.'

Lt Gen Javed Nasir had also claimed that:

'*In April 1993 the US threatened to declare Pakistan a terrorist state unless he [Javed Nasir] was removed. It was therefore at the behest of the US government's official demand that he was prematurely compulsorily retired from service by the caretaker government of Mir Balkh Sher Mazari on 13th May 1993.*'

Lt Gen Javed Nasir was the ISI Chief from March 1992 till May 1993.

The court did not take any action on the petition. Contrarily, the honourable court should have initiated proceedings against him on the charge of 'divulging state secrets'.

Scenario 39

LEGAL FRAMEWORK ORDER (2002)-II:

It has been stated in detail on the preceding pages that Gen Musharraf himself changed his own assignment from Chief Executive to the President of Pakistan on 20th June 2001, under the Provisional Constitutional Order (PCO) by sending Rafiq Tarar home not allowing him to complete his five-year tenure. With immediate effect he dissolved the suspended Senate, National and Provincial Assemblies and dismissed the Chairman of the Senate and the Speaker of the National Assembly. After assuming the new office as President, Gen Musharraf had announced that:

> 'The change will augur well for the future of Pakistan and I think I have a role to play; I have a job to do here; I cannot and will not let this nation down.'

In the meantime 9/11 tragedy occurred. Washington suddenly and direly needed Gen Musharraf's support to combat with alleged and concocted 'anti-terrorism campaign' and to crush the Taliban in Afghanistan. He could not stand the American pressure and just on a phone call from Washington he promised to extend all cooperation and offered for which the 'Americans had not even demanded. As a result the Taliban were ousted from Afghan capital and the Americans succeeded to establish a pro-US government, under the control of one Hamid Karzai, in Kabul and Gen Musharraf offered all possible help to the new government.

Gen Musharraf ordered for general elections in October 2002 after getting mandate from the Supreme Court. After general elections, Pakistan's National Assembly and Senate met in November 2002 for the first time since 1999's coup. Then he also relinquished the post of Chief Executive when Zafarullah Khan Jamali was made Prime Minister of Pakistan the same month but Gen Musharraf continued to hold the offices of Chief of Army Staff and Chief of the Staff Committee.

The then opposition parties had refused to accept Legal Framework Order (LFO) 2002 as it empowered the President to sack the prime minister; dissolve the parliament and also recognize him [Gen Musharraf] as both head of the army and head of the state. Some of the provisions of the LFO were unconstitutional and illegal [though some were very good, purely democratic], and against the sovereignty of the

Parliament. As a result, the business of the parliament went in deadlock and remained so for a year.

In December 2003 the ice melted and this deadlock ended after negotiating a deal with MMA (*Muttahida Majlis e Amal*) to end the stand-off, Gen Musharraf agreed that he would step down as military head of the country on 31st December 2004. After getting vote of confidence from parliament and the four provincial assemblies, Gen Musharraf was entitled to serve full five-year term as President till 2007 after the 17th Constitutional Amendment was passed by a two-third majority of the Parliament. He secured 658 votes out of 1,170 members of parliament and the four assemblies amid MMA's abstention and opposition's boycott.

The major constitutional amendments which Gen Musharraf got approved from the puppet National Assembly of 2002 were the focus of his stay ensured through 17th Amendment in the Constitution of Pakistan which largely included reframing of the articles 43(1), 63(1)(d) and (k). Article 63(1)(d & k) were related to the office of the President when read with Article 41(2) with or without the uniform. The said Articles were suspended for different periods under Article 41(7)(a & b) through the same Amendment. Of all the suspended articles, Article 63 (1)(d) was to come into force on 31st December 2004, while Article 43(1) and 63(1)(k) would stand restored in mid-November 2007 when the President's tenure would expire.

[The original Article 43(1) of the Constitution says, "Conditions of president's office: The president shall not hold any office of profit in the service of Pakistan or occupy any other position carrying the right to remuneration for the rendering of services."

Similarly, the original Article 63(1)(k) says, "A person shall be disqualified from being elected or chosen as, and from being, a member of parliament, if he has been in the service of Pakistan or of any statutory body or any body which is owned or controlled by the government or in which the government has a controlling share or interest, unless a period of two years has elapsed since he ceased to be in such service."]

Since the Article 43(1) had to come into force in November 2007 and the president would have no immunity from other related articles as provided through Article 41(7)(a & b) after the completion of his tenure, he was not able to get himself elected in any circumstances unless he managed these constitutional amendments.

The fact remains that Gen Musharraf had sailed smoothly after Article 63(1)(d) was restored on 31st December 2004, which warranted the president to quit one office immediately under the constitutional proviso of the Article 41(7)(b). This spin was given to the law under the trick of 'Validation of Presidential Act'. He had gone too far to please the American President, then Mr Bush, and his team in that arena of 'War on Terror' philosophy; so much that later the magazine *'TIME' of 29th April 2006* included his name in 'top 100 personalities' of the world who had influenced the world opinion most.

One can recall the history when Gen Ziaul Haq had managed to hang Z A Bhutto through judicial gimmicks, the Americans were quite happy over that episode. The Americans had declared Gen Ziaul Haq as their right hand statesman because the Russian threats to Afghanistan were not 'fully cleared' then. But what were their inner feelings about the General, certain paragraphs from a CIA report of 1982 (since declassified) have been given in the last chapter of Volume I in detail. Just for a moment, if one inserts the name of Gen Musharraf where Gen Zia's name was placed, the said statement of 1982 was holding well during 2003-2007.

Military, during Gen Musharraf's era, which was holding both power and guns, was not able to play a key role in shaping the future course of events. It should have proactively understood that its continued interference in politics and economy had weakened the Federation and institutions as World Economic Forum's Global Competitiveness Report, 2005 had (once more) indicated by rating quality of Pakistan's public institutions at 102 out of 104 countries.

Coming back to our original topic, in Pakistan, Lt Generals retire at the age of 57 or on completion of four years as Lt Gen, whichever is earlier. Gen Musharraf granted himself an extension on 6th October 2001 when he was due for retirement as the COAS and was supposed to hand over power to an elected political leadership before 12th October 2002, in accordance with the judgment of the Supreme Court. That day has never seen dawn, Gen Musharraf was there as COAS (& President) whereas all threatening Lt Generals were sent home.

One shouldn't be surprised, if concerned over this prospect, the US had planned so. It made no difference to the US if Gen Musharraf was continuing in power as the President in uniform or a non-political civilian elected in a sham election, functioning as the Prime Minister so long as the things were continuously delivered in the upkeep of US interests. That was exactly the same what Gen Ziaul Haq did during his rule.

For thirty six out of sixty years of existence Pakistan has been under military rule. The military has been responsible to a great extent for Pakistan's continuing deadlock. If there is any hope, it lies in the fact that despite its domination the military has somehow been restrained from turning security into a means of terrorizing its own citizens. Throughout his rule of eight years, Gen Musharraf has been stressing his commitment to human rights, religious tolerance and a free press. But the time proved that all his steps moved to concentrate power in his own hands, and while he talked largely of accountability he has allowed no space for holding the army or any of his corrupt army officers accountable and all the superior judiciary remained silent indirectly providing strength to the illegal and illogical military rule.

GENERAL ELECTIONS OF 2002:

Gen Musharraf announced for general elections in Pakistan scheduled to be held on 10th October 2002. More than 70 parties vowed to take part in those parliamentary elections but the mentionable were PPP (Parliamentarian Group), PML(N), PML(Q) better known as pro-Musfarraf or King's Party, *Muttahida Majlis e Amal* (MMA): an alliance of six religious political parties, Imran Khan's Pakistan *Tehrik e Insaaf* and Tahir ul Qadri's Pakistan *Awami Tehrik*. Several regional parties with strongholds in their own provinces included the Sindh based Muttahida Qaumi Movement (MQM), Awami National Party (ANP) in Khyber PK (then NWFP), Jamhuri Watan Party, factions of Baluchistan National Movement and Pashtunkhwa Milli Awami Party.

The National and Provincial elections were held on the same day. More than 72 million registered voters aged 18 and above from a population of 140 million, had elected 272 members for the National Assembly seats and 728 members for the four Provincial Assemblies. A total of 2,098 candidates contested for the said seats of the National Assembly. The remaining 60 seats were reserved for women and 10 for non-Muslim minorities. These seats were to be allocated on the basis of proportional representation to parties bagging at least five per cent of the total general seats.

In the Provincial Assemblies: out of 371 seats of the Punjab Assembly, 66 were reserved for women and eight for minorities, in 168 seats of the Sindh Assembly 29 for women and nine for minorities, in 124 seats of the NWFP Assembly 22 for women and three for minorities and in 65 seats of the Baluchistan Assembly 11 for women and three for minorities.

The elections were observed by hundreds of local and 300 international observers, including observers from European Union and the Commonwealth. These elections were different from the previous ones on many counts. Only educated candidates having at least a Bachelor's degree could submit the nomination papers. Pakistan's leading political personalities Benazir Bhutto and Nawaz Sharif were barred from the contest under the new electoral laws. The age limit of voting in these elections was also lowered from 21 to 18 years. For the first time since 1977, the minority communities that included Christians, Hindus and Parsees had voted for all general seats in the National and Provincial Assemblies.

The election results were declared with mysterious delay which invited un-necessary criticism. Unexpectedly, large number of seats were won by the Islamic parties; MMA secured 51 seats in the National Assembly after PML(Q) with 76 seats, PPPP with 62 seats and the PML(N) won only 14 seats. The MMA got a clear-cut majority in NWFP [now Khyber PK] and Baluchistan provinces where it easily formed government on their own. In the other two Provinces, coalition governments were formed as no party could surface with enough majorities to form sovereign governments.

Despite government assurances that the elections would be fair, free and transparent, different political parties alleged that the elections were engineered by the ISI and the military government was involved in massive rigging. The elections had a low turnout of less than 25 percent as compared to 35.42 percent in 1997 general elections. Allegations of rigging were mainly raised by the PML(N) because they got much less seats than expectations in a way sanctifying 1999's military take over.

With no party emerging with a simple majority, Pakistan faced menace of a hung parliament. A coalition government was, however, set up with Mir Zafarullah Khan Jamali of PML(Q) as the Prime Minister of Pakistan with the help of MQM, a number of independent candidates and 10 members of the PPPP who defected from the main PPP to form 'Forward Bloc'.

ZAFARULLAH JAMALI MADE PM:

The PM Jamali was elected as the 21st Prime Minister of Pakistan on 21st November 2002; Gen Musharraf administered the oath at the

Presidency. A political deadlock had prevailed as no party had won with an overall majority. The President did not call the National Assembly session until the creation of PPP's forward bloc and the floor-crossing law was held in abeyance. Maulana Fazlur Rehman of the MMA, Shah Mahmud Qureshi of the PPPP and Mir Zafarullah Khan Jamali of PML(Q) were the main contenders for the Prime Minister's slot.

Mir Zafarullah Khan Jamali went successful by securing 172 votes out of 329 votes, against 87 bagged by Maulana Fazlur Rahman and 70 by Shah Mahmud Qureshi. Mir Z K Jamali was however, able to get the desired number of votes only after 10 members of the PPPP had defected from their original party PPP to form their own forward bloc in order to support Mir Jamali.

PM Jamali continued with Gen Musharraf's economic and foreign policies, particularly in supporting the ongoing international war against terrorism. He reiterated Pakistan's support for the US and said that *'Pakistan has become a frontline state, and will remain one'*. PM Jamali then announced a 25-member Cabinet which included four unelected advisers and several legislators who had defected from the PPP. The PPPP's group of dissidents got the best ministries in the PML(Q)'s Government. Rao Sikandar and Faisal Saleh Hayat were given the Ministries of Defence and Interior. Out of the ten PPPP dissidents, six had been accommodated either as full Federal Ministers or Ministers for state.

PM Jamali's Government faced tough challenges; not only from a strong opposition on the Assembly's floor but also in keeping his fragile coalition together while sharing power with Gen Musharraf. The President had the ultimate power, with the authority to dissolve Parliament and sack the PM and his government any time. On 29th December 2002, the PM Jamali won the vote of confidence of 188 members in the Assembly of 342 seats. It is a tribute to PM Jamali's pleasing personality that even the main Opposition like MMA, while sticking to its own political agenda, had pledged publicly not to destabilize his Government so that the democratic dispensation takes firm roots. PM Jamali, despite enormous pressures, remained firm in sticking to two principles:

Firstly: not to take any major step in policy formulation without consulting the opposition parties on the floor.

Secondly: making sure that his political opponents would not be dragged in false criminal cases as per previous practices in Pakistan.

These two simple principles at length led to the strengthening and functioning of a sustainable democracy. Though the PM Mir Jamali who did bear confidence of the majority in the Parliament and tried to maintain amicable terms with the most powerful President as well as the Opposition with his traits of humility and decency, could not complete his five-year term and was forced to resign on 26th June 2004 and dissolved his cabinet, too. He was replaced by Ch Shujaat Hussain of PML(Q), a major ally of Gen Musharraf. Mr Hussain continued for an interim period of about three months and then vacated the slot for Shaukat Aziz, the then Finance Minister in the dissolved cabinet. Mr Aziz was set to win a seat in the National Assembly as he was a senator then. Mr Aziz had returned from living abroad as a senior Citibank executive in 1999 at Gen Musharraf's request.

During Shaukat Aziz's tenure as the Finance Minister, Pakistan's economy had one of its best performances, the public was told; the gross domestic product grew at 6.4% in 2003-4, well above the target of 5.3%. [However, poverty remained high for about one-third of the population] For advocates of democracy in Pakistan, Gen Musharraf's refusal to let Mr Jamali finish his term was a blow, emphasizing again that Parliament had less power than the president.

Referring to the *'NY Times'* of *27th June 2004*: *'you cannot in a parliamentary democracy have a head of state running the show. Parliament must be sovereign.'* The problem was not between the two men, but in the system Gen Musharraf had created. He was facing a rising law & order problem in Karachi, a nationalist movement and a pro-Taliban government in Baluchistan, and an ongoing conflict with Al Qaeda militants and their supporters in the NWFP. Gen Musharraf had been eager to avoid having to remove Mr Jamali through a parliamentary vote of no confidence, because there was no guarantee of the outcome. The opposition had indicated it would support Mr Jamali.

Mr Jamali was Pakistan's first prime minister from Baluchistan, a province that had a tense relationship with the governments since long. His departure had further aggravated anti-government sentiments among Baluchi nationalists.

Gen Musharraf had held general polls in Pakistan to fulfil his promise to return the country to the democratic path but it was a brand of democracy that suited the General better than anyone else. He reframed the election rules to disqualify the two former Prime Ministers Nawaz Sharif and Benazir Bhutto, and threatened them to go in jail if they returned from abroad. After the polls were over, the PM Jamali's government worked under an amended constitution, which had given ultimate powers both to him [Gen Musharraf] and a new militarized National Security Council.

Gen Musharraf reiterated that he was merely trying to prevent corruption and bad governance; critics said he had no intention of letting elected civilians run Pakistan. Thus PM Jamali acted as a show face. Amidst such criticism, Gen Musharraf had successfully diverted public attention away from the elections by involving army and media in dreadful news of their nuclear missile race with neighbouring India those days.

In Pakistan, the Muslim Leagues and the PPP combined normally get more than 50% of the popular vote, but during 2002 elections their camps were apathetic, producing one of the dullest campaigns in Pakistan's parliamentary history. Gen Musharraf did not expect that but the vacuum was filled by an alliance of six hard-line religious parties called MMA; the wholesome anti American in the back drop of their crackdown on *jihadis* in Kashmir.

As per analysis of the western media, Pakistani religious parties seldom grabbed more than five percent of votes in the past elections because most Pakistanis were moderate and of secular folk. The fact also remains that most Pakistanis are poor and uneducated who traditionally vote as per their feudal lord's command. With the absence of two big parties, the hard-line religious coalition got a chance to lead the whole lot of voters to the booths; thus the MMA could win 51 National Assembly seats. They were not in majority but in a splintered Parliament, it was enough to give the clerics a few berths in a coalition government.

The *Time Magazine of 7th October 2002* had written that:

> 'The six hard-line party leaders of the MMA were rivals. They stormed each other's mosques over ideological disputes dating back to Islam's early days. Their differences were stark: some worship at the tombs of local Sufi saints; the personalities of the party leaders have also clashed. Qazi Hussain Ahmed from the Jamaat e Islami is a cultured, well-travelled cleric who speaks with the measured finality of a judge passing a grim sentence.

> Several of his new brethren, in contrast, are unquestionably flamboyant. Maulana Fazlur Rehman wears robes of golden thread and was dubbed 'Maulana Diesel' after allegations were made though never proven that he was involved in a fuel scam. They have differences, some are centuries-old but they have enough in common.

Under their guidance the people of Pakistan had started crying that Americans are killing our Muslim brothers and sisters in Afghanistan; soon, they will come here!'

The MMA's stronghold was based in the tribal band at Pak-Afghan border. Its Baluch and Pashtun supporters were ethnically and ideologically tied to the former Taliban rulers in Afghanistan, thus their anti-Americanism. Guns were in plentiful supply there as ever. An enlightened educated tribal youngster had once told the Time's reporter that:

'Of course I carry an automatic pistol. That doesn't mean I'm a terrorist; but I refuse to bow to the Americans. This is our land'.

Even though, the MMA clerics and their followers had termed Gen Musharraf as *'an American agent and a puppet'*. They resented the General for allowing the US to use Pakistani military bases in Baluchistan and NWFP as staging posts in its Afghan campaign. It angered them that the agents of FBI wiretap Pakistani telephones and organize raids on suspected al-Qaeda hideouts. They knew that cameras at the Karachi airport were feeding images into CIA computers. What irritated them most was that Gen Musharraf had buckled to US pressure and this was against Pakistan's sovereignty.

In and around 2002 elections, Gen Musharraf had plainly given the religious groups more free rein in the campaign than the PML and the PPP had provided during their respective regimes and the same relaxations tightened the noose around his neck fiver years later.

There are numerous articles available in media suggesting that the America has ultimately lost the so called War on Terror in Afghanistan and has planned to quit much before 2014 as is being suggested by his cronies and concocted think tanks in America. After sustaining hundreds of deaths of the American and NATO soldiers, loosing $113 trillion in the un-winning war and killing more than 35,000 civilian lives of falsely occupied territories, what they got; humiliations and another black dot of defeat. The above lines appearing in the Time, the most read & circulated magazine in the West, had clearly indicated as early as in 2002 that sons of the soil were not favouring foreign boots on their land.

Americans should have heard those innocent voices and should have read in between the lines being a 'wise & superior' nation, which they have proved otherwise.

Scenario 40

PAK ARMY & JUDICIARY IN 2003:

PBC's White Paper against Judiciary:

8th March 2003: Due to open partisanship of the two consecutive Chief Justices with the military regime, the Pakistan Bar Council (PBC) once decided to boycott the Supreme Court (SC) by refusing to challenge any constitutional question before it; reason being that PBC was not expecting a fair and impartial decision from the SC. The matter did not end there; the lawyers had observed 8th March 2003, the day the Chief Justice of Pakistan, Sh Riaz Ahmed had to originally retire before the three-year extension, as a black day.

The PBC also held conventions throughout Pakistan against the judiciary and brought out a white paper in which it described their 'noble deeds & decisions'. These measures by the legal community were unprecedented in the history of Pakistan. The matter reached such a stage was unfortunate but the situation raised a number of questions. The PBC charged that corruption had plagued the institution of judiciary for the past 55 years but the pestilence peaked after Gen Musharraf came to power in October 1999. The PBC held that:

'Chief Justice Sheikh Riaz Ahmad and his predecessor Irshad Hassan Khan have destroyed the institution of judiciary which should have been an effective and independent organ of the state, and now corruption and incompetence in the judiciary have become the order of the day'.

'Daily Times' quoted from the 83-page White Paper, the first such to be released by the Pakistani Bar in the judicial history of Pakistan. The document said:

'The judiciary, due to its role and performance for the last three years, has relegated itself to the position of subservience to the military rulers. Its role has been to support the regime of Gen Musharraf without any regard for the constitutional dictates and the law laid down by the Supreme Court in its previous cases.'

The said white paper on the then prevailing scenario stated that:

'The inclusion (in the constitution) of provisions relating to the president's powers to dissolve the assemblies, simultaneous holding of

two offices of the army chief and president by one person, three-year extension in the superannuation age of judges of superior courts and the constitution of the National Security Council was aimed at enslaving the constitution and the people's will.

The white paper also charged that '*In most cases, a corrupt judge, if he happens to be a chief justice, can easily be manipulated by a dictatorial regime, which maintains dossiers on the judges*'. This reference was pointing to the then Chief Justice Sh Riaz Ahmad, who had administered oath of the office to Gen Musharraf just before last year's general elections. The General was previously given an additional three years to remain in office by the previous CJP.

The Bar Council's words were also spread out to the judicial minds of the world. Later the *'Daily Mail' (UK) dated 6th May 2005* said that:

'*By the continuing of Chief Justice Sheikh Riaz Ahmad for three more years, he (Gen Musharraf) can count on a pliable chief justice to manage a verdict favourable to him in case he dissolves the National Assembly (NA) under his discretionary powers to get rid of a hostile or recalcitrant parliament. Thus the judiciary has been reduced to the level of being a protector of a military ruler who is bent upon "contaminating" the Constitution to perpetuate his rule*'.

At another occasion the same article said that:

'*The [Pakistani] judiciary is acting under the dictates of the military ruler in defiance of the constitutional provisions and the Supreme Court's own previous judgment. Ironically, the chief justice administered oath of office to the president under the Constitution before the NA had met and the election to the senate had taken place.*

This was done despite the existence of his own judgment in a reference case, in which the chief justice had maintained that the consequences of the referendum would be settled by the parliament'.

The other newspapers of the west had also hailed the PBC's effort to show mirror to the then military regime. In fact the judiciary had miserably failed to protect, preserve and defend the Constitution and the oath of office that members of the judiciary make at the time of induction as judges. The judiciary had thus reduced itself to the position to bring protector, preserver and defender of the unconstitutional acts and orders of the military regime.

The powers of the chief justice to form benches had been misused throughout the history of Pakistan but it was abused to the maximum during the years from 2000 till then. It was generally felt that the military government of Gen Musharraf needed the services of only five judges; chief justice of the Supreme Court and the four other like minded judges to obtain a favourable verdict. Gen Musharraf had also ensured that he had five judges predisposed towards him and that they would and had actually managed verdicts beneficial to him throughout his tenure till then. The chief justice of Pakistan alone could manage all the verdicts desired by the military rulers. Chief Justice Sheikh Riaz Ahmad blatantly established how the power to constitute sympathizer benches could be exercised.

It was apparent that the then Pakistan Bar Council had full grip on the legal and constitutional matters which needed immediate attention. All the subjects were mentioned in the white paper to attract the attention of judiciary and the parliamentarians for a better Pakistan. The subjects included:

- Proclamation of Emergency October 1999,

- Oath of Office (Judges) Order 1999,

- President Succession Order 2001,

- Legal Framework (Amendment) Order 2001,

- Extracts from the judgment in Syed Zafar Ali Shah's case,

- Extracts from the judgment in Qazi Hussain Ahmad's case,

- Letters addressed to the CJP Sheikh Riaz Ahmad; Justice Qazi Mohammad Farooq, a Supreme Court judge and Justice M Ashraf Leghari, judge of the Sindh High Court, requesting them to lay down robes in view of their having attained the age of superannuating under the 1973 Constitution.

- Army role in politics,

- Implementation of Hamood ur Rehman Commission Report,

- *Suo-moto* powers of the CJ when he was retiring,

- Elevation of junior judges to the Supreme Court,

- Appointment of J (Rtd) Irshad Hassan Khan as the Chief Election Commissioner.

President of the Supreme Court Bar Association Hamid Khan told that the entire lawyer's fraternity had worked very hard to gather data for the White Paper saying that *'we are ready to face the consequences of publishing this paper'*. The white paper also held:

> *'The military regime seems happy over corruption in the judiciary because it thinks that judges with 'compromised integrity' will not question their [the military's] corruption.'*

Realistically, the PBC had cogent weight in their arguments. The Council was of the opinion that the litmus test of the judiciary's independence would lie in its decisions against the dictators when they were still in power. But the Supreme Court had continuously failed that test when it upheld all martial laws and military take-overs alike; as for in the cases of Gen Yahya, Gen Ziaul Haq and then of Gen Musharraf.

In the latest test when the military takeover by Gen Musharraf was challenged, the Supreme Court not only justified it but also granted three years to the military regime to implement its program; in addition to granting the right to make amendments to the Constitution; a right even the Court did not possess itself. It is noteworthy that though the Court did not stipulate the removal of the then President Rafiq Tarrar in its judgment, but the later was removed and Gen Musharraf was administered oath as President by the Chief Justice of Pakistan. The act was patently unconstitutional.

Most observers noticed that the then Chief Justice Irshad Hassan Khan was rewarded for this bounteousness and generosity by Gen Musharraf when he was made the Chief Election Commissioner after retirement.

It had come possible partially through concerted efforts of the then Federal Law Secretary, Faqir M Khokhar, who was also given an out of turn appointment as a Supreme Court judge even though he was a junior judge of the Lahore High Court. This was in clear violation of the principle laid down in the 1996 Judges' Case which had stipulated the seniority rule in the matter of appointment of judges. This and other appointments of junior judges were challenged but were turned down by a special bench presided over by Chief Justice Sh Riaz Ahmad himself.

By granting extension to the judges of the superior courts, Gen Musharraf violated his commitment to the nation that no amendment would be done in the Constitution in ordinary course of nature.

Interestingly, the extension period corresponded with the period granted by the judges to Gen Musharraf as the Chief Executive. It was not the extension itself granted by the military but rather the manner and the method in which it was granted. This was so because it clearly smacked of a bribe for 'services' rendered by judges; the bar and the parliament were not involved in the process.

On 31st March 2003, Pakistan Country Report on Human Rights for the year 2002 was released mainly stating that:

> *'Former Prime Minister Benazir Bhutto's husband Asif Zardari waited for more than 5 years for the start of his trial on charges of killing his brother-in-law, Murtaza Bhutto in 1997. In April 1999, Zardari was tried and convicted separately on corruption charges. In December 2001 Zardari received bail but was not released; the NAB ordered his continued detention on suspicion of corruption. Despite government claims that NAB cases would be pursued independent of an individual's political affiliation, NAB had taken a selective approach to anti-corruption efforts.*
>
> *Gen Musharraf's NAB was created in part to deal with $4 billion (PKR 208 billion then) that was estimated to be owed to the country's state owned banks by debtors, primarily from among the wealthy elite. The Musharraf Government stated that it would not target genuine business failures or small defaulters but the NAB acted otherwise with selective accountability.'*

MEETING THE PRESIDENT BUSH (2003):

During a meeting at Camp David in mid June 2003, Gen Musharraf was offered by the US President George Bush a package of conditional $3 billion provided:

- Firstly; the Congress gives its approval.

- Secondly; Gen Musharraf continues to arrest Islamic militants and support the US military occupation of Afghanistan;

- Thirdly; Pakistan makes no trouble with India over Kashmir;

- Fourthly; Pakistan doesn't supply nuclear technology to North Korea.

In an article appeared in media on **30th June 2003** captioned as **'Soldier of the RAJ'**, an American columnist **Eric Margolis** had clearly written that Mr Bush had mentioned of the first clause because the American Congress used to hate Pakistan the most as country but had decorated Gen Musharraf with the labels of 'statesman' and 'the friend of freedom' for the time being.

At so many public occasions, deliberately making it a public insult, President Bush had refused his 'friend and ally Gen Musharraf' to release F-16 fighters bought by Pakistan in 1989. Pro-Israel members of the Congress had blocked delivery of those aircrafts to punish Pakistan for its nuclear program. The same Congress heads had once assured the US that Iraq was bristling with deadly weapons that could annihilate the US and UK 'in 45 minutes'. Later the world had known about truth in it.

In his concluding paragraph, Eric Margolis wrote that Gen Musharraf used to plead Mr Bush to help resolve the Kashmir dispute - the world's most dangerous crisis that risks nuclear war between India and Pakistan – but was ignored. *'Take your money, go home, arrest more militants and don't cause trouble,'* was Washington's dazzling & stunning send-off message to Gen Musharraf.

On 25th July 2003, two civil judges and a magistrate were killed by prisoners of the Sialkot District Jail while they were on an official visit to the jail premises accompanying a heavy contingent of the local police.

Why did they have to kill the judges? Dr Farrukh Saleem, an Islamabad based economist and analyst, rightly pointed out that: '.......... *It is important for the judiciary to peep into their own history for answers.'*

On 23rd September 2003: Pakistan and the UK judiciary signed an agreement under which both the countries would establish a body in each country to help the parents and abducted children of Pakistani origin British nationals. The agreement was signed by the CJP Sheikh Riaz Ahmad, and Dame Elizabeth Buttler Sloss, president of the Family Division of Courts of Appeal and Wales. The agreement was signed in furtherance of protocol signed by the Pakistan and British judiciary in January 2003.

[*Under the judicial protocol if a child is removed either from Pakistan to the United Kingdom or from the United Kingdom to Pakistan, the child would be sent back to the country of his / her habitual residence. If a court of country of habitual residence of the child, passed any restraint order, the court of the country to which the child has been removed, would not exercise jurisdiction over the child and order him to return.*]

From Pakistan, Justice Munir A Sheikh was appointed as liaison judge, and Lord Justice Matthew Thorpe from the UK side. When a naughty media person asked that Pakistan's judiciary bore allegiance to one man and did not represent the nation as it has not taken oath under the Constitution, the British delegation refused to take the question saying *'Don't ask such questions'*.

PAK ARMY CAUGHT IN FATA:

In 2003, the army had negotiated a deal with the Taliban in the Pak-Afghan border area and as a result 213 soldiers were handed over by the militants to the *Jirga* at *Tiarza* village in the *Mahsud* tribal territory, and then driven in 13 vehicles to Wana. In Wana, the freed soldiers were handed over to the military authorities. The militants gifted a pair of new *shalwar-kameez & chappals* to each soldier before seeing them off at *Tiarza*. Among the freed soldiers were six army officers; including a colonel, majors and captains. Colonel Zafar led the military convoy that was seized by the militants.

It was a deal of the prisoner's swap, militants & Pak Army soldiers; became possible when the government agreed to release 25 of their tribesmen which were collected from different jails in various cities and brought to Dera Ismail Khan before being flown to Wana in a helicopter. These men were then handed over to the tribal *Jirga* which brought them to Tiarza to complete the prisoner's swap deal. Contrary to the claims by government officials, almost all of them were booked on terrorism charges and jailed.

These 25 men included one Suhail Zeb, a cousin of militants' commander Baitullah Mahsud. He was arrested by the police from a bungalow on Canal Road in Dera Ismail Khan along with three suicide bombers reportedly wearing explosives-filled jackets. They were later tried in a court and sentenced to 24 years imprisonment. Two of these 25 men were arrested in Karachi and were being held in a jail there.

30th December 2003: Through the 17th Amendment passed on this day, the three-years extension in the retirement age of the judges of the higher judiciary was withdrawn and Chief Justice of Pakistan Sheikh Riaz Ahmed, Justice Munir A Sheikh and Justice Qazi Muhammad Farooq were asked not to hear cases. Before the extension was awarded, the chief justice was supposed to retire on 8th March 2003, Justice Munir A Sheikh on 1st July 2003 and Justice Qazi Muhammad Farooq on 5th January 2003. According to the agreement signed between the government and the MMA, the constitutional bill was to be enforced from 1st January 2004.

Gen Musharraf had to appoint the new chief justice under Article 177 of the Constitution by 1st January 2004. Justice Nazim Hussain Siddiqui was poised to be the new chief justice of the apex court after the retirement of CJP Sh Riaz Ahmed and the other two senior judges. The new chief justice later administered the oath to Gen Musharraf as the president.

[*Gen Musharraf as the chief executive of Pakistan had amended the Article 179 and 195 of the Constitution through his Executive Order No 24 of 2002 under the Legal Framework Order during the night between 9th October and 10th of 2002, a few hours before the general elections of the national and provincial assemblies. With that amendment, the retirement age of the Supreme Court judges was extended from 65 to 68 years and the age of High Court judges was extended from 62 to 65 years.*]

Opposition parties and the legal fraternity strongly opposed that extension and Gen Musharraf had agreed to withdraw the amendment at an appropriate time. The General had used the judiciary in his favour and then was looking for the moments to throw them away like a used toilet tissue; 17th Amendment was the proper occasion to do that.

17th AMENDMENT FINALLY PASSED (2003):

17th Constitutional Amendment was basically the confirmation of LFO of 2002 that was accepted with minor modifications to become part of the 1973 Constitution. A year-old constitutional deadlock was broken only because of 'flexibility' shown by Gen Musharraf and the top MMA leadership. The amendment allowed Gen Musharraf to serve out his five years term as President, which ended in 2007. This amendment had also formalized special powers he had decreed himself giving him the right to sack the prime minister and disband the parliament. In return, Gen Musharraf had committed to step down as army chief by 31st December 2004 which he never fulfilled.

A vote of confidence was passed in favour of the President on 1st January 2004 by members of both National Assembly and the Senate as per requirement of the 17th Amendment. Despite the fact that MMA abstained from giving the vote of confidence to the President, it had indirectly accepted him as elected president by allowing vote of confidence from both houses of parliament and provincial assemblies. At the same time the MMA was a bit successful in getting a probable action of dissolution of assemblies referred to the highest court. Under Article 58(2)(b):

'The President, in case of dissolution of the National Assembly shall, within fifteen days of the dissolution, refer the matter to the Supreme Court and the Supreme Court shall decide the reference within thirty days whose decision shall be final'.

Similar provision was made in Article 112 of the constitution in respect of the provincial assemblies. Gen Musharraf had also managed to get indemnity to all his actions since military action of 12th October 1999 as according to the amended Article 270AA, the Parliament had:

'Affirmed, adopted and declared to have been duly made by the competent authority ... all laws made between 12th October 1999 and the date on which the Article comes into force'.

It was widely perceived that the PPP's government, after coming in power in 2008, would give priority to plan of removing the stigma of 17th Amendment from their original Constitution of 1973 but, as per disclosures of the WikiLeaks, President Zardari in a meeting with US Ambassador Anne Patterson had told her that he was not interested in abolishing the same. Mr Zardari had openly told the US Ambassador that:

'He does not want to transfer the Presidential powers [of Article 58(2)(b)] to the Prime Minister Gilani though he had demanded it through many public meetings. Opposition Leader Nawaz Sharif had also joined that orchestra with PM Gilani in the name of popular public demand. He would also try to limit the powers of Chief Justice of Pakistan Iftikhar Chaudhry'.

It may be remembered that Gen Musharraf's term as the army chief technically had expired firstly on 6th October 2001 and by stretch in August 2003 when he reached retirement age, but the 17th Amendment in the Constitution of Pakistan, manoeuvred by him with the help of Muslim league (Q) and Maulana Fazlur Rehman, Leader of the Opposition in the Parliament and MMA, allowed him to carry on as both president and army chief until 15th November 2007.

Ten (10) laws were added by the LFO to the Sixth Schedule: the 'laws that are not to be altered, repealed or amended without the previous *sanction of the President.'* After 17th Constitutional Amendment, five of those laws would lose their Sixth Schedule protection after six years. Laws to be freed included the four laws that established the system of democratic local governments. Those in favour of this change had argued that it would enable each province to evolve its own system till then. Opponents feared that authoritarian provincial governments could dis-empower or even dismantle the system of local democracies. However, it was left at the whims of Gen Musharraf and his military advisors.

Astonishingly, once Justice Saeeduzzaman Siddiqui, Justice Fakhruddin Ebrahim and others in 1999 had suggested about the ability of the Supreme Court to strike down a constitutional amendment while Barrister Akram Sheikh had cited Justice Sajjad Ali Shah's suspension of the 13th and 14th Amendments in 1997 as an argument. Those were the special circumstances when PM Nawaz Sharif had desired to get the judicial verdict on assigning himself as *Ameerul Momineen*. Some how the move could not get mature due to other political exigencies then cropped up. Much later, a cogent reply came from the Supreme Court's own judgment on the 17th Amendment Case. This judgment upheld Aitzaz Ahsan's contention that the Parliament was empowered to change the basic structure of the Constitution.

Justice Iftikhar Chaudhry was one of the five Supreme Court judges on the bench who had delivered this judgement. This judgment had dismissed all petitions questioning the legality of the 17th Amendment. Justice F G Ebrahim had told the media that:

> *'In the latest example of 17th Amendment, the court has held that it can only point out the flaws in the constitutional amendment though in India, a principle has been laid down that the courts can strike down an amendment.'*

It was urged by the petitioners that the 17th Amendment in its entirely or at least specifically, Article 41(7)(b) and Article 41(8) should be struck down as violative of the basic structure of the Constitution; but it was held, quoting numerous cases of the past, that this Court did not have the jurisdiction to strike down provisions of the Constitution on substantive grounds.

Let us travel back to history for a while, may it help us comparing:

> *[After the crash of Gen Ziaul Haq in 1988, as the Constitution was operative, there was smooth transfer of power and Chairman Senate*

Mr Ghulam Ishaq Khan took over as acting President and elections were held in the normal course. From 1988 to 1999, for about 12 years, there was no martial law in the country because of the presence of Article 58(2)(b) in the Constitution, which was introduced by Gen Ziaul Haq and which empowered the President to dismiss the Prime Minister at his discretion and hold elections within 90 days.

Four Prime Ministers were dismissed by the respective Presidents and finally that provision was undone by the 13th Amendment in the Constitution of Pakistan, manoeuvred by the then PM Nawaz Sharif, opening the way for military intervention yet again.]

In all parts of the world where the countries had been subjected to army rule in the past, the pages of history lead us that the rate of economic growth and pace of social developments remained below the optimum level during military regimes. The military dictators did paint very glorious pictures of prosperity but the people could not get any fruit. The corruption and under-hand deals remained the hallmarks of their rule though the media concerns were forced to print and praise their cooked figures of pseudo developments and mega projects. When military rulers were sent home then each country had proved that the people were pushed into quagmires of rosy figures and statistics and nothing practical beyond that.

Many countries can be named which adopted a real path of progress and socio-economic growth when democracy prevailed there. Pakistan is one of those unlucky mentionable states where every type of fashion comes late except the military form of government. Once it comes here then it does not go without bloodshed or a major tragedy. In early 80s Pakistan was not the only country ruled by a General, so many other countries were there to taste this fruit. Argentina was run by Gen Gattieri, Chile by Gen Pinochet, Philippines by Marcos, Nigeria by Maj-Gen Buhari, Brazil by Gen Figueiredo, Bangladesh by Gen Ershad, Turkey by Gen Kenan Erven, South Korea by Gen Chun, and Poland by Gen Wojciech Jaruzalski to name a few. A little more details:

- In Argentina elections were held in 1983 and democracy has survived despite huge economic crisis.

- In Chile, Pinochet lost referendum in 1988, stepped down as head of state in 1990 and relinquished his army office in 1998. Since then, there has been a functioning democracy in the country while Pinochet was brought to justice for human rights abuses in 2000.

- In Philippines, Marcos had to lift martial law in 1981 and held elections in 1986 which paved the way for return of democracy.

- In Nigeria, military rule ended in 1999 and first free legislative elections held in 2003.

- In Brazil, elections were held under an electoral college set up by military in 1985 and since then it remains on democratic path.

- In Bangladesh, Gen Ershad's rule ended in 1990 and democracy was restored in 1991 (the General was convicted and jailed afterwards). Despite domestic crisis and partisan politics, Bangladesh continues to march along the democratic path.

- In Turkey, elections were held in 1983 and since then military's influence has gradually weakened ant still the democracy prevails.

- In South Korea, the constitution was amended in 1986 to allow direct election of President and later free parliamentary elections were held in 1988. Despite East Asian crisis of 1998 and several scandals, South Korea has stayed on democratic course.

- In Poland, martial law was lifted in 1983 and in 1989 roundtable talks held among the Solidarity, Communists, and the Church led to free elections and today Poland is a member of the EU as a democratic state.

Each country has moved forward by breaking the cycle of military interventions and made considerable economical progress. In fact, most of them faced serious political and economic disasters in the last ten years. But their adherence to civil and democratic system largely stems from the consensus within military leadership and society based on the past experience that military rules end up creating more and bigger problems than what they seek to address through take-overs.

In an age of empowerment and information revolution, people have to be given primary responsibility for running the affairs of society through representative political structures. Unfortunately, Pakistan is one such country which defies this logic and where what was written in 1982 about it by the CIA applies word to word even after quarter of a century.

When this power game in Pakistan would end, no body knows. Military take-overs attract the people because they consider the politicians, belonging to all major parties like PPPs and PMLs equally corrupt, their leaders take their parties as their family business [*18th Amendment is an example under which the political parties are not bound to hold elections within parties*]. All have their business interests, families and homes abroad. When the military comes, they start their rule seriously but after a year or so, trying to stick to the personal power gains, contacting the *jagirdars* and feudal stalwarts belonging to the same secret mafias of white collar crimes, indulge in the same kind of political corruptions, bargains and compromises.

Let us hope for a sun shine.

Scenario 41

PAKISTAN'S JUDICIARY IN 2004-05:

An extract of *Report N°86 dated 9th November 2004* compiled by *the International Crisis Group* which had categorically stated that when military coups ended democratic rule in Pakistan the judiciary not only failed to check extra-constitutional change, but also endorsed and abetted the consolidation of illegally gained power. Gen Musharraf's government had deepened the judiciary's subservient position among national institutions, ensuring that politics trumped the rule of law, and weakened the foundations for democratic rule.

Since Chief Justice Muneer's days in 1955, Pakistan's higher courts have been playing a critical political role by reviewing the legitimacy of unconstitutional take overs- or continuity. To eliminate potential judicial challenges, the successive military governments devised ways to keep the judiciary weak. The executive always exercised control over the courts by using the system of judicial appointments, promotions and removals to ensure its allies fill key posts. Immediately after all military coups, the judiciary was washed out of judges who might have opposed the military's unconstitutional assumption of power.

Such cleaning actions were accomplished by requiring judges to take an oath to military ruler's Provisional Constitutional Order, an oath that required judges to violate oaths they had all previously taken to uphold the 1973 Constitution. Fear, that another oath would be used to remove more judges, brought limits to the bench's freedom. Moreover, new judges were more cautious because the executive would remove them after one or two years by declining to 'confirm' their appointments.

During Gen Musharraf's regime, his political allies filled key judicial positions, particularly the posts of Chief Justices of the Lahore and of the Sindh High Courts. Compromised by this political bargain, the superior judiciary was unable to address creeping financial corruption within its own ranks. Dysfunction in the superior judiciary also hampered reform in the subordinate judiciary, which comprises the trial courts in which the mass of ordinary judicial business was handled. Endemic corruption in the subordinate judiciary led to agonising delays in the simplest cases and diminished public confidence in the judiciary and the rule of law.

In some subject areas and in some territories, the government simply bypassed the ordinary courts by establishing parallel judiciaries as had been done in Nawaz Sharif's era. In 1997 and 1999 respectively, the government had established separate [and parallel] anti-terrorism and accountability courts, amazingly headed mostly by the serving army officers.

In fact, PML's political government had gone too far by establishing military courts during democratic rule. Those tribunals contained procedural shortcuts that made them too attractive to overzealous police and prosecutors. On the other hand, the gesture had created rift and misunderstanding between the judiciary and executive. CJP Sajjad Ali Shah's row with PM Nawaz Sharif had taken start from the point of establishing these courts in mid 1997 which ended with attack on the Supreme Court in November of the same year and the Chief Justice winding up his baggage.

17ᵗʰ AMENDMENT UPHELD:

On **13th April 2005**, a five member Bench of the Supreme Court of Pakistan delivered a Judgment, known as *Pakistan Lawyers Forum vs Federation of Pakistan* and through this bunch of different petitions, the constitutionality of 17th Amendment was challenged before the apex court. One of the grounds was that the 17th Amendment was violative of the basic structure of the constitution. The five member bench had also included two judges named Justice Iftikhar Mohammad Chaudhry [later the CJP] and Justice Javed Iqbal [*both were the victims of 3rd November 2007's Emergency later reinstated in March 2009*].

Gen Musharraf's Uniform cum Presidential Office [*quite analogous to Mr Zardari's dual Office: President's portfolio & PPP's Acting Chairperson's designation*] was also challenged in the same petition and were dismissed accordingly. Supreme Court's wisdom as to how it handled that question in 2005 was ignored at the time when Gen Musharraf's above mentioned petition was placed before the SC's bench in 2007 in which the same two judges aforementioned were also sitting with the only difference that one of them was the Chief Justice.

The five member bench in 2005 dismissed the petition and upheld the 17th Amendment. The court held that the Indian Doctrine of Basic Structure of the Constitution had never been accepted in Pakistan's judicial history; and that the Court could strike down a Constitutional Provision only if it was not passed in accordance with the procedures provided by the Constitution itself. Once an amendment is passed, it is left to the wisdom of the Parliament which passed it to change it in future according to the aspirations of the people of Pakistan.

The following are the paragraphs taken from that judgment of 2005, numbered as original being easy to comprehend. [*Had the Supreme Court turned down the 18th Amendment later, as it was a roaring demand through media and other political pressures, it would have come up with a very strong reasoning for deviating from its own judicial precedents.*]

32. As to the issue of striking down the 17th Amendment on procedural grounds, it is observed that an Amendment to the Constitution, unlike any other statute can be challenged only on one ground: it has been enacted in a manner not stipulated by the Constitution itself.

41. It has been urged by the petitioners that the 17th Amendment in its entirely or at least specifically, Article 41(7)(b) and Article 41(8) should be struck down as violative of the basic structure of the Constitution. It may first be noted that it has repeatedly been held in numerous cases that this Court does not have the jurisdiction to strike down provisions of the Constitution on substantive grounds.

*46. A challenge to the Fourth Amendment to the Constitution on the ground of the doctrine of basic structure was rejected by the High Court of Sindh in Dewan Textile Mills v. Federation (**PLD 1976 Karachi 1368**).*

56. The superior courts of this country have consistently acknowledged that while there may be a basic structure to the Constitution, and while there may also be limitations on the powers of the Parliament to make amendments to such basic structure, such limitations are to be exercised and enforced not by the judiciary (as in the case of conflict between a statute and Article 8), but by the body politic, i.e. the people of Pakistan.

In this context, it may be noted that while CJP Sajjad Ali Shah had observed that 'there is a basic structure of the Constitution which may not be amended by the Parliament', he nowhere observes that the power to strike down offending amendments to the Constitution can be exercised by the superior judiciary. The theory of basic structure or salient features, insofar as Pakistan is concerned, has been used only as a doctrine to identify such features.

57. The conclusion which emerges from the above survey is that prior to Syed Zafar Ali Shah's case, there was almost three decades of settled law to the effect that even though there were certain salient features of the Constitution, no constitutional amendment could be struck down by the superior judiciary as being violative of those features. The remedy lay in the political and not the judicial process. The appeal in such cases was to be made to the people not the courts. A constitutional amendment posed a political question, which could be resolved only through the normal mechanisms of parliamentary democracy and free elections.

58. It may finally be noted that the basic structure theory, particularly as applied by the Supreme Court of India, is not a new concept so far as Pakistani jurisprudence is concerned but has been already considered and rejected after considerable reflection as discussed in the cases noted hereinabove. It may also be noted that the basic structure theory has not found significant acceptance outside India, as also discussed and noted in the Achakzai's case.

More specifically, the Supreme Court of Sri Lanka refused to apply the said theory in a case, reported as in the 13th Amendment to the Constitution and the Provincial Councils Bill (1990) LRC (Const)1.

Similarly, the said theory was rejected by the Supreme Court of Malaysia in a case titled Phang Chin Hock v. Public Prosecutor (1980) 1 MLJ 70.

59. The position adopted by the Indian Supreme Court in Kesva Bharati case is not necessarily a doctrine, which can be applied unthinkingly to Pakistan. It has been the consistent position of this Court ever since it first enunciated the point in Zia ur Rahman's case that the debate with respect to the substantive vires of an amendment to the Constitution is a political question to be determined by the appropriate political forum, not by the judiciary. That in the instant petitions of this Court cannot abandon its well settled jurisprudence.

85. The petitioners also argued that the statute be struck down because it was not a 'good thing'. This Court, however, held in Zia ur Rahman's case that 'it is not the function of the judiciary to legislate or to question the wisdom of the Legislature in making a particular law'. This Court has consistently held that the wisdom or policy of the legislature is not open to question in exercise of the power of judicial review.

87. Lastly, the petitioners argued that the statute be struck down because that would be the more appropriate thing to do and would be in consonance with popular demand. This Court has, however, always held that statutes are not to be struck down lightly. The Court must make every attempt to reconcile the statute to the Constitution and only when it is impossible to do so, must it strike down the law.

88. Statutes are presumed constitutional and the burden of proving otherwise is on the petitioners. This Court has never struck down a statute on subjective notions of likes and dislikes or what is popular and unpopular. That is not its function. It is as much its duty to uphold a statute, which is constitutional as is its duty to strike down an unconstitutional statute.

90. This Court must have due regard for the democratic mandate given to Parliament by the people. That requires a degree of restraint when examining the vires of or interpreting statutes. It is not for this Court to substitute its views for those expressed by legislators or strike down statutes on considerations of what it deems good for the people. This Court is and always has been the judge of what is constitutional but not of what is wise or good. The later is the business of the Parliament, which is accountable to the people.

92. In consequence, the petitions are dismissed. Above are reasons for the short order announced on 13th April 2005.

However, such juggleries are often seen in Pakistan. The rulers, military and civil both, get the legislations on paper as per their own suitability, sometimes through higher courts and sometimes through the Parliament. During 17th Amendment Gen Musharraf got suitable verdict from the SC and for 18th Amendment, the politicians from both treasury and the opposition benches, got the law suitable to them but from the Parliament.

The tragedy with Pakistan is the greed and incompetence of mostly ruling politicians belonging to all sects and parties. Due to their incompetence there were four 'martial laws' in which a nexus of Generals, judges and a section of the press having 'good relations' with ISI or GHQ were visible. Once Justice Ramday of the Supreme Court of Pakistan had opined that:

'Whereas the higher judiciary gave a temporary reprieve to military rulers, parliaments gave them permanent relief'.

Ayaz Amir, in *'the News' of 16th July 2010,* had not considered it as the whole truth. The fact remained that the parliaments which sanctified the actions of military dictators were the creatures of those dictators and shaped by them but the judges who legitimized military takeovers were not under such compulsions. They were on their benches before those takeovers. In the next paragraph Ayaz Amir opined that:

'No constitution in the world says there should be elections in political parties; not even American which poses as champion of democracy. Yet their lordships [would] observe that with the provision of party elections deleted from the constitution, the command of the Pakistan's constitution is affected.'

At this point the intelligentsia also felt disturbed, genuinely raising a point that though the elections in political parties are not mentioned in the written constitutions world over but:

• *Is there any true democracy in the world where elections are not held in the political parties though not provided in the constitution.*

• *Is there any true democracy in the world where the party is transferred by the chairpersons to their sons and daughters in succession like a family property as in Pakistan.*

• *Is there any true democracy in the world where elections in political parties are made optional by constitutional provisions as in Pakistan vide 18th Amendment. Like the worldly constitutions, the mention of party elections was not required with either sense.*

Ayaz Amir, widely respected for his democratic thoughts, always struggled for the people's genuine will and never hesitated to differ even with his own boss Nawaz Sharif of PML(N) to which party Mr Amir belonged; neither in 2001 nor in 2011 as the media witnessed.

HIGH COURTS vs FEDERAL SHARIAH COURT:

In 2004, a controversy appeared in Lahore chapter of Pakistan's judiciary that whether the high court could review or re-assess the judgments passed by the Federal Shariat Court (FSC). A question was also taken up that whether the expression 'decision' in Article 203(GG) of the Constitution included the 'judgment' or order or the sentence passed by the FSC and whether the same would be binding on the High Court and its subordinate courts.

The cause of controversy: that numerous judgments of the superior courts especially the FSC were available on record that an adult *sui juris* Muslim girl could contract a valid *'Nikah'* on her own and consent of guardian or near relations was not needed. This judgment was incorporated in the Constitution of Pakistan in 1982 by virtue of Article 203(GG) but was not being normally followed [and still it is so] by the subordinate courts under the threat of local feudal community.

The said Article [203(GG)] says that any decision of the FSC in the exercise of its jurisdiction under the Chapter 3-A of the Constitution would be binding on the High Court. Article 203(D) describes the original jurisdiction of the FSC and Article 203(DD) empowers the Court to call for and examine the record of any case decided by any criminal court under any law relating to the enforcement of *Hudood* for the purpose of satisfying itself as to the correctness, legality or propriety of any finding, sentence or order recorded or passed by any such criminal Court. Article 203(DD)(3) lays down that *'the Court shall have such other jurisdiction as may be conferred on it by or under any law'*. Thus exercising the appellate jurisdiction, the FSC in fact is exercising jurisdiction conferred by Article 203(DD)(3), a part of Chapter 3-A.

Moreover, the expression 'decision' in Article 203(GG) seems to have been used in a generic sense which would include the reasons of an order: say of confiscation of property, and / or an order regarding compensation or sentence of imprisonment or fine. Of course, the High Court can take up scrutiny of the judgments or orders or sentences imposed by the FSC but keeping in view the cost of repetition, in terms of both time and money, such an ugly situation has to be avoided.

When the above matter was brought before the Supreme Court, Justice M Ajmal Mian maintained that:

> 'The FSC is a Constitutional Court and it is at least undesirable and inappropriate, if not illegal that another Constitutional Court (like High Court) should hold FSC's judgments as without jurisdiction. Even in normal course the point of jurisdiction has to be urged before the same Court and adjudication obtained. The Constitution provides appeal to the Shariat Appellate Bench of this Court and the question of jurisdiction could have been urged there. Additionally, under the provision of Article 203(E)(9) of the Constitution, added through Presidential Order No. 5 of 1981, the FSC has the power of review which could have been moved, if desired.' *(P L D 2004 SC 219)*

Justice M Ajmal Mian also held that Muslim Personal Law cannot be examined by the FSC and Muslim Personal Law in Article 203(B)(c) means (i) statutory law of Muslim and (ii) it is the personal law of a particular sect; if these two conditions are not present, the matter can be examined by the FSC.

However, in the following two highly trumpeted cases, the Constitutional provisions and the ruling passed by the Supreme Court of Pakistan were over-turned first by the LHC and then the apex court itself.

MUKHTARAN MAI CASE (2002-05):

Customary and extra-judicial practices are always a source of abuse of women in Pakistan. In June 2002, a tribal *Jirga* (local council) in southern Punjab overlooked the gang rape of one **Mukhtaran Mai**, a young woman. Four men, including one of the tribal council members had then allegedly raped Mukhtaran Mai which was intended as 'punishment' for the suspected conduct of her under 18 brother named Abdul Shakoor. Abdul Shakoor was accused of an illicit relationship with a woman named Salma of another tribe called 'Mastoi'.

The subsequent story came up that earlier on that day of 22nd June 2002, Shakoor was abducted by three Mastoi men, was taken at the *dera* of one Abdul Khaliq (Salma's brother) and each of whom sodomized him. The medical report had testified that Shakoor had indeed been sodomized and assaulted. [*Abdul Khaliq and the two others were convicted later in a separate trial*] Shakoor shouted for help in that dragging and his relatives heard his cries. Many women including Mukhtaran Mai rushed outside and urged Abdul Khaliq to release Shakoor but he refused. Mukhtaran's mother then sent her brother to get the local police from the Jatoi Police Station, 18 km away from there.

Members of Mukhtaran's clan also came there and were told that Shakoor had been accused of illicit sex with Salma. On the other side about 200 men of Mastoi tribe also gathered and a Mastoi tribal *jirga* formed immediately under their clan chief, Faiz M Mastoi, known as Faizan. The police arrived before sunset, freed Shakoor from the Mastois and took him to the police station for further probe.

Mukhtaran's family proposed to settle the matter with the Mastois by marrying Shakoor to Salma, and marrying Mukhtaran to one of the Mastoi men, and if Shakoor was found guilty, to give some land to Salma's family. This proposal was conveyed to Faizan but Abdul Khaliq

461

refused the offer and insisted that illicit sex must be settled with illicit sex as per their tribal rules. The *Jirga* decided that the Mastoi would accept the proposed settlement, if Mukhtaran Mai would personally come and apologize before the gathering. Mukhtaran Mai agreed and it was settled that her family should be forgiven.

Immediately after, Abdul Khaliq armed with pistol and with two others, forcibly took Mukhtaran Mai into a nearby stable where she was allegedly gang raped. About an hour later, she was pushed outside wearing only a torn shirt and paraded naked before hundreds of onlookers. Her father covered her up with a shawl and took her home. [*Her clothes were later presented as evidence in the court after medical examination of Mukhtaran and chemical analysis of her clothes.*] That same night, the police were informed that the two clans had settled their dispute, and that Mastois were withdrawing their complaint against Shakoor.

In next Friday's prayer, the local *imam* named Abdul Razzaq condemned the gang rape incident in his sermon, got a local journalist Mureed Abbas to meet Mukhtaran's father, and persuaded the family to file charges against the rapists. On 30th June 2002, Mukhtaran and her family went to Jatoi Police Station and filed their complaint. Within few days the story became headline news in Pakistan media. On 3rd July, the BBC picked up the story; the Time magazine published the front page article on it in mid-July 2002 and major international print & electronic media jumped in.

The police went proactive then, case hurriedly investigated, culprits picked up and the trial conducted. The alleged rapists including Abdul Khaliq and members of the Mastoi *jirga,* six men in total, were sentenced to death by the Dera Ghazi Khan Anti-Terrorism Court (ATC) on 1st September 2002. [*Four men were found guilty of rape and two others, who were part of the tribal council, were found guilty of aiding and abetting the crime but all were sentenced to be hanged which was not considered fair by any court practice*] Eight other accused men were released. Mukhtaran Mai filed an appeal the very next day in Lahore High Court (Multan Bench) against the acquittal of the eight men set free.

On 3rd March 2005, the Lahore High Court reversed the judgement of the trial court on the basis of insufficient evidence and subsequently five of the six men sentenced to death were acquitted, however, the Pakistani government decided to appeal the acquittal.

Mukhtaran Mai was lucky enough to be represented by the highly acclaimed panels of lawyers. One such team was headed by Pakistan's Attorney General [Makhdoom Ali Khan] and the other panel was led by Aitzaz Ahsan, a veteran politico-lawyer of the PPP but the alleged rapists were found not guilty. The accused were subsequently released. The Federal Sharia Court (FSC) decided to suspend the said decision of Lahore High Court on 11th March on the pretext that Mukhtaran's case should have been tried under the Islamic *Hudood* laws. Three days later the Supreme Court ruled that *'the Federal Sharia Court has no authority to overrule the High Court's decision'* and decided to hear this case in the Supreme Court.

On *6th June 2005, the Lahore High Court ruled* that the accused persons could be released on payment of Rs: 50,000 (£450 then) bonds, however, the men were unable to come up with the money, and remained in jail while the prosecution appealed their acquittal. Two weeks later, the Supreme Court intervened and suspended the acquittals of the five men (which were originally sentenced to death) as well as the eight others who were acquitted in the original trial of 2002 by the ATC. All 14 were placed at the mercy of the Supreme Court.

On 21st April 2011 the Supreme Court upheld the Lahore High Court verdict.

Mukhtaran Mai's case was not the only case of chequered cultural perspective of Pakistan. Earlier in 2001, the same kind of case was reported in the NWFP commonly known as Zafran Bibi Case.

ZAFRAN BIBI CASE:

Daily the *'Guardian' of 12th May 2002* stated that Human Rights Commission of Pakistan estimates that every two hours a woman in the country is raped but very little thought has been paid as to how it is possible for innocent illiterate young female victims to be so thoroughly abused by Pakistan's judicial system. Given the inherent weaknesses in the investigation system, with a zero per cent chance of punishment to the assaulter, hardly any rape case is reported to the police. In Zafran Bibi Case she was convicted with the maximum punishment available under any law in the country divulging that how a rape case could be twisted to a perverse conclusion under the prevailing legislation. The victim reported that she was subjected to a crime against her will while the police insisted that she was a consenting party. What could be the consequences then?

On 26th March 2001, one Zafran Bibi, aged 28 years, had reported in the police station concerning with the village Kerri Sheikhan of Kohat in NWFP [now Khyber PK] that one Akmal Khan [*a villager involved in a long-running dispute with her family*] had overpowered her in the nearby fields and raped. After the report, Zafran Bibi was referred to a hospital for an examination. The medical officer there found her to be over seven weeks pregnant. Given the discrepancy in the period between the alleged rape and her pregnancy, the police accused Zafran Bibi as an accused along with Akmal Khan under the Zina Ordinance 1979. The allegation was that she had consented to sex with Akmal Khan but had only disclosed it when she became pregnant.

During the trial, however, Zafran Bibi told the truth that it was in fact Jamal, her brother-in-law, who had raped her repeatedly, but her father-in-law implicated Akmal Khan to save his son. The trial court acquitted Akmal Khan and on the basis of circumstantial evidence and her statement *sentenced Zafran Bibi to death by stoning u / s 5 of the Zina Ordinance*. The court ruled that she had not been raped but had committed adultery, which entailed that punishment.

When Zafran Bibi's in-laws felt that the person whom they implicated had been acquitted and the victim was adamant that the actual culprit was her brother-in-law, her husband gave a new twist to events by telling the superior court through an affidavit that his wife was pregnant by him. He stated that although he was imprisoned but worked at the residence of the Jail Superintendent where his wife frequently visited him and they had sex there, resulting in the pregnancy; the story no body believed because if there were any wrongful act on the part of the victim she would have never reported the matter to police.

The superior courts held that '*a mere delay in reporting is no basis for drawing an adverse inference. In this case, the delay has also been plausibly explained in the First Information Report itself.*' Thus the conviction order of the Additional Sessions Judge Kohat, Anwar Ali Khan, was set aside by the Federal Shariat Court (FSC) which acquitted Zafran Bibi as there were material irregularities in the procedure adopted by the lower court. The FSC, interalia, observed that:

- Firstly, the Pakistani *Hudood* Laws are clearly discriminatory, as they exclude altogether the testimony of female witnesses in awarding the punishment of *hadd*. If a woman is raped in the presence of any number of women, the rapist cannot be punished under the Ordinance.

- Secondly, rape in the absence of any witness is no crime at all under the provisions of Zina Ordinance 1979.

- Thirdly, as the offence of Zina is based on the injunctions of Islam it comes within the domain of Muslim personal law. Hence, non-Muslims should be exempted from this law, which at present they are not.

- Fourthly, the law does not protect a child victim who has not attained mental maturity. The only criteria set forth by the Ordinance are that a male be aged 18 years while a female be aged 16 years or have attained puberty. This means that a 12-year-old girl can be punished with having had wilful sexual intercourse out of wedlock if she has started menstruating. The Ordinance does not in any way account for the girl's mental maturity, which in criminal law is a fundamental requirement to construe criminal liability.

- Fifthly, the law does not contain a single word about the possible compensation or rehabilitation of the victim, neither as a result of being raped in the first place, nor subsequent to wrongful prosecution and all of the suffering and anguish that it has caused.

Gen Musharraf, the military ruler, knew nothing about the case until he was questioned by foreign journalists that if he had planned to reform the adultery laws, introduced in 1979 in a wave of Islamisation led by another military dictator Gen Ziaul Haq. *'Frankly, I haven't given it such deep thought, let me admit,'* said Gen Musharraf who had worriedly insisted that Bibi would not be executed. But hundreds more women who had reported rapes till then were held in jail under the same adultery laws. The foreign reporters were sure that the military regime, despite its promise to eradicate that misuse of Islamic judicial provisions, was unwilling to reform the specific laws for fear of angering his religious friends around the government.

Chairman of the Human Rights Commission of Pakistan, Afrasiab Khattak urged in that Zafran Bibi's case that:

> *'She is not the first case and she is not going to be the last. If Gen Musharraf really wants to do away with extremism, then there is no alternative to doing away with the structures created by Gen Ziaul Haq, which include the so-called Islamic laws. Even if Zafran Bibi returns to her village now, the stigma is so severe that it will be a very harsh life for her and her children.'*

The misuse of the Hudood Ordinance of 1979 was effectively highlighted internationally when Zafran Bibi, was charged with adultery and sentenced to death by stoning. Pakistani women's rights groups rallied around the case and formed an alliance for the repeal of discriminatory laws, especially the Hudood Ordinance of 1979. It was after an active campaign led by national women's rights groups, the Federal Shariat Court of Pakistan had opted to hear the case and then overturned the sentence and acquitted Zafran Bibi in June 2002. However, the law that led to her conviction remained in effect and continued to be a major source of abuse against women victims of violence.

HASBA BILL (2005)

In July 2005, the **Hasba bill** (Accountability Bill) was proposed by members of the NWFP assembly of the Mutahida Majlis e Amal (MMA) [an alliance of six religious parties endorsing a system of Islamic justice (sharia)]. In 2003 the Hasba Bill (Sharia Implementation Bill) was approved by the same assembly; which mandated sharia in the province; thus the Hasba bill was intended for overseeing the implementation of Sharia Act of 2003 approved by the same assembly. The bill was blocked by the Supreme Court of Pakistan. CJP Iftikhar Chaudhry declared it to be unconstitutional as the then Attorney General Makhdoom Ali Khan had appeared on behalf of the President of Pakistan who challenged the bill using his powers as Referring Authority.

The proposed bill was drafted by the MMA leadership strongly advocating that it would bring a pleasant change in the society and it will ensure that all miseries of masses will be solved in a short span of time. The opposition and the civil society organizations criticized the bill declaring it unconstitutional; the Marshal Law of Maulvies and a parallel legal system that would spread anarchy and chaos in the society and would deprive the general public of their rights and liberties.

It was astonishing to note that regardless of its tall claims, the government avoided to present the bill in the assembly since 2003. The Governor had once forwarded it to the Council for Islamic Ideology (CII) for review. The council held a detailed discussion on the bill in August 2004 and sent their comments to Governor NWFP through a letter no PSG-1(2) 2004/324-25-WF openly asking for its rejection.

The main scheme was to establish the offices of Mohtasibeen (Ombudsmen) on provincial, district, tehsil and local levels under the bill. The governor as per the advice of Chief Minister was to appoint of a Mohtasib for a term of four years who would in turn appoint an advisory council consisting upon two religious scholars, two lawyers and two senior serving government officers in grade 20. Similar set ups were to be established at down levels of hierarchy to achieve the desired results. There was a mention of twelve clauses in detail earmarking the sphere of Mohtasib's administrative powers.

The summary of comments of the CII on the proposed Hasba bill was that:

- The said bill would contribute to make Islamic laws disputed in the society giving an edge to the government to utilize it for its vested interests in an unjust manner.

- The inclusion of controversial matters concerning interpretation of Islamic teaching would make Hasba unpopular amongst masses; it would lead to sectarian disputes on grounds of unjust treatment by the powerful groups.

- The 27 sub articles mentioned under clause 23 of the proposed bill were not clearly defined and were left on the discretion of Mohtasib and Hasba force.

- The definition of vice and virtue in Islamic perspective was not equally acceptable to all the existing sects in the country.

- The Jafaria sect had no definable concept of Hasba.

- The bill contradicted many articles of the constitution of Pakistan particularly articles 75 (3) related to the independence of judiciary.

- The responsibilities of Mohtasib were similar to that of judges; therefore, he should possess the required qualification as described for the judges of Sharia court. The term 'certified scholar' (Mustanid Aalim e Deen) was not enough.

- Article 12 of the bill stated that any of Mohtasib's decisions could be challenged in any court of law, which would create anarchy and victimization at large.

- The term Hasba force (volunteers) and their responsibilities were not defined.

- The institution of Mohtasib already existed in Pakistan so it would be taken as a parallel institution creating wide misunderstanding.

- The appointments of Mohtasibeen on district and tehsil levels would lead to open confrontations with existing local government system.

- The CII recommended that power to remove Mohtasib should rest with the supreme judicial council and his tenure should not be extendable.

A thorough review of the above mentioned points raised many crucial questions concerning the establishment of the Hasba institutions, capacity of the government to deliver and implement the existing laws; moral, legal and constitutional and other practical aspects of the bill. Some opined that there would be no need of provincial assembly or other departments in the province because the ultimate concentration of legislative, judicial and administrative powers in Mohtasibeen would lead establishment of clergy rule in the province. It would have deteriorated the relationship of the federal and provincial governments and the selective use of religious teachings had the potential to further polarize the society opening more avenues for the exploitation of religion for political gains. Unknowingly it would have brought defame and criticism for certain Islamic sects.

The Mohtasibeen would have been virtually ruling the entire province but the women and minorities had greatly suffered because it was unlikely that they would have got due representation in it. Thus the implementation of the bill could have eroded the people trust in the democratic process and the relevant institutions. More so, the powers of Mohtasibeen were likely to be used to obtain the desired results in the upcoming local bodies' elections. Thus the proposed bill had little relevance with the ground realties, ill conceived, vague, and contradictory in nature. No link was seen between its objectives, the proposed structure and the job description of the Mohtasibeen. Furthermore, a component party of MMA was opposing it publicly.

It was definitely a politically motivated and aimed at to establish a totalitarian rule in the province in the name of religion and its implementation would have isolated the province from the rest of the world viz a viz increasing polarization in the society. It will not be out of context to mention that the MMA government faced a big embarrassment when its Sharia bill, passed by the present assembly in 2003, was labelled as a replica of an earlier bill passed by the then

Parliament in PM Nawaz Sharif era. The same group of people were involved in that exercise wasting enormous amounts of the public funds in that exercise ended in futile.

Going back to its origin; the then Governor NWFP had not agreed with the Hasba bill; had it got the governor's assent, the bill would have been through. The bill's main accomplishment was the creation of Mohtasibs at various levels of government to 'promote virtue' and to eliminate un-Islamic practices; putting ban on alcohol and music in commercial vehicles and similar like things. Actually, this bill was about power: both of the 'traditional' political kind as well as the religious. One newspaper mentioned it as *'extremism is hardly being rolled back by the King's Party. It is actually creeping in under its door like a stain of blood.'* Creeping was right. 40 km south of Peshawar, two girls' schools were closed down on the day the bill was floated, with threats extended that further closures could be on the way. And the Supreme Court had done its bit to water the original Hasba Bill down; good it was. The daily 'Dawn' had said: *'it is the duty of everyone opposed to this law to resist it, however they can'.*

Thus; it remains a history now.

Scenario 42

NAB: A DECADE OF MISUSE:

[*Accountability is something you do after the damage is done. Good governance is measures you adopt that prevent things going wrong, and in case they do, then the discrepancy is quickly detected and tackled.* (Riaz A K)]

TRAGEDY OF JAVED HASHMI:

In October 2001, PML(N) decided to join hands with certain politico-religious parties of Pakistan under the guidance of its Acting President Makhdoom Javed Hashmi [*as the original leadership of the PML(N), Sharif family, had slipped away to Saudi Arabia under a dubious deal with Gen Musharraf in December 2000*] to raise loud voices against the then military rule. As per decades old power practice in Pakistan, Javed Hashmi was picked up by the NAB people through a police raid at his residence at 2AM on 31ˢᵗ October instant. [*Javed Hashmi was staying in Nawaz Sharif's house in Islamabad at the time of his arrest*] No charges were read over to Mr Hashmi at the time of his arrest; even the raiding officers didn't know much about details.

Later, ISPR's spokesman Gen Rashid Qureshi told that Javed Hashmi was arrested for amassing *'assets beyond his mean'*, and was being held by the NAB but the media knew it well that his detention was related to turning political developments. In those days, Gen Musharraf was contacting secular political parties frequently attempting to broaden his political base during the rising crisis in Afghanistan in the back drop of 9/11 events.

[*However, all Pakistanis knew that Javed Hashmi was a man of character; rather he was the only clean person (or one of very few like Siddiq ul Farooq) in the PML(N). After five years he was cursed, objected, neglected, annoyed, irritated and shunted out of the party by the sole proprietors of the PML(N) because he had once said in a live TV program that 'all politicians including Sharifs should truly declare their assets, here & abroad, for the sake of Pakistan'.*]

The **Washington Post of 1st November 2001** had opined that Gen Musharraf's decision to abandon Pakistan's support for the then ruling Taliban in the War against Terrorism had angered Pakistan's Islamic parties, which had sympathies with Afghanistan's ruling Taliban militia. Moreover:

'The religious groups had launched protests with regular street demonstrations all over Pakistan. Javed Hashmi and PML(N) had not taken a stand with Gen Musharraf's decision to support the US-led campaign against the Taliban; contrarily they had decided to participate in the strike of 9th November being organized by the religious parties against the government. Javed Hashmi was arrested a few hours after that decision; he was the third prominent politician to be arrested, as part of the military leader's effort to prevent an escalation of the anti-government protests. The heads of two leading Islamic groups were also kept under house arrest.'

This was the scenario for which the NAB was given special powers under 1999's amendments to create an atmosphere of threat and coercion for politicians so that no one should be able to challenge the military rule. Nawaz Sharif had also done the same, rather he was the pioneer of that criminal extortion through Saifur Rehman's Ehtesab Bureau in 1997, which was polished and improved by Gen Musharraf. So it was the NAB of civil and military rulers, making fool of the whole nation in the name of accountability.

Lt Gen SHAHID AZIZ'S CASE:

Lt Gen Shahid Aziz, a former Chairman NAB, while speaking to media [referring to 6th & 8th Dec 2009 live on GEO, the News & Dawn] after expiry of two year's mandatory period that prevented him to discuss service matters, revealed that he was constantly pressurized to hand over the lists of politicians being probed by the NAB, but he refused to do so. However, Parliament's Standing Committee later ordered NAB to provide the updated lists naturally for the consumption of the PM Shaukat Aziz and Gen Musharraf. Moreover, he told that:

'I was appointed as the NAB chairman with a pre-condition that I would not open old cases against politicians and other prominent people and was pressurized into formally closing down cases against politicians supporting Gen Musharraf. I was told repeatedly not to create problems and not to destabilise the government, otherwise the system would collapse. They (the president & his team) gave a strange logic that corruption and economic development goes hand in hand.'

Lt Gen Shahid Aziz quoted Lt Gen Khalid Maqbool, a former NAB Chairman and Governor Punjab, as saying while trying to convince him that:

"If you stop corruption, there will be no development. If ministers and politicians are not given personal benefits in contracts, why would they pursue development schemes? They have to be given personal incentives...contracts to their sons and kinship."

Once Gen Musharraf had personally called Lt Gen Shahid Aziz, the Chairman NAB, and asked him that:

'.... drop the name of one Malik Riaz Hussain from the exit control list. (Riaz Hussain was one of the prime accused in a multi-million land scam) As President of Pakistan, I give my personal guarantee that he (Malik Riaz) would not run away. Isn't a personal guarantee of the President of Pakistan sufficient to satisfy you'?

(Ref: daily 'Dawn' of 6th December 2009)

Malik's name was removed from the ECL subsequently.

Lt Gen Shahid Aziz was appointed NAB chairman on 10th November 2005 for a period of four years. According to the NAB Ordinance of 1999, the NAB Chairman cannot be removed before the expiry of four years except if he resigns but it never became clear that whether he himself opted to resign or he was forced to resign. But the record told that he was not attending his office since May 2007 due to undue interference of the government in NAB's affairs.

Lt Gen Shahid Aziz's predecessor Lt Gen Munir Hafeez had left NAB on the eve of his retirement from the army. Lt Gen Shahid was succeeded, first time in eight years, by a civil bureaucrat Nawid Ahsan, who was General Secretary Finance in the Federal Government. The appointment of Nawid Ahsan, a civilian Chief of NAB, was made in the backdrop that the President himself was planning to come out of his military uniform (An army officer, retired or serving, remains answerable to the Army Chief). Gen Musharraf had planned to keep the control of NAB exclusively with him as a civilian President.

The fact remains that Lt Gen Shahid and the then PM Shaukat Aziz were not easy with each other. The PM had once reprimanded the Chairman NAB in a public meeting not to insult senior bureaucrats on the pretext of investigation. Some reports speak out that the tussle between the two started in 2006 when the NAB under his command tried to conclude investigations against some top politicians, including Asif Ali Zardari, Nawaz Sharif, Shahbaz Sharif, Ch Shujaat Hussain and Humayum

Akhtar etc on various counts; of course new cases in addition to the old files. Lt Gen Shahid was going to collect and incorporate important features and facts about those top politicians when his cousin Gen Musharraf had shown him the exit door in an un-ceremonial way.

At that time, the main issues were of sugar crisis and edible oil shortage. Chairman NAB was initially asked to close the files on the pretext that *'the prices of sugar, edible oil and petroleum products would go all time high if the investigations continued'*. In the cases then opened by the NAB Ch Shujaat Hussain, Sharif's family members, Humayun Akhtar, Jehangir Tareen, Altaf Saleem, Nasarullah Dareshak, Anwer Cheema and Mian Azhar were alleged to have hoarded about 315000 tons of sugar and the prices were taken up from Rs:20 to Rs:45 per kg for consumers.

[Lt Gen Shahid Aziz was known as an upright person. To judge his spirit of nationalism and sincerity to cause one should not forget his talk to the media to divulge on certain untold stories of Gen Musharraf's earlier era. He, being the Chief of General Staff (CGS) from Oct 2001 to Dec 2003, had revealed that the Army as an institution was kept in complete dark about what was going on between Washington and Islamabad after 9 / 11 and on 'War on Terror' deals.

GHQ and the top Army commanders had strongly opposed the handing over of Pakistanis to the US, but Gen Musharraf did so at his own. Though Office of the CGS was always taken as the nerve centre in GHQ but then it did not know most of the controversial things Gen Musharraf did.

Lt Gen Shahid told the media that while the Pakistan Army used to catch the targeted foreigners and locals and handed them over to the ISI for interrogation, they were passed on to the Americans without the knowledge of the GHQ. It caused a lot of resentment in the top echelons of the Pakistan Army when they found this was happening. Gen Musharraf kept the ISI engaged to collaborate with American CIA without the knowledge of other commanders.

Gen Musharraf had also allowed the US drones to use the Pakistani airspace for intelligence sharing besides permitting the American intelligence agencies, the CIA and the FBI, to recruit their agents in the tribal belt of Pakistan. Despite strong opposition from the GHQ, Gen Musharraf granted this permission in the name of intelligence sharing. The same drones had then carried out strikes inside Pakistan, killing hundreds of people, including innocent women and children.

Lt Gen Shahid Aziz felt no hesitation to disclose that when initially consulted after 9/11, the top commanders had decided to stay out of the conflict. However later, because of compromises by Gen Musharraf, the Army was dragged in that odd situation.

Gen Musharraf had compartmentalised the Army to such an extent that even the CGS would not know many things directly assigned by the Army Chief to other departments. Since he (Gen Musharraf) was also holding the government, the Army as an institution was not consulted on many things that were being agreed between Islamabad and Washington.]

The government did not like the media briefings by retired army officers against their policies then what if anti-national. As per usual practice in Pakistan, Lt Gen Shahid was also taken to task on lines earlier mentioned in the context of Javed Hashmi, country's typical hallm ark. Baseless accusations were listed against him; investigations into alleged *'misuse of powers by a former chairman NAB'* were launched and given a booster start on 9th December 2009, within 24 hours he had appeared in the live TV program of GEO to tell the truth about Gen Musharraf and his way of managing the NAB; using it for arms twisting of any one who could dare to oppose the military ruler.

The allegations included that Lt Gen Shahid Aziz had allotted quota of LPG for himself, while his son-in-law purchased a few plots from three housing societies in lacs but sold them for millions of rupees, while the societies had allegedly given his son-in-law special discount; the General himself had manoeuvred to get a five-kanal house worth a rent of Rs:0.5 million per month for only a monthly rent of Rs:60,000 and had taken away its furniture worth Rs:15 million when he left it. The revengeful team of investigators within one night detected a fraud done by the former Chairman in official registry of that land on which he was constructing a house. Investigations on all those closed files were immediately opened which were closed during his tenure and many more things like that.

Lt Gen Shahid Aziz rejected all the allegations levelled against him. He simply stated that he had no house when he was transferred to Lahore and he used to live at the house of his daughter, so what issues of rent or furniture.

In year 2002, after the evolution of National Anti-corruption Strategy, identification of root causes of corruption were also incorporated into the anti corruption mechanism that empowered NAB to undertake prevention and awareness of corruption and corrupt practices. The fact remains that in early days of Gen Musharraf's take over, some of the NAB officers had strictly and harshly pursued the NAB agenda to eradicate corrupt practices but it was allegedly & purposefully propagated that it had offended the business community thus hindering the economic growth. During Lt Gen Maqbool's tenure as Chairman, compromises were struck with the business community and significant politicians. Thus Khalid Maqbool's tenure was marked with peculiar reputation of striking deals and negotiating under the table compromises in the name of 'plea-bargains' in NAB's history.

[*On 9th December 2004, Senator Sanaullah Baloch asked how much money had been recovered under plea bargains from politicians and civil and military officers on the orders of the court. It was revealed that whereas an amount of Rs:432 million had been recovered from politicians and nearly Rs:2 billion had been recovered from the civil-military bureaucracy under pleas bargain. During a reply to a question on 15th February 2004, it was told that the NAB had paid Rs:390 million as fees to lawyers during the past five years.*]

Though there was a high-powered committee consisting of Chairman NAB, Principal Secretary to the President, Governor of State Bank etc who were also supposed to know the 'important' suspects in cases of 'high volume corruption' but practically the mechanism was not given the required transparency. The Presidency, NAB & ISI continued to deal with the business tycoons and politicians in getting their favours to prolong the military rule of Gen Musharraf. The NAB remained after the wealthy targets like Admiral Mansoor ul Haq to do plea-bargains, and it became a routine practice those days. The media and judiciary knew it well; rather the details of certain 'big deals' had also appeared in the foreign press but judiciary purposefully kept mum and compromised.

HASAN WASEEM AFZAL'S DUBIOUS ROLE:

To cut and avoid NAB's budget unto millions on account of dubious foreign trips, the government had to abolish the Special Operation Division (SOD), a subsidiary of the NAB, which was investigating matters related to illegal foreign assets and offshore bank accounts of politicians, including Sharif Family assets, Benazir Bhutto and of Asif Ali Zardari.

[*During the last two years till that date the NAB officials had made forty eight (48) foreign trips at the public expense costing over Rs:10* *million for the government exchequer. One senior officer alone made 16 foreign trips that cost the exchequer Rs:3.3 million. Twenty five (25) visits were undertaken for participation in seminars, conferences and conventions in various world capitals. The NAB officials made three trips to Riyadh and Dubai to attend Pakistan Day celebrations only. A senior officer of the Bureau, during several journeys to European countries, had also **travelled to Dubai ten times for 'the special purposes'.**]*

This SOD was created on a misleading advice of one DMG officer named Hasan Waseem Afzal who was made its incharge when it came into being. Initially the officer had landed in Nawaz Sharif's Ehtesab Bureau of 1997 just to save his brother in law's skin [named Javed Zia of Gulberg III Lahore] who was nominated and the only culprit in an FIR registered with FIA Rawalpindi on 5th September 1995. Waseem's only brother-in-law was involved in two fraud cases then:

Firstly; for selling out Cotton Mills Okara's open land after converting it into a private housing colony without clearing his bank loans.

Secondly, Mr Zia was involved in selling out a Cessna to the Punjab Government on double market price and masterminding 'commissions' in the name of the then Chief Minister Manzoor Watto.

The first and remarkable job of Hasan Waseem Afzal was to get that FIR quashed with the help of the then Chairman Saifur Rehman of Ehtesab Bureau. Then he offered his special services to Saifur Rehman to fabricate the Swiss Case against Benazir Bhutto and Asif Ali Zardari during the tenure of Nawaz Sharif compelling Benazir Bhutto to leave the country. He had managed it through the services of his 'family' friend, a tarnished judge of the High Court named Malik Qayyum. [*Allegations on J Malik Qayyum have been given separately on the earlier pages along with his contentions whatsoever*]

Mr Hasan Waseem Afzal was then awarded the *Tamgha e Imtiaz* by the government of Pakistan for his services against Bhuttos and was made Deputy Chairman NAB when the government wished to penalise Benazir Bhutto who was exerting pressure on Gen Musharraf-led government for her return. He again activated cases against Benazir Bhutto and Zardari in Swiss courts, and paid tens of visits to Switzerland. The facts also appeared in media that, during his apparent visits to Switzerland and London, he had managed to strike a secret deal with Ms Bhutto and had perhaps succeeded. When the facts reached Gen Musharraf, Mr Waseem was asked to relinquish charge of his assignment in NAB and kicked out.

One may be able to find out Hasan Waseem's place in between the above paragraphs. Once on 9th December 2006, NAB organized an anti-corruption march on Constitution Avenue in Islamabad. Abdul Sattar Edhi came to lead it and the call was 'Unite against Corruption'. Earlier that day, PM Shaukat Aziz attended the formal Anti-Corruption Day function in which he openly abused NAB for its misdeeds. Later during tea, when the PM had gone away, the news reporters gathered around the Chairman and asked why the PM was so furious with NAB. Then they themselves uttered *'we know Sir, it is because you are doing POL inquiry against him.'* The video film of whole of that tea function is still available in NAB's office. Hats off to Lt Gen Shahid Aziz again.

Pakistan's NAB had been involved more in political victimization than in actual accountability since its inception, no doubt. The draconian provisions of the NAB Ordinance and their selective implementation had often brought criticism and never praise.

On *5th December 2003*, a question was raised about the military officers working in civil departments against whom cases had been registered by the NAB. The 14 military officers on the list included a former lieutenant general heading a civil department, as being 'under investigation for accumulating assets beyond his means.' The investigations, however, never concluded.

On *2nd December 2004*, a question was asked about the status of NAB cases against sitting members of Parliament, if any. Nine sitting MPs were named against whom there were cases of corruption, misuse of authority and accumulation of assets beyond their known sources of income. All these enquiries ended up in twisting arms in Gen Musharraf's favour. Lt Gen Shahid Aziz when took over as Chairman NAB, had issued directions:

> 'Not to continue to chase the gunahgars [sinners] *but to go after the shiateen* [devils], *because the shiateen here in Pakistan point fingers at the gunahgars so that all appear as one and no distinction remains.'*
> Correct it was. Our history is depleted with such truthful instances.

Federal Ministers Faisal Saleh Hayat, Aftab Sherpao, Rana Nazir Ahmad, Jehangir Khan Tareen and Liaquat Ali Jatoi were named in the above referred list. All had been the target of the NAB until they joined the King's Party; were rewarded with ministerial jobs and let off the hook. The chairman of the Senate Committee on Foreign Affairs, Syed Mushahid Hussain, had also been named as being involved in a case of "misuse of authority." The case was closed in May 2002 after over two years of investigation. On a privilege motion, two meetings were called to discuss the case but were subsequently cancelled or held without the attendance of the Chairman NAB; no results whatsoever.

The Supreme Court once asked the NAB's Chief Prosecutor whether petitioner Siddiq ul Farooq [the Information Secretary of PML(N)] was in NAB custody and what the status of investigations against him was. In reply, the Prosecutor General admitted that the petitioner was in NAB custody but he could not inform the Court that where Siddiq ul Farooq had been 'dumped' and what the status of investigations was.

The hallmark conclusion was that while the NAB was carrying out investigations, open or secret, an accused may roam free or be made a cabinet minister or 'dumped' and forgotten; depends upon the sweet will of the rulers not the law. *South Asia Tribune of 29th April 2005* had indicated various mega scandals during the military regime of Gen Musharraf but the NAB kept their lips tight because certain army generals were named then.

Hats off to the Corps Commander of Lahore, Lt Gen Shahid Aziz, who had once started a serious investigation against his predecessor, the last Corps Commander of Lahore then posted in GHQ, Lt Gen Zarrar Azim [known in the real estate world of Lahore as Gen Zarrar Zameen (land)] who was so deeply involved in the scam of Lahore Defence Society that in the price of every plot of land allotted in the society, a fee of Rs:600,000 (then £7500) had to be built-in, almost automatically, meant for the Corps Commander's office. The out-going CC was using a junior officer, Major Lodhi as his front man. This major had the backing of Gen Aziz of Kargil fame who was related to Gen Musharraf as his coup partner.

The details of these Defence Society scams were mind boggling. Thousands of plots of land were designated in official files as Defence Society land and the same were then sold and re-sold on files. More paper Housing Societies were registered and approved and they claimed vast tracts of land without owning a square yard. In Lahore, there were about 12,000 files of plots for Sectors 7, 8, 9 and 10 for which there was no land actually available on the ground. As per SAT referred above:

'An on going joke in the Army Mess Circuit then prevailing was; the last request Gen Musharraf made to Indian Prime Minister Manmohan Singh in Delhi was to give him 8,000 acres of land from the Indian territory across the Wagah-Atari border, 30 miles from Lahore, in

return for Kashmir and Siachin, because "my boys have already sold this land" in the files'.

Gen Musharraf's another commander, Lt Gen Tariq Wasim Ghazi of Karachi became notoriously famous for similar land scams in Defence Society Karachi, including Creek City and allotment to two special people, Humayun Butt and Fareed Veerani. Who were these specials and what their involvement was, no body was sure.

In Lahore, the Mayor Mian Amer Mahmood had claimed on 24th April 2005, that he had succeeded in vacating 3,000 kanals (375 acres) of land belonging to schools from a 'big land mafia', most of the people knew that who were that mafia - the brokers using army's name. In the same row, the former head of the NAB Lt Gen (retd) Amjad Hussain was himself accused of massive corruption in the corporation he has been heading. This charge of corruption was levelled in the Parliament involving the Fauji Foundation, undeniably the largest corporate body of Pakistan which was then heading towards buying the largest public sector company, Pakistan State Oil (PSO). It was regarding the sale of the Khoski Sugar Mills; the Parliament was told that en enquiry had been ordered in that respect but results never made open because Pak Army's name was frequently discussed allegedly involved.

While the above details show that in-service Generals and Corps Commanders were being investigated for corruption, another officially announced corruption case was against the management of the South Asian Federation (SAF) Games, interestingly consisting of all military officers headed by Lt Gen Arif Hassan. The financial irregularities to the tune of Rs:201 million were also including undue benefit to be provided to certain private firms through 'verbal agreements'; daily 'Dawn' told quoting an audit report. The 9th SAF Games were managed by its Chairman Lt Gen Arif Hassan, Chiefs included Brig Amjad Javaid, Lt Col Syed Mujtaba Tirmizi, Brig Ahmad Raza Siddiqi, Brig Abid Hussain Bhatti, Lt Col (retd) M Yahya, Lt Col Mansoor Abbas, Lt Col Umer Farooq, Lt Col Azhar Dean, Brig Arif Rasul Qureshi, Brig Khalid Rasheed Lodhi and Engr Col Usman Saeed. None of the very well qualified civilians players was found suitable for any slot.

In a military regime, obviously the Corps Commanders and senior Generals were the top Government and if scams and scandals involving those top men were officially exposed, some in the National Assembly and others by leaks to the media by their own juniors; the tall claims of Gen Musharraf to eliminate corruption were a mockery and NAB was there to provide them shelter.

During the decade of 2001-10, the Bank of Punjab (BoP) scam was taken up by the Supreme Court of Pakistan in which Chaudhrys of Gujrat were also named. Stunning details told that what our politicians have been doing with poor economy of Pakistan. The BoP scam had uncovered the multi-billion scandals of Harris Steel loan (Rs:9 billion); the controversial sale of Phalia Sugar Mill of the Chaudhrys of Gujrat for Rs:2.2 billion with BoP money borrowed by a sitting director of the Bank and the mind-boggling lending of over Rs:18 billion to five sitting directors of the BoP in violation of the Bank policy; then popped up with another Rs:1.8 billion eating up.

Lt Gen KHALID MAQBOOL's CASE:

Lt Gen Khalid Maqbool's era as Chairman NAB is marked with 'corruption within ranks' in the name of dubious plea bargains. Adml Mansoorul Haq's case is widely quoted as an instance in which the NAB recovered from him only a few thousand dollars [on record] against an allegation of $7.2 million kickback. An amount of $2.65 million was recovered from one Mr Jamil [country rep of the French Firm] in Agosta submarines case and set him Scot free without mention of his name in the record even. Kamran Khan is quoted for 'The Facts of May 2004':

> 'NAB officials said that the plea bargain deals are meant to recover the looted money in exchange for some grace to the accused persons who get the benefit of not going through the public trial and exposure of their misdeeds in public. But the process is attracting some criticism, as it allows the senior NAB officials to exercise their discretion in settling the amount for the plea bargain.

> In Irfan Puri, Usman farooqi and Admiral Mansurul Haq cases the money recovered by the NAB may match their ill-gotten wealth, but in some cases some key suspects won their freedom at a cheap cost. For instance Huzoor Buksh Khalwar, a former Karachi Metropolitan director, who was arrested after a NAB investigation found that he had allegedly amassed wealth to the tune of hundreds of millions of rupees, was set free after a brief (according to the NAB standards) three months' confinement and a nominal payment of Rs16 million. Khalwar was one of the beneficiaries of a Rs600 million octroi fraud unearthed in the KMC in 1998.'

During late 2010, some latest revelations had shown that the son in law of former Punjab's Governor, Lt Gen (retd) Khalid Maqbool got a whopping Rs:1.8 billion loan from the said bank and wilfully defaulted. The Bank of Punjab's Special Asset Management (SAM) wing approached the NAB of Lahore seeking an inquiry against one Ahsan Latif [the son in law of Lt Gen Khalid Maqbool] for not returning the Rs:1.8 billion loan that was given to his company (M/s Gas Naturale) on political pressures. The written complaint of the BoP contained:

"M/s Gas Naturale (Pvt) Ltd through its directors has obtained a loan amounting to Rs:1.8 billion. The loan was awarded in an unorthodox manner, and the BoP stepped in as a sole lender to the project because of political pressure exerted by the party who happens to be son-in-law of the then Punjab Governor. Due to lending at such a large scale without merit, the loan is in default now causing loss to the bank and the project is completely stuck. The borrower is not paying its portion of equity nor is ready to transfer the project to the BoP."

Lt Gen Khalid Maqbool and Ahsan Latif were not then available to the NAB for questioning as they were abroad. The fact remains that following political pressure, the Bank management had to give loan to Ahsan Latif's company despite the fact that the company was financially incapable to support such a mega project. However, it also talks of managerial incapability of the BoP to handle the project as the company had no significant experience in the said field or business of that scale in any other industry. The BoP maintained that misleading and factually incorrect information was submitted to the bank, with wilful intent to deceive the bank authorities.

It is also on record that while this project was suffering from escalation and delays, the BoP allowed another loan of Rs:28 million to M/s Synergy Power belonging to the same group [Gas Naturale (Pvt) Ltd].

The documents also show that Lt Gen Khalid Maqbool, during his governorship, had entered into an agreement with the BoP under which he had rented out his commercial property at the Defence Housing Scheme Lahore, to the BoP for Rs:620,000 per month. The said agreement was signed between Khalid Maqbool, the then Governor, and the BoP on 1st March 2008 but subsequently cancelled on 4th April 2008.

When the contents of BoP scam having mention of Lt Gen Khalid Maqbool's son in law was published at the 'Defence Journal of Pakistan', a military's official internet site, no body came forward to comment on it because it was a story about a General's power twisting role. If he were a son of a politician or bureaucrat, the thread would have got 100s of comments criticizing the whole political and bureaucratic nexus. It was a mini mention of 'power corruption' in Pakistan. He was a retired General; he was a governor at that time, so why raising voices so loud though some say that he should be held accountable.

This was not the first case and won't be the last. People from all walks of life have done corruption in Pakistan; all should have been held for it but since Pakistan experienced the same oligarchs coming and going while running the country, the NAB would prefer to go for 'targeted accountability' again.

A report by Transparency International (TI) had once claimed that Gen Musharraf's military regime was perceived as more corrupt than its military or civilian predecessors. The *Corruption Watchdog's 2006 Report* on Pakistan was based on a sample of 4,000 urban and semi-urban citizens in all the four provinces. Asked about the then government, 33 percent of the respondents thought that it was corrupt in 1999-2002, but when asked to assess the period 2002-06, more than 67 percent thought it was corrupt. Yes, it was true 67% - the highest ever rating given to a government in Pakistan for corruption.

In a statement, the then ruling PML(Q) partner had told the media that despite rating as first in corruption according to Transparency International, the regime was not facing a single NAB case. This proved that the NAB was for political and not for corruption purposes. The then PPP had pledged to wash that image when voted into government. The PPP spokesman had said that:

'Transparency International findings also rejected the military regime's view that military dictatorships are honest. When military regimes of Ayub, Yahya, Zia and Musharaf were the most corrupt, creating from twenty two families to a high of sixty seven percent corruptions, it meant that the lower scores showed that the political governments had improved on the situation although there is still a long way to go. The issue of corruption should be separated from politics. The history of Pakistan shows that the corruption prevails because laws are mocked and political parties broken by abuse of the word while the actual corruption proliferates'.

But the PPP is in power since four years now. The stories of corruption during PPP's this rule has beaten all the previous records. See the media reports; when this govt goes, more scams for billions will be unearthed.

[Part of this essay was published at www.Pakspectator.com as a 'Lead Story' on 19th October 2011]

Scenario 43

SARDAR BUGTI ASSASSINATED (2006):

In January 2005, scuffles between Pakistani security forces and resentful Bugti tribes in the Sui region of Balochistan again cropped up in which eight paramilitary security men were killed and four seriously wounded. The military government maintained that the tribesmen want more royalties from the gas taken from their lands. In the light of the past five years brawling history, Gen Musharraf finally opted to wipe out all rebels once for all with force and re-establish its writ through permanent army positioning. The rebels also desperately wanted to deliver a knockout blow to the rulers, both Pakistan's civil government and military.

DR SHAZIA RAPED BY ARMY MEN:

Amidst this state of insurgency, an alarming rape case was quickly grabbed by many Balochi tribes to instigate a war against Pakistan's establishment; a reaction and resentment against the army.

> *'During the late hours of 2nd January 2005, Pakistan Army's Captain Emad and three soldiers from the Defence Security Guards (DSG), gang-raped a lady doctor, Dr Shazia Khalid serving in the Pakistan Petroleum Limited (PPL) as an employee during night times. These army men had beaten her and kept her unconscious for several hours. Since an army officer was involved in the case, Major Mukhtar of the DSG hushed up the case by influencing the PPL management. They shifted the doctor to Karachi and she was not allowed to meet anybody so that nobody would know the reality.*
>
> *Even the first information report (FIR) was not allowed to be registered with the police; and when after 12 days it was registered, it was a 'blind' FIR in which unknown rapists were mentioned. The case spread all over the area and the Baloch Liberation Front (Baloch Liberation Army) took things into their hands, attacked DSG camps, annihilated them and demanded that all foreign elements should leave the area immediately. The event was taken as against the Baloch culture. The lady doctor was there to serve the humanity thus taken as honourable guest.'*

When the Bloch people attacked the DSG Camps to register their protest and anger, the Pakistan army, instead of contacting Nawab Bugti, their

Tribal Chief, preferred to send 36 trucks loaded with army men from nearby cantonments as show of power. At Sibi air base, six gunship helicopters, military aircrafts and 12 artillery tanks were placed to reach Sui at call; to eliminate the dissenting voices once and for all. Referring to the *Asia Times dated 15th January 2005*, Nawab Bugti [while giving an interview to (late) Saleem Shehzad] told that:

'They [Pakistan government] think that natural resources are national assets, and we think they are Baloch assets, and whoever wants to use them must do so through us, not by direct possession. Call for a Greater Balochistan movement is a stunt against us.

It is [attacks on DSG Camps] just a reaction and resentment shown by the Baloch nation to a heinous crime committed on our land. Dr Shazia was not Baloch but the Punjabi cannot understand our culture and codes. What respect we give to women, irrespective of her caste, religion or ethnicity, no Punjabi can understand.

You may have read about many incidents that happened in Punjab, reported in newspapers, that on the issue of personal enmity somebody entered into the house of his enemy and brought the women of his enemy naked in public, and the Punjabi public, instead of reacting or putting clothes on the naked women, clapped. We are alien to this kind of culture, and therefore when our men learned of the heinous crime they bombed the criminals' nest [DSG] and we say: Get lost back to your Punjab and do whatever you like, but not on our lands.'

Starting from January 2005, the surge in insurgency continued in Balochistan.

DETAILS OF SARDAR BUGTI'S ASSASSINATION:

A media version of the ISPR dated 26th August 2006 claimed that in a usual counter insurgency operation in Bugti area of Balochistan, an army helicopter came under fierce attack from the rebels while over-flying the region. The army contingent retaliated and the resultant battle led to the caving in of a mud bunker where Nawab Akbar Bugti along with his men had taken shelter.

The electronic media had also released the breaking news that *'the driving force behind the anti-government rebellion in Balochistan'*, was killed in a massive military operation in the Bhambore Hills, an area between the cities of Kohlu and Dera Bugti.

It was officially stated to the press that during the army operation Akbar Bugti and a number of other terrorists were killed at the spot as a result of heavy fire exchange and all were left buried in the same cave including Nawab Bugti and his top aides. An ISPR statement once more reiterated that two army helicopters, flying over the general area of Tartani in Kohlu on 23rd August were fired upon from the ground and one helicopter was damaged. Another chopper was then dispatched to investigate and was also hit, but returned safely.

Federal Information Minister Mohammad Ali Durrani later told that:

'Gen Musharraf was told just before 12am on Sunday that Nawab Bugti had been killed. As many as 21 army commandos and 37 rebels had also been killed in the same operation, which targeted 50 to 80 of Nawab Bugti's closest family members and top commanders. Balochistan Liberation Army (BLA)'s Chief Balach Marri and Nawab Bugti's grandsons Brahamdagh Bugti and Mir Ali Bugti were also killed in the fighting. Nawab Bugti's location was discovered only three days earlier by the security forces; they had besieged the hills where he was hiding in. Nawab Bugti's whereabouts were established by monitoring satellite phone intercepts.' [Later reports told that Brahamdagh Bugti was not there in the cave but was in Afghanistan then]

According to the foreign press; the military launched air strikes against a cave in the mountains on the border of Dera Bugti and Kohlu districts, where Nawab Bugti was said to be hiding. There was little fighting on the ground. The missile raid destroyed the entrance to the rocky hideout and Special Forces moved in [next day] to carry out a 'cordon and search operation'. Heavy fighting broke out as the insurgents returned fire, killing several soldiers including the leader of the commando team.

The foreign press continued to say that the soldiers eventually secured the area and ascertained that Nawab Akbar Bugti was among the dead. Around 24 Marri and Bugti tribesmen, including Nawab Bugti, were killed and 37 injured. The injured were taken into custody by security forces. However there was no immediate information about the custody of the dead bodies. Six officers were also among the 21 security force personnel who were killed in that operation.

After four days another official version given out by the government spelled out that Nawab Bugti was not targeted by the military and the intention was to apprehend him alive but the cave, in which he was hiding, collapsed owing to a mysterious blast, just as military personnel were entering it. However, these conflicting statements raised suspicions amongst media and the general public especially when the government consumed five days to recover the dead body of Nawab Bugti.

Some of the family members of Bugti tribe had opined that Nawab Akbar Bugti was not killed in the cave as the government claimed but in an encounter in the open, or in custody after being apprehended, but there was no evidence with them to place before the media.

A news brief dated *18th September 2011*, available at internet media under the title: *'Akbar Bugti Committed Suicide; Not killed By Army'*, however, said that:

> *'A close aide of late Baloch nationalist leader Nawab Akbar Bugti, Wadera Muhammad Murad Bugti has told a private TV channel that a rocket fired by Bugti caused the explosion that led to the nationalist leader's death. When security forces entered the cave where he (Sardar Bugti) was hiding, he attempted to fend them off by firing a shell. This caused a massive explosion, which resulted in the cave-in that led to the death of Sardar Bugti, one colonel, two majors and three commandoes. The late Bugti had decided that he would rather die fighting than surrender to the security forces. When forces besieged his cave on 26th August 2006, he asked his comrades to leave the cave and let him fight them alone [but then it was too late].'*

"Instead of a slow death in bed, I'd rather [opt for] death come to me while I'm fighting for a purpose," Nawab Bugti himself said before going to cave with his armed men in 2006. He was 79 years old warrior tribal chief, the biggest tribe in Balochistan.

The diverse media reports created more suspicion because the dead body of Nawab Bugti was brought to Dera Bugti on 1st September 2006 and the public was not allowed to have a look at the dead body. His remains were buried in a locked and sealed coffin, opened only briefly to allow the *Imam* leading the funeral to take a look. The security forces took the plea that due to blast in the cave Nawab Bugti's body was torn into unidentifiable pieces whereas the tribal people around kept the opinion that the security forces had used some chemical weapon while targeting the cave; again no proof surfaced.

The western media immediately released their bulletins saying that Gen Musharraf wanted to establish his writ by force in the province by eliminating that Baloch Tribal Chief who was allegedly being supported by foreign powers to threaten the integrity of Pakistan. Balochistan's Governor Owais Ghani had categorically assured the Balochi populace, just a few weeks earlier, that the government had no intention of harming Nawab Bugti as he was a respected figure for every one in politics, academies and the general populace.

After being informed that Nawab Bugti had been killed and his body was lying buried under the rubble of a stone cum mud cave, Gen Musharraf, in a shocking show of insensitivity and complete lack of tact, cheerfully congratulated the secret service chief who had carried out this operation, knowing fully well that Sardar Bugti was a much-loved leader for a considerable section of Pakistan's population. This unfortunate episode was not an occasion for cheer but a time for concern and mourning all over Pakistan. One should have pondered that how things came to such a stage that a popular leader had to be killed by the country's armed forces.

Nawab Bugti was one of Pakistan's most charismatic politicians; one of the most genuinely loved leaders of his people and one of the most awe-inspiring warlords.

One would be able to remember that most of the sub-clans of the Bugti tribe had disowned Nawab Bugti in a *jirga* on 24th August 2006, as the leader of the Bugti tribe and had announced an end to the *sardari* system but the people had the suspicion if that *jirga* was government sponsored. A plain clothed group of people had earlier made an unsuccessful attempt on Sardar Bugti's life in March 2005 by targeting his residential complex in Dera Bugti with as many as 17 shells. Sardar Bughti's hideout was again attacked in July 2006, but he had survived both these attacks.

Many analysts and opposition leaders had portrayed Bugti's killing as a major threat to the federation and had taken as a replay of the events that led to the loss of East Pakistan in 1971. In its report dated 14th September 2006, the International Crisis Group (ICG) had appealed to the international community to urge Gen Musharraf to end military rule in Pakistan. Gen Musharraf had initially congratulated the army contingent on its success in eliminating Nawab Bugti, but later turned around. Some media reports had mentioned that satellite phone trackers were used to find the location of Nawab Bugti before the attack. As neither the military regime then in power nor the subsequent political government of the PPP ever considered to nominate a judicial commission to probe into the death of Nawab Bugti, so the matter is still going mysterious even after six years.

Nawab Akbar Khan Bugti, the chief of the largest Baloch tribe, had launched the Baloch resistance to the military regime of Gen Musharraf when the clashes around Sui village got intensified in January 2005. He was rather considered a collaborator by the mainstream Baloch nationalists for his willingness to cooperate with Islamabad during the previous phases of the Baloch insurgency.

An earlier report of *'daily times' dated 15th November 2005*, compiled by Sarfraz Ahmed says that Nawab Akbar Bugti once seriously tried to unite disgruntled Baloch Sardars to form a single Baloch nationalist party working for the Baloch people's rights in the wake of approaching army action in Sui and Dera Bugti. According to the rebel leaders their rights were continuously usurped by Islamabad or the Punjab through army actions. Hence, the Jamhoori Watan Party (JWP)'s central working committee decided at a two-day meeting in Dera Bugti on 12th & 13th November 2005 to contact Sardar Ataullah Mengal, Nawab Khair Bux Marri, Dr Abdul Hayee and Mir Ghulam Mohammad Baloch and convince them to form a single party to speak for Balochistan.

Sardar Bugti was ready to immediately dissolve its own JWP. This move was considered difficult because Sardar Bugti had been labelled as 'an agent of the Establishment' for the role he had played during the 1970s against the National Awami Party (NAP), which was banned on 10th February 1975. The Supreme Court of Pakistan, on 30th October 1975, had held that the NAP was working for an independent *Pakhtunistan* at the cost of Pakistan's territorial integrity [*a point to ponder that if the Supreme Court's all judgments are always right; think Bhutto's case also*].

Prior to the Supreme Court's verdict of 1975, the Z A Bhutto's government had set up a special tribunal popularly known as the Hyderabad Tribunal. The NAP's whole leadership including Khan Abdul Wali Khan, Ghous Bux Bizenjo, Nawab Khair Bux Marri and Sardar Ataullah Mengal were arrested and subjected to trial. The Baloch Sardars then alleged that Sardar Bugti, on 31st January 1973, had claimed at a public meeting at Mochi Gate Lahore that:

> *'Wali Khan and Ataullah Mengal shared with him the* **Independent Balochistan Plan,** *through which Balochistan could be placed under the control of some foreign power. The foreign headquarters supporting the Greater Balochistan Plan were to be located in Baghdad'.*

The above piece of Sardar Bhugti's speech and alleged evidence obtained from the Iraq Embassy was used as a pretext for the dismissal of the then provincial government of Sardar Attaullah Mengal and the subsequent military intervention in Balochistan.

On the basis of Sardar Bughti's 'disclosures' in public, the above named Baloch Sardars were arrested and sent to face Hyderabad Tribunal, therefore, the other Baloch nationalist leaders were not having trust in his person. Some Baloch leaders had also an impression that Nawab Akbar Bugti had served as an agent of the federal government [*but Pakistan's Constitution also say so*] when he was appointed Governor Balochistan by Zulfikar Ali Bhutto at the time of the insurgency and that he never spoke in favour of Baloch rights or more provincial autonomy.

Sardar Bugti had contended that:

> '*I resigned on 31st December 1973, shortly after PM Bhutto launched the army operation in Balochistan. I am not absolving myself. I was governor. You can't change history. You can't belie history. I don't say I did something great or something fine. No great or fine things happened during that period of his governorship*'.

The fact remained that Nawab Akbar Bugti had lost a number of his ons and grandsons to the assassin's bullets but he remained an uncompromising feudal lord, who showed no mercy to his opponents, civil or military or his tribal rivals. During 1950s he was the only Baloch in the Pakistani cabinet holding the Home and then the Defence portfolios. In the 1960s he took an active part in the opposition to the Pakistani government. In the 1970 elections, having been convicted for murder, he was barred from contesting the elections but contributed immensely towards the election campaign of the National Awami Party (NAP), led by Khan Wali Khan; later developed differences with them.

He was thereafter appointed as the governor of Balochistan but during this period the guerrilla war against the government went intensified. He resigned from the governorship on 31st December 1973 having served for ten months. A plus point for Nawab Akbar Bugti remained that he had not become a separatist [*though he and one of his sons were falsely labelled with that charge by security forces*] and continued his demands for greater autonomy, parity and more resources for Balochistan within Pakistan. During the 1980s, he made a personal protest against Gen Ziaul Haq's military regime by refusing to speak Urdu, Pakistan's national language till elections of 1988.

In the 1988 elections, he led the Baloch National Alliance (BNA), won majority of seats in the provincial assembly and by joining hands with

Jamiat Ulema e Islam (JUI) got the chief minister's slot in Balochistan. He held that seat till 1990. In 1990, he contested elections from his newly established Jamhoori Watan Party (JWP), got many seats and continued to dominate politics. Akbar Bugti had been attempting to get all Baloch nationalist parties under one umbrella but his efforts were resisted by other Baloch Sardars who did not trust him due to his role in 1973 as has been mentioned above and more due to Hyderabad Tribunal episode.

HYDERABAD TRIBUNAL (1975):

In 'Hyderabad conspiracy case', the **Hyderabad tribunal** (1975) was made by the then PM Zulfikar Ali Bhutto to prosecute opposition politicians of the National Awami Party (NAP) on the charges of treason and acting against the ideology of Pakistan. It was ultimately wound up after Gen Ziaul Haq overthrew Bhutto in July 1977.

A total of 52 people were arrested including Khan Abdul Wali Khan, Khan Amirzadah Khan, Syed Kaswar Gardezi, Ghaus Bakhsh Bizenjo, Nawab Khair Bakhsh Marri, Mir Gul Khan Nasir, Sardar Ataullah Mengal, Habib Jalib, Barrister Azizullah Shaikh, Aslam Baluch, Aslam Kurd, Saleem Kurd, Sher Mohammad Marri (General Sherof), Najam Sethi, Saleem Pervez, Majid Gichki, Mir Abdul Wahid Kurd, Sultan Mengal and several other patriots. In addition, several members of the Muslim League and even prominent critics of Z A Bhutto within his own PPP were also arrested.

The PM Bhutto got the 3rd Amendment to the Constitution of Pakistan passed which gave wide legal scope to the state to define anti-state activities. In Article 10(7), the definition of 'enemy' was extended to include:

> 'A person who is acting or attempting to act in a manner prejudicial to the integrity, security or defence of Pakistan or any part thereof or who commits or attempt to commit any act which amounts to an anti-national activity as defined in a Federal Law or is a member of any association which has for its object, or which indulges in any such anti-national activity'.

In 1974, Z A Bhutto's close ally and Governor of the NWFP Hayat Sherpao was killed in a bomb blast at Peshawar University. PM Bhutto was made convinced that NAP and its Chief Khan Abdul Wali Khan were responsible for that murder. Within Balochistan tribes Nawab Khair Bux Mari and his son, Balaach Mari, went tilted towards Moscow and India; and Nawab Akbar Bugti had allegedly developed interests with Iran.

The Hyderabad Tribunal was headed initially by Justice Aslam Riaz Husssain and subsequently by Justice Mushtak Ali Qazi, while the government was represented by Attorney General Yahya Bakhtiar; the defence counsel consisted of noted lawyers Mahmud Ali Kasuri and Abid Hassan Minto. During trial Khan Wali Khan withdrew from any defence arguing that the tribunal included biased judges and that a decision to convict had already been made.

The trial was widely considered discredited. Khan Wali Khan was also charged for an allegation that he was paid Rs:20 million by the then Indian Prime Minister Indira Gandhi which was never proved nor there was any truth in that. The government used extensive means to validate the charges levelled against the NAP, but nothing was proved. The fact, however, is available on record that:

> 'The Prime Minister Bhutto warned the judges that the responsibility of the consequences will be of the Supreme Court and the judges should they reject his reference against NAP'.

'This conspiracy allegation' ultimately forced the NAP towards joining the Pakistan National Alliance (PNA) which ended the Bhutto's government in 1977 at last. Some available record suggests that the then Federal Interior Minister (1973–1977) Abdul Qayyum Khan had played a key role in triggering Z A Bhutto's confrontation with the Baloch nationalists which also provided false grounds for army intervention in Balochistan.

SARDAR BUGTI vs ARMY IN 2000s:

Coming back, Nawab Akbar Bugti could not develop a working relationship with the military regime of 2000s. Over the past 50 years Islamabad tried to balance their mutual conflicting interests by granting royalties, and concessions or through political bargains in the corridors of power but could not fully succeed. Bugtis continued with their anti-government resistance from their tribal territory Dera Bugti. In early 2006, Nawab Akbar left Dera Bugti, riding a camel, with his armed followers and tribesmen and saddled in the mountains to fight Gen Musharraf's army.

Unexpected for Gen Musharraf and his forces, Nawab Akbar Bugti's killing caused a spontaneous outbreak of violent demonstrations mainly in Quetta and Karachi. The protesters burnt vehicles, banks and petrol pumps and blocked roads. A curfew had to be announced in Quetta and Kalat. A total shutter down and wheel-jam strike was observed throughout Balochistan on 28th August 2006. In Karachi, riots had erupted in all Baloch dominated areas.

Nawab Akbar Bugti's assassination brought various diverse tribes at one platform. Even Raisani tribe, which had feudal clashes with the Bugtis for decades killing several members from each side, had expressed solidarity with the Bugtis. He became a martyr for Baloch nationalism like Nauroz Khan fighting for Baloch cause despite the military regime's repeated attempts to paint him as feudal tyrant. Gen Musharraf had underestimated the Baloch nationalism earning a permanent enmity and hatred for his person and the whole army.

Nawab Akbar Bugti's death helped the Baloch nationalists to unite together whereas he might have failed to achieve during his lifetime. The killing of Nawab Bugti was a case of terrible miscalculation. It had weakened Pakistan army's stand before the nation. Not a single politician, even from Gen Musharraf's allies PML(Q) & MQM, had accorded approval for that blatant murder though the forces had done so in the name of army's security operation. Surprisingly, many retired army officers had strongly criticised the government over that serious historical mistake.

Nawab Akbar Bugti's killing had precipitated a furious reaction in Balochistan and added fuel to an already escalating unfriendliness and a sense of separation. A number of Baloch nationalist leaders had tendered their resignations from the provincial and national Assemblies. PML(Q) Secretary General Mushahid Hussain had openly condemned the killing of Nawab Bugti terming it sad and unfortunate. It was taken as a deliberate move to weaken the federation as Nawab Bugti's martyrdom continued to remain masked in mystery.

The beginning of the end for Nawab Bugti's life actually took place in early 2005; provoked by the rape of Dr Shazia Khalid by a Pakistani army officer at Sui; as has been narrated earlier. He started a violent insurrection against the authority of the army and the Pakistani government. Nawab Bugti launched successful raids against elements of the infrastructure and military installations. Frequent subversive attacks on gas pipelines caused widespread outrage throughout the country with forced closure of industrial production and blockade of commercial activities throughout Pakistan.

Gawador Port was another case point in sight. It has been Pakistani government's priority project of constructing a warm-water gateway to the coveted gas and oil destinations of Central Asia coupled with creation of enormous business opportunities and voluminous employment for all Balochis. Here Nawab Bugti erred in understanding the real acumen of Balochistan province and this Chinese-assisted grand undertaking was subjected to terrorist activities about one hundred times since its inception, because it stands nearly 100% funded by China; thus neither America nor the regional countries want its development.

Nawab Bugti had in fact looked upon this project and some more developmental projects like that, with suspicion simply because he never wanted to encourage settlement of more non-Baluchis in Balochistan. Of course, the big stake holders of Dubai and especially the Americans never wanted that Gawador port should be developed and that too with the Chinese aid; not at all. They had encouraged Bugtis and other tribal chiefs to create hindrances in smooth running of the projects when possible.

The successive Pakistani governments had record that all the family members of Bugti and Murri tribes keep British or American nationalities. Gen Musharraf's government remained successful in convincing the world media and the people of Pakistan that the mortar guns, anti-aircraft missiles, night-vision rifles and their ammunition available with the dissident people of Balochistan, including Bugtis, were actually provided by the Americans through Indian Consulates inside Afghanistan borders. It was all *'Oppose China'* game because the port would be the nearest one to the Central Asian states with the potential to attract international traffic, which previously went to Port Abbas in Iran, to Oman, or to the UAE in most cases.

Gawador project was opposed by Bugtis on two other counts also. Firstly, the Bugtis consider them the most respectable tribe in Balochistan. A Gawador project about 900 km away from Dera Bugti, when developed, would provide more importance to the nearby tribes; thus was a matter of humiliation for Bugtis. Secondly; Bugtis are financially rich in Balochistan due to royalties from government of Pakistan for Sui Gas supply. Naturally the Gawador project would bring much more money for the rival tribes of Balochistan at the cost of Bugtis.

Such distracted approaches towards Gawador project and above mentioned one rape event were the primary reasons for the bursting of the Bugti's sentiments that were simmering in rage and resentment.

The army contingents deployed on developmental duties had also suffered continuously through subversive attacks on Gas, Highways and Communication projects; hundreds of lives were lost and jobs halted for months. Both sides were annoyed thus a lasting clash was there.

Nawab Bugti had loads of grudge against civil and army governments in Islamabad but he had also served as the Chief Minister and Governor of Baluchistan for various tenures. Other Baloch tribal chiefs considered his reigns as disappointing and dull. Despite his complaints against Islamabad for ignoring his area's development, he himself failed to perform when he had the opportunities to do so.

As usual, contradictory versions of Nawab Bugti's death from government sponsored media spokesmen started pouring in immediately after the event. Thus by eliminating a political leader of Bugti's stature, the military government, might be unintentionally, had strengthened certain ranks of the nationalists cum militants in Balochistan. Consequently many innocent Punjabis residing in Balochistan were killed in the violent protests and the menace is still continuing today. The future of the federation is at stake since then and the hostilities growing day by day; but the provincial and federal governments are not bothered about it.

Pakistan army have taken over the affairs of Balochistan in their hands at countless occasions since the Pakistan came into being. Significantly, the army was sent here in 1973 during PPP's rule under Z A Bhutto and Nawab Akbar Bugti, the then Governor Balochistan had resigned in protest. The military and civil leaderships have learnt no lesson from history and the events of 1971's East Pakistan but have been continuing with the same policies of oppression and strategies of disintegration. The rulers at the helm of affairs should minutely go through the Hamood ur Rahman Commission Report before taking any untoward decision for this region.

The critics and intelligentsia keep opinion that Nawab Bugti could mean different things to different people: an opportunistic politician of nuisance value to many middle-class Pakistanis; a traitor to the Generals sitting in Islamabad; and a terrorist-like figure to CNN-watching Americans. But for Baloch people he was a hero. He was the head of the Bugtis, a warrior tribe that looked upon Islamabad with distrust and had always resented what it perceived to be the heavy-handedness of the Punjab.

In 1992, Sardar Akbar Bugti had allegedly killed more than hundred members of an enemy tribe for the revenge of his son's assassination in the city of Quetta; but no details available on record.

Like many other non-Punjabi citizens of Pakistan, he believed rightly or wrongly, that the National Government as well as Pakistan's army had always exploited the resources of other provinces to fill the coffers of Punjab. Still there prevails a widely accepted assumption that the wealth produced from Baluchistan's natural resources, such as its vast gas reserves, had never been used to invest in the development of that province. It is this grievance which Islamabad had consistently failed to address and the consequence of which could be disastrous.

Baloch people are being exploited, no doubt, but for some of the atrocities their Sardars (tribal chiefs) and Sardari System could be held responsible. In fact the Balochis are being subjugated and demoralized by both factions equally; firstly the successive military and civil governments and secondly by their own tribal chiefs. No doubt that the province is inadequately compensated for its natural resources but what meagre amounts come, they are kept by their tribal chiefs in the name of royalties. Nawab Akbar Bugti used to get the major chunk but not a single penny was spent on their tribe's local needs except ammunition, it is widely perceived.

The Baloch tribes ever remained split and mostly with daggers drawn at each other but the underlying grumbling is common against the governments. At all occasions the army believes that defeating the dissidents this time would make the things easier for ever. Here they are mistaken. Each time they manage to get arms and shelter from various stake holders of international stature. Thus every time Pakistan army's self-satisfaction and contentment brings disaster and displeasure for their political bosses. More than six brigades deployed in Balochistan only piles up the cost and expenditure; no results since 50 years at least.

One *Alok Bansal* from the neighbouring country opines at the internet pages that:

> *'In fact, an independent Balochistan is being seen as a future reality by some US experts. A paper recently published [2006] in the US Armed Forces Journal not only recommends redrawing the borders of the Middle East but also speaks of an independent Balochistan. The future course would depend on whether the Pakistani Army would step back and implement the recommendations on Balochistan made by the high profile parliamentary committee in 2005, or choose confrontation and set the country on a disastrous course.'*

Much later a formal FIR [for murder of Nawab Akbar Bugti] was got registered in a police station of District Sibi on the instructions of the concerned District & Sessions Judge. Gen Musharraf and the then PM Shaukat Aziz stand nominated in that FIR and the Warrants of Arrest have also been issued as a due process. The case is under investigation with the Crime Branch Quetta of Balochistan Police.

In early October 2011, a judicial magistrate, on the request of the Crime Branch, had also issued an arrest warrant for Balochistan's former home minister, currently a member of the provincial legislature, Mir Shoaib Nausherwani in the same Nawab Bugti's murder case. Mr Nausherwani was one of the accused nominated in the FIR. The team contacted the Speaker of the Balochistan Assembly to ask the former home minister to cooperate in the investigation, but he refused. The investigating team had written to the provincial home secretary to seek his approval for obtaining arrest warrants for the others.

Besides former Home Minister Nausherwani, Gen Musharraf and former PM Shaukat Aziz; former Federal Interior Minister Aftab Sherpao, former Balochistan Governor Owais Ghani and former Balochistan's CM Jam Mir Muhammad Yousaf were also nominated in the FIR. The Balochistan government had requested Islamabad to get Gen Musharraf extradited but his arrest warrants were required by Interpol to move ahead. Gen Musharraf is in the UK with which Pakistan government holds no 'Extradition Treaty'.

Let us hope for a better perspective for our true Balochi country men, the common Balochis, too.

Scenario 44

JUDICIARY vs ARMY 2007-I:

CHIEF JUSTICE SENT HOME:

On **9th March 2007**, the history of Pakistan took another turn, unprecedented and un-imaginable. Gen Musharraf, who has been ruling the country for the last eight years in army uniform but using the shield of office of the President of Pakistan to paint a picture of democracy for the outside world, held a meeting with the Chief Justice of Pakistan (CJP), J Iftikhar Mohammad Chaudhry at Army House Rawalpindi. He was asked to resign from his office.

When the CJP refused to oblige Gen Musharraf, he was pressurized by the heads of the army and civil intelligence agencies to bow his head. The CJP was detained at the Army House for five hours. During this time a reference was prepared against him and the same was filed with the Supreme Judicial Council of Pakistan (SJC) in haste on the same evening. The CJP afterwards contended that he had been "illegally detained" and that the Chiefs of Pakistan's intelligence services spent five hours urging him to resign after he told Gen Musharraf he would not do so; the media reported the event on the same day telling truth to the whole world.

The sequence of events was later narrated by the CJP himself in an affidavit which moved away curtain from the facts while covering four day's hell that he faced from 9th to 13th March 2007 when he was rendered non-functional. This affidavit, filed in support of a constitutional petition filed by the CJP under Article 184(3) of the Constitution, told that on 9th March 2007, he headed bench No 1 of the apex Court as chief justice and heard several cases till about 10.30 AM. The bench rose briefly and had to reassemble for the day except the CJP who left for the Army House Rawalpindi to meet the president.

The CJP arrived at the Army House at about 11:30 AM along with his protocol staff and was shown to a waiting room. After five minutes of his arrival, Gen Musharraf, wearing his military uniform, came into the room along with his military secretary and ADC. As soon as the General took his seat, a number of TV cameramen and photographers entered into the room. They took several pictures and made movie footage of meeting between the two giants as it was the routine activity of the Army House.

In the meeting, while discussing the SAARC Law Conference and the concluding session of the golden jubilee ceremony of the Supreme Court, the General said that a complaint against him had been received from a judge of the Peshawar High Court. The CJ replied that it was not based on facts as his case had been decided by a two-member bench and that attempts were being made to maliciously involve other members of the bench as well. On this, the president said there are a few more complaints against him and after saying so; he directed his staff to call the other persons.

The other persons, who entered the room on Gen Musharraf's direction, included the Prime Minister Shaukat Aziz, Director General Military Intelligence (DG MI), Director General Inter Services Intelligence (DG ISI), Director General Intelligence Bureau (DG IB), COS and another official. All officials (except DG IB & the COS) were in uniform. At this moment, the president started reading from a small piece of paper. The allegations, which were being put to the CJP, had been taken from the contents of a letter written by an advocate Supreme Court Mr Naeem Bukhari. The CJP strongly refuted the allegations as being baseless and engineered to defame him personally and the judiciary as a whole.

Gen Musharraf said that the CJP had obtained cars from the Supreme Court for his family, however, the CJP vehemently denied the allegation, too. Gen Musharraf went on to say that the CJP was being driven in a Mercedes, to which the CJP promptly replied; *"here is the Prime Minister. Ask him, he has sent me the car himself."* (The CJP stated in his affidavit that the PM did not reply even by a gesture) The President then forwarded the last allegation that the CJP had interfered in the affairs of the Lahore High Court and had not accepted and taken notice of most of the recommendations made by the Chief Justice of the LHC.

Gen Musharraf then asked the CJP to resign and in case of his resignation, the former would accommodate the later. He was told that in case of refusal to resign, the CJP would have to face a reference, which could be a bigger embarrassment for him. The CJP resolutely said that he wouldn't resign and would face any reference since he had not violated any code of conduct or any law, rule or regulation. *"I believe that I am myself the guardian of law. I strongly believe in God who will help me"*. This ignited the fury of Gen Musharraf who stood up angrily and left the room along with his MS, COS and the PM, saying that others would show evidence to the CJP.

The meeting of Gen Musharraf and the CJP continued for not more than 30 minutes. The DG MI, DG ISI and DG IB remained behind and continued to sit with the CJP but did not show him a single piece of evidence. The DG MI and the DG ISI insisted that the CJP should resign while the CJP continued to assert strongly that the allegations were baseless. The CJP was forced to stay in the same room during the subsequent hours till 5 pm and despite requests, he was not allowed to see his protocol officer.

Sometimes, all the persons would leave the CJP alone in that room but would not allow him to leave. Despite several attempts to leave the room at the Army House, the CJ was made to stay there on one pretext or the other and was kept there 'absolutely against his will'. Thereafter, DG MI came in again and told the CJ that his car was outside to drive him 'home'. DG MI came out of the room and once outside, told the CJ that:

> 'This is a bad day, now you are taking a separate way and you are informed that you have been restrained to work as a judge of the Supreme Court or Chief Justice of Pakistan'.

The CJ's car was stripped of both the flags of Pakistan and the emblem. His staff officer informed him that Justice Javed Iqbal had taken oath as the Acting Chief Justice and it had been shown on TV.

> [*The driver also informed the CJ that he had been instructed not to take him to the Supreme Court while on the way to his residence.*]

The CJ directed the driver to go to the Supreme Court but an Army official prevented his car from proceeding further near the Sports Complex. Meanwhile, Tariq Masood Yasin, Senior Superintendent of Police Islamabad appeared and ordered the driver to come out of the car so that he could drive the CJ and also asked the CJ's gunman to come out of the car. The CJ said:

> 'Okay, I will not go to the Supreme Court but my driver will drive my car and my gunman will escort me home'.

SSP Islamabad Mr Tariq agreed to let the car be driven by the CJ's driver. SSP himself was being instructed and controlled by the Military Protocol Officer on duty following that cavalcade.

The CJ reached home at 5:45 pm and was shocked to see police officials and agencies personnel in plain clothes all around his residence. Landline phones had already been disconnected; cell phones, TV, cables and DSL had been jammed or disconnected. The CJ and his family were completely cut off for several days from the outside world.

It might be a mind blowing fact for some that Gen Musharraf had not performed that act of detention of judges first time. In 2000, after his take over as military dictator in October 1999, he had issued the same like PCO and the judges of the higher courts were asked to take fresh oath if they wanted to stay on roll.

The then Chief Justice of Pakistan Saeeduzzaman Siddiqui told Gen Musharraf that they had already taken oath as per constitutional provisions so they would not go for the fresh oath on PCO. He was subjected to immense pressure through various means but he did not agree. Some of the judges from each high court had also declined to take the PCO oath. At that moment, too, the army troops were sent to besiege the residence of the CJP and he was only allowed to come out of his residence after the oath ceremony of the new Chief Justice was over.

BRIEF CAUSES OF CJP'S REMOVAL:

In short, under the Chief Justice Chaudhry's smudge, the Supreme Court took action on its own initiative to question the military government on the role of the ISI and apparent instances of injustices. He launched investigations into cases of 'forced disappearances' arising as part of the 'WOT' in which the Pakistan military and its ISI had allegedly imprisoned hundreds of persons without due process; most of them were from Balochistan Province where an insurgency was underway. The apex court's efforts had resulted in the return of some missing persons.

In another major ruling against the government, in August 2006, the Supreme Court under the CJP Iftikhar Chaudhry also prevented the sale of a state monopoly, Pakistan Steel, to private investors, based on allegations of kickbacks. Chief Justice Chaudhry ruled interalia that:

> 'While exercising the power of judicial review, it is not the function of this Court, ordinarily, to interfere in the policy making domain of the Executive ... relatable to the privatization of State owned projects... However, the process of privatization of Pakistan Steel Mills Corporation stands vitiated by acts of omission and commission on the part of certain State functionaries reflecting violation of mandatory provisions of law and the rules framed hereunder which adversely affected the decisions qua prequalification of a member of the successful consortium ..., valuation of the project and the final terms offered to the consortium which were not in accord with the initial public offering given through advertisement.'

Going far back in 2005, the NWFP provincial Assembly had passed a controversial bill, known as the *'Hasba Bill'*, which had raised concern in other parts of the country. The Bill established a sort of ombudsman not only to inquire into corruption and maladministration by provincial government departments, but also to carry out moral and religious policing to ensure the protection of Islamic values. A number of the moral policing provisions were declared unconstitutional by the Supreme Court and it asked the Governor of the province not to sign the bill and thus avoided making it into law.

As stated elsewhere, the most significant issue providing the real reason behind the attempted removal of CJP Chaudhry, was the fear that the Supreme Court would prevent Gen Musharraf from retaining his position as the Army Chief and running for President for another term. This fear was based on an address of Chief Justice Chaudhry in February 2007 when he told the trainee military officers: *'he was of the opinion that Gen Musharraf should not continue as army chief if he runs again for the [President's] office'.*

The media had blown this address [& opinion of the CJ] with high trumpeted analysis thus Gen Musharraf had to move for 9th March 2007's action just within one month of CJ's speech.

PROCEEDINGS AGAINST A CJP:

10th March 2007, Justice Iftikhar M Chaudhry received a 'Notice' from the Supreme Judicial Council (SJC) whereby he came to know that a reference had been filed by Gen Musharraf (in the capacity of President of Pakistan) before the Council. There was also a copy of the order passed by the SJC whereby Justice Chaudhry had been restrained to function as a judge and as the Chief Justice of Pakistan. This order was passed in a meeting of the SJC convened on 9th March 2007 after 6 PM in an indecent haste.

> *"In fact, no meeting had been called by the secretary of the Council namely Dr Faqir Hussain. No one had issued either agenda for the meeting or notice thereof."*

Justice Chaudhry was kept detained along with his family members including his young child of seven years from the evening of 9th March till 13th March 2007. He could not use any vehicle since there was none and he had to walk till the other end of the road where a police officer confronted him and manhandled him as was established later by a

501

judicial enquiry on the subject issue. An attempt was being made to fabricate evidence against Justice Chaudhry through the Supreme Court staff attached to him by coercive means and even employees working at his residence were taken away and made to appear before the 'agency' officials.

The CJ's chamber was sealed and certain files lying therein were removed and some of them handed over to the ISI under the supervision of the newly appointed registrar. No one was authorized to meet Justice Chaudhry, even his colleagues were not allowed access to him. His children were not allowed going to school, college and university. He and his family members were deprived of basic amenities of life, i.e. medicines and doctors, etc. They were made to go through a lot of mental, physical and emotional agony, torture and embarrassment.

All these tactics were used to put pressure on him to tender his resignation 'but after **13th March 2007,** when Justice Chaudhry succeeded in establishing some contact with his lawyers team during a brief appearance before the Council, the ongoing pressure to resign from the office was released to some extent. One of his daughters failed to appear in her 1st year exams while the other was not being allowed to take her examination (1st semester) at Bahria University.

Analysts held that Gen Musharraf wanted to suppress an independent judiciary in view of the coming elections that year. Justice Chaudhry's sacking was done in the backdrop of a concerted whispering that he was going to 'adversely consider' some cases like Gen Musharraf's re-election in uniform from the sitting assemblies.

Most of the charges listed against Justice Chaudhry were contained in a letter written by the lawyer Mr Naeem Bokhari to the CJ. The later developments proved that it was part of a vilification campaign against the CJ and was believably written on government's instance. The said letter was purposefully but 'secretly' leaked to the press. Moreover, some of Justice Iftikhar Chaudhry's rulings did comprehensively embarrass the government. However, his intervention in cases of public importance and human rights violations (especially *suo moto* proceedings on about 250 missing persons which were allegedly picked up by secret agencies without keeping them on official record) was taken as the basic cause of this episode.

Justice Chaudhry, sworn-in as the Chief Justice in June 2005, was sent home just after 21 months. He was to hold the office for another six years till 2013 and to become the longest serving chief justice.

[*Until 9th March 2007, the media liked Justice Chaudhry's fondness for judicial activism on public interest and human rights issues. Journalists were hugely entertained by his habit of passing harsh comments on senior government functionaries and frequently embarrassing them publicly in his court room. But he was no public hero. Not at all, that is, until the government took action against him. In the past he was seen very much as a supporter of Gen Musharraf.*

J Chaudhry was among the half of the Supreme Court judges who validated Gen Musharraf's 1999 military coup against an elected government. The other judges [had] resigned in protest.

Later, when Gen Musharraf held a referendum to install himself as the President; the act was challenged in the SC. J Chaudhry was on the bench that decided in favour of the General. These actions brought J Chaudhry closer to the military rulers. He was never seen as a threat to the legitimacy of Gen Musharraf's rule until 9th March 2007 at least.]

Coming back, Justice Abdul Hamid Dogar and Sardar M Raza Khan, Judges of the Supreme Court, Chief Justice Lahore High Court Chaudhry Iftikhar Hussain and Chief Justice of Sindh High Court Justice Sabihuddin Ahmed attended the meeting as members of the SJC. Acting Chief Justice Javed Iqbal presided over the meeting as available next senior most judge of the Supreme Court.

Some of the alleged charges against the CJ Iftikhar Chaudhry were related with his son's police career while he was a doctor on the pay roll of Baluchistan government (*taken up from Mr Naeem Bokhari's letter mentioned above*). When the reference against CJ was brought to the SJC then those in the government who had been facilitating the son of the deposed CJ in his pursuit of a police career were ready to speak against him. They were tight-lipped in the past, defending Dr Arsalan's police training despite his not being a police officer. Seeing the man falling, those officers who were silent in the past suddenly started speaking out.

Interior Minister Aftab Sherpao, whose ministry had issued orders to treat Dr Arsalan extraordinarily [*just to please the CJP*], right from his posting from Balochistan to the FIA, and then allowing him to get police training along with probationers of the Police Service of Pakistan (PSP Cadre) said that the junior VVIP got special treatment because of his father.

*[It is a known typical characteristic of Pakistani bureaucracy that they would go to the last extent to please their sitting bosses by saying anything, mostly twisting the facts and sometimes turning to 180 angles in their narrations. Every member of this bureaucracy tries to take a role of approver in the changing power scenarios amidst getting higher rewards for themselves and their kinship. It has become a distinctive trait of Pakistan's elite now. **Lotacracy** has very deep roots in the Superior Civil Service of Pakistan, too.]*

Whereas the fact remained that Dr Arsalan, CJ Iftikhar Chaudhry's son, was appointed in the FIA on deputation after seeking the consent of the DG FIA but his induction was processed by the Secretary Interior and with Interior Minister's written consent. The FIA Director General Tariq Pervaiz had rightly held that it was the interior ministry's initiative which led to the appointment of the Balochistan official as Assistant Director in the FIA. No doubt, such developments do not happen in vacuum and of course, such opportunities are not available ordinarily; but it had been the practice in Pakistan since early ages and still in vogue.

CJP Iftikhar Chaudhry was not the only judge to avail those fruit of their elevated positions; there were more examples available from the past. The son in law of CJP Sajjad Ali Shah (1994-97) was a clerk in CM Sindh Abdullah Shah's office. The CJP got him inducted in the civil service as Assistant Commissioner under Benazir Bhutto's special orders. He was sent to Peshawar for training and was kept at Supreme Court Rest House for nine months. CJP Sajjad Ali Shah used to send Justice Bashir Jehangiri and Justice Fazal Elahi to hear cases at Peshawar bench because they both were residents of Peshawar. None of them needed the rest house otherwise CJP's son would have suffered with discomfort.

The CJP Sajjad Ali Shah had also availed an official residence at Karachi which was beyond his entitlement. In Rawalpindi the CJP had taken possession of CJ's official residence attached with old SC Building on Peshawar Road. Previously that residence was kept by J Nasim Hasan Shah for years and when it got vacated it went in the hands of J Sajjad Ali Shah. Legally both could live in only one official residence and just for one month after retirement.

CJP Sajjad Ali Shah had moved a case for change in his date of birth and he announced that he would continue living there till the decision on his petition comes up. Such benefits, including Arsalan Iftikhar's transfer to FIA, could be considered minor but in confrontations these are exploited.

A CJ SEEKS RELIEF FROM HIS OWN COURT:

26th March 2007: The deposed Chief Justice had planned to give first public appearance to the Rawalpindi Bar Association, on the 17th day of historical judicial crisis in Pakistan. Ladies and gentlemen lawyers were occupying their seats in the Bar Room in a dignified way when a veiled lady sitting with the women lawyers, suddenly stood up, dramatically unveiled her face and announced:

> '*I am Sajida Chaudhry, serving Civil Judge Gujar Khan* (a town 30 miles away from Rawalpindi), *and have come here to show solidarity with my Chief Justice of Pakistan.*'

The announcement received a thunderous applause. She calmly told the reporters:

> '*I came here to welcome the chief justice, and it is my duty. Gen Musharraf should resign; he who is occupying the country illegally.*'

The Punjab government, next day, placed her under suspension but she was successful in delivering a clear message to the incumbent judges of the Supreme Court. She was the first drop of rain in desert.

14th April 2007: During the second public appearance, Justice Iftikhar Chaudhry was to attend an annual dinner of the Sindh Bar Association Sukkur (a town 300 miles away from Karachi). On this day, the history unfolded a new leaf. Two judges of the Sindh High Court, Justice Zia Pervez and Justice Nadeem Azhar Siddiqui, had decided to follow their junior colleague Sajida Chaudhry of Gujar Khan and decided to speak about the military tyranny in Pakistan.

18th April 2007: CJ Iftikhar Chaudhry filed a petition before the Supreme Court raising the issues of:

* "Constitution of the Supreme Judicial Council without the CJP,

* The personal bias and prospects of advancement of some members of SJC,

* Alleged *malafide* of the referring authority and PM Shaukat Aziz,

* The haste with which the referring authority (the president) acted against the CJP,

- Illegal suspension and forced leave of sitting Chief Justice,

- Illegal assumption of office by the Acting Chief Justice,

- The executive's assault on the independence of judiciary, AND

- In-camera proceedings of the SJC."

Justice Chaudhry had also *'requested the Supreme Court to restrain the SJC from hearing the reference as some members harbour bias against the petitioner, rendering them ineligible to be a member of the SJC.'*

Justice Chaudhry's petition under Article 184(3) of the Constitution of Pakistan was floated through Chaudhry Aitzaz Ahsan and Barrister Gohar Ali Khan, carrying 132 points of law. In his petition he had challenged his suspension and replacement with acting chief justice, his forced leave and composition of the SJC with 'biased judges'. Apart from seeking stay order against the proceedings of the SJC, Justice Chaudhry had also sought a declaration that no reference could be filed by the referring authority or examined by the SJC against the chief justice under Article 209 of the Constitution and an acting chief justice could not head the Supreme Judicial Council.

The President, the Federation, the Supreme Judicial Council, the Registrar of the Supreme Court, the Registrar of the Sindh High Court and the Registrar of the Lahore High Court were made respondents in the petition. The petition was admitted for regular hearing.

19th April 2007, the petition was taken up by a three-member bench comprising Justice Sardar Mohammad Raza Khan, Justice Chaudhry Ijaz Ahmed and Justice Hamid Ali Mirza. The bench issued notices to the respondents to the petition and adjourned its proceedings till 24th April 2007.

21st April 2007: The deposed Chief Justice reached Peshawar after a journey of nine hours from Islamabad (normal journey time is 1.5 hours). He was showered with rose petals all the way by ordinary people, political workers and lawyers at different places during his journey. Excited people lined up all the way from his official residence in Islamabad to the Peshawar High Court building, in scorching temperature and under a blistering sun. Ten (10) judges of the Peshawar High Court welcomed him. The Chief Justice of Peshawar High Court led the reception of the deposed CJ.

[*Two judges of the Peshawar HC were absent from this reception. One, Justice Talat Qayyum was a heart patient. The other one, Justice Jehan Zeb Rahim, was a party against Justice Iftikhar Chaudhry. He had written a letter against Justice Chaudhry to Gen Musharraf.*]

During this high profile judicial crisis, it was also a beginning of a new chapter of Pakistan's judiciary when Munir A Malik, President of the Supreme Court Bar Association (SCBA), invited the sitting judges to join struggle with Justice Chaudhry for withdrawal of the reference and upholding the rule of law. It was the first time that judges were formally invited to join hands with the legal community.

This call got an immediate response from the Sindh High Court judges. The very next day, 15 judges of the provincial Sindh High Court were present at the reception of the defunct CJ at Hyderabad. The provincial law officer, the Advocate General of Sindh, also attended the function. Leaders of the legal community demanded unconditional withdrawal of the presidential reference and release of lawyers and other people arrested while protesting against filing of the reference.

24th April 2007, Mr Justice Sardar Mohammad Raza Khan declined to head the bench because, as a member of the Supreme Judicial Council, he was '*a signatory to the Supreme Judicial Council's endorsement of the presidential reference.*' It appeared this was a reference to the Supreme Judicial Council's order restraining the Chief Justice from functioning in his official capacity. He requested the Acting Chief Justice to '*form a full court or a larger bench to hear a number of identical petitions challenging the formation of the SJC and the reference against the suspended chief justice.*'

On **26th April 2007**, Justice Chaudhry filed an application before the Supreme Court seeking constitution of a full court, comprising all the judges on the Supreme Court, to hear his petition.

On **28th April 2007**, the Acting Chief Justice Rana Bhagwandas, taking action on that application, constituted a five-member bench headed by Justice M Javed Buttar, and additionally comprising of Justice Nasirul Mulk, Justice Raja Fayyaz Ahmed, Justice Ijaz Ahmed and Justice Hamid Ali Mirza.

On **2nd May 2007**, Gen Musharraf's government also requested a full court, arguing that the five-member bench was too junior to hear such an important matter.

On **7th May 2007** Justice M Javed Buttar, heading the five-member bench of the Supreme Court mentioned above, took up 23 identical petitions challenging the filing of reference against the CJ, composition of the SJC and its competence to try the CJ. The bench halted the proceedings of the SJC and referred the constitutional petition of Justice Chaudhry along with other identical petitions to the full court. This decision was appreciated on two counts. Firstly: for suspension of the SJC proceedings, and secondly with the request for constituting a full court to consider this matter, i.e. a bench comprising all the sitting judges of the Supreme Court, excluding those who were members of the SJC.

Next day the Supreme Court constituted a 14-member full court to hear the constitutional petition of Justice Chaudhry against the presidential reference along with 22 other identical petitions. The full court announced to take up these petitions from 14th May on day-to-day basis.

The full court was headed by Justice Khalilur Rahman Ramday and comprised Justice Muhammad Nawaz Abbasi, Justice Faqir Muhammad Khokhar, Justice Falak Sher, Justice Mian Shakirullah Jan, Justice M Javed Buttar, Justice Tassadduq Hussain Jillani, Justice Saiyed Saeed Ashhad, Justice Nasirul Mulk, Justice Raja Fayyaz Ahmed, Justice Ch Ijaz Ahmed, Justice Syed Jamshed Ali, Justice Hamid Ali Mirza and Justice Ghulam Rabbani. However, Acting CJ Rana Bhagwandas, Justice Javed Iqbal, Justice A Hameed Dogar and Justice Sardar Muhammad Raza Khan, were not made part of the full court because of being party to the proceedings of the SJC.

The suspension of the SJC proceedings was an initial legal victory for the deposed CJ Iftikhar Chaudhry against Gen Musharraf and was widely welcome for the following reasons:

- Under established norms of judicial conduct, members of the SJC with a manifest conflict of interest should have voluntarily dissociated themselves from the reference proceedings. The Supreme Court's decision to stay the SJC proceedings was thus welcome, because such proceedings were tainted by allegations of bias and were unlikely to further the cause of justice irrespective of the outcome.

- The SJC was a disciplinary judicial body constituted to investigate charges of misconduct against judges of the higher judiciary and accordingly make recommendations to the president for disciplinary action; a constitutional prerequisite for removal of a judge who is offered security of tenure by the Constitution. Thus it was not a court as such.

- The Supreme Court was the apex constitutional body that had the last word on what the Constitution meant. The Supreme Court could not shrug off its responsibility to resolve elementary constitutional issues, to name a few, such as:

  ○ whether the SJC was competent to investigate allegations of misconduct against the Chief Justice of Pakistan,

  ○ the appropriate composition of the SJC in a reference against the chief justice,

  ○ whether or not the SJC could be constituted by someone other than the Chief Justice,

  ○ whether or not the head of the judiciary could be suspended from office by a head of the executive, while allegations of misconduct were pending investigation etc.

  ○ It was logical to determine the constitutionality of the reference and the scope and composition of the SJC before it was allowed to proceed with the presidential reference. The whole set of proceedings by the SJC would have ended in futile had the SC observations surfaced otherwise later.

On **12th May 2007**, Justice Iftikhar Chaudhry was scheduled to be in Karachi to address lawyer's community at the premises of Sindh High Court but he was not allowed to come out of the airport lounge. Outside lounge there were blockades done with containers & long vehicles and propelled riots throughout Karachi. The day ended with 43 deaths and hundreds wounded. A full description is available on separate pages under the title of *'Karachi Greets a Chief Justice'*.

On **14th May 2007**, the full bench started conducting daily hearings on the case but on that day, at the first hearing of this bench, Justice Falak Sher refused to sit on the bench citing:

'On account of seniority and being the senior-most judge in the country, it would be improper for him to hear a case in which the chief justice is a party, who like other judges of the Supreme Court is junior to him from four to nine years.'

Nevertheless, the hearing continued with 13 judges.

During the night between 13-14th May 2007 the Personal Staff Officer of Justice Iftikhar M Chaudhry, named Hammad Reza, was shot dead at his official residence in Islamabad. He was a DMG officer of 1996 batch but had been taken on deputation by the Supreme Court with a rank of Additional Registrar. He was killed allegedly by the mighty secret agencies, every one believed but no body could dare to express openly.

The Supreme Court felt embarrassed, took cognizance of the issue, asked the investigation officer to put up progress report to the SC on daily basis and ordered a senior police officer to supervise the investigation but could not get justice for Reza's family. The government wanted to convey a message to the Court through this brutal act but the bench had not taken any effect. Mr Reza had told his family and friends during the last two months that on a number of occasions he was summoned by agencies who were trying to get information about the alleged 'wrong doings' of Justice Chaudhry. He, according to his friends, was being pressurized to give evidence in support of reference.

Meanwhile, another chaos surfaced when the news came out that:

> *'The federal government is seriously considering the filing of another reference against [the Chief] Justice Iftikhar Chaudhry over politicizing the presidential reference.'*

It was based on reports that most of the lawyers with Justice Chaudhry were affiliated with political parties and they were using the presidential reference for their peculiar objectives. Daily *'the News'* of *15th May 2007* also opined that the reference was ready against the judges who had participated in the functions of Justice Chaudhry while hearings were under way in the SJC and the Supreme Court against him. Due to timely intervention of advisors the government dropped the idea at the last moment.

On **16th May 2007**, Sharifuddin Pirzada, the President's Counsel, giving an overview of the judicial history of the country with regards to references filed against judges, argued against the maintainability of Justice Chaudhry's petition.

Mr Pirzada had argued before the full Court that the first reference in the judicial history of the country was filed against Justice Hasan Ali Agha in the Federal Court of Pakistan during 1951; the second reference was filed against Justice Ikhlaq Hussain, the third against Justice Shaukat Ali while the fourth one was filed against Justice Safdar Ali Shah. Justice Ramday, however, observed that all those references were filed during the martial law regimes except the one against Justice Hasan Ali Agha that was filed in a civilian regime and he was exonerated of all charges in 1951.

[*The reference against Justice Ikhlaq Hussain was made out in Gen Ayub's regime; Justice Shaikh Shaukat Ali faced reference in Gen Yahya's regime and Justice Safdar Ali Shah in Gen Ziaul Haq's regime. All these cases were made out in peculiar circumstances and were settled on different grounds. In all the three references filed during respective military regimes, the judges were sent home. Justice Shaukat Ali was removed on the basis of the reference but the decision of his removal remained controversial and he was later elected president of the bar.*]

It may not be out of place to mention that during the days of his turmoil, while his petition was being contested by Aitzaz Ahsan and his helping barristers in the Supreme Court, Justice Chaudhry remained busy in having by-road tours in Punjab and NWFP provinces of Pakistan. The lawyer community made his tours successful by boycotting the courts, arranging huge gatherings of people around and taking frequent help from workers of anti-Musharraf political parties. On the main roads wherever J Chaudhry passed, the crowds of people welcome him with banners and flags but he deliberately avoided to address them.

Justice Iftikhar Chaudhry's tours were covered by the local and western world's media moments by moments and two Urdu TV private channels named ARY and GEO constantly telecasted his live movements which were otherwise viewed throughout the world.

The media coverage spoiled Gen Musharraf's image worldwide and the feedback of extensive criticism from all corners disturbed the government. The general populace started processions in favour of Justice Chaudhry and raised voices against the army rule openly violating the law and order. The proceedings in the Supreme Court were also covered by the media alive and the arguments forwarded by Justice Chaudhry's panel of barristers were hailed by intelligentsia and the general public equally.

GEN MUSHARRAF ATTACKED MEDIA:

Getting annoyed over the situation Gen Musharraf's regime took another turn by imposing censorship on the print and electronic media through an ordinance from the president's camp, which was government's new tactic to keep the people in dark over the CJ's popular move. Warnings to the media in the name of 'national interest' do not work in this age; rather they go thoroughly counter-productive and only exacerbate an already tense situation.

The reason for the clampdown on media was the thinking then prevailing in military junta's circles that the whole crisis had been blown out of proportion by the media and hence it would be deflated once the media, especially the TV channels, are brought under the censorship restraints. Till that moment the general populace of Pakistan had gone genius enough to frame their minds for:

- Gen Musharraf made the Chief Justice of Pakistan non-functional.

- Gen Musharraf threatened the Chief Justice in military General's uniform in the Army House and did not allow him to leave the Army Camp Office for 5/6 hours.

- In a wrong manner an action against the Chief Justice was taken and a presidential reference filed before the Supreme Judicial Council.

- The charges that the CJP was fond of extra protocol or that he asked for favours for his son were true; the same could have been dealt with in a dignified way. [*The CJP could have been called to explain or proceeded against separately for any such charge without calling him in person at the Army House and asking him to resign. The requirement was to uphold the rule of law whatsoever*]

- Attacks on the office of Geo TV and the top newspaper in Islamabad were wrong; thus condemned.

- Army spy chiefs confronted the Chief Justice on 9th March at the Camp Office and tried to impress on him to quit his post.

- Gen Musharraf stood by and idly watched as 43 people lost their lives in Karachi on 12th May 2007; did nothing as the offices of a TV channel came under attack by armed men for several hours on 12th May and then proceeded to hold a 'National Unity' rally the same evening in Islamabad, where PTV showed participants doing the *bhangra* (a Punjabi folk dance) and having a generally fun time.

- Army sponsored administration prevented the chief justice from leaving the premises of Karachi airport on 12th May for address.

- Uncharitable remarks against judges of the Sindh High Court were raised after the court took *suo moto* notice of the tragic events of 12th May [*till today there is no report or final outcome of that court proceedings, what a mockery of justice*].

- Those days the Sindh government illegally prevented Imran Khan from entering Sindh and confined him to Lahore for three days.

- Gen Musharraf got declared names of 12 prominent journalists for calling them enemies of the people and placed bullets-filled envelopes in the cars of three of them.

Referring to an editorial note of '*the News*' of 3rd June 2007', more questions could be added to the above list. Gen Musharraf's team was unable to grasp the fact that the media was a mirror and was bound to reflect reality. Also, if for the sake of argument, it is accepted that the media was presenting an unbalanced anti-military version then what about coverage in world media.

Next day the lawyer's forum including the Supreme Court Bar Association, who was boldly handling the CJ's issue, announced that the lawyers of the whole country would also fight this censorship against the media taking it another army attack on the fifth pillar of democracy in Pakistan. How the world media reacted to Pakistan's situation in those days, an opinion of '*Nigerian Observer*' is placed below:

> "*Pakistan's recent and ongoing experiences in the last two months in its Judiciary is proof, if any were needed, that once a military man always a military man, whether in or out of uniform. Sometime in March this year, President Pervez Musharraf (dressed in military uniform) tried unsuccessfully to force Pakistani Chief Justice Iftikhar Muhammad Chaudhry to resign.*
>
> *When the Chief Justice refused to be intimidated, the President placed him on a highly controversial and contestable compulsory leave, skipped the next senior Justice said to be on a visit to neighbouring India and appointed another Justice to do his bidding as Chief Justice. Since then Pakistan has been thrown into the chaos which is brought daily into our living rooms via satellite television.*

Today, Musharraf has exposed himself as a wolf in sheep's clothing. A military mindset brooks no divergent views; it is used to giving orders and being obeyed without question. President Musharraf's misguided attempt to humiliate and tame the Judiciary has backfired and several prominent lawyers have declined to represent the government. To worsen his embarrassment, the whole world is watching the unsavoury drama, and ahead of this year's national elections Musharraf is not looking too good."

(Ref: Nigeria: Avoiding the Pakistani Pitfall by Funke Aboyade appearing in *'This Day' of Lagos dated 14th May 2007*)

For the military adventurers of the future, there were many lessons.

Scenario 45

PAKISTAN'S CJ GREETED IN KARACHI:

[*In this essay the author depended less on Pakistani and more on foreign media to keep intact the impartiality & his personal opinion non-existent unless some authentic enquiry report comes up*]

On **12th May 2007** Karachi had launched an uproarious greet for a chief justice by offering him a banquet of 43 dead bodies amidst other nearly dead or mutilated 'tributes'. Let us recall those gloomy and miserable moments in the name of Justice - Hurray, Justice in Pakistan - Zindabad.

Referring to a magazine *'Slate' dated 17th May 2007* which told that on 12th May 2007 with the help of press, electronic media, and Internet blogs, the real face of MQM was exposed. Upon the orders of an army dictator, with complete support from intelligence agencies, once MQM used to blame those for all evils, resulted in huge political damage for Altaf Hussain and his MQM. To minimize the damage, MQM crafted a video presentation for its supporters that other political groups were also involved in this heinous crime of killing innocents, which was not termed true. Detailed account of events presented by foreign press on the very next day told the whole truth.

Question arises that was it really MQM's job; if so, had MQM alone performed that task.

Nicholas Schmidle, the author of *Two Tumultuous Years in Pakistan*, released on 12th May 2009 writes his account of arrival on 11th May night as:

"I arrived in Karachi at 2 am on Saturday. The MQM had blocked every possible exit and entry point to the airport using shipping containers, buses, and water tankers. There were no taxis. People were sleeping in the terminal, and babies screamed. Food and water supplies at the airport were already running low, 10 hours before the chief justice was expected to land.

It seemed entirely possible that these people would be marooned at the airport for a day or two. Fearing that I would be stuck there, too, I shouldered my luggage and headed in the direction of the main road. On the way, a security guard warned me that there was gunfire and burning tires just outside the airport. Karachi is not a city that you walk around on a good day; but the longer I waited, the tighter the blockade would be.

Fortunately, I met a moustachioed man in his 40s along the road who happened to be a police officer. He said he had a jeep, with an armed guard, waiting on the other side of two layers of MQM-arranged cordons. After a few minutes, we reached the jeep and began navigating through back alleys and roads still under construction, any path that the MQM might not yet have blocked.

There were no vehicles on the streets other than the commandeered tankers and buses, most of which flew the MQM's tricolour flag. The trip from the airport to the hotel where I was staying typically takes about 15 minutes. I finally checked in at 4:30 am."

Question arises again that was it really MQM's job; if so, had MQM alone performed that task.

In the last week of November 2009, the then Provincial Home Minister of Sindh, Dr Zulfiqar Mirza, announced in a press meeting that his PPP government would order an inquiry into the events of 12th May 2007 and would like to unveil the real faces behind that utter cruelty. That dawn was never seen.

Let us peep deep into that page of our forgotten history........ When chaos had gripped the streets of Karachi on that day! The day when Justice Iftikhar Chaudhry, the then suspended Chief Justice, had landed at Karachi Jinnah International Airport for onward move to Sindh High Court premises to address the Karachi Bar Council. Karachi had witnessed 'orchestrated mayhem', a well organized event, wherein about 43 lives were lost, and about 150 were injured, threatening a complete breakdown of law and order in Pakistan's largest and most volatile city.

Referring to UK's daily *The Telegraph's* '*Pakistan on brink of disaster as Karachi burns*' appearing on *13th May 2007:*

'Karachi with plumes of black smoke billowing over the city of 12 million people, there were extraordinary scenes as gunmen on motorbikes pumped bullets into crowds demonstrating against ...., while police stood by and watched.

Bloodstained corpses lay where they had fallen in the streets and bodies piled up in hospital morgues. As the sense of crisis deepened, the military General resolved to send in Pakistan rangers (paramilitary troops) to restore order, and to place the army on standby.

Yesterday's violence erupted as 15,000 police and security forces deployed in the city stood idly by as armed activists from Karachi's ruling party, Muttahida Qaumi Movement (MQM), a coalition ally of Gen Musharraf, blocked Mr Chaudhry's exit from the airport and took control of the city's central district.'

When events of killings in Karachi were published in the Daily Telegraph of UK on 13th May 2007, the MQM Chief Altaf Hussain had called the news people at Edgware Road London to correct the facts. That interview with The Daily Telegraph was published on 14th May 2007 in which Altaf Hussain had insisted that they held a 'completely peaceful gathering' and that it was opposition supporters who provoked the violence, in which at least nine MQM activists were (also) killed. Mr Hussain addressed the party at Karachi on telephone that day and *'it was a completely peaceful gathering by MQM supporters that was targeted by a collaboration of three other parties.'*

[In the same newspaper another report titled **'Violence as Musharraf's power fades'** said in the (Karachi) city's Jinnah Hospital yesterday, Adil Bashir, aged 23, was recovering from three bullet wounds after narrowly escaping a street execution. *'He said he had not taken part in the rally but was rounded up by armed, teenage MQM activists along with four others. He alleged that he and others were lined up against a wall before being sprayed with automatic gunfire. He and one other survived.'*]

Question arises that were they MQM's boys really; if so, who might have ordered them to act so.

That article of daily *'the Telegraph' dated 14th May 2007* ends with the conclusion that *'the actions of the MQM may have been not so much a sign of support for the eight-year rule of Gen Musharraf, but a demonstration of its own power in what could be the first round of a new turf war in Karachi. Gen Musharraf's options are becoming more and more limited as he struggles to have himself re-elected and to continue as army chief.'*

The MQM's most senior leader in Pakistan, Farooq Sattar, said that *'the opposition wants to show that Karachi does not belong to the MQM. We have accepted the challenge.'*

The fact remained that despite denials by the MQM, almost all the British newspapers of 13-14th May 2007, in their reports, comments and editorials put the blame of violence on MQM workers and had asked that *'to what extent the man running MQM from London could be responsible'*. Imran Khan in his statement accused the British PM Tony Blair of giving sanctuary to a politician whose party he claimed was linked to killings in Pakistan. However, Mohammed Anwar, head of international relations for the MQM, denied that Altaf Hussain was responsible for any violence in Karachi, saying:

> *"He is living here [in Britain] since 1992 so how could he stir up violence when he is not even living in Karachi? If we wanted to commit carnage, would we bring our mothers and sisters and daughters [Pointing towards the women and children in MQM's rally in Karachi that day] on to the streets with us? It simply isn't plausible. Imran's criticism of Altaf was motivated by the MQM's success in making inroads into other parts of Pakistan".*

It was a factual belief that Gen Musharraf had hoped to create a compliant judiciary ahead of elections which he had promised to hold later that year. But it started as a political confrontation then emerged from the purposefully instigated ethnic rivalry in Karachi. Referring again to the above quoted article of *'the Telegraph'*;

> 'Inside Mr (Justice) Chaudhry's intended destination, Sindh's High Court, hundreds of lawyers, some of them bloodied after being beaten up by MQM supporters, milled about chanting slogans and receiving news on their mobile phones about the trouble engulfing them. Outside, MQM activists with pistols tucked into their jeans, blocked the entrance.'

Again question arises that were they MQM's activists really; how the Telegraph people assessed so.

The record later revealed that Gen Musharraf, PML(Q) government at Islamabad and an army officer [subsequently known as Brig Huda] controlling the Sindh Home Department had purposefully allowed conflicting rallies to go ahead to create the requisite level of disorder to justify the declaration of an emergency or Martial law.

LIVING EPISODES OF 12th MAY 2007:

The prologue to violence was familiar to Karachi, where hundreds of people were killed in ethnic violence in the 1990s but first time in

Pakistan live television cameras captured the situation for viewers to see government tankers used to block off routes to the airport, police and rangers prominent by their absence or standing idle as armed men ran armed & free on the streets of Karachi; corpses and wounded bodies lying by the wayside in pools of blood.

The security plans chalked out for that day were abandoned overnight. The Sindh Home Department withdrew the weapons of most law enforcement personnel in Karachi. Armed only with batons, the 15,000 policemen deployed in the city avoided the violent areas. Rangers who were to hold key positions on the 'flyovers' on the main airport road were nowhere in sight. Instead, armed men in civilian clothes held those posts, and fired into the crowds trying to reach the airport to receive the Chief Justice stranded inside.

Over at the Sindh High Court, as a lawyer Ayesha Tammy Haq witnessed, at about 5 PM the things were getting worse. Judges were not leaving the premises as there would be a rampage. City courts were being attacked. The lawyers were expecting to have army rule in Karachi. Later it transpired that:

> *'.... It was a part of "the political activity" of a party attempting to show its strength to its constituency and of course a loyalty show to see and feel by Gen Musharraf too.'*

> *'Not only was the Sindh High Court under virtual siege by armed activists, but lawyers attempting enter the Court were repeatedly beaten and roughed up. The armed activists did not even spare the Judges of the High Court.*

> *One judge was held at gun point and his car damaged. "While holding me at gun point, the youth called someone and stated 'Yeh bolta hai kay High Court ka judge hai...kya karun is ka? ...... achaa theek hai, phir janay daita houn.' (He says he's a judge of the High Court. What should I do with him? .... Ok then; will let him go)."*

> *Many judges, unable to drive to the Sindh High Court, had to leave their official 'flag' cars and make their way through menacing crowds and climb over the court's back wall in order to reach their chambers.'*
> (Ref: an interview with **Talat Hussain, 'Aaj TV', 18th May 2007**)

An extract from an essay titled *'Story at the airport'* appeared in *'the News' of 20th May, 2007:*

[*Munir A. Malik and his fellow 24 lawyers accompanying Justice Chaudhry from Islamabad to Karachi were forced to remain inside the airport. The Sindh government representatives offered to transport the Chief Justice by helicopter but this offer was for him alone. Since the lawyers with him had already foiled the attempts of 'two uniformed officers' to 'snatch the CJP and take him from the other side;' he refused.*]

Armed men attacked lawyers at Malir District Bar, Justice Chaudhry's scheduled first stop in Karachi, killing a lawyer and injuring several others, including female lawyers. Justice Chaudhry and his team, of course, were 'extradited' to Islamabad after arguing and struggling for several hours at the airport.

Late that night; residents in the low-income housing of 'Ranchore Lines' were awakened by loud banging on their doors. One resident narrated that it was two young boys distributing freshly cooked '*biryani and suji*' in plastic bags: "*Yeh chief justice ki wapsi ki khushi mein hai*" (This is to celebrate the Chief Justice's return [to Islamabad]).

Another account can be seen here:

"On the Karachi streets, Uzi's press card had saved her again at around 05:00 pm as she and a colleague tried to reach the Rangers Headquarters in Dawood College. "A car chockfull of ammunition passed in front of us, stopped, backed up and stopped in front of us, Kalashnikovs pointing at the two of us from the windows. We showed our press cards and the car moved on. NEVER in my LIFE have I felt more grateful to my press card than I did then."

At around 06:00 pm, she and her colleague were trapped by gunshots all around. "Short of climbing the walls and entering one of the houses around, there really was no other place for us to go." They stopped a police mobile and asked which way would be safe to go. The answer, accompanied by laughter: "You can be killed wherever you go. Choose your place."

(Ref: **Eyewitness: Karachi 12th May 2007 by Beena Sarwar**
published in www.Chowk.com dated 30th May 2007)

In published reports, journalists prudently avoided naming the parties involved. See another reference:

'*Young men toting flags and banners had set up camp outside the airport departure lounge. They hid, however, when policemen came by. Reporters in the vicinity were asked whether they had seen any political activists around. Munawar Pirzada (from "Daily Times") said that he had seen some nearby.*

After the policemen had left, the activists came up to the reporter, dragged him by the hair and took him aside. They then proceeded to threaten him with dire consequences if he said anything the next time the policemen came around.'

(By *Urooj Zia in 'Daily Times': 14th May 2007*)

But the affiliation of these gangs was visible in the live coverage provided by several private television channels, which showed plainclothes men brandishing weapons on the deserted roads, using government tankers as cover, exchanging gunfire with unseen opponents, the tri-colour MQM flag visible on their motorcycles.

After *Aaj TV*'s continuous live coverage of such scenes, armed men attacked the television station, firing at it for several hours. Instead of stopping the coverage, *Aaj* showed live footage of reporters ducking behind a desk, shots being fired at their office, as anchor Talat Hussain provided an account of the situation on phone. Reporters in the area asked the Rangers posted nearby to help the *Aaj* workers trapped inside their building. The answer was:

'*We're helpless. We can't do anything unless we have orders from above.*'

Another eye-opening narration:

'*The local media received a call from a hospital, apparently sent by a doctor who had been at work for several hours attending to multiple gunshot wounded victims in his hospital lobby, where a makeshift emergency room had been set up. Nothing but he told:*

'*Struck down my soul more than what nine fully armed workers of a local political party along with 2 sector office bearers did. They tried to drag out a wounded and dying body of a 'poor politico-religious worker' (whose identity they later learnt) for presumably finishing him off.*'

The protesting doctors were slapped around and dragged by their legs to the back of the gurney alley. With shotguns, pistols and ak-47's in hand, the men ran back to the lobby presumably to find their target again.

The doctor ran out to the rangers and police at hospital's front gate. Their answer was:

'Jaante ho inn logon ko phir bhi kyon larte ho...hamain upar se order hai ke inn ko char baje tak karne do jo karna hai. Char baje ke baad kuch dekhainge' (When you know who these people are; why do you still fight them; we have orders from above to let them do whatever they want until 4pm. After 4pm we will see).

As a previous party supporter, the doctor had recognized some of the assailants and called a friend related to their deputy leader Farooq Sattar. Five minutes later the men received a phone call and left; threatening the doctors (and stealing one of their cell phones, "Chikna set hai" – (it's a costly set, isn't it).

The guy they had come looking for had been shot one more time in the head. The OT dress we had dressed him 10 minutes earlier was freshly bloody.'

(Ref: www.***karachi.metblogs.com*** / archives / 2007)

Those were the MQM's men as the media undoubtedly believed so; but who was controlling the Rangers in Karachi then.

There was a story behind each of those who were killed, some belonging to one or the other political party, and others just because they were there. Masked men stopped ambulances and sprayed them with bullets, killing an Edhi Ambulance driver, Faizur Rahman Khan, aged 65, when he refused to throw out a wounded person he was transporting to hospital from near the airport; the wounded man was also shot again. Armed gangs herded passers-by into an alley and shot dead a young over-lock machine operator along with another man, in front of two colleagues who were also shot but survived to tell the television source.

As per written facts in '*They shot us one by one...*' by **Munawar Pirzada** in the '**Daily Times**', there have been reports about an SHO who guided a procession into an ambush and a pregnant woman who had to deliver her baby in the car when armed men refused to let her proceed to the hospital with her husband. The Pakistan Press Foundation (PPF) reported that several journalists were manhandled and nine wounded.

Some TV cameramen were beaten and their cameras snatched or damaged, mostly in front of the police and Rangers.

Zaffar Abbas was correct when he wrote that Karachi was only at peace for the past many years because it suited its militants.

> 'Finger pointing is necessary, because throughout our history, instead of a catharsis, we simply go through a 'jo ho gaya ab bhool jaao, aagay daikho' (forget what has happened; look ahead) attitude. Already, with the President's pat on the back at an emergency meeting of the ruling party in Islamabad (on 14th May 2007) the MQM is back on the front foot.
>
> Although it is unlikely that the perpetrators of Saturday's violence will ever be brought to justice, at least they should continue to be exposed before the entire country. More importantly, they should face the consequence of such exposure.
>
> Public image is very important to the MQM and the national outrage at their conduct may be the best prospect of compelling them to change their ways'.

(Ref: 'Back to the Future?' Published in *Daily the 'Dawn' of 14th May 2007*)

In the light of above facts, narrations, opinions and analysis one can read in between the lines. MQM's activists were no doubt there to participate in the killing spree of that day but questions arise:

- Were all the armed activists or killers really belonged to the MQM? [The facts should have been ascertained that no other political party or ethnic or religious group was involved in that mass murder.]

- Did MQM's high command really wanted to 'show their strength' through street killings?

- Could a political party like MQM aspiring to move at national level adopt such harsh strategies?

- Who was controlling the Rangers & ISI & IB and the Police on that particular day? [The fact remains that MQM could muster the Police but Army and Rangers NEVER accept orders from any one except their own commanders; it is in-built in their training.]

- Who were the army OICs at ISI, Rangers and Home Department (only police comes under Home Deptt.) making 'contingency plans' to control the CJ's visit to Karachi that day?

- What was the possibility that some hidden hands had used the MQM activists 'on payment' without knowledge of the MQM or under an 'implied consent'.

- What were the possibilities that some of the 'hired killers' might have crossed their limits when once MQM commanders had asked them simply to 'help the agencies'.

One would like to find the answers of above questions and many more similar; see below.

Later Gen Musharraf was in the Chief Minister House Karachi to review the law and order situation following 12th May carnage. At that occasion a Provincial Minister Irfanullah Marwat (from Pakhtun Community) asked Gen Musharraf to order an inquiry into who had opened fire, arrest the culprits and take action against the elements responsible. The minister stressed that the people would not be satisfied till the arrest of the elements responsible and strong action against them.

The Pakhtun Action Committee Chief Shahi Syed stated on the occasion that all it was due to Adviser to the CM on Home Affairs MQM's Waseem Akhtar. The Advisor kept silent giving an impression of denying charges; virtually he was the Home Minister with all the powers more than the delegated.

Gen Musharraf heard it and that's all; military people find it hard to say sorry. In 2008, MQM joined hands with the PPP as a coalition partner and raised voice that MQM was not involved in the incident. MQM also asked for the enquiry which never held, at least till today. In Pakistan enquiries are never held when the fools and poor political workers are targeted in daylight on roads because never a political leader's kin is killed or even fired at in Pakistan.

AGENCIES DID THAT ALL?

Dr Zulfikar Mirza, later the PPP's Sindh Home Minister, was probably pointing out towards this core issue on the basis of his personal knowledge being a staunch political worker of the PPP and may be depending upon the reports of western press as quoted above. Being a

Home Minister he had definitely got access to the secret 'Special Branch' reports of the Sindh Police and floated his wish of conducting this enquiry at such belated stage so vigorously.

Whether MQM was involved in that whole scenario or not; is a subject of detailed enquiry based on solid evidence but the people still consider that the master mind behind that episode was Gen Musharraf, who had claimed those killings as *'his success and show of power'*. Hats off to his Army Commanders in Rangers & ISI or elsewhere in Karachi too, who were bent upon to prove their loyalties for their Army Chief. Reference is being made to an open *jalsa* [big gathering] held, organized and patronized by the PML(Q) at Islamabad on the same evening of 12th May 2007 showing strength of Gen Musharraf.

Very few people know that it was one Brig Huda of the ISI who had contributed most in show of power in Karachi on 12th May 2007 and was given due credit by Gen Musharraf the same evening.

Initially, the MQM was reluctant to hold a rally in Karachi on 12th May. The then DG ISI Gen Ashfaq Kayani also had the same opinion that MQM should not come out on the streets when Justice Iftikhar Chaudhry would visit Karachi. *It was Brig Huda who played an important role in convincing the MQM not to cancel its rally.* He assured the MQM leadership that there will be no riots on that day; but it happened and the whole episode brought bad name for Pakistan [and of course for the MQM too, may be inadvertently] in the world media mainly due to that extra-loyal Brigadier.

Fact remains that the Chief Secretary of Sindh, Shakeel Durrani, had strongly opposed the 'counter productive' strategy of the provincial government designed for 12th May 2007. He had written in advance to his seniors, proposing that hurdles should not be created and that the CJ be given a smooth passage. His recommendations were in clear contradiction to the ill-conceived strategy already worked out by the *Sindh Home Department, headed by former Commander of Military Intelligence, Brig (rtd) Ghulam Muhtaram.* The Home Department, due to unknown secret planning in top minds, insisted that the CJ should not be allowed to come out of the Karachi Airport.

Shakeel Durrani's recommendations, however, got a deaf ear from those who mattered in decision-making in Sindh. Durrani had also held responsible his provincial government for Karachi mayhem. Meanwhile, the Sindh government had refused to order a judicial inquiry into the killings. Prime Minister Shaukat Aziz wanted to order a judicial inquiry into the incident and for that purpose he had especially gone to Karachi with this plan but faced opposition from his ruling allies in Sindh.

The PM had gone to Karachi with a plan to announce the judicial inquiry in a press conference after holding meetings there. Information Minister Mohammad Ali Durrani and Interior Minister Aftab Sherpao had also accompanied him during this visit. The PM's plan could not materialize following stiff opposition from his allies in Sindh who said that such an order would open up a new Pandora's Box.

The then Federal Secretary Interior Division, Kamal Shah, had miserably failed in estimating the real danger incorporated in 12th May's situation of Karachi or he wilfully played in the hands of 'certain hidden people'. Reasons understood were that earlier the MQM had desired to join the Islamabad rally but was stopped by the Interior Ministry. Some MQM lawmakers blamed the 'bureaucracy at Islamabad' for 'pushing' them to hold a separate rally in Karachi instead of joining the PML(Q) rally in Islamabad held the same day. Thus an enquiry was direly needed into the Karachi affairs of that day to unearth such hidden planned 'green signals' from 'some' to keep the history intact.

The MQM kept the feeling that the 12th May incidents had left an adverse impact on their strategy to expand to other provinces so as to become a mainstream political party. The Karachi tragedy had put the MQM in dock as its offices in the Punjab and rural Sindh faced a virtual closure following protests by the public of respective areas who blamed them for this bloodbath in Karachi. MQM leadership should not be so wrong to take such negative decision of killing the innocents in the open streets; sane politicians would not like to cut their own wings at the brink of their flight at least. A serious mistake was done by the MQM; OR 'secret agencies' used them in a brutal way; only a thorough probe into the events could have revealed.

Why the enquiry was not ordered by the Sindh or Federal Governments; or by the PPP's new regime; or even by the superior courts; or by the provincial or national assemblies though all the stake holders, *including the MQM*, have been raising their demands to do that. Till today, tens of cabinet meetings have been held in the Presidency and the Prime Minister Secretariat; dozens meetings have been convened by the Federal Interior Minister Rehman Malik in the Governor House and CM House at Karachi on the subject of these killings but no body ever dared to seriously order for an investigation into the said affairs.

The Chief Justice Iftikhar Chaudhry, in whose honour a tribute of 43 dead bodies and about 150 injured persons were presented, stands comfortably saddled back in his mighty chair since March 2009 but the SC could not find time to ask CJ Sindh HC that what happened to those proceedings which were initiated in this respect. SC is always pleased to call the Chief Secretary, Sindh Home Secretary, IGP Sindh, DG Rangers, DIG City Karachi and others in less important *suo moto* actions into kidnapping of girls or beating of women by cruel husbands but never considered to call any of the above officers to come with FIRs of 12th May 2007 (if any case was then registered); and if registered, with the final reports of those cases or any one case got through investigation.

The Chief Justice Iftikhar Chaudhry himself was an eye witness to the whole scenario; he himself was kept in illegal confinement along with 24 prominent lawyers in Karachi Airport Building. Many of his judges at Sindh High Court were beaten & manhandled and lawyers killed, but no action.

The CJ, the judges and courts who cannot ensure 'Rule of Law' [just to keep the soldiers happy] being the witnesses themselves, can hardly provide justice to the people; thus we'll continue to suffer, my countrymen.

[*Part of this essay was published at www.ciriticalppp.com (LUBP) on 29th November 2009*]

Scenario 46

'OPERATION SILENCE' AT RED MOSQUE (2007)

In mid 2011, Gen Musharraf, permanently settled in London, vowed to go back to Pakistan on 23rd March 2012, because [as per his miscalculated assessment] the poor people of Pakistan at large and some fools need him. He was totally lost, misinformed and misplaced. In mid December 2011, he again reiterated that he would be landing there in January 2012; again a misguided belief he was adhering to. The secret reports were there that he was urging his ex-subordinate General and at present the Army Chief Gen Kayani to provide him shelter and immunity from the arrest warrants in Nawab Akbar Bugti's & Benazir Bhutto's murder cases; might be he had got clearance but a big question mark prevailed; now the January 2012 had passed long ago.

The Guardian of 2nd August 2007 had rightly narrated a story in the back drop of *Lal Masjid* (Red Mosque) episode in which 102 people [as per government's press release 68] had died on 10th July 2007. On the same day, there was a great debate in the National Assembly on the issue pointing towards the portrait of Mr Jinnah, the founder of Pakistan, on the wall. The paper wrote:

> '*On 14th August 1947 Jinnah founded Pakistan in the hope of forging a homeland where the subcontinent's Muslims could live in peace and harmony. Sixty years later, it was going badly wrong. The military ruled the country for about 36 years and in 2007 the situation was the same when Pakistan was being headed by a dictatorial and unpopular General named Pervez Musharraf. Huge protests had filled the streets, the courts were defiant and fearing the Taliban control over the tribal belt; al-Qaeda and the United States were threatening to use force.*
>
> *Suicide blasts had rocked the big cities and worse was to come. The western media had reached a conclusion that the country hasn't had a crisis of this magnitude since the 1970s when East Pakistan split off and Bangladesh came into being. End of the country was being spelled endangering a civil war.*'

On 7th July 2007, Gen Musharraf sent a message to the Islamic militants holed up in *Lal Masjid* (Red Mosque) Islamabad to 'Surrender or Die'. Negotiations started between the two factions without interruption and former Prime Minister Ch Shuja'at Hussain and a group of *Ulema* continued to convince Maulana Aziz and Ghazi Abdul Rashid, the custodians of the Red Mosque, but of no avail. Ch Shuja'at Hussain had offered militant mosque leader Maulana A Rashid Ghazi one last chance to surrender. *'I am returning very disappointed,'* said Mr Hussain. *'We offered him a lot, but he wasn't ready to agree to our terms.'*

The Economist of 12th July 2007 described the situation as under:

> *'When last-ditch negotiations broke down in the early hours of 10th July 2007 [at 3 AM], about 200 army commandos stormed the compound. A battle like situation was seen by the alert media because the resistance was fierce. The compound, far from being a madrassa (religious school) housing harmless women and children, was a bunker for well-armed extremists. Some were from banned religious parties and groups, and some linked to al-Qaeda and the 'Taliban' militias terrorising the tribal belt between Pakistan and Afghanistan.'*

When negotiations failed, **'Operation Silence'** was launched. Here are the eye-witnessed accounts!

With the restricted access to local hospitals, the government's refusal to release an updated official death toll added to fears that the actual number of fatalities could still be much higher than 68 as official figure which was estimated by the media as 102 after some days. The local city admin maintained that there had been just one group of around 30 women and children inside the compound, led by Umme Hassan, the wife of Maulana Abdul Aziz [who was captured by the forces trying to flee the mosque under a *burka* (veiled dress) a week earlier]. They were housed in one room when the Special Forces attacked and they were allowed to leave the compound alive.

During encounter with the armed forces, Commandos killed Abdul Aziz's brother and the mosque leader Ghazi Abdul Rashid, at the climax of what became a blistering battle for control of the complex in central Islamabad. Mr Ghazi, a university-educated cleric who tried to enforce *Sharia* Rule on Islamabad, was shot twice as the Commandos stormed his basement hideout. On refusing to answer calls to surrender, a second volley of bullets killed him.

The operation to storm the mosque began in darkness at 4am, minutes after last efforts for a peaceful end to the siege by 12,000 policemen and army soldiers had collapsed. The Special Services Group (SSG) had led the attack, striking from three sides. The elite forces immediately came under a hail of fire from heavily armed militants bunkered behind sandbagged positions on the roof and firing through loopholes in the walls. The military commanders had thought the 'Operation Silence' would be over within four hours; wrong calculation it was. The explosions and thunderous gunfire and bullet echoes continued to simmer through the whole day continuously.

Ghazi Abdul Rashid was holed up in one of the mosque's basements, surrounded by girls & children from the women's school serving him as a last-ditch propaganda campaign. Ghazi had told media reporters that he was prepared to be a *Shaheed* (martyr), though only few perceived him as such.

A group of hard-core girl students took up positions inside *Jamia Hafsa*, an extension in the mosque compound. Some were armed with guns and rockets; several areas were 'booby-trapped' like professional fighters. Fleets of ambulances continued to ferry the dead and wounded to hospitals not very far off. Moments after the assault started, Maulana Ghazi had called a local TV network accusing military troops and saying that *'the government is using full force. This is naked aggression; my martyrdom is sure now.'*

For more than 13 hours, the sound of fierce fighting had rattled the capital. The militants were responding with RPGs (rocket launchers), machine gun fire and petrol bombs. The religious education complex, which included a women's academy [*Jamia Hafsa*], was trapped with landmines, and militants were shooting from the minarets. Eight soldiers had died as well.

> [*It was the Jamia Hafsa which the British schoolgirl Misbah Rana, also known as Molly Campbell, was reported to have been interested in joining after arriving in Pakistan at the centre of an international custody row.*]

Pakistan's Prime Minister Shaukat Aziz, declared the Red Mosque siege over saying that:

> *'The government forces had regained full control of the compound after a 36-hour assault. The operation is over. Everybody who was inside is out, but the security forces were still surprised by the ferocity of the resistance. These were trained, hardcore militants, a number of foreigners; Uzbeks, Chechens, Tajiks and Afghans, had been arrested and were undergoing interrogation. We have not found any [dead] body of a woman or child yet.'*

Ghazi Abdul Rashid was hoping that an Islamist revolution would be sparked at his death but nothing happened. Instead the people got the enlightenment to ponder that what kind of Islam was being taught here in Red Mosque where the guns, mortars and grenades were also given in the hands of students. Under what provisions of Islam and under what state laws the two Maulana brothers were authorised to Islamize the capital city of Islamabad by use of armed force. Who had supplied them these arms and from where had they procured so much ammunition.

The state had to enforce its writ where it was being so criminally flouted. For western observers, religious extremism was a curse which had laid Pakistan low amongst nations and must be eliminated. But there were as many who insisted that the militants should have been pardoned and Muslim lives saved. Naturally, this school of thought & camp included clerics and conservatives. There were, however, signs of anger from militants around the country. The opposition coalition of Islamic parties, *Mutahida Majlis e Amal* (MMA), had announced three days of mourning starting from 11th July in NWFP.

Some critics, however, suggest that the fabrics of the Red Mosque students had served as a convenient distraction from Gen Musharraf's dipping popularity. One Brig (rtd) Shaukat Qadir opined that:

> *'My impression is that if it was not in collusion, the government was at least encouraging this event. The judicial crisis [Gen Musharraf vs Justice Iftikhar Chaudhry] had grown to enormous proportions, and the General wanted to re-establish that fact that he was essential to country; but somewhere along the way things got out of hand.'*

BACKGROUND OF LAL MASJID:

The Red Mosque was built in 1965 in the capital city of Islamabad and was named for its red outer walls and red carpets inside. Red Mosque is one of the oldest Mosques in Islamabad and one Maulana Abdullah was appointed its first imam. Abdullah was critical of all governments except Gen Ziaul Haq with whom he was very close. During the Soviet war in Afghanistan (1979–1989), the Red Mosque played a major role in recruiting and training *mujahideen* to fight in Afghanistan. Throughout its existence, it has enjoyed patronage from influential members of the government, prime ministers, army chiefs, and presidents. Several thousand male and female students live in adjacent seminaries.

After Abdullah was assassinated in 1998, his sons Abdul Aziz and Abdul Rashid Ghazi took over the mosque, making it a centre for hard-line teaching and open opposition to the government. Abdul Aziz remained the official *Khatib* of the mosque until he was removed in 2005 for issuing a controversial fatwa stating no Pakistani Army officer could be given an Islamic burial if died fighting the Taliban.

Original Red Mosque was built on a small piece of land. With the passage of time, the mosque managers encroached upon the surrounding area and a big complex like a fort was constructed. Due to influence and strong connections, the Capital Development Authority (CDA) remained unable to get the encroached land vacated till end 2006. In early 2007, CDA strongly persuaded the encroachment matter and issued a vacation notice to the premises managers.

Maulana Abdul Aziz and Ghazi Rashid retaliated the move by taking possession of the nearby Children Library, a CDA owned campus, by using the female student force. These students were motivated in the name of religion and thus the visible conflict started. All this was to force the government to come to some compromise, to the Maulana's terms.

Maulana Ghazi wanted to become hero of the Islamist rebellion in the garb of defying Gen Musharraf's rule in an attempt to install *Sharia* law in the city. Six months ago they placed themselves and the 8,000 students who attended their seminaries in Islamabad on a collision course with the government by launching an anti-vice campaign in the city. A week after clashes broke out between armed students and the military, resulting in more than 20 deaths. Gen Musharraf initially sought to negotiate but then had to send the militants an ultimatum to surrender or die. Mr Ghazi chose the later path.

The campaign began in January 2007 when they occupied the Children's Library near their Red Mosque, referred above, to include it in their Islamic *Jamia* Campus. Negotiations to get it vacated continued for weeks raising an impression that government had gone scared. In the next step hundreds of *burka-clad* women and stick-wielding girl students at the *'madrasah'* (Jamia Hafsa) took to the streets, kidnapping prostitutes, intimidating movie store owners and down-grading the western diplomat's wives for 'spreading nudity' by wearing sleeveless shirts.

Abdul Rashid Ghazi's girl students, known as *'Danda Bardar Force'* (heavy wooden sticks carrying force), had once abducted seven Chinese nationals working in a local massage parlour, which deeply embarrassed Gen Musharraf before a key ally country China. In fact that was the day 'Operation Silence' was thought and planned. The crisis had sparked deep international concern also.

The *Guardian of 11th July 2007* had quoted the EU Foreign Policy Chief Javier Solana saying that:

> '*He was gravely concerned that fighting could spill over into neighbouring Afghanistan. After the killing of three Chinese nationals in Peshawar a day before, Beijing publicly urged Pakistan to protect its citizens.*'

In the context of this military operation, one conflicting voice was of Benazir Bhutto from London. She supported the storming of the mosque as necessarily a strong message to extremists; but she qualified her endorsement by arguing that religious extremism was a consequence of army rule, and only civilian democracy could counter it effectively. However, the subsequent rule of the PPP for more than four years, under the iron hand of her husband Mr Zardari, proved she was wrong.

Liberals and NGOs were anyway opposed to the military rule of Gen Musharraf, and human rights activists did not approve the 'brutish' army operation but without suggesting any alternate remedy to that open lawlessness. At the same moment they hoped that the said operation would make the army realise that:

> '*It is time to end its alliance with religious forces. Even the army must see the dangers the jihadists pose. They have made desperate attempts to derail the peace process with India; to assassinate Gen Musharraf himself; to Talibanise the frontier regions; and now to enforce their brand of Shariah law in the federal capital by armed blackmail*'.

The *'Time' magazine of 10th July 2007* had, however, opined that:

> '*The government's cautious handling of the siege has worked in President Pervez Musharraf's favour. Security forces have clearly done their utmost over the past week to protect the lives of civilians, offering negotiations, amnesties, cash and even alternative schooling to students who surrender but all the efforts were continuously & blatantly discarded for eight long days.*'

However, alarming incidents in the tribal areas at the hands of Taliban; a possible machine-gun attack on Gen Musharraf's plane while he was ready to fly to the flood-ravaged province of Baluchistan [a day before]; armed tribesmen blocking the Karakoram Highway near the northern border with China; in Multan, hundreds of religious students blocking roads with burning tyres and chanting '*Down With Musharraf*; clerics at several radical mosques denouncing what they felt as law enforcement agencies attacking fellow Muslims; the banned militant group *Tehrik Nifaz e Shariat e Mohammadi* (TSNM) using FM radio stations in Swat and instructing its followers to carry out jihad against the government and many more such news had an accumulating effect on the military government demanding stern action against the miscreants using the religious platforms as their shields.

Moreover, when Gen Musharraf had announced his support for America's 'war on terror (WOT)', Red Mosque had become the centre of calls for his assassination. One of such speeches was delivered by Maulana Masood Azhar, whose *Jaish e Mohammad* (JeM) fundamentalist group members were later involved in several failed attempts on the life of Gen Musharraf. *In an interview, Ghazi Rashid had said that they had the support of the Waziristan Taliban and any action against the mosque would generate an 'appropriate response'.*

Once in July 2005, Pakistani security forces had tried to raid the mosque following suicide bombings during 7/7 episode in London. The security personnel were met by baton-wielding women, who refused to let them enter the mosque or seminary compound. Authorities said the security forces were investigating a link between the seminary and one Shehzad Tanweer, one of the 7th July bombers.

'OPERATION SILENCE RESUMED:

Coming back to the details of Operation Silence; as the negotiations were not progressing, it was clear that military action was not far away. While it was still dark, a barrage of explosions was followed by sustained gunfire as commandos moved into the sealed-off complex. The security forces had conducted the operation cautiously because of concerns about killing the women and children still inside. More than 70 separate rooms inside the mosque complex were bolted from inside when the forces were around in the premises.

Supported by paramilitary units, the commandos first seized the mosque itself. While they were freeing about 20 children inside the building, they came under fire from militants positioning in the minarets. The troops next moved against gunmen on the roof of the adjoining school building. Those 20 children were ultimately rescued from the mosque. Twenty-six women were rescued by troops including wife of Maulana Aziz.

About 70 militants were captured or surrendered. Federal Minister for Religious Affairs Ejazul Haq, one of the negotiators, told that women and children had been locked up on two floors of the *Jamia Hafsa* religious school by five 'hardcore terrorists' at least. He also told that one person killed on the first day of the siege belonged to *Jaish e Mohammad* (JeM), an outlawed radical Muslim group linked with al-Qaeda.

Those were days when the tension continued in the capital and security was stepped up at targets considered vulnerable to retaliation, as there were series of reports of periodic gunfire coming from the mosque as militants mounted a final defence in the basement of the complex's residential area; military was bound to move into the final phase of the operation at last.

The daily *'Independent'* of UK *dated 11th July 2007* cited about an interview of Ghazi Rashid with their correspondent saying that:

> 'Mr Ghazi led the way into his office, passing an area of the Lal Masjid in which sat a number of bearded young men with AK-47s. Mr Ghazi, too, had an automatic weapon propped against his desk; in that interview [less than three weeks ago] the erudite said that "The thing is, we are convinced the system in Pakistan is a total failure," he said in excellent English. "It's not giving justice; it's not giving the basic necessities. It's not giving basic education for the people."
>
> When the interview was over and their guest left, they (the armed students) waved goodbye.'

After 'Operation Silence' the mosque was taken through repair and renovation with its colour changed from red to off-white, but the enraged mullahs had again painted its outer walls with red *'jihadi'* slogans written on it. Emotional scenes were witnessed as parents and relatives of those who died during *Lal Masjid* operation dug out body parts, bones, blood stained clothes, pages of religious books and torn prayer mats from the debris of demolished *Jamia Hafsa*. They also found damaged books, broken utensils; of course, *jackets of militants were also scattered around in the debris.*

On the second Friday prayers after operation, the clerics and students again attempted to take control of the Red Mosque and started chanting slogans against Gen Musharraf and in favour of *Jihad*. They also started painting outer walls of the mosque red and wrote pro-jihad slogans. The exchange of stones that ensued outside the mosque between police and the former seminary students was followed by intense teargas shelling that affected residents in the nearby localities with suffocation.

The government should have cleared the debris of demolished *Jamia Hafsa* before opening the mosque for general public. The scene of the remains of bodies charged the people and they reacted with strong protests. Most of the people living in the nearby government quarters were critical of the government.

[*To celebrate the first anniversary of Lal Masjid episode, a suicide attacker killed 16 people during the first week of July 2008; twelve of them police officers, during a protest rally near a market place marking last year's Pakistani government raid. The rest of those killed were civilians; fifty-three people injured, mostly police personnel they were. The police were stationed at the outermost security perimeter, part of a protection cordon set up by the government for that rally of about 12,000 people.*]

MUSHARRAF RAN OUT OF OPTIONS:

The Red Mosque raid of July 2007 was intended to rout out Islamic extremists who hoped to establish a Taliban-style rule across the capital but instead, it increased suicide attacks on civilians, police and security forces. It also led to the collapse of a controversial cease-fire between Gen Musharraf's government and tribal leaders in the tribal territories along Pakistan's border with Afghanistan. The 2006 truce was blamed for establishing a safe heaven for Taliban & al Qaeda in Pakistan's frontier regions.

A secret meeting between Gen Musharraf and the exiled opposition leader Benazir Bhutto in UAE in the last week of July 2007 had triggered speculation of a power-sharing deal. Neither side had confirmed the details but supporters said it could offer a peaceful transition to full democracy; critics called it military rule under another name. Time schedule was settled for her come back to Pakistan but Benazir Bhutto perhaps did not stick to the timetable. As a result, Gen Musharraf got angry and thus the planning was made to teach her a lesson through **attack of 18th October 2007** in Karachi.

[*When she continued to flout the terms of that secret Dubai agreement of July 2007, she was ultimately eliminated on 27th December 2007 in Rawalpindi; it is widely perceived.*]

The gravest threat came from the tribal belt where pro-Taliban militants had declared war on the state. Since 3rd July 2007, the first day of the Red Mosque siege, suicide bombers killed more than 200 people, mostly tribal policemen and soldiers. Al-Qaeda was blamed as usual. The fighting was most intense in Waziristan, a mountainous area along the Afghan border where al-Qaeda was allegedly regrouping. Islamabad had no control there. Pakistani soldiers were largely confined to their bases and when they venture out, they were attacked. The defiance was spreading and the pro-government leaders in the tribal belt were beheaded. A big chaos was there all over the country.

On the other hand, the civilians had shattered Gen Musharraf's impression of authority during the same days, led by an unlikely hero the Chief Justice Iftikhar M Chaudhry whose defiance had prompted protests that swelled into a powerful movement. Black-suited lawyers took to streets across the country, hurling insults at the General. The kindest called him a dog. The lawyers were bolstered by the rickshaw class; ordinary people tired of soaring food prices.

An explosion of private television channels had also revolutionized Pakistani politics. Previously coverage was censored but then lively debates used to appear every hour. Live coverage of riots in Karachi on 12th May 2007, when armed government men or its supporters had killed 43 innocent citizens & leaving more than 150 injured; and an open public meeting in Islamabad the same day with Gen Musharraf fostering a triumphant speech was enough to show him his end.

The civilian revolt reached its climax on 20th July 2007 when, against all expectations, a Supreme Court bench headed by Justice Khalilur Rehman Ramday had thrown out Gen Musharraf's case against the Chief Justice Chaudhry. Never before it happened against a sitting military dictator in Pakistan. Gen Musharraf was down & silent; the US and British policies excusing the military dictatorship went up in smoke.

Gen Musharraf remained under continuing ferocious pressure from the White House because they had given him $10.65 billion in aid. Soon they frustrated with Gen Musharraf's slippery gimmicks. US Congress had to pass aggressive legislation to link American aid with 'do more' approach. Some key US officials had suggested unilateral strikes on al-Qaeda bases in Waziristan. Lee Hamilton, a member of President George Bush's Homeland Security Advisory Council, went too far to give this idea a practical shape but the Pakistan government got angered and alarmed declaring this strategy as counter productive. Pakistan's Foreign Minister Khurshid Kasuri told the media loudly that:

'This may be election season in the United States but it should not be at our expense'.

One of the core problems with Gen Musharraf was that he had no say in the financial matters. The Pakistan's military had consumed a large proportion of the GDP: probably more than 50%.

[*The CIA then commented that much of the Pakistani military budget was hidden in other ministries: much of the salaries and retirement / health accounts, which would be classified as 'military expenditure' in Western accounting systems was not accounted as such in Pakistan.*]

The monstrous military expenditure in Pakistan usually came at the cost of investment in education. This led to *madrassas* taking on educational burden which, as per western research, gave propagation to more extremism. True; that weapons do not provide stability when the people are on the breadline. Anti-American hostility was becoming deeper and bitterer. A general perception in those days had prevailed all over Pakistan that:

'*Red Mosque & Waziristan: all being manipulated by America, they've just been playing us since 9/11; paying dollars and turning the Pakistani army into killers of Muslims.*'

On the other side, Gen Musharraf wanted a return from his rubber-stamp parliament, the product of a rigged vote in 2002, to elect him as president for another five years term later that year. For this he needed a deal with Ms Bhutto, and had promised to withdraw long-standing corruption charges against her. The US and Britain were behind him, apparently convinced Gen Musharraf was still their best bet but the Supreme Court could easily shoot it down thus it was a high-stakes game for Ms Bhutto.

Benazir Bhutto was in exile since nine years. She was also risking a revolt from supporters who considered Gen Musharraf to be a political poison. This was very demoralising move and could undermine the whole process. The intelligentsia was of the view that Benazir Bhutto had bracketed herself among the opportunists. Her support was likely to dip, and the religious parties were in row to pick the fallen ripe fruit out of this compromise; PML(N)'s Sharif family was the first to avail that opportunity.

Nevertheless, the huge welcome of 18th October 2007 at Karachi Airport and the subsequent massive and un-precedented mob following her suddenly changed the whole wishful thinking of the military ruler and a suicidal attack was manoeuvred on immediate basis which left 157 people dead and 300 injured in Karachi.

Brig Huda, the then OIC of Karachi's ISI chapter, had [once more after 12th May's bloodshed] successfully played his role by subverting Benazir's show into a living graveyard amidst roaring cries, scattered human pieces and pools of blood.

Benazir Bhutto, however, got the message.

After two weeks, a mini martial law in the name of 'Emergency' [of 3rd November 2007] was announced for which it had already been placed on record in July 2007 by the International Crisis Group, that:

'Such emergency would accelerate the slide towards a military-led, failing state status prone to domestic unrest and export of Islamic radicalism domestically, regionally and beyond'.

It was OK for Gen Musharraf because he wanted to avoid the fate of the last military ruler, Gen Ziaul Haq, who was blown in ashes in a mysterious plane crash on 17th August 1988 near Bahawalpur.

The post attack [on Benazir Bhutto dated 18th October 2007] sensation among the general masses all over the country had proved that the former commando, Gen Musharraf was running out of options. A poll by the Washington-based International Republican Institute had announced about Gen Musharraf's popularity at 34% - down 20 points since February 2007. It was evident that if politics would fail, he could impose an emergency.

It was the sharp beginning of the end for Gen Musharraf.

And in fact, a month after the Red Mosque raid, Gen Musharraf did consider imposing a state of emergency in Pakistan citing the growing security threat in the tribal regions but the US Secretary of State Condoleezza Rice had asked him to refrain from such measure. He eventually imposed the same [emergency] on 3rd November 2007, suspending the constitution and sacking dozens of judges. That move ended up rallying more Pakistanis behind Gen Musharraf's political opponents and helped the PPP win the 8th February 2008 elections.

Scenario 47

JUDICIARY *vs* ARMY (2007)–II:

CJP GETS RELIEF – REINSTATED:

26th May 2007: The Sindh High Court (SHC), taking *suo moto* notice of the government's failure to remove the siege of the High Court and City Courts buildings by mobs on 12th May 2007 summoned the Attorney General, the Advocate General Sindh, the Chief Secretary Sindh, the Home Secretary, DG Rangers, IG Police Sindh, City Police Officer, and TPO Saddar for explanation. The *suo moto* notice was taken by SHC CJ Sabihuddin Ahmed on a report of the In-charge Registrar of SHC, submitted to him regarding the 12th May blockade. The court converted the registrar's report into a petition and constituted a seven-member full bench for hearing it.

The bench comprised Justice Sarmad Jalal Osmany, Justice Anwar Zaheer Jamali, Justice Mushir Alam, Justice Azizullah Memon, Justice Khilji Arif Hussain, Justice Maqool Baqar and Justice Ali Sain Dino Metlo. The court had directed the officers and respondents to appear in person on the next working day with the plausible explanations.

On the same day the Sindh High Court had taken another step towards making of Independent judiciary in Pakistan by taking a decision that *no Judge of the SHC would officiate as Acting Governor in absence of the Governor Sindh*. The decision was made at a meeting of the SHC judges presided over by CJ SHC Sabihuddin Ahmed. The decision was immediately conveyed to the Sindh government and the federal cabinet secretary. The meeting observed that:

> *'The judicial work is affected when a judge or CJ is asked to officiate a s the Acting Governor. Besides, it also violates the very principle of separation of the Judiciary from Executive provided in the Constitution.'*

On the same day of **26th May 2007** at Islamabad, regarding a law point as to whether the Chief Justice Iftikhar M Chaudhry could move the Supreme Court under Article 184(3) of the Constitution, Justice Khalilur Rahman Ramday had observed that the full court was concerned with the determination of its jurisdiction for hearing of the chief justice's case. It was held that the matter involving bloodbath on streets could not be termed a matter of no-interest for public; however, the point was that to what extent, the court could exercise its jurisdiction.

Justice Khalilur Rahman Ramday headed the 13-member full court to hear the said case. CJ Iftikhar Chaudhry's counsel Ch Aitzaz Ahsan submitted that under Article 209 of the Constitution, opinion of the president on the reference was not final rather the SJC had to review it.

In 1989's Haji Saifullah case, Wasim Sajjad had delivered a message of the then Army Chief Mirza Aslam Beg, to a judge of the Supreme Court J Nasim Hasan Shah. The Army chief had asked Justice Nasim Hasan Shah not to restore the PM M K Junejo's government on a petition against the dissolution of the then National Assembly. [*Wasim Sajjad, later, had however denied the said statement of COAS Mr Beg.*]

While hearing Justice Chaudhry's petition against the presidential reference in the Supreme Court, a 13-member full court, on 2nd July 2007 banned intelligence agencies' personnel from entering the superior courts of the country. The court commanded that no unauthorized person, including officials of the intelligence agencies of whichever department of the state, would enter the offices of the apex Court or of the high courts and that no one would seek access to any record of the superior courts.

The bench ordered the registrar of the Supreme Court and the registrars of the respective high courts to ensure compliance of this order. The bench ruled that the concerned registrar would be personally responsible and liable for any deviation or non-compliance of this order. The full court also ordered the DG IB to inspect the premises of the apex Court and residences of the judges regarding presence of any bugging instruments or devices and submit a personal affidavit about their non-existence within one week.

Strangely Barrister Aitzaz Ahsan had relied much on the arguments of Sharifuddin Pirzada, which he had once given in the Zafar Ali Shah's case. (Quite opposite to it, in the current scenario Mr Pirzada was appearing as the counsel for Gen Musharraf opposing the maintainability of the CJ's petition) In the Zafar Ali Shah case, Sharifuddin Pirzada had argued that the power of judicial review could not be ousted despite ouster clauses while discussing a peculiar situation.

Referring to Justice Yaqoob Ali's verdict, it was a historical fact for Pakistan that *'when tyrannical system comes in the hands of usurper, then the courts and people become silent.'* Earlier, in Zafar Ali Shah case

Sharifuddin Pirzada had supported doctrine of necessity and in Haji Saifulah case it was held that although the Assembly was dissolved illegally, but the court was not going to restore it. Chief Justice Nasim Hasan Shah had later uttered in one of his interviews that *we should have restored the Assembly*.

On **20th July 2007**, while announcing re-instatement of Chief Justice Iftikhar M Chaudhry, full bench of the Supreme Court of Pakistan headed by Justice Khalil ur Rehman Ramdey issued a Short Order regarding Constitutional Petition No. 21 of 2007 filed by the Chief Justice of Pakistan and other 22 related petitions. For detailed reasons to be recorded later, the following issues arising out of this petition were decided:

* Maintainability of CoP#21 of 2007 filed under Art. 184(3) of the Constitution:

  This petition is unanimously declared to be maintainable.

* Validity of the reference issued by the President under Art. 209 of the Constitution: By a majority of ten to three (J Faqir Muhammad Khokhar, J M Javed Buttar, and J Syed Saeed Ashhad dissenting), the said direction to reference in question dated 9th March 2007, for separate reasons to be recorded by the honourable judges so desiring, is set aside.

* Vires of Judges (Compulsory Leave) Order (President's Order No. 27 of 1970) and the consequent validity of the order dated 15th March 2007 directing that the Chief Justice of Pakistan shall be on leave: The said President's Order No. 27 of 1970 is unanimously declared as ultra-vires of the Constitution and consequently the said order of the President dated 15th March 2007 is also unanimously declared to have been passed without lawful authority.

* Validity of the order of the President dated 9th March 2007 and of the order of the same date of the Supreme Judicial Council restraining the Chief Justice of Pakistan from acting as a Judge of the Supreme Court and as Chief Justice of Pakistan: Both these orders are unanimously set aside as being illegal. However, since according to the minority view of the question of the validity of the direction of the reference in question, the said reference has been competently filed by the President. Therefore, this court should pass a restraining order under Article 184(3) read with Article 187 of the Constitution.

- Validity of the appointment of the Honourable Acting Chief Justice of Pakistan in view of the annulment of the two restraining orders and the compulsory leave order in respect to the Chief Justice of Pakistan: The appointments in question of the Honourable Acting Chief Justices of Pakistan by notification dated 9th March 2007 and the notification dated 22nd March 2007 are unanimously declared to have been made without lawful authority. However, this invalidity shall not affect the ordinary working of the Supreme Court or the discharge of any other constitutional and / or legal obligation by the Honourable Acting Chief Justices of Pakistan during the period in question and this declaration is so made by applying the de-facto doctrine.

- Accountability of the Honourable Chief Justice of Pakistan. It has never been anybody's case before us that the Chief Justice of Pakistan was not accountable: The same issue does not require any adjudication and other legal and constitutional issues raised before us shall be answered in due course through detailed judgments to follow.

Order of the Court: By majority of ten to three (J Faqir Muhammad Khokhar, J M Javed Buttar, and J Saeed Ashhad dissenting), this original Constitutional Petition No. 21 of 2007 filed by Mr Justice Iftikhar Muhammad Chaudhry, the Chief Justice of Pakistan is allowed as a result of the above mentioned direction the reference of the President dated 9th March 2007 is set aside.

- As a further consequence thereof, the petitioner Chief Justice of Pakistan shall be deemed to be holding the said office and shall always be deemed to have been so holding the same.

- The other connected petitions shall be listed before the appropriate benches in due course for their disposal in accordance with law.

[Signatures of judges on the 13-member bench]
20th July 2007

Next day Justice Iftikhar Chaudhry had taken over his seat as Chief Justice of Pakistan exercising his full control on judiciary and judicial matters with restored grace and honour.

Lawyers and civil society activists whooped with joy at the verdict in favour of Justice Chaudhry, the first time in Pakistan's 60-year history that a civilian had challenged a military leader in the court and won. This was a defining moment for Pakistan, first time the people had true liberty and raised high slogans of **'Go Musharraf Go'**

> *'Gen Musharraf said he would respect the verdict and would adhere to. Mr Chaudhry, a stubborn judge with a tendency to rambling speeches, became an unlikely national hero when Gen Musharraf tried to fire him in March'*; commented **daily 'the guardian' of 21st July 2007.**

Gen Musharraf's support had actually plunged on 12th May 2007 after his supporter's sparked violence in Karachi which left 43 dead. A veteran human rights activist and a lawyer, Asma Jahangir, commented that there was a 'clear divide' between civilians and military. *'Not only should Musharraf resign, I think he owes this country an apology too,'* she said.

Another potential winner / beneficiary from this decision were exiled opposition leader Benazir Bhutto. She described it as one of the most remarkable judgments in Pakistan's history; the legal protest had become a *"struggle against dictatorship".*

The detailed judgment in the case of the restoration of the Chief Justice of Pakistan [on 20th July 2007] was written by Justice Ramday after about 30 months when all the team resumed their portfolios in March 2009. The detailed judgment revealed some stunning facts which were, though known to the people, but were not believed.

The Supreme Court also made it clear that the case had nothing to do with army as an institution but concerned with acts of one person who happened to be the Army Chief. The judgment said regarding the statement of Ch Shuja'at Hussain [*'it was a matter between army and judiciary'*] that:

> *'This, in our opinion, was a naive attempt to create a wedge between two important and indispensable arms of the State and to put them on a war-path. What was in question before us was an act of the President and it was just an accident or a coincidence that the said President also happened to be the Chief of Army Staff. The matter had obviously nothing to do with the Army as an institution.'*

A retired General who was close to Gen Musharraf afterwards told that the later tried to expel the chief justice because he wanted extension in his tenure that was expiring; election results of his own desire and government of his own choice. Gen Musharraf had used his senior colleagues, to press the chief justice to quit. The then DG MI Gen Nadeem, who was also a relative of Gen Musharraf, crossed all limits in dealing with the opponents of the former dictator. The DG MI was the strong man of Gen Musharraf and the government had taken aggressive steps against judiciary on advice of the DG MI, who was in fact responsible for spoiling Gen Musharraf's all matters related to judiciary. The DG IB had also gone too far in bid to protect the interests of his boss, Gen Musharraf.

The fact remains that under Gen Musharraf's pressure the DG MI Nadeem, DG IB Ejaz Shah, the then secretary interior Kamal Shah and some others had submitted affidavits in the Supreme Court against the chief justice. DG ISI, Gen Ashfaq Kayani, did not submit an affidavit. The army on the whole hailed the chief justice and the members of his court; all deserved praise and esteem for showing rare courage. Justice Khalilur Rehman Ramday also mentioned the reasons for delay in writing the detailed judgment.

In short, Gen Musharraf had become a lesson for others that even Washington, to whom he had sold his soul and served even at the cost of damaging Pakistan, had abandoned him. US special envoy to Pakistan and Afghanistan (late) Richard Holbrooke had once said *'President Pervez Musharraf is now history and that the US will not come to defend him'.*

The reputation of Pakistan Army was at its worse when Gen Musharraf handed over the military command to the incumbent Army Chief Ashfaq Parvez Kayani, who took no time to get the army out of politics and repeatedly proved military's neutrality in political and government related matters. Gen Kayani, kept army out of any electoral manipulation though Gen Musharraf was keen to rig the elections to get his choice parties elected, especially the JUI & PML(Q).

GEN MUSHARRAF'S 2 PORTFOLIOS CHALLENGED:

Those were the days of 2007 when Pakistani masses under the banner of 'Judiciary's Freedom' went so volatile that everywhere the army and Gen Musharraf were being discussed in derogatory sense. The trend went so popular that the people started taking pride in abusing army and the military junta of Pakistan. Taking stock of this alarming situation Gen Musharraf called a meeting of Corps Commanders at GHQ Rawalpindi. At a time when the opposition parties and the legal fraternity were hurling contemptuous and disdainful criticism on president's cannons and policies, the top military commanders minced no words in lending their support to Gen Musharraf and standing behind him.

The Corps Commanders, in its routine monthly meetings at GHQ, used to discuss the internal situation in the context of an outburst against the national security institution, its chief and the president. Held at the General Headquarters (GHQ) Rawalpindi, Gen Musharraf used to chair all the meetings attended by corps commanders and principal staff officers (PSOs). A threadbare discussion used to be there with detailed briefing on the country's situation, including 'behind the scene' attempts to chop up the system by politicizing chief justice issue.

The wind against Gen Musharraf's tyrannical rule was aggravated by an alarming domestic security threat because about 285 people had died since 3rd July 2007, when the Red Mosque siege in Islamabad triggered a violent backlash from Islamists. Killing and kidnapping numerous civilians and soldiers in suicide attacks in North Waziristan and Bajaur Agency were in addition. This upsurge of violence also chased the Chief Justice's supporters, with a bomb blast in a rally at Islamabad killing 18 people at the spot.

In early September 2007, Qazi Hussain Ahmed, Chief of *Jamat e Islami* (JI), approached the Supreme Court of Pakistan with a writ petition that *'Gen Musharraf cannot hold two offices (of President of Pakistan & the Chief of the Army Staff) at one time, and that he should resign from one post immediately'*. The petition was admitted for hearing.

In fact this petition was meant to reconsider two earlier judgments given on the same subject by the apex Court in the past. One of these was reported in **PLD 2005 SC 719**, titled *"Pakistan Lawyers Forum vs. Federation of Pakistan and others"* and decided on 13th April 2005, by a bench of five judges perhaps also including the CJP Iftikhar Chaudhry as a judge. This was based on yet another decision, titled *"Qazi Hussain Ahmad vs. General Pervez Musharraf Chief Executive and others"* and reported in **PLD 2002 SC 853**, which also included Justice Iftikhar Chaudhry in the nine-member bench.

The question placed before the Supreme Court of Pakistan in September 2007 was:

'Whether a person who is disqualified under Article 63(1)(d) of the Constitution of Islamic Republic of Pakistan 1973, and also Article 63(1)(k), can be allowed to contest the elections'.

This matter had earlier surfaced in the issue of former president *Rafique Tarar vs. Justice Mukhtar A Junejo*, acting Chief Election Commissioner of Pakistan and six others. In this judgment it was held that:

> 'Article 41 of the Constitution does not by itself provide disqualification from contesting the election to the office of president but adopts the method of what is commonly known as legislation by reference, and provides that a candidate to the office of president must be qualified to be a member of the National Assembly' .... 'That the qualifications and disqualifications are not inter-changeable terms and have separate and distinct connotations. Qualification is a virtue while disqualification is a vice.'

In the light of above judgment, the provisions of Article 63 of the Constitution were not made applicable to Gen Musharraf. This was so held in Qazi Hussain Ahmad's case by seven judges of the apex Court and then was repeated in the Pakistan Lawyer Forum's case comprising five judges and when the 17th Amendment was enforced on 31st December 2003, it incorporated a proviso to Article 41(6)(h) of the Constitution which reads as follows:

> ' .....Provided that Para d of Clause 1 of Article 63 shall become operative on or from the 31st day of December 2003'.

The Parliament approved this judgment of the Supreme Court then.

> 'It was an act of omission or a deliberate act, whereby the dictum of the Supreme Court of Pakistan was given effect by the legislature to the extent of only Para d of Clause 1 of Article 63 of the Constitution'.
> (Ref: An opinion appeared in *'the News' dated 24th Sep 2007*)

18th September 2007: Mr Sharifuddin Pirzada, Gen Musharraf's counsel in the Supreme Court, submitted a written undertaking on behalf of the President that 'Gen Mushaff will leave the post of the Army Chief If he would be elected as president by the sitting assemblies in the coming days'. It categorically meant that leaving one portfolio was conditional. A nine-member bench hearing the case was told that:

> 'If elected' the president "shall relinquish charge of the office of the Chief of Army Staff soon after election, but before taking oath of office of the President of Pakistan for the next term".

This scheme to re-elect the president was relying on certain questionable measures. These involved the Election Commission of Pakistan which, two days earlier, had regrettably shown it to be working in a manner not entirely similar to being independent of the executive. First blow was its notification of a change in rules governing the president's re-election whereby it amended them to exempt the president from being subject to Article 63 of the Constitution. A bar on a person was that:

'Who has been in the service of Pakistan or of any statutory body or any body which is owned or controlled by the Government or in which the Government has a controlling share or interest from contesting an election for public office until at least two years have passed since the individual ceased to be in such service'.

It meant that the said condition was not going to be applied to the president. One could imagine who other than Gen Musharraf would benefit from such an amendment. This was followed by another amendment, which curtailed the power of returning officers to reject, on the basis of Article 63, the papers of a candidate who stands for the president's slot.

ANOTHER BLACK DECISION OF SC IN 2007:

28th September 2007: Supreme Court's 6-3 verdict rejecting the petitions filed by Qazi Hussain Ahmed, Imran Khan and the Pakistan Lawyers Forum challenging Gen Musharraf's eligibility for the presidential election scheduled for 6th October brought a massive relief for Gen Musharraf and his supporters, especially Ch Shuja'at's PML(Q). For the opposition, especially the All Parties Democratic Movement (APDM) and the lawyers opposing military rule and those who campaigned for the restoration of the chief justice and for a large section of civil society, the verdict came as a surprise and disappointment. The grounds for rejecting the petitions were given as *'non-maintainable'*.

[Normally, in court cases, the maintainability or otherwise of a petition is adjudged before regular hearings commence: in fact, common sense would dictate that it was a pre-requisite.]

The people wondered that if non-maintainability was to be cited as being the reason then why several hearings, beginning from 17th September, were held to examine the petitions. The fact was that the question of maintainability of the petitions had already been settled. The demand of natural justice was that the apex Court should have given a ruling that:

'General Musharraf must first relinquish the post of army chief and then seek re-election.'

It was more appropriate especially when Gen Musharraf's lawyer had earlier told the court that *'while he would contest the election as army chief, if successful, he would take the oath of the president's office as a civilian.'*

Harsh comments immediately came from the opposition politicians and lawyers. Right after the announcement of the verdict, many lawyers and others inside the court room began shouting *'not acceptable, not acceptable'* and cries of *'shame shame'* rang out as well. One top lawyer named Ali Ahmed Kurd told the media right after the announcement of the verdict that: *'the ruling was written and sent from Aiwan e Sadr and would be seen as a black mark on the country's judicial history.'*

The full judgment was, of course, to be written later, but going by what the judges had said during the hearing, the 17th Amendment was a major consideration before them. The MMA leadership was to blame itself for a bad bargain while voting for the 17th amendment in December 2003: it made the entire Legal Framework Order part of the Constitution in exchange for such minor concessions as those relating to the NSC, the judge's age and action under 58(2)(b) being made justifiable.

It may not be out of place to reclaim that the past 3 year's political sins of top MMA leaders had once again given a second lease of political life to Gen Musharraf at a very crucial phase, as the infamous 17th Amendment became the basis of the Supreme Court's decision of 28th September to allow a uniformed president to get himself re-elected for next five years from the dying assemblies.

On 28th September 2007, it was felt that the Supreme Court had again taken a turn like Pakistan's old character of judiciary since Justice Munir Ahmed's days. It was a day when the apex Court provided a fulcrum to Gen Musharraf to become a candidate for President's office while at the same time being an Army Chief. Going by the decision the question was:

> *'Whether the top court goes back to its old ways of behaving like a junior partner of the Army? The Chief Justice of Pakistan might be in a minority in the court'.* A question was posed by M B Naqvi in Daily *'the News'* of 3rd October 2007.

Their lordships might have a hard time swallowing many observations about doctrine of 'State Necessity' being dead. This rejection of Qazi's petition was [allegedly deliberately made] on technical grounds: the 17th Amendment and the 'Two Offices Act' allowed the General to become the President until 2012. The SC was hiding behind technicalities and had chosen to fight each day as it came. These petitions were based on major principles: natural justice makes a good law (and the Constitution); the principle of the general scheme, spirit and natural justice underlying the Constitution override hasty or ill-considered amendments. The SC had ignored these precepts once for all.

The jurists may give any explanation for it but historians would remember that through this decision the SC had permitted a serving General to rule for five years more just as Justice Irshad Hussain had earlier given three years to the same army General to rule & ride Pakistan. The apex Court provided him another smooth sail through 6th October's election. He needed another 14 votes only in addition to his loyal party's votes. Those could be begged, bribed or coerced; after all, the NAB and ISI had enough experience and powers to persuade weak politicians. There was enough time to stitch a deal either with Maulana Fazlur Rahman's JUI or Benazir Bhutto's PPP whatsoever.

Leaving aside the local press, the reactions in the world media was much robust and strapping because the Pakistan's Supreme Court had provided them enough laughing stock. Some parts of an article written by Declan Walsh in '*the guardian*' of *29th September 2007* are being placed below:

> '*Pakistan's supreme court cleared the way for President Pervez Musharraf to seek another five-year term yesterday when it threw out a major legal challenge to his controversial re-election plans. Inside the normally quiet courtroom, lawyers cried "Shame! Shame!" and "Go, Musharraf, Go!" after six of the nine judges rejected a tangle of petitions against General Musharraf standing in next Saturday's poll.*
>
> "*This is shameful. It is not a judgment, it is the dictation of a dictator,*" *said Ali Ahmad Kurd, a prominent anti-military advocate, addressing supporters from a courtroom bench. Outside the mood was equally black as opposition supporters threw eggs and tomatoes at the [Supreme Court's] building.*'

Roedad Khan, a retired civil servant openly said that:

> '*They have given this judgement at gunpoint. It proves that as long as Gen Musharraf is there no institution can be free in Pakistan*'.

The intelligentsia and the media analysts grilled that the decision was a blow to hopes of driving out the military from politics. An eminent columnist *Ayaz Amir* noted that:

'Pakistan's Prague Spring has come to an end in September [2007]. His election should be smooth sailing from now on.'

Gen Musharraf's electoral woes might have diminished but the political crisis rumbled on, with enraged opposition leaders vowing to take their protests to the streets. *'We will not simply go home. We will launch a protest movement. With the support of the people he will be overthrown,'* said Javed Hashmi of PML(N), who was then freed after four years in jail. But the opposition had proven incapable of mounting large rallies since four months, when a lawyer-led anti-military movement fizzled out after the Chief Justice Iftikhar Chaudhry was reinstated and his portfolio was restored on 20th July 2007, but his fellow judges had simply proved themselves coward sheep in tiger's skins always at the look out at issuing contempt notice to any one to show their false strength.

On that black day of 28th September 2007, the nine member bench of Supreme Court of Pakistan, which in a 6-3 spilt verdict held that petition as non maintainable comprised of Justice Rana Bhagwandas as head of the bench [dissenting], Justice Mian Shakirullah Jan [dissenting], Justice Sardar Muhammad Raza Khan [dissenting] whereas other six stooge judges were Javed Iqbal, Abdul Hameed Dogar, M Javed Buttar, M Nawaz Abbasi, Faqir Muhammad Khokhar and Falak Sher.

For the presidential elections to be held a week later [on 6th October 2007], although 43 people had put their names forward but the only serious contender was Gen Musharraf. The lawyers had nominated Wajihuddin Ahmed, a retired Supreme Court judge who had refused to validate Gen Musharraf's 1999 coup, as a protest candidate.

The *'Time' magazine of 28th September 2007* had commented that the lawyers who only two months ago had been celebrating the Supreme Court judges for standing up to Gen Musharraf by reversing his dismissal of the popular and independent Chief Justice Iftikhar Chaudhry [who did not preside in this case] denounced the ruling as 'despicable.' It was not an independent decision at all because the Supreme Court had maintained the legitimacy of the dictatorship.

Outside the Supreme Court building members of one religious party had hoisted a coffin on their shoulders emblazoned with the words JUSTICE and SUPREME COURT. *"This coffin is a symbol of the death of the Supreme Court,"* explained one Khalid Abbasi, a telecom engineer from Islamabad adding that *'Justice has died in Pakistan today.'*

A lawyer and talk-show host Ayesha Tammy Haq said that:

'It means that from now on we can always have a military leader running for the office of President. The only people left with any credibility are the lawyers. They are the only ones taking a stand, and they will win in the end. The court decision is a setback but we have not lost hope.'

The 'Time's reporter at another place noted that:

'Not all were dismayed by the decision. Some lawyers at the court expressed relief, explaining that while a decision against Musharraf may have upheld the integrity of the Constitution, the consequences for the country could have been devastating. No one knows what Musharraf would have done had the court ruled against him, but rumours were rife that he would declare martial law, suspending basic rights and civilian institutions [which he otherwise did after 35 days].'

The poor 'Time' reporter had no idea that in Pakistan most of the rulers; Generals and civil, are characterless creature. The reporter might be repenting on his assessment or analysis when he had learnt later that 'even then Gen Musharraf had promulgated (mini) martial law on 3rd November 2007, just 35 days after that decision". For some of them the minutes of the meeting or agreed political announcements are not 'Quru'an & Hadith', a meeting between the PPP & PML(N) leaders at Murree a year after can be cited here.

'The war is not over. It was a skirmish. It was disappointing. But we will be back,' said Munir Malik, President of the Supreme Court Bar Association. But everybody knew that it was difficult to derail Gen Musharraf after the controversial verdict from the Supreme Court in Qazi Hussain Ahmed's petition.

In addition to the taunting narrations from the foreign press, the Pakistani press also roared while taking the people back to the same kind of situation in 2004. With the background facts that at the time of passage of the Legal Framework Order (LFO) in 2004 after the MMA leaders decided to betray the political forces engaged in desperate struggle against the rule of Gen Musharraf, it was widely assumed that it might be only one-time 'political sin' of the MMA leaders. But, later the SC verdict confirmed the wild doubts of critics of the MMA that the country was continuously suffering from the havoc created by the so-called two champions of Islamic rule in the country. This background politics in the garb of Islam was explained better by Rauf Klasra through following words:

> 'The MMA, nicked named as a "B team" of General Musharraf, had given a false impression after the 2002 elections that it would fight for the supremacy of the Parliament when President Musharraf would push his LFO for approval from the Legislature.
>
> Qazi Hussain Ahmed and Fazlur Rehman simply hijacked the agitation movement of the opposition parties to oppose Gen Musharraf and his LFO in the Parliament. The movement became so aggressive and popular in nature that at one stage, it emerged that Gen Musharraf might yield to the rising political power of these forces.

(Ref: **Rauf Klasra's** opinion in *'the News'* dated
30th September 2007)

Rauf Klasra's article further divulged that the international media and community were giving serious attention to the political turmoil in Pakistan amidst the rising pressure from the Commonwealth and the European Union on Gen Musharraf to get legitimacy from the Parliament or he might lose their vital support. The agitation movement within and outside the Parliament against the LFO was so effective that it crippled PM Jamali's government. At that time, Gen Musharraf appointed two of his top and trusted generals, Major Gen Zaki and Maj Gen Ehtasham Zamir, assisted by S M Zafar, to negotiate a secret deal with the MMA.

> [*Qazi, Fazl and Liaquat Baloch started meeting these Generals late nights. Finally, a deal was brokered between the Generals and the MMA, which exclusively benefited both the parties. The rewards were the continuation of the MMA-led NWFP government, share in the Balochistan cabinet and slot of the Opposition Leader in the National Assembly. MMA also got the references against its MPs blocked after certain forces tried to get them disqualified on account of [fake] educational qualifications.*]

It was also [and rightly] opined that after initial dents in its lost credibility, the MMA leaders once again revived their political credentials using Nawaz Sharif who, too easily, accepted their role as a major opposition figure [*referring to the All Parties Conference at Nawaz Sharif's residence at London in mid 2006*] when he started giving them more importance despite being partners of Gen Musharraf in the government. Despite being part of Gen Musharraf regime, Nawaz Sharif and those MMA leaders had later formed an alliance (named APDM) with them. But, afterwards Nawaz realised that he was only being used by smart and shrewd politicians of the MMA as none of them turned up at the Islamabad airport on 10th September 2007 to receive him.

And the poor guy, Nawaz Sharif, was expelled back just after 3 hours stay at the Airport.

The most-important thing was that verdict of the Supreme Court had justified the claim of Gen Musharraf that *'let the agitators do their job, he would have the last laugh'*.

The critical role of the MMA in facilitating the rule of Gen Musharraf in uniform was so irritating that during the two week [2nd half of September 2007] long proceedings on the case, some judges did not forget to keep on reminding the religious parties about their 'deeds' during December 2003 followed by their tyrannical partnership with the General. However, it is interesting to note that the MMA leaders were so smart that they had not only been facilitating Gen Musharraf in power but they had also been successfully acting as the 'real opposition' to the regime in the Parliament and outside, as PML(N) did for the PPP in the Parliament during 2008-12.

Scenario 48

SC ALLOWS SHARIFS TO COME BACK:

Sharif brothers and their families had left Pakistan under a clandestine deal on 10th December 2000 to settle in Saudi Arabia. It was a package including the exile deal, the presidential pardon and remission of sentence and undertakings of Nawaz Sharif and Shahbaz Sharif then sponsored by Saudi prince ruler but the deal was negotiated through Lebanon's PM Rafiq Hariri. When the wind went against Gen Musharraf after CJP Iftikhar Chaudhry's mishandling and Red Mosque episode of Islamabad, Nawaz Sharif vowed to come back to Pakistan in the back drop of Musharraf-Benazir deal of the last week of July 2007 in UAE. Drawing benefit from the situation, the Sharifs then moved a petition in the Supreme Court of Pakistan for their come back.

The SC admitted the petition and a judgment dated 23rd August 2007 by a seven-member bench of the Supreme Court, headed by Chief Justice Iftikhar Chaudhry, was announced stating: *'the former prime minister's release from prison and his journey to Saudi Arabia after getting a presidential pardon due to an undertaking cannot be described as forced exile.'* The detailed judgment dated 17th October 2007 by the apex court in the same case to prove its contention that the Sharifs had left the country under a deal or not was also available with the media then.

It was held in the judgment of 23rd August 2007 that the Sharif brothers could return as no restraint could be placed on a Pakistani citizen to return to his country and the undertaking given by them had no constitutional legitimacy as such the petitioners can't be prohibited from coming to Pakistan. But the court order had also mentioned:

'In view of the chequered history of the case, the undertaking furnished by the petitioners cannot be ignored altogether on the basis whereof they had proceeded abroad. Had this undertaking not been in field, the position would have been different and sentence awarded in various cases would remain intact. In such view of the matter, the journey to Saudi Arabia could not be termed as 'forced exile'. The move was never challenged for a couple of years as the petitioners were aware of the undertaking which culminated in their release from jail.

Whatever terminology, i.e., deal, negotiation, mediation, third-party intervention, undertaking or agreement may be used, there is no denying the fact that the petitioners had proceeded abroad at their own.'

The Supreme Court had announced its verdict a day after Gen Musharraf regime had submitted [on 22nd August 2007] the documents of the alleged deal made between the Sharif brothers and Gen Musharraf's government, in line with the apex court's desire dated 16th August 2007. As per contents of the exile deal produced before the apex court by the then Attorney General of Pakistan Justice (Retd) Malik Qayyum, the Sharif brothers had voluntarily agreed to live out of the country for ten years. A copy of an undertaking seeking permission to proceed abroad by Nawaz Sharif and Shahbaz Sharif was also filed in the apex court the same day which revealed that the Sharif brothers had left the country for 10 years on their own choice and agreed not to be engaged in any business or political or any other activities of any nature whatsoever against the interests of Pakistan.

Nawaz Sharif's exile agreement produced before the apex court was as under [verbatim]:

> *"I, Muhammad Nawaz Sharif, accept the help by a personality for negotiation for the release from imprisonment in Pakistan. I am satisfied with this whole process of the negotiation. In the country where I would adopt residence, there I would not take part in any business or political activity and nor would take part for ten years in any politics, regarding imprisonment or against the interests of Pakistan. I will not proceed to another country without any permission of the country where I will reside for ten years outside Pakistan, and that I will come back in the same country. I will not tell anything to anybody about the personality and the country, through which the agreement has been made."*

Two separate but identical one-page *"Confidentiality and Hold Harmless Agreements"* carried the signatures of the Sharif brothers. There was no other signature on them. Sharifs pledged in these papers that they would not disclose the identity of *"either the gentleman or the country involved in their release from Pakistan and relocation except with their prior written consent."* During the hearing of the case, the Attorney General was stopped by Gen Musharraf from revealing the identity of the "gentleman" mentioned in the agreement who had arranged the agreement that let the Sharif family leave Pakistan in 2000. But in his book titled *"In the Line of Fire"*, Gen Musharraf had clearly stated that the deal was arranged by Crown Prince Abdullah bin Abdul Aziz Al Saud.

According to the pardon documents produced in the apex court by Gen Musharraf regime on 22nd August 2007, it was on the basis of a 4-page application signed by Nawaz Sharif, Shahbaz Sharif, Abbas Sharif and Hussain Nawaz, that the then Chief Executive of Pakistan Gen Musharraf had advised the then President Rafiq Tarar on 9th December 2000 to remit the sentences awarded to Nawaz Sharif under Art 45 of the Constitution, which he remitted.

The text of the 4-page petition signed by the Sharifs was as under:

"The President

The Islamic Republic of Pakistan

Dear Sir,

That petitioner No 1 (Nawaz Sharif) along with others was tried for offences under sections 120B, 212, 121A, 123, 365, 402B, 109 and 324 of Pakistan Penal Code and section 6/7 of the Anti-Terrorism Act 1997 by the Anti-Terrorism Court No-1 Karachi.

The other co-accused of petitioner No. 1 were acquitted but petitioner No 1 was, by the judgment dated 6th April 2000 of the said court, convicted for offences under section 402 PPC read with Section 7 of the Anti-Terrorism Act 1997 and sentenced as under.

Offence under Section 402(B) PPC:

  (i) Rigorous imprisonment for life.

 (ii) Fine of Rs:5,00,000 (in case of non-payment of fine R.I of 5 years).

(iii) Confiscation of entire property.

Offence under Section 7 of Anti-Terrorism Act:

  (i) Imprisonment for life.

 (ii) Fine of Rs:5,00,000 (in case of non-payment of fine R.I for 5 years).

(iii) To pay Rs:29,00,000 as compensation to all passengers of flight PK-805 in equal shares.

That on appeal by petitioner No.1 against the judgment the court maintained conviction under Section 402(B) PPC read with Section 7 of the Anti-Terrorism Act and modified the sentences as under:-

(i) Imprisonment for life.

(ii) Fine of Rs:5,00,000 (in case of non-payment of fine R.I for five years).

(iii) Forfeiture of property (movable and immovable to the extent of the value of Rs:500 million).

That on a reference filed by the National Accountability Bureau under the NAB Ordinance 1999, petitioner No 1 has been tried by Accountability Court Attock Fort and convicted for an offence under section 9(a)(v) of the NAB Ordinance and sentenced as under:-

(i) R.I for 14 years.

(ii) Fine of Rs:2,00,00,000 (in case of non-payment of fine R.I for 3 years).

(iii) Disqualification for 21 years for seeking or from being elected, chosen, appointed or nominated as member or representative of any public office or any statutory or local authority of the government of Pakistan.

That the petitioner No 1 has developed serious health problems. That certain inquiries and investigations against conduct of petitioner No.1 and petitioners No 2 to 4 are pending with the investigating agencies and investigations may culminate into the petitioners' prosecution.

In view of the above it is requested that the sentences of imprisonment of petitioner No 1 may be waived to enable him to proceed abroad for medical treatment and the petitioners may not be prosecuted in respect of any alleged past conduct.

(Signed) Mian Muhammad Nawaz Sharif - petitioner No 1.

(signed) Mian Shahbaz Sharif - petitioner No. 2.

(signed) Mian Abbas Sharif - petitioner No. 3.

(signed) Hussain Nawaz - petitioner No. 4." [9.12.2000]

On 9th December 2000, the then Chief Executive Secretariat wrote to the president:

"Subject: **Grant of Pardon**

In terms of Article 45 of the Constitution of Islamic Republic of Pakistan the president is advised to:-

(a) Remit the sentence of imprisonment for life awarded to Mian Muhammad Nawaz Sharif by the High Court of Sindh in its judgment dated October 30, 2000 in Special Appeal No 43 of 2000 under Section 402B of the Pakistan Penal Code read with section 7(ii) of the Anti-Terrorism Act, 1997 and

(b) Remit the sentence of R.I for 14 years awarded to Mian Muhammad Nawaz Sharif by the Accountability Court Attock Fort in its judgment dated July 22, 2000 in reference No 2 of 2000 under Section 9(a)(v) of the National Accountability Bureau Ordinance 1999.

(Signed) Pervez Musharraf,

Chief Executive of Pakistan and CJCS and COAS

December 9, 2000."

On this the-then President [Rafiq Tarar] wrote:

"Approved. Sentences remitted. (Signed)."

CJP COMPENSATED SHARIFs:

From above it was evident that Sharif brothers had left the country under a deal and had voluntarily surrendered their properties to the NAB but after their return in 2007, the Sharifs had filed an appeal before a division bench of the Lahore High Court, contending that since the corruption cases against them had been disposed of, their properties should be released.

[The court consequently ordered the release of their properties on 4th October 2011 besides asking NAB to return property documents of the Sharif family, which were seized in 2001 to recover fine imposed on Nawaz Sharif in two cases; the NAB challenged the LHC decision in the apex court.

A three-member bench of the Supreme Court of Pakistan, headed by Chief Justice Iftikhar M Chaudhry, on 18th January 2012 ordered the release of seized assets of the Sharif brothers by dismissing the National Accountability Bureau (NAB)'s appeal and upholding the decision of the Lahore High Court (LHC). During the hearing, the court held that 'NAB cannot take over Sharifs' property against the punishment. NAB had no right to seize their property'.]

The Lahore High Court and the Supreme Court were able to understand that in the above 'mercy appeal' Gen Musharraf had categorically recommended only the remission of imprisonment sentences and not the punishments of fine or confiscation of the property. The then President Rafiq Tarar had also agreed with Chief Executive's advice while remitting the imprisonment sentences under Art 45 of the Constitution and nothing more. But as the apex judiciary wanted to oblige the Sharifs so they used their prerogative. The PPP government alleged that the CJP wanted to compensate Sharifs in the name of 'independent judiciary'

[The NAB's prosecutor K K Agha placed all the above metioned documents before the apex court on 18th January 2012 again but allegedly the CJP Iftikhar Chaudhry discarded them for unknown reasons.

The media roared that:

> 'The CJP wanted to oblige the Sharifs, he did so and upheld the LHC's decision. Judiciary has gone independent in Pakistan; the decisions would be taken at the sweet will of the judges, may not be on facts. Paying back the blessings of March 2009's long march was not over yet; though it was the lawyer's show not of Sharifs, they were the beneficiaries of the fall out.']

Nawaz Sharif himself, once talking to the Geo News from Germany on 22nd August 2007, (a day before the apex court announced its 23rd August 2007 verdict) had spoken on the deal documents produced in the court by the government. He had used diplomatic phrases saying that:

> 'General Musharraf is blackmailing and threatening us by presenting fake and fraud documents in the Supreme Court to keep us from returning to Pakistan. The entire government drama is meant to blackmail us and the entire nation. **However, I do acknowledge that there was an understanding with the Saudi Arabian government** at that time, but I can't reveal that because it is a very sensitive issue.'

Such blatant lie was not expected from a politician of such high stature like Nawaz Sharif who had been the prime minister of a country twice. He forgot then that the mercy petition of condoning punishments dated 9th December 2000 was not only signed by him but also other three respectable members of his family. On the same day Gen Musharraf had written his recommendatory remarks over it and then got approved from PML(N)'s own slave president Rafiq Tarar using his powers under Art 45 of the Constitution. The official record was to be maintained in the President's Secretariat, Attock Jail from where Sharif family was released and GHQ as Gen Musharraf was the Army Chief then too.

If those documents could be fraud or concocted then think about the Pakistani judiciary on the same footing too.

In a *live TV program of ARY News dated 19th January 2012*, the veteran lawyer Asma Jahangir, the former president of the Supreme Court Bar Association, had opined that:

> 'The apex court's decision can also be wrong. In the past history the Supreme Court's many decisions were wrong. Still they are behaving differently by targeting only one 'corrupt person' [pointing towards Mr Zardari] and has not questioned even a single other known corrupt politician for justice. Is he the only corrupt man in Pakistan and no one else?'

PML(N)'s Senator Mushahidullah Khan told the viewers that *'Nawaz Sharif's whole kingdom of wealth is genuine wherever it lies in Pakistan or abroad (?). Nawaz Sharif's business in London is being looked after by his son to whom he [Nawaz Sharif] had given 1.5-2 billion rupees from his own savings.'* Afzal Chan, a parliamentarian from the PPP, also present in program, had questioned that why the Supreme Court was not inquiring into that 'golden process' under which a shopkeeper of Brandreth Road Lahore was able to foster billions of pounds in UK and elsewhere just in ten years.

The intelligentsia stands nowhere to comment upon the judgment of the Supreme Court but, in their opinion, the CJP Iftikhar Chaudhry could have handled the case in another honourable way to enhance the respect and prestige of the apex court. The appeal was launched in the court just in December 2011 and it was assigned so much priority that it was fixed for 18th of January 2012 and was decided in the first hearing and that too by the CJP himself. Already there prevails an impression that the CJP Iftikhar Chaudhry leaves no stone unturned to please the Sharifs whenever an occasion arises to reciprocate the March 2009's long march gesture after which the defunct judiciary was reinstated. There were numerous more examples to quote in that regard.

Had the said appeal be heard in routine and through any other bench, the result might have been the same but at least the Supreme Court could have avoided itself from finger pointing and undue criticism.

The insiders also felt smilingly that on the same day of 18th January 2012, the CJP Iftikhar Chaudhry had very graciously ordered *'to postpone for indefinite period another old case file praying for disqualification of Nawaz Sharif.'* The said petition was placed before the Supreme Court by one Iqbal Jaffery Advocate in 1990 and still waiting for hearing since 22 years. In the petition it was then prayed that:

• Nawaz Sharif had sent his ill-gotten wealth worth billions in foreign countries.

• Nawaz Sharif had allotted state lands in an illegal way.

Thus he [Nawaz Sharif] was no more 'honest' as per definition given in the constitution. He should be disqualified and should be barred to contest elections for the rest of his life; it was prayed.

The CJP Justice Chaudhry once again sent the file to the cold room for an indefinite period saying that *'the cover page of the said file is missing'*. Pakistani Justice-hurray!

JAPAN'S LOAN [YEN 32 b]: NO CLUE?

Let us take another count in this regard.

Referring to *'the News' dated 21st December 2009*, the PML(N) had categorically contradicted a similar news report then appeared in the media in the aftermath of the Supreme Court's decision on NRO on 16th December that there were outstanding bank liabilities against Sharif brothers. It was maintained by PML(N) leaders that:

'They were not the defaulters of any bank in Pakistan and the issue discussed in media pertained to the settling of financial liabilities through handing over of valuable properties to the high court under mutual agreement with the banks. Even at that time their assets worth Rs:10 billion were in custody of the committee set up by the high court while their total outstanding liabilities were about Rs:2.2 billion only.

During their rule in 1990s, they instead of getting their loans written off, had set an unparalleled example in the political history of Pakistan by surrendering highly valuable assets of his family to the banks. Moreover, no stay order existed from 1999 to 2005 when Gen Musharraf, the President of Pakistan and the CM Punjab Ch Pervaiz Elahi were at liberty to deal with their properties in appropriate manner.'

The PML(N) maintained that Nawaz Sharif, despite being in power, had decided to surrender his properties to repay the loans otherwise it was an open secret that during the rule of Benazir Bhutto all the commercial banks of the country had been stopped from opening letters of credit of business concerns of Sharif brothers due to which they suffered a loss of billions of rupees and were virtually closed. He said that the Jonathan ship incident was one of the sad reminders of this era.

But from where those assets of Rs:10 billion [as per their own admission and that too in Pakistan only] gathered in Sharifs till 1999. Sort out the link below; a tip of the iceberg!

During the same days, the media brought forward a special report once published in the **'South Asia Tribune'** under the title *'Dar defends his Govt in missing Rs:11 billion scam'* saying that Mr Ishaq Dar [the former Finance Minister in the PML Cabinet, then the PML(N)'s Senator in 2006 and once again the Senator of the PML(N) in March 2012] had denied the *SAT* story published on 23rd September 2002 trying to wash out the dirty linen of Sharif's financial schemes.

Mr Dar had known the details that how a Japanese Loan of $250 million taken by PML(N) government in 1998 had mysteriously disappeared and even the military Government had failed to trace it.

The said Japanese loan of $250 million was signed on 27th March 1998 and handled by the then Finance Minister Sartaj Aziz but later looked after by Ishaq Dar, the new Finance Minister from November 1998. The fact remains that all sums, whether loans or other receipts, of the Federal Government were to be taken in the Federal Consolidated Fund under the provisions of Article 78(1) of the Constitution of Pakistan. This amount of Yen 32 Billion was a Structural Adjustment Loan to be spent [along with Counterpart Fund in Pak rupees] at projects approved under the Public Sector Development Program (PSDP), as mutually agreed between the GoP & Japan.

The State Bank of Pakistan (SBP) had converted the said loan amount into Pak rupees amounting Rs:10.94 billion. The above mentioned amount remained throughout with the SBP as part of the Consolidated Fund but in papers only and was never transferred to Federal Government's Accounts till at least 12th October 1999.

Nawaz Sharif had once launched 'Qarz Utaro Mulk Sanwaro' Scheme (National Debt Retirement Program or NDRP) in February 1997 and had the following three components:

- An outright donation with no payback.

- Qarz-e-Hasna deposits for a minimum period of two years; no interest payments but principal repayments could be taken in Rupees or foreign currency.

- Profit bearing deposits for a minimum period of two years.

All funds in the aforesaid NDRP were directly received in the Federal Government's account with the SBP and the largest receipt was in profit bearing deposits. Inflow of funds under this Scheme virtually stopped in June 1998. The foreign exchange component of this NDRP was never generated or sent to the reserves of the SBP. Instead Nawaz Sharif's Government paid Rs:1.7 billion in 'national debt service' as it was propagated to some media sources. Most of the economists held that if the above said amount [of Rs:1.7 billion] was (really?) paid, it was paid to either Muslim Commercial Bank of Mian Mansha or the National Bank from where the Sharifs and their close friends had taken huge loans against bogus collaterals.

The Pakistani people still do not know that how much amount was totally collected in NDRP and where the rest of the money gone.

On 21st November 2002, **SAT's Correspondent Ahmed Khan,** again replied from Islamabad that perhaps Mr Ishaq Dar was not aware of the fact that OECF [Japan] loan under question was transferred to Pakistan after the SBP had opened a separate "Counterpart Fund Account", already in existence on 27th March 1998 at the time of signing the contract. The amount was never put in the Federal Consolidated Fund as Mr Dar had wrongly claimed. The Auditor General of Pakistan (AGP) had given its findings after audit which was forwarded to the SAP Coordinator Mushtaq Khan by the DG Audit SAP, Shabbir Ahmad Dahar, vide his DO letter No: DGA / SAP-II / FSS Planning / 99 - 2000 dated 21st November 2000, clearly saying that:

'The GoP received a loan of Yen32 billion (equivalent to $250 million or Rs:11 billion) as loan from OECF on 27.3.1998; the amount was to be utilized by 27.3.2000 but the loan was not accounted for. Neither the equivalent amount credited to the Counterpart Fund nor allocation for utilization arranged. [The Audit letter had also recommended that] In view of this serious problem, an in-depth inquiry was inevitable.'

Ishaq Dar's claim that the amount was meant for PSDP was, therefore, not correct. The issue turned serious when the missing of billions was brought to the notice of the Chief Executive Secretariat. The Secretariat through its letter No 689 / Dy Dir (D.1) CES / 2000 dated 27th September 2000 asked the Secretary Planning Fazal Qureshi to immediately submit a report on the bungling done by the previous Government (of Nawaz Sharif). The report submitted later by the Planning Division pointed out to the CE Secretariat that:

'Under the agreement, borrower (GoP) was required to deposit the equivalent in Pakistani rupees in the Counterpart Fund which was opened with the SBP but only Rs:10 million was deposited in the account against Rs:11 billion. The Auditor General of Pakistan has not been able to conduct financial audit of the accounts of schemes or programs under Japan loan in compliance with the loan agreement as Counterpart Fund for the project have not been provided by the Finance Division.'

The Planning Division report was enough to prove that Ishaq Dar was trying to cover up the matter. At a meeting held in Economic Affairs Division (EAD) on 10th June 2000, the provinces had raised hue and cry for non disbursement of Japanese money to them and Mr Dar had no answer except embarrassment.

During ending 2002, the issue of the billions collected under the *"Qarz Utaro, Mulk Sanwaro"* scheme was again raised in the Public Accounts Committee where the Finance Ministry was asked to give details of how much money collected under the scheme had been used for debt retirement. "Not a single penny", came the startling answer from the then Secretary Finance.

History would also remember the event of man-handling of the then SAP Chief, Mr Qizilbash, by Captain Safdar the son in law of the PM Nawaz Sharif and his Political Secretary Muthaq Tahir Kheli, when he was picked from his office and brought to the PM Secretariat where he was physically beaten and made to help the PM and his Finance Minister, Mr Dar to 'cook up' the figures for the record.

Pakistan's history is saturated with such planned episodes; is there any judge or court to take accountability of such events.

(One part of this essay was published at www.pakspectator.com on 20th July 2011 under title: 'A Forgotten Page of Pakistan's History')

(2nd Part of this essay was published at www.Pakspectator.com on 21st January 2012 under Title 'Supreme Court going choosy')

Scenario 49

PAKISTAN: NRO DEAL (2007-09)

In the words of Salahuddin Shoaib dated 21st October 2007 available at internet media:

> 'In 1987, Benazir married Asif Ali Zardari, little known then for anything but a passion for polo with huge social and financial differences by family backgrounds; Zardari's family was of modest means with limited holdings and a rundown movie theatre named Bombino Cinema in Karachi. Zardari's only experience of higher education was a stint at a commercial college in London. In part, the marriage was intended to protect Benazir's political career by countering conservative Muslims' complaints about her unmarried status.'

In 1988, Benazir Bhutto became Pakistan's first female Prime Minister when Gen Ziaul Huq was killed in a plane crash but twenty months later she was dismissed by President Ghulam Ishaq Khan (GIK) on grounds of corruption and misrule. When Benazir Bhutto took office as 2nd time prime minister in 1993, Asif Zardari became her alter ego; though having no formal powers until PM Benazir appointed him Investment Minister in July 1996 but he was otherwise every thing. Since first day in the PM House Zardari exploited arms contracts; power plant projects; the privatization of state-owned industries; the granting of export licenses for rice & cotton; the purchase of planes for PIA; the assignment of textile export quotas; the granting of oil and gas permits; permits to build sugar mills, sale of government lands and many defense procurement deals like Agosta submarines. Benazir Bhutto had to assign approvals but by writing orders on yellow Post-It notes and attaching them to official files. After the deals were completed, the notes were removed, destroying all traces of involvement. No formal agreements were signed, no written sanctions or orders issued.

COTECNA & SGS SHIPMENT DEALS:

During Benazir Bhutto's first term, Pakistan entrusted pre-shipment 'verification' of all major imports to two Swiss companies with blue-ribbon reputations, Societe Generale de Surveillance SA [SGS] and a subsidiary, Cotecna Inspection SA. The service was quickly turned to generating profits for the Bhutto family's accounts, as both the companies got into making fabulous amount of cash by issuing certificate on under invoicing and sharing the profit with the politicians in power. During her 2nd term, Benazir Bhutto revived the same contracts with the same two companies. This time the deal went in black & white by negotiating 'commissions' totaling 9% to three offshore companies controlled by Asif Ali Zardari and Nusrat Bhutto [Benazir's mother].

A Cotecna letter of June 1994 had stated:

> 'Should we receive, within six months of today, a contract for inspection and price verification of goods imported into Pakistan, we will pay you 6% of the total amount invoiced and paid to the government of Pakistan for such a contract and during the whole duration of that contract and its renewal.'

Similar letters were sent by SGS in March & June 1994, promising 'consultancy fees of 6% and 3%' to two other offshore companies controlled by the Bhutto family.

The NAB report contained that the two Swiss companies had dealt in for about $15.4 billion in imports into Pakistan from January 1995 to March 1997, making more than $131 million. Zardari + Bhutto family's off-shore companies made $11.8 million from the deals. For SGS, with 35,000 employees and more than $2 billion a year in earnings, the relationship with the Bhutto family had been painful.

Benazir Bhutto's two terms in office had brought a range of overseas properties to her husband like the Rockwood, a 355-acre estate south of London and a $2.5 million country manor in Normandy (known as House of the White Queen in France) in the names of Hakim Ali Zardari and Zarrin Zardari, Benazir Bhutto's parents-in-law. Others included a string of luxury apartments in London, a country club and a polo ranch in Palm Beach County, Florida (worth about $4 million then); all were bought by them in 1990s.

The innocent PPP workers always discarded accusations against Benazir Bhutto & Mr Zardari as a frame-up but the educated lot started changing their opinion when the incorruptible Swiss federal prosecutors once announced that the two PPP leaders had hidden at least 20 million Swiss francs (till 2011 it was $1.5 billion as per French Press) made from money laundering, illegal payoffs, and possibly drug dealing in their accounts in Geneva. Benazir Bhutto herself was once worried saying that:

'Few people believed the Pakistani government charges until the Swiss investigation but that [Swiss prosecutor's statement] changed everything.'

These accusations of massive bribery and drug dealing had caused pain to Benazir's many ardent supporters in Washington and the western media, whom she was seeking to enlist to her cause; gave her the cold shoulders. It was a significant loss for her future plans in politics.

In nut shell, during their two terms of rule, Benazir Bhutto & Asif Ali Zardari, had acquired cash and property worth a few hundred million dollars mostly located in Europe and Middle East. Some sharp person had stolen the 'concerned' documents from the Geneva office of Jens Schlegelmilch, Bhutto's family's attorney in Europe since 20 years and a close personal friend. The said documents were sold to 'somebody' [in Pakistan's High Commission London] for $one million cash. The documents included: statements for several Citibank accounts in Dubai and Geneva; letters from executives promising payoffs, details of the percentages to be claimed; notes of meetings where 'commissions & remunerations' were agreed on, records of the offshore companies used as fronts in the deals mostly registered in the British Virgin Islands, their business deposits in UK's Barclay's Bank and Union Bank of Switzerland as well as Citibank in Dubai, New York and Geneva etc.

Those documents were actually bargained by Gen Musharraf's front officer; which were ultimately transferred to GHQ for study and future consumption. When on American pressure, the General finally agreed to negotiate with Benazir Bhutto; he had all the details of those documents in mind thus had an upper hand.

Being convicted during Nawaz Sharif's era, Benazir Bhutto had lost her right to run for politics and thus her extensive personal property in Pakistan. By signing a secret understanding with Gen Musharraf, Benazir was not only able to re-attain her right to be in politics but also going to bury all corruption charges, proved by the NAB authorities.

Even before the Supreme Court ruled on 28th September 2007 that the presidential election should go ahead as planned, Gen Musharraf had emerged as a political winner. He had successfully taken revenge on Zulfikar Ali Bhutto by destroying the traditional political role of the Pakistan People's Party (PPP), founded in 1967 against a military dictator Gen Ayub Khan. The critics had rightly opined that the PPP would become another PML(Q) to play on the tunes of army Generals putting back their manifesto and traditions built and developed during the last 40 years.

Three decades ago, when Musharraf's father Syed Musharrafuddin was posted in a senior position at the Pakistan's Embassy in Jakarta, the then Prime Minister late Zulfikar Ali Bhutto had allegedly suspended him on the charges of irregularities. Gen Musharraf always hated the senior Bhutto for humiliating his father without solid evidence and declared him a fascist in his book *"In the Line of Fire."* Bhutto was later hanged through a team of handpicked judges of Gen Ziaul Haq in April 1979 with the support of the then US administration. Bhutto's name became a symbol of resistance in Pakistani politics and his death was declared a "judicial murder" by many top international jurists. The history remembered him.

Like former Indian Prime Minister Indira Gandhi and Bangladeshi Prime Minister Sheikh Hasina Wajid, Bhutto's daughter Benazir Bhutto too used the political legacy of her father to become prime minister of Pakistan twice. The hard luck was that she was not allowed to complete her terms on both occasions, and each time her government was dismissed on corruption charges with the active support of some army Generals. Gen Musharraf also kept on declaring Benazir Bhutto a thief for seven years and never allowed her to come back. Her husband Mr Asif Ali Zardari was kept in jail in Karachi on similar charges during that period. During her decade-long exile, Benazir Bhutto had also accused Gen Musharraf of nuclear compromising and supporting terrorism many times.

Benazir Bhutto had gone so deep in accusing the army regime that she preferred to join hands with her old political rival Nawaz Sharif who had caused her exile when she got convicted from the courts. During her nine years exile, Benazir had also accused Gen Musharraf on his dubious reservations for nuclear policy. Most of the corruption charges against Benazir Bhutto were initially made public by her own Brutus named Farooq Leghari in 1996, (who was sent to the presidency by Benazir Bhutto herself). The same charges were afterwards developed, extended and comprehensively trumpeted by Nawaz Sharif and his aide senator Saif ur Rehman when they assumed power in February 1997.

AGENCIES BROKERED THE NRO DEAL:

Hats off to Major Gen Nadeem Taj of the ISI who had initiated talks with the PPP in 2005 to break the possible alliance of the PPP &

PML(N). These talks were followed and continued by Lt Gen Ashfaq Parvez Kayani who was the DG ISI then. Their efforts materialised and the anti-establishment credentials of the PPP were buried by the Pakistan Army on 5th October 2007, by an ordinance through which Gen Musharraf, though having all the Swiss documents in mind, pardoned Benazir Bhutto from all the corruption charges levelled against her.

It was a soothing breeze for Benazir Bhutto brought by some people like Rehman Malik around her who remained constantly in touch with the establishment. Mr Malik played this game sincerely or with bad intentions but he had no experience of doing bargains in political situations though his efforts prevailed. Tariq Aziz, the closest aide of Gen Musharraf was also in contact with Mr Malik since 2000 at least. In this game, they all protected the interest of Gen Musharraf more than Benazir Bhutto or the PPP and forced her to accept the conditions of establishment without any political achievement. *Not a single political demand of Benazir Bhutto was accepted by Gen Musharraf.* She only got some personal relief for herself and for her husband.

There were three main items on agenda when Gen Musharraf and Benazir Bhutto met each other in Dubai on one fine Friday of ending July 2007:

1. Gen Musharraf would not be in uniform when PPP comes in power after election.

2. Article 58(2)(b) would not remain in force throughout the PPP's governance.

3. Gen Musharraf would allow amendment in the constitution for the PM to enable Benazir Bhutto holding premiership for the third time.

Despite her tall claims, PPP's exhaustive statements and their best efforts, Benazir Bhutto could not make Gen Musharraf agree to any of the three points. Gen Musharraf's uniform was to stay there as such till his own discretion. Article 58(2)(b) was to prevail in the constitution as presidential prerogative. Even her wish to take over the premiership for the third time was not acceded to straightaway but with a promise of positive consideration once Benazir would land in Pakistan; even then she agreed to make a deal.

Pakistan's spy masters had done the whole exercise with a key goal in their minds that Ms Bhutto would be given a toast of 'constitutional facility' to become a third time prime minister and her parliamentary colleagues would, in turn, choose him as President for another term of five years. However, if at all Benazir Bhutto wanted to achieve any of the above objectives, there was only one way open for her. It was through general elections and after getting two third majority in the Parliament. She needed at least 256 votes in a house of 342 for changing the laws relating with Art 58(2)(b) and a third term for a prime minister. *PPP's top legal expert Aitzaz Ahsan was of the view that Gen Musharraf was actually trying to destroy the credibility of Benazir Bhutto through an ordinance, which was against the constitution.* Any time it was subjected to challenge in the superior courts.

[*The subsequent political developments proved so. Even if she would be alive, her chances of becoming a third time prime minister would have been remote because a two-third majority from the National Assembly was needed to enable her enjoy the slot.*]

Despite all the shortcomings, the NRO was promulgated on 5ᵗʰ October 2007. At that time PPP's Chairperson Benazir Bhutto was facing a number of National Accountability Bureau (NAB) cases, one of which was popularly known as the 'ARY Gold Reference'. Another case against her was commonly known as the 'Assets Case'. According to the prosecution, she had filed a miss-declaration of assets before the Election Commission for the 1988 elections and failed to submit complete details of assets she owned. The most importantly she was also facing charges for the alleged commissions taken from SGS & Cotecna (as detailed in the beginning) through offshore companies. In this case, the Swiss government had once decided to continue prosecuting the case despite the government of Pakistan's withdrawal.

Oil for Food Program Scandal:

The actual game had taken start much earlier. An extract from *'Daily Times' of 31st May 2007* is placed below as food for thought:

'When Rehman Malik fled to UK and claimed asylum in the year 2000, he managed to come much closer to Benazir Bhutto in London. His office in Crown House at North Circular Road used to be a hub of such political and business activities in which Benazir Bhutto's finances were being invested. Numerous local and off-shore companies floated jointly by them for various activities including one named 'Petro-line'. Its office was also linked or opened in Vienna city of Austria to streamline money transactions originated from Swiss accounts of Benazir Bhutto.

As per news appeared in the media, the National Accountability Bureau (NAB) had withdrawn their complaint from a Swiss court allegedly because of lack of evidence, concerning a $150 million corruption case against former PM Benazir Bhutto and two others, Rehman Malik and S Jaffari [they were made directors of the company].

Lawyers hired from Spain had filed an application in the Swiss court stating that NAB no longer wished to be a party to the case. The court accepted the application but continued with the case proceedings. The NAB application had stated that the company allegedly used in the $150 million scam of 'UN Oil for Food Program' scandal, was registered at Dubai in the name of 'Petro Line' [having name of Mr Zardari as the key figure]. Ms Bhutto was the managing director of the company whereas Mr Malik and Mr Jaffari were the directors.

A NAB team under Bureau's Deputy Chairman Hassan Wasim Afzal had spent millions of dollars investigating the case. The withdrawal of the case was a clear indication that the government and Ms Bhutto had reached a 'deal' for a future game in Pakistan's politics.'

The NRO was promulgated by Gen Musharraf's just one day before his presidential election; but interestingly, before his deposition on 3rd November 2007 Chief Justice Iftikhar Chaudhry had issued a stay order against the NRO on two petitions challenging it and had directed the authorities that no relief could be offered to anyone under this controversial law till the final disposal of petitions. CJP Chaudhry was dethroned. The new CJP A Hameed Dogar's Supreme Court had vacated the stay order and allowed the beneficiaries of the NRO to get relief.

The beneficiaries of NRO got relief but both the petitions remained there pending final decision. PPP came in power in early 2008. It was a fatal mistake and rather incapability of PPP's ruling elite including Mr Zardari that they did not bother to get those two petitions decided in their favour despite the fact that their pro-PPP CJP A Hameed Dogar remained in chair for complete one year. It also happened by chance that PPP leaders in the then Sindh Assembly of Gen Musharraf's regime; Nisar Khuhro, Murad Ali Shah and Saleem Hingoro were accused of beating a government MP who had insulted a PPP's lady MPA by passing her a 'friendly' note in the House with objectionable remarks over the PPP-military relations.

Mr Zardari, was also a beneficiary from NRO as he was facing four cases in Sindh. These included a famous smuggling case commonly known as the 'Container Case'; the murder cases of Mir Murtaza Bhutto and his seven supporters, the double murder case of Justice Nizam Ahmed & his son Nadeem Ahmed and the murder case of one Alam Baloch, the former Secretary Food of Sindh. Benazir Bhutto's father-in-law, Hakim Ali Zardari, was facing at least two cases before Karachi's Accountability Court. Benazir Bhutto's sister-in-law Faryal Talpur's husband, Mir Munawar Talpur, was facing cases before the Hyderabad Anti-Corruption Court. He was an MP and was a minister in the CM Abdullah Shah's cabinet.

NAB had made out a list of about 50 for the politicians, bureaucrats and businessmen involved in different corruption cases who could stand to benefit from the NRO. They could include former provincial minister for excise and taxation Agha Siraj Durani, Chaudhry Sharif of FIA, NDFC's former Chairman M B Abbasi, former Chairman of the Employees Old Age Benefits Institute Shaikh Barkatullah, former Chairman of the Hyderabad Cantonment Board Riazur Rehman Hashmi, an officer of the same board Badar Alam Bachani, former General Manager of the Port Qasim Authority Irshad Ahmed Sheikh, former Director General of the Agriculture Extensions Malik Akram and former Director of the Export Promotion Bureau Nayyar Barri . Most cases had stemmed out from political rivalries between the PPP and the PML but the military government brewed benefit out of them.

Other PPP leaders facing cases of corruption or misuse of authority included former Sindh Law Minister Pir Mazharul Haq and former federal minister Syed Khursheed Shah. Former Sindh Assembly Speaker Syed Muzaffar Hussain Shah and former Chief Minister Syed Ghous Ali of Nawaz Sharif's PML(N) were also there to face the NAB cases, again mostly political. Some bureaucrats accused of swindling public money or granting land allegedly at throwaway prices were also facing trial. Former Secretaries Ramesh Udeshi, Salman Farooqui and former Chairman Pakistan Steel Mills Usman Farooqui [father of PPP's advisor Sharmila Farooqi] were also some of the accused in such cases allegedly for financial corruption but more due to their political affiliations with the PPP.

The beneficiaries from Balochistan included former prime minister Mir Zafarullah Jamali, who faced corruption allegations in the Kech Flour Mills scandal, former Chief Minister Mir Jan Mohamed Jamali, dozens of former ministers, some sitting ministers and former members of the parliament. Jam Yusuf also faced serious corruption charges when he was the Chairman of the District Council; all ill conceived on political grounds.

A former Chief Minister, two federal ministers and a provincial minister were to benefit from the NRO in Punjab. Though not claimed but were likely to get benefit from the NRO included former Chief Minister Punjab Shahbaz Sharif; PPP's Secretary General Jahangir Badar for illegal appointments and illegal assets; former Principal Secretary to Bhuttos Ahmad Sadiq; ex-MNAs Abdul Hameed, Mian Rashid, Rana Nazir; ex-MPAs Tariq Anees, Chaudhry Zulfiqar and his business partner and former NWFP MP Haji Kabir.

Amongst the bureaucrats, mostly there were such who became victims of the political change during the second tenure of PM Nawaz Sharif. When he assumed power in early 1997, he immediately got prepared a list of 87 bureaucrats who remained engaged in digging out the ill gotten wealth of Nawaz Sharif and his family members. Numerous cases were registered starting that how from an ordinary foundry to the biggest industrial giant of Pakistan, the Sharifs had travelled along. The main cases were Rs:21 billions right off by Gen Ziaul Haq, siphoning of Rs:5.6 billions from Motorway Project and more as per reports of the Public Accounts Committee in ending 1980s.

Amongst the bureaucrats made retired or dismissed, then arrested and sent to jails or to Accountability Cell's secret 'Drawing Rooms' to undergo third degree treatments under the able guidance and control of Mian Saif ur Rehman were Rahman Malik, facing two cases before Accountability Court IV in Rawalpindi; Inam R Sehri who had completed investigations against Sharif's corruption in Motorway Scandal, Ittefaq Foundries, Hudaibya Paper Mills etc; Sajjad Hyder for making reports on behalf of Rehman Malik and keeping record of all cases concerning Sharifs; Saad ullah Khan and Rahat Naseem Income Tax Commissioners for doing tax-related investigations against Sharifs; Akhtar H Jaffery of FIA for doing investigations of 'Import of scrap scandals' of Sharifs, Ejaz Chaudhry for doing investigations of MCB's loans given to only those industries who were to buy sugar machinery from Ittefaq Foundry only and many more.

Of course, there were former bureaucrats with tainted reputation also like Salman Farooqi & Usman Farooqi; Personal Staff Officer Siraj Shams-ud-Din; former finance secretary Talat Javed; former NBP president & Chairman NDFC M B Abbasi etc but they were able to get even better slots in compensation [as their price] from the PPP's government after take over of Zardari as president in August 2008.

Gen Musharraf's Interior Minister and former confidant of Benazir Bhutto, Aftab Sherpao; Water and Power Minister Liaqat Jatoi; Federal

Ministers Faisal Saleh Hayat & Nilofer Bakhtiar and others; some of them were formally sentenced by the Accountability Courts but were offered attractive and the most lucrative slots in the cabinet of that military regime for obvious reasons; just to buy the PPP persons turning against Ms Bhutto.

There were two intimates of (late) Pir Pagaro who were also to be the beneficiaries of that amnesty. They were former CM Sindh and the speaker of the provincial assembly, Muzaffar Hussain Shah, and former provincial minister Islamud Din Sheikh. There were around 26 corruption cases against Mr Sheikh. He had entered into a plea bargain with the NAB in a number of cases. One or two cases against Sheikh were alive and he was on bail at the time of NRO. They were, of course given benefits for unknown reasons by the NAB chiefs then.

PML(N) leader Mian Shahbaz Sharif were also to be benefited from that amnesty as there were three corruption references against him then pending with the accountability court in Rawalpindi though he afterwards claimed himself innocent. May be files had moved away or the courts might have been 'toned down' to throw out the cases as has been the PML's old tested policy.

Over two-third members of the federal cabinet in Gen Musharraf's regime were firmly opposed to the clinching of National Reconciliation Ordinance (NRO) as a result of deal between Gen Musharraf and Benazir Bhutto. In an informal cabinet meeting chaired by Prime Minister Shaukat Aziz in October 2007, only 13 out of total 46 ministers raised their hands in favour of the NRO. An equal number supported lifting of ban on two times prime minister serving for the third term. However, 20 ministers had approved an overall deal with Benazir Bhutto while 26 opposed it.

Nawaz Sharif and his associates had though condemned the NRO, none of them or their party had shown the guts to challenge the shameful ordinance in the court of law if they were really against it. Mere condemnation was nothing but politics while the reality was that the PML(N) leadership was also the beneficiary of the amnesty. If the Sharifs wanted to come clean on the issue and were sincere to face the cases against them in the court of law then what prevented them to knock the door of the superior judiciary to undo the amnesty as they did in ending 2011 on memo-gate issue.

The Sharifs and the members of the Redco group, Senator Saifur Rehman & associates, were shouting loud because rogue judges like

Malik Qayyum had given them the clean chit in the first six months of their governance in 1997 closing all those cases which were investigated, proved and placed before the courts for trial by the FIA's teams subsequently sent home in 87 bureaucrats list.

If one analyse the whole pendency of NAB cases, he would be surprised to know that in NAB the entire lot of politician's cases are related with those who were associated with the PPP and only two files were concerned with PML(N)'s politicians because Nawaz Sharif was angry with them [Gaus Ali Shah & Muzaffar H Shah of Sindh]. **Can one imagine that in politician class only PPP's members were corrupt and rest of all including PML(N), PML(Q), Fazal ur Rehman's JUI and retired Generals cum politicians and their sons were saints, *waliullahs*, seraphs and angels.**

It was the jugglery of Justice Malik Qayyum and Saifur Rehman Ehtesab that NAB & Accountability Courts have been living on PPP's cases only since the last twelve years; look at these parasites.

NRO FAILED IN PARLIAMENT:

Going into orderly details of the NRO; the CJP Iftikhar Chaudhry assumed office again in March 2009 and the court work started in routine. It was the decision of the Supreme Court of Pakistan dated 31st July 2009 which turned the tables in Pakistan politics. According to this decision the entire 'Emergency' announced on 3rd November 2007 by Gen Musharraf and its all associated steps were declared unlawful.

NRO of 5th October 2007 was also included in the list of those 34 ordinances, issued by the military dictator, which were to be placed before the Parliament to give them shape of a proper act otherwise would stand nullified. The Supreme Court had given 120 days for getting through those ordinances and the last date of approval by the Parliament was worked out as 28th November 2009. The PPP government tried to table the NRO for approval in the Parliament through a standing committee but could not come up to the level of discussion or voting so was finally withdrawn. Reasons were manifold.

The PPP had not enough strength of MsNA and senators with them. First of all it was their coalition political party Muttihida Qaumi Movement (MQM) which announced that they would not favour this black law in the Parliament. PML(N), another coalition party in Punjab, but was then extending cooperation to the PPP in the centre, openly announced to reject the NRO if placed before the Parliament. After two weeks the JUI, another coalition partner of the PPP also defected.

Another game was played within the PPP. A group of staunch workers, but big stake holders in party like Senator Safdar Abbasi, Naheed Khan and others, under the able guidance of Barrister Aitzaz Ahasan and allegedly with secret backing of the sitting Prime Minister Mr Gilani, openly held press conferences, issued media statements and appeared in live TV talk shows to display that NRO should go. This group of influential politicians candidly made demands of resignations from those cabinet members [*mostly aiming at Rehman Malik being considered trespasser and intruder in the party*] who were among the beneficiaries of NRO. Result was obvious. The PPP, instead of taking it through, abandoned it in the Speaker's office, never followed it and calmly waited for 28th November 2009 till its natural death.

At the same time Gen Musharraf, who was the main person to propagate this evil, had admitted his "mistake" saying that his decision to promulgate the NRO was wrong. Answering the questions on his 'facebook' website he wrote:

> *"The one clarification that I will make is that I committed this mistake on the strong advice of the political leadership at that time [pointing towards PML(Q)], who now blatantly disowns connections with it. My interest was only national, with absolutely no personal bias or agenda. He would keep a more detailed response pending for the time being because of certain political sensitivities. However, I promise that I would take the nation on board at the appropriate time.*
>
> *NRO may have allowed Asif Zardari or corrupt politicians to contest elections, but it certainly was not the cause of their coming to power. NRO is not responsible for electing the PPP as the majority party or allowing Asif Zardari to win an election. NRO is not responsible for corrupt politicians sitting in assemblies or being appointed as ministers."*

SC'S VERDICT ON THE NRO:

The decision of the Supreme Court dated 16th December 2009, setting aside the NRO from the day of its promulgation was generally hailed by the Pakistani public at large and particularly applauded, highly praised and much admired by *Jamaat e Islami* and both major factions of PML. Articles were written in the newspapers and TV programmes were anchored on all private channels appreciating to the extent of flattery and showing their strength to the Supreme Court and its judges. All cannons of criticism were aimed at firing or at least mud slinging on Mr Zardari and Rehman Malik.

However, there were very powerful voices from the intelligentsia who may otherwise be happy with the result but were critic over methodology or the way the issue was tackled. For example, the Chairperson of Human Rights Commission of Pakistan (HRCP) Asma Jahangir said:

> *"The Supreme Court in its verdict on NRO has targeted the whole democratic structure by extending its power and crossing the constitutional limits. Independence of judiciary means they should be seen as impartial; independence means when they give judgment there should be reasoning for it; basically two things do not suit the Supreme Court i.e. being one-sided or giving a constitutional decision which is a bit controversial.*
>
> *The movement against dictator Musharraf was launched because he did not respect separation of power and attacked the judiciary, whereas in its NRO verdict the judiciary, too, has made a sort of attack on the legislature and extended its own jurisdiction.*
>
> *Thus, (referring to the removal of DG FIA Tariq Khosa by the government and issuance of Notice for Contempt of Court to the Minister of Interior asking him to explain that why Tariq Khosa has been transferred) assuming all power is a dangerous trend, no matter PPP remains in power or not. Judiciary can ask the government to remove a person who is not working properly, but it cannot ask for appointment of a specific person of its choice.*
>
> *One should not ignore the NRO verdict's political fallout and marginalising of political forces. The judiciary has crossed its limits and it is a dangerous precedent that the Supreme Court passed a verdict on parliamentarians' morality, more surprisingly through a unanimous verdict, showing that all 17 judges had the same judicial mind."*

(Ref: 'the News' dated 23rd December 2009)

Both the above views speak about two different aspects of the issue; both are self explanatory and guide us to peep into the visions of decision makers. It also points out towards the 'betrayal' of our PML(Q) leadership who were the guides of Gen Musharraf and a propelling force for NRO when they were in saddles of the government in 2007. When they felt that the Supreme Court was going to throw it out of their corridors, they immediately changed their stance and started speaking against the NRO to attract the sympathies of the general populace.

On the other hand the *PML(N), whose commanding leadership went abroad after signing a same kind of NRO in December 2000 with the same army dictator Gen Musharraf*, accepting many humiliating, mortifying and embarrassing conditions of not taking part in politics for ten years etc, when came back to Pakistan in 2007 using Benazir Bhutto's NRO as fulcrum, turned around and became flag bearers of Judiciary's 'just decision' against the same NRO. What a character of our political parties.

On 16th December 2009, the SC set aside the NRO for which the PPP suffered a lot and would continue to suffer for another decade or two; hats off to the PPP's advisors like Rehman Malik & Babar Awan.

In early December 2011, government's review petition on NRO was also declined by the apex court. In January 2012 it was expecting reports on the implementation of its judgment; more serious issue than the Memo-gate scandal. Aitzaz Ahsan's assessment came true. The same happened as he had predicted. When the Supreme Court had dismissed the National Reconciliation Ordinance (NRO), the PPP and especially Mr Zardari & his close associates lost their credibility; still the humiliation is going on.

LOAN DEFAULTERS' CASE:

Let us see the other side of the coin:

Gen Musharraf's military government, immediately after the 12th October 1999's coup, had launched an intensive drive against the loan eaters who were given one month ending in mid November 1999 to voluntarily return their loans. As per government's report, a recovery of Rs:8 billion [6% of the actual base defaulted amount] was made out of Rs:146 billion. The then Governor SBP, Mukhtar Nabi Qureshi, had told that about 325 defaulters owe more than Rs:100 million each amounting to Rs:72 billion. About 590 legislators were defaulters of Rs: 9.64 billion mostly of Agricultural Development Bank of Pakistan (ADBP); 263 members were from those who were sent home then.

In November 1999, the National Accountability Bureau (NAB) was entrusted to recover the loans from the defaulters; they had arrested some of them mostly feudal, politicians, a few retired army officers and former bureaucrats. The list included Legharis, Saigols, Dreshaks, Khokhars, Kakars, Magsis, Mians, Rehmans and Farooquis. Jaffar Leghari [a suspended senator] and Malik Asad Khan, two close relatives of former President Farooq Leghari, who had been crying for a non-discriminatory accountability at the top of his voice, were also among those who were nabbed by the NAB.

In the beginning, Gen Musharraf's team was impartial thus former CM Punjab Manzoor Wattoo and former federal ministers Anwar Saifullah & Faisal Saleh Hayat were also arrested along with one former Air Marshal Viqar Azim. It was perhaps the first time in Pakistan's history that such a forceful crackdown had been launched against wilful loan defaulters but then the compromises, nepotism, deals and negotiations empowered; NAB became another FIA of Rehman Malik's era for friends and foes. Many arrested MsNA & MsPAs were given ministerial slots and that NAB game continued for another eight years.

Referring to the *'Express Tribune' of 18th June 2010,* a three member bench of the Supreme Court headed by the CJP Iftikhar M Chaudry heard the loan defaulters case and remarked that *'the apex court wants to hear the case as it involves public money of Rs:256 billion'.* The Supreme Court sought the details of people who got their loans written off in the duration between 1971 and 2009.

The whole nation knew that the superior courts were never solemn in taking that case seriously throughout the last sixty years. During the hearing of the NRO case in December 2009, the apex court was pointed out that it should also take cognizance of those corrupt politicians who had eaten up the poor people's savings worth billions in the name of bank loans then got waived off. The Supreme Court had ordered then to produce the lists of loan defaulters *'since 1971, we'll see'.* The apex court's orders of 12th December 2009 are on record.

May not be based on facts but the PPP had publicized on media that the judgment of 16th December 2009 on NRO was hastily announced because it was mainly against the PPP and Mr Zardari in person. The loan defaulter's list was placed before the apex Court on 22nd December 2009, but deferred because SC's dear party members like Sharifs were named in the list; purposefully spread that due to them the CJP Iftikhar Chaudhry was there in saddles. It was merely a perception in which judiciary's shoulder was used to bear the gun; the future time would reveal the facts. The court, however, directed the SBP to provide details of all the loan cases being heard by the banking courts; adjourned the hearing till 2nd August 2010 without recording any progress. Time went on.

In the 3rd week of October 2010 during another hearing, the CJP's serious warning was that *'those who had their loans written off have built empires. If they don't pay back the loans, their names should be put on the exit control list (ECL) and they be put behind bars.'* Nothing doing till today; Pakistan's superior courts are known for such gimmicks.

The State Bank's counsel, Iqbal Haider, produced a list of 50 defaulter companies and one Barrister MS Baqir apprised the court that Indus Sugar, a company owned by former MPA of the PML(Q) Nasrullah Dareshak, had Rs:820 million in loans written off through eight different banks upon which, the court summoned Mr Dareshak to the court on next hearing. Nothing happened in the next hearing as usual. The fact was that the State Bank had never become interested in getting the money back but always preferred to defend the loan defaulters.

A Senior lawyer Hafeez Pirzada contended that the present PPP government had written-off loans worth Rs:50 billion without any authority, adding that the move was also endorsed by the Executive Director of the State Bank, Inayat Hussain declaring that it was part of an ongoing scheme. [*The State Bank had issued a total of 33 circulars since 1972 to 2007 in that respect.*]

Astonishingly, the State Bank did not have the details of all companies and individuals concerned, the CJP went furious and remarked that if the banks concerned did not share the information, why their licenses should not be cancelled and the list containing names of defaulters should be published in newspapers. The CJP had also warned that if they did not pay their loans back, their properties should be confiscated and auctioned and they should be put behind bars in Adiala Jail; but which loan eater bothers for court orders in Pakistan.

It was observed by the court that the State Bank had been ostensibly misused Circular No 29. The said *suo moto* case was initiated on the call of Altaf Hussain of the MQM who had urged that there was a need to give equal rights to everyone to improve the economy and that billions of rupees should not be given for personal benefits of some influential. According to Section 25 of the Banking Ordinance, a loan write off case should be sent to the Parliament but this section had continuously been ignored since decades.

The Chief Justice said that there was a need to enact new laws to give big loans against small securities. Knowingly that the whole Parliament was comprising of the *jageerdars, waderas* and such industrialists who are the proven loan eaters then who would make such laws. If Parliament has not made the required laws in 62 years, the apex court should have made these laws much earlier.

During the 2nd week of March 2011's hearing, the Supreme Court approved the State Bank's request for constituting a commission for loan recovery and sought the opinion of banks and their customers and loan defaulters within four days. The State Bank's governor agreed to form a 3-member commission headed by Justice (retd) Saleem Akhtar. It was proposed that:

> 'The commission should be empowered to impose heavy financial penalties on loan defaulters and to send them behind bars because that is what they are afraid of. Only a powerful commission can ensure that the loans are recovered. Citing Circular 29, it was considered a viable document on banking laws but it has been misused. Banking rules need to be amended through legislation to stop misuse of loans and to increase the number of banking courts.
>
> People don't pay taxes, why would they return their loans.'

[*In Pakistan it is very old and tested technique that if the government or the court wants to thin out some issue, or to detract people's attention from it, or to make the fools forget corruption; make out a commission or committee. The poor people will forget every thing.*]

Hurray! Till today [the last day of March 2012] not a single loan has been recovered; not a single property confiscated, not a single man is jailed or convicted. SC's immediate orders are for the bureaucrats and the PPP while directions of commissions are for PML (N) & (Q) members.

Let us keep on chasing the NRO, why the decision has not been implemented yet.

[*One part of this essay was published at www.Pakspectator.com on 23rd December 2011*]

Scenario 50

JUDICIARY vs ARMY (2007)-III

LAWYERS' PROTESTS AGAINST ELECTIONS:

After **28th September 2007,** when the Supreme Court of Pakistan gave verdict of legitimacy for Gen Musharraf to contest the presidential election in uniform, there was a big chaos in Islamabad. In the office of the Chief Election Commissioner, the nomination papers of Gen Musharraf as a presidential candidate were admitted amidst a big roar of objections filed by the other two main candidates. All the objections were straightaway rejected.

The Constitution Avenue Islamabad on that day presented the scene of a virtual battlefield. The blood of journalists and lawyers soaked the ground who fell victim to the worst-ever brutality of police in the capital's history. All this happened because large contingents of the police, both in uniform and plain clothes, were deployed at the main route of the Constitution Avenue and all the main routs around that day. The lawyers had gathered in front of the Election Commission building where they wanted to protest against the nomination papers of Gen Musharraf for another term in office. Many media persons were there to cover the event.

Marvat Ali Shah, the Police Incharge Islamabad, was himself heading his force at that moment. It was alleged that he had issued orders to target Aitzaz Ahsan, Ali Ahmad Kurd, and others by name but no evidence was there beyond media reports. However the situation worsened when the Police teams manhandled Ali Ahmad Kurd while he was trying to enter the Election Commission building. Aitzaz Ahsan was also there. One stone hit his belly. This infuriated the lawyers who went to argue with the police. Odd situation was there. A group of lawyers, including Zamurrad Khan MNA, managed to drag away Aitzaz Ahsan from the scene.

On that day, the police stopped journalists and media persons to enter the premises of the Election Commission. Some of them were allegedly beaten. As many as 34 media persons and 80 lawyers, including common citizens sustained serious injuries. Earlier, Ali Ahmed Kurd, before moving to the premises of the Election Commission, had burnt the said order (dated 28th September 2007) of the Supreme Court allowing Gen Musharraf to contest the presidential election. He had bitterly criticized the decision of the six judges who had declared the petitions as not maintainable.

29th September 2007: Chief Justice of Pakistan had taken *suo moto* notice of police violence against lawyers, newsmen and representatives of the civil society at Constitution Avenue of Islamabad on a drafted report of his Registrar. The Police and civil administration of Islamabad then held that the Supreme Court had taken notice of the police action just to cover its own misgiving for that black decision, to take away their shame and sorrow and to continue playing with the tunes of army's orchestra; the Supreme Court of Pakistan did another odd.

The lawyers who had raised their voices and hurled shouts at the judges by name; the media members who had torn out the Supreme Court's humiliating orders; the political activists who had burnt the copies of SC's judgment and so many others – all were found noble, innocent, guiltless and blameless but only police was found offender because they were the symbol of authority; because they were easy to be shouted at in the court; because they all religiously attend the court to tender their unconditional apologies; because they help the sheepish courts to 'be known as strong and powerful' and because they are poor and are not able to bring costly pleaders to save their skins. Weigh the strength of the judges calling only the police to answer; hurray Pakistan's judiciary!

Most people understand that why the superior courts behave so; to hide their own embarrassment and regret without realising that history is cruel; keeps track of the events and paints a very ugly picture of some jackals sitting on certain honourable echelons. It was enough to confirm that the higher courts could do anything to please the khaki uniformed people, as ever before, but would shout, scream and screech at poor police just to pretend that they are powerful and arrogant. What a show of power and what degree of cowardice at the same moment — what kind of history they wanted to make. Whom should one blame?

The Court had summoned Secretary Interior, Advocate General Punjab, Chief Commissioner Islamabad, IG Police, DC and SSP Islamabad to appear before the court. They were directed to submit their security plans and FIRs to the court. The Chief Justice had also issued directives to doctors of PIMS and Polyclinic Hospital to submit their reports to the court about patients admitted in their hospitals and nature of their injuries registered during the days of turmoil.

Many people believe that the SC was blackmailed by the 'mighty intelligence agencies' of Pakistan to get the 28th September's judgment in favour of Gen Musharraf. News appeared in *'The Australian' of 12th November 2007* under the caption: **Pakistan: judges 'filmed having sex'** is reproduced below verbatim:

> *"ISLAMABAD: Some of Pakistan's Supreme Court judges and their children were secretly filmed in compromising positions with lovers and prostitutes as part of a dirty tricks campaign by the country's feared military intelligence, it was reported yesterday.*
>
> *Videos were sent to at least three of the 11 judges in September as they were deciding whether Pervez Musharraf was eligible to run for president while still army chief. One showed a judge with his mistress while another was of a judge's daughter with a boyfriend, London's* **Sunday Times reported.**
>
> *"The message was clear," a British barrister who learned about the tapes from a Pakistani counterpart told the paper. "If you rule the wrong way, these will become public and your family destroyed."*
>
> *The judges gave an ambiguous ruling, allowing General Musharraf to be elected but declaring that they would decide on his eligibility later.*
>
> *It was fear that this ruling, due last week, would go against him that led General Musharraf to declare the state of emergency.*
>
> *Although he claimed he acted to prevent extremists taking over the country, the judiciary appeared to have been his principal target, the paper said.*
>
> *No jihadi leaders have been arrested, but General Musharraf sacked chief justice Iftikhar Chaudhry and eight of the 11 Supreme Court judges, and scrapped the constitution.*
>
> *Since declaring the state of emergency, General Musharraf has placed most of the top judges and human rights activists under house arrest. The sacked judges have been replaced by others who swore an oath of allegiance.*
>
> *According to Western diplomats, it was General Musharraf's intelligence chiefs who talked him into imposing emergency rule by convincing him the Supreme Court was about to overturn his re-election as president."*

[No rebuttal or denial was ever seen from the apex court or the 'agencies', thus no comments from the author.]

5th October 2007: The Supreme Court of Pakistan unanimously decided holding of Presidential elections on 6th October as per schedule. In a short order, the larger bench of the apex court disallowed staying the presidential poll. However, it added that results of the election would not be notified by the election commission till decision of all related petitions.

The text of the order said:

> 'Having heard the learned counsels for the parties at length, it is unanimously resolved and directed that the election process already commenced shall continue as per schedule notified by the Chief Election Commission of Pakistan but the final decision of the election of the returned candidate shall not be issued till the final decision of these petitions.'

The main petitions were set down for hearing on 17th October 2007. This short order was passed by a ten member larger bench of the Supreme Court headed by Justice Javed Iqbal and comprising of Justice Abdul Hameed Dogar, Justice Khalil-ur-Rehman Ramday, Justice Muhammad Nawaz Abbasi, Justice Faqir Muhammad Khokhar, Justice Tassaddaque Hussain Jillani, Justice Nasirul Mulk, Justice Raja Fayyaz Ahmed, Justice Syed Jamshed Ali Shah and Justice Ghulam Rabbani.

6th October 2007: When on 28th September 2007, the Supreme Court of Pakistan had given clearance to Gen Musharraf for presidential election; the Election Commission of Pakistan started accepting applications from Presidential candidates next day. 43 candidates in all applied for the slot.

Justice (R) Wajeehuddin Ahmed was from Lawyer's group whereas the PPP fielded its vice president Ameen Faheem as a candidate stating that he would withdraw his candidacy if Gen Musharraf were approved as a candidate. On 29th September 2007, the Election Commission scrutinised the nomination papers of all 43 candidates. Gen Musharraf and both of his major opponents (Justice W Ahmed and Ameen Fahim) were approved along with three others; the official list of candidates was publicised on 1st October 2007. The final list of five candidates was:

- Gen Pervez Musharraf, the incumbent in uniform, for the Pakistan Muslim League (Q);

- Justice ® Wajihuddin Ahmed, for an association of lawyers opposed to Gen Musharraf;

- **Ameen Faheem** for the [Parlimentarian] <u>Pakistan Peoples Party</u>;

- **Muhammad Mian Soomro**, Chairman <u>Senate</u>, as Musharraf's backup candidate;

- **Faryal Talpur**, Deputy Mayor of <u>Nawabshah</u>, as Amin Fahim's backup candidate.

On Election Day, 80 opposition party members had resigned from the Parliament, protesting that Gen Musharraf was running for re-election while being head of the army. Complete results were announced only 80 minutes after the five-hours-long voting process had been finished, with 685 of the 1,170 eligible lawmakers participating. The results were Pervez Musharraf: 671 votes, Wajihuddin Ahmed: 8 votes, Invalid: 6 votes. The Supreme Court had rejected all challenges to the legality of the election, with the last ruling made on 22nd November 2007.

Gen Musharraf easily won a vote to be re-elected Pakistan's President, even though it was unclear if his candidature was legal. He had won all but five of the votes cast in parliament's two houses and swept the ballots in the four provincial assemblies whereas opposition MPs abstained or boycotted the vote, calling it unconstitutional.

Chief Election Commissioner Qazi M Farooq told the National Assembly that Gen Musharraf had won 252 of 257 votes cast in the upper and lower houses. His nearest rival, Wajihuddin Ahmed, had won just two votes in the National Assembly and the Senate. Three votes had been rejected. A similar picture prevailed in the provincial assemblies of Punjab, Sindh, North West Frontier and Balochistan.

A deal had been announced earlier that, as a result of July 2007's meeting between Gen Musharraf and Benazir Bhutto in Dubai, members of Pakistan People's Party (PPP) would not join opposition boycott but abstain from voting while remained seated in the Parliament. The PPP did exactly as settled. Under the deal, Gen Musharraf had to drop corruption charges against Ms Bhutto, a stride towards power-sharing arrangement which had surfaced as NRO a day earlier.

PML(N) had boycotted that presidential election. Nawaz Sharif had attempted to return to Pakistan before the election [10th September 2007] but was deported back into exile by the ruling government because of a gross violation of the agreement he had signed with Gen Musharraf in December 2000 to stay out of Pakistan and its politics for a period of ten years.

After the Election Commission's announcement, Gen Musharraf lodged an appeal to the people to end protests against his rule and once more revived his offer of reconciliation to all political parties. The opposition parties rejected Gen Musharraf saying *'We will not accept him as president... He is a person who has hardly any respect for the rule of law'*. Opposition parties and lawyers called for protests. In Peshawar city, the police had to fire tear gas at lawyers protesting near the provincial assembly building. However, Political observers believed that Gen Musharraf got himself re-elected as the president on 6th October only because of the MMA leaders who had decided to vote in favour of 17th Amendment after striking a deal with a uniformed General and distorted the Constitution of 1973.

Gen Musharraf once again was grateful to the MMA leaders, particularly Qazi Hussain Ahmed and Maulana Fazlur Rehman, whose single act not only gave him the crucial support when he needed it most, but it continued to yield results when he once again needed it.

The Supreme Court had said that no winner could be declared until the decision whether Gen Musharraf could stand while being the army chief. This ruling had dragged the presidential election into confusion for a while but subsequently, on 17th October's hearing, nothing happened.

[It may be remembered that since early 2007 Gen Musharraf had started exploring different options to retain both offices for another term, but none of them were likely to stand up in a court of law. It should be available on PPP minutes of Dubai mutual meeting of July 2007 that another parliamentary exemption was worked out and it was offered to him by the Pakistan Peoples Party (PPP), the largest political party in the country but it asked him to give up his army post and settle for reduced presidential powers.

Gen Musharraf, instead, preferred to order his intelligence agencies to try to ensure a similar parliamentary victory for him through PML(Q) party loyalists by rigging the elections and this option cum strategy went successful.]

14th October 2007: Pakistan's Supreme Court ruled that legal challenges to Gen Musharraf's re-election in uniform should be heard by a larger bench headed by the Chief Justice, adding to the uncertainty over a new five-year term. An 11-member bench of the apex court headed by Justice Javed Iqbal, which took up five petitions challenging Gen Musharraf in the 6th October presidential poll, decided to ask Chief Justice Iftikhar M Chaudhry to constitute a full court to hear the matter.

Among those who filed the petitions taken up were PPP leader Makhdoom Amin Fahim and retired judge Wajihuddin Ahmed, who had unsuccessfully contested the presidential poll. Justice Ahmed's counsel told the court that the petitions were of the highest national importance as they involved the role of the army in Pakistan's politics and constitutional affairs and deserved to be heard by a full court. Attorney General Malik Qayyum, however, opposed this contention and said the government would object to the inclusion of four judges if a full court was constituted.

EMERGENCY OF 3ʳᵈ NOV 2007:

On **3rd November 2007**, Gen Musharraf declared a state of emergency in Pakistan, suspending the constitution, replaced the Chief Justice before an expected crucial Supreme Court ruling on his future as president, and cutting various private Tele-Channels all over Pakistan other than state-controlled PTV. Telephone service in the capital, Islamabad, was also cut. Gen Musharraf's leadership was threatened by an increasingly defiant apex court and his 'Emergency Order' had accused some judges of *'working at cross purposes with the executive and weakening the government's resolve'* to fight terrorism.

Going into details; during the hearing of Gen Musharraf's eligibility case, the Supreme Court had once announced that it might postpone the hearing until 12ᵗʰ November due to a personal engagement of one of the judges on bench. However on 2ⁿᵈ November, the court reversed its decision to break and called the bench on 5ᵗʰ November to resolve the political situation quickly. On the same day [of 2ⁿᵈ November 2007], Barrister Aitzaz Ahsan placed an application before the Supreme Court separately asking that the army be restrained from imposing martial law in Pakistan. On this petition a seven member's bench was formed headed by CJP Iftikhar Chaudhry himself which issued a stay order next day against the imposition of an emergency or martial law. The other members of the bench were Justice Rana Bhagwandas, Justice Javed Iqbal, Justice Mian Shakirullah Jan, Justice Nasirul Mulk, Justice Raja Fayyaz, and Justice Ghulam Rabbani. Attorney General Malik Qayyum while representing Gen Musharraf had assured the court that there was no planned move by the government to indulge in any such extra constitutional activity.

This stay order was ignored; before the court's next proceeding on 5ᵗʰ November, Gen Musharraf, acting as Chief of the Army Staff, declared a state of emergency as per Article 232 of the constitution on the evening of 3rd November 2007, and issued a Provisional Constitutional Order (PCO) which replaced the constitution. Under the order, the Constitution was suspended, the federal cabinet ceased to exist, and the justices were ordered to take an oath to abide by it. Those who failed to do so would be dismissed.

[*The Constitution's Article 232 allows only the President of Pakistan (and not the Army Chief) to declare a State of Emergency when he is satisfied a situation exists that warrants its imposition. In the case that a President of Pakistan declares a State of Emergency, the National Assembly has to approve it within 30 days.*]

Following was the text of the Proclamation of Emergency declared by Chief of the Army Staff Gen Pervez Musharraf:

- WHEREAS there is visible ascendancy in the activities of extremists and incidents of terrorist attacks, including suicide bombings, IED explosions, rocket firing and bomb explosions and the banding together of some militant groups have taken such activities to an unprecedented level of violent intensity posing a grave threat to the life and property of the citizens of Pakistan;

- WHEREAS there has also been a spate of attacks on state infrastructure and on law-enforcement agencies;

- WHEREAS some members of the judiciary are working at cross purposes with the executive and legislature in the fight against terrorism and extremism, thereby weakening the government and the nation's resolve and diluting the efficacy of its actions to control this menace;

- WHEREAS there has been increasing interference by some members of the judiciary in government policy, adversely affecting economic growth, in particular;

- WHEREAS constant interference in executive functions, including but not limited to the control of terrorist activity, economic policy, price controls, downsizing of corporations and urban planning, has weakened the writ of the government; the police force has been completely demoralized and is fast losing its efficacy to fight terrorism and intelligence agencies have been thwarted in their activities and prevented from pursuing terrorists;

- WHEREAS some hard-core militants, extremists, terrorists and suicide bombers, who were arrested and being investigated, were ordered to be released. The persons so released have subsequently been involved in heinous terrorist activities, resulting in loss of human life and property. Militants across the country have, thus, been encouraged while law-enforcement agencies subdued;

- WHEREAS some judges by overstepping the limits of judicial authority have taken over the executive and legislative functions;

- WHEREAS the government is committed to the independence of the judiciary and the rule of law and holds the superior judiciary in high esteem, it is nonetheless of paramount importance that the honourable judges confine the scope of their activity to the judicial function and not assume charge of administration;

- WHEREAS an important constitutional institution, the Supreme Judicial Council, has been made entirely irrelevant and non est by a recent order and judges have, thus, made themselves immune from inquiry into their conduct and put themselves beyond accountability;

- WHEREAS the humiliating treatment meted to government officials by some members of the judiciary on a routine basis during court proceedings has demoralized the civil bureaucracy and senior government functionaries, to avoid being harassed, prefer inaction;

- WHEREAS the law and order situation in the country as well as the economy have been adversely affected and tri-chotomy of powers eroded;

- WHEREAS a situation has thus arisen where the government of the country cannot be carried on in accordance with the Constitution and as the Constitution provides no solution for this situation, there is no way out except through emergent and extraordinary measures;

AND WHEREAS the situation has been reviewed in meetings with the prime minister, governors of all four provinces, and with Chairman of Joint Chiefs of Staff Committee, Chiefs of the Armed Forces, Vice-Chief of Army Staff and Corps Commanders of the Pakistan Army; NOW, THEREFORE, in pursuance of the deliberations and decisions of the said meetings, I, General Pervez Musharraf, Chief of the Army Staff, proclaim Emergency throughout Pakistan.

2. I, hereby, order and proclaim that the Constitution of the Islamic Republic of Pakistan shall remain in abeyance.

This Proclamation shall come into force at once.

Text of PCO 2007:

Following is the text of the Provisional Constitutional Order (PCO) promulgated by Chief of the Army Staff Gen Pervez Musharraf:

1. In pursuance of the Proclamation of the 3rd day of November, 2007, and in exercise of all powers enabling him in that behalf, the Chief of Army Staff, under the Proclamation of Emergency of the 3rd day of November, 2007, is pleased to make and promulgate the following Order:

   - This Order may be called the Provisional Constitution Order No 1 of 2007.

   - It extends to the whole of Pakistan.

   - It shall come into force at once.

   - 2. (1) Notwithstanding the abeyance of the provisions of the Constitution of the Islamic Republic of Pakistan, hereinafter referred to as the Constitution, Pakistan shall, subject to this Order and any other Order made by the President, be governed, as nearly as may be, in accordance with the Constitution.

   - Provided that the President may, from time to time, by Order amend the Constitution, as is deemed expedient:

   - Provided further that the Fundamental Rights, under Articles 9, 10, 15,16,17,19 and 25, shall remain suspended.

   - (2) Notwithstanding anything contained in the Proclamation of the 3rd day of November, 2007, or this Order or any other law for the time being in force, all provisions of the Constitution of the Islamic Republic of Pakistan embodying Islamic injunctions including Articles 2, 2A, 31, 2O3A, 227 to 231 and 260 (3) (a) and (b) shall continue to be in force.

   - Subject to clause (1) above and the Oath of Office (Judges) Order, 2007, all courts in existence immediately before the commencement of this Order shall continue to function and to exercise their respective powers and jurisdiction:

- Provided that the Supreme Court or a High Court and any other court shall not have the power to make any order against the President or the Prime Minister or any person exercising powers or jurisdiction under their authority.

- All persons who immediately before the commencement of this Order were in office as judges of the Supreme Court, the Federal Shariat Court or a High Court, shall be governed by and be subject to the Oath of Office (Judges) Order, 2007, and such further Orders as the President may pass.

- Subject to clause (1) above, the *Majlis e Shoora* (Parliament) and the Provincial Assemblies shall continue to function.

- All persons who, immediately before the commencement of this Order, were holding any service, post or office in connection with the affairs of the federation or of a province, including an All Pakistan Service, service in the armed forces and any other service declared to be a service of Pakistan by or under Act of *Majlis e Shoora* (Parliament) or of a Provincial Assembly, or Chief Election Commissioner or Auditor General, shall continue in the said service on the same terms and conditions and shall enjoy the same privileges, if any, unless these are changed under Orders of the President.

- 3. (1) No court, including the Supreme Court, the Federal Shariat Court, and the High Courts, and any tribunal or other authority, shall call or permit to be called in question this Order, the Proclamation of Emergency of the 3rd day of November, 2007, the Oath of Office (Judges) Order, 2007, or any Order made in pursuance thereof.

- (2) No judgment, decree, writ, order or process whatsoever shall be made or issued by any court or tribunal against the President or the Prime Minister or any authority designated by the President.

- 4. (1) Notwithstanding the abeyance of the provisions of the Constitution, but subject to the Orders of the President, all laws other than the Constitution, all ordinances, orders, rules, bye-laws, regulations, notifications and other legal instruments in force in any part of Pakistan, whether made by the President or the governor of a province, shall continue in force until altered, or repealed by the President or any authority designated by him.

- 5. (1) Any ordinance promulgated by the President or by the governor of a province shall not be subject to any limitations as to duration prescribed in the Constitution.

- (2) The provisions of clause (1) shall also apply to an ordinance issued by the President or by a governor which was in force immediately before the commencement of the Proclamation of Emergency of the 3rd day of November.

After the proclamation of Emergency & the PCO; out of 18 Supreme Court justices, only five judges took oath on the PCO. Initially in Islamabad, Abdul Hameed Dogar who was inducted as the new Chief Justice, J Nawaz Abbasi, J Faqir M Khokhar and J Javed Buttar took the oath under the PCO. Later in the evening, in Karachi J Syed Saeed Ashhad also took the oath on the PCO on the same day. From the remaining judges, Justice Javed Iqbal, Justice Falak Sher, Justice Sardar Muhammad Raza Khan, Justice Mian Shakirullah Jan, Justice Tassaduq Hussain Jillani, Justice Nasirul Mulk, Justice Chaudhry Ejaz Ahmed, Justice Raja Fayyaz, Justice Syed Jamshed Ali and Justice Ghulam Rabbani declined invitation to take oath on the PCO. All judges of the High Court of Balochistan had taken oath on the PCO.

The Chief Justice Iftikhar Chaudhry, Justice Rana Bhagwandas and Justice Khalil ur Rehman Ramday were not offered to take oath. On 3rd December 2007, a notification of removal of the said three judges was issued without any retirement privileges. On the same day, the federal government issued another notification that in pursuance to Article 3 of the Oath of Office (Judges) Order No. 1 of 2007, 24 judges of the High Courts of Sindh, Punjab and NWFP had ceased to hold office, with effect from 3rd November 2007.

Strong public opposition was seen to imposition of the state of emergency. 67% demanded Gen Musharraf's resignation where as 71% said they opposed suspension of the Constitution. More than 70% people surveyed said that they were opposed to closure of private television channels and arrest of judges. International broadcasts and local phones were blocked in main cities like Islamabad where barriers & barbed wires were erected at important points. PPP's Aitzaz Ahsan was detained at home and key opposition figures & senior lawyers were also placed under house arrest but were released after a day or two.

Similar actions were taken all around in Pakistan after proclamation of the emergency; prominent lawyers, human rights activists and politicians including Asma Jahangir at Lahore and Kh Asif at Sialkot were house arrested. Reports from inside Karachi stated that the situation remained peaceful showing entirely different picture than rest of the Pakistan due to MQM's standing along with Gen Musharraf. On 21st November

2007, two thousand detainees under the Emergency were released, but 3,000 remained in detention, according to the media reports.

Police blocked entry to the Supreme Court building and later took the deposed Chief Justice and other judges away in a convoy and placed them in house arrest at their official residences cordoned by Police and Rangers while cutting off their tele-connections and jamming their mobiles. Gen Musharraf also said that Pakistan was at a 'dangerous' juncture as its government was being threatened by Islamic extremists.

The Supreme Court was immediately placed under occupation and control of military personnel and the Chief Justice J Iftikhar Chaudhry, who was re-instated half heartedly by Gen Musharraf on 20th July 2007, was told that *'your services are no longer required.'*

Secondly, the military had also suffered devastating defeats against Islamic militants in Waziristan and Swat, the northern areas of Pakistan. They reportedly had thousands of troops in fierce fighting over the last two or three months, and just one day before proclamation of this emergency, had forced into signing a ceasefire. Why so; because the militants had captured two police stations in Matta Sub Division of Swat from the military forces and had paraded 48 captured paramilitary personnel in streets – bringing the total military personnel captured to more than 300. This development had brought the writ of the military government to zero level in fact.

The critics declared that the judiciary herself had called the cause of that Emergency giving their decision of 28th September 2007. Riots had immediately started from the court room when the decision was announced and then continued for days. Next day, on 29th September, the apex court at its own had taken *suo moto* notice terming those riots as 'contempt of court' and all the high ups were called in.

The Contempt of the Court case was kept going on its pace. One fine morning of last week of October 2007 Justice Rana BhagwanDas announced punishments for all the police and administrative officers who were involved in that day's exercise of allegedly beating the shouting lawyers. Commissioner and the Deputy Commissioner Islamabad got punishment till the rising of the Court whereas the IGP Iftikhar Ahmed, the SSP, DSP and inspector etc got fifteen days imprisonment.

That was the day when the police force got demoralized as an institution because many higher courts had heard tens cases of contempt of court on one pretext or the other but the matter always ended with submission of unconditional apology. First time in the history of Pakistan police officers of such high stature were punished for such issue.

The police force was justified to recall the judicial murder of Z A Bhutto's case where Nawab Ahmed Khan was not killed by Mr Bhutto in person but even then he was hanged by the judiciary. Similarly here the IGP had not touched the Chief Justice on the alleged day of contempt but he was simply punished because he was over-all in charge of the police contingent deployed on duty.

This decision of the Supreme Court was also one of the factors which provided stimulation to Gen Musharraf to call for 'Emergency of 3rd November 2007' just four days after announcement of the decision.

The *'TIME' magazine of 3rd November 2007* had opined that:

*'Pakistani President Pervez Musharraf declared a state of emergency Saturday, citing growing militant attacks and **interference in government policy by members of the judiciary**. But far from a solution to Pakistan's problems, Musharraf's move to consolidate power has plunged the country into a deeper constitutional crisis.*

The declaration of a state of emergency by Musharraf, who remains head of the army eight years after seizing power in a bloodless coup, suspended the constitution, blacked out independent television news stations and cut some phone lines.

The emergency declaration came as Pakistan's Supreme Court was expected to rule in the next two weeks on the legality of Musharraf's candidacy for another term as President. Chief Justice Iftikhar Chaudhry, a thorn in Musharraf's side since the President suspended the judge earlier this year only to see him reinstated after massive public protests, was removed from his job and placed under house arrest.

Members of the Supreme Court were required to sign a new provisional constitutional order that would mandate the state of emergency. But most of the justices instead signed a declaration calling the state of emergency illegal.'

"The Supreme Court was going to rule against him," president of the Supreme Court Bar Association Aitzaz Ahsan told TIME by cell phone from jail, where he was taken after being served a month-long

detention order. "Constitutionally he had no right to run as President while staying a General. This is the end of the road for him."

The state of emergency announced by Gen Musharraf brought America in an increasingly uncomfortable position. The Bush Administration had long backed Gen Musharraf as a key ally in the war on terror, while regularly calling for a return to democracy. Gen Musharraf's move made that balancing act harder to keep up. Secretary of State Condoleezza Rice told the media soon after that emergency news:

'The US has made clear it does not support extra-constitutional measures because those measures take Pakistan away from the path of democracy and civilian rule. Whatever happens we will be urging a quick return to civilian rule and a return to constitutional order and the commitment to free and fair elections.'

Just a day before declaration of emergency; as Gen Musharraf and his regime was rigorously following the "war on terror" dictates of Washington, the Engineering & Technical Branch officers & workers of Pakistan International Airlines (PIA) suddenly went on strike and in one day 92 scheduled flights including 21 for foreign destinations were cancelled demonstrating a total chaos on all the airports of Pakistan. On the same day in Karachi, 200 doctors at one hospital started an indefinite strike and elsewhere about 300 workers and activists went on protests against killing of some textile worker's leader reportedly on the behest of government sponsored agencies.

In the country, there was a very strange scenario because, while releasing the emergency pack, it was declared that the 1973's Constitution of Pakistan had been suspended; but at the same time it was announced that the Parliament and the Provincial Assemblies would continue working, the Prime Minister and the Provincial Chief Ministers would remain in place, the Governors would continue to occupy their seats, the Federal and Provincial Cabinets would continue to carry on their assignments but the Judges of the Supreme Court and respective High Courts would be required to take a fresh oath under the provisions of new PCO.

The Speaker of the National Assembly issued call notice for meeting of the Assembly to be convened on 6th November 2007. The world intelligentsia was reluctant to understand the developments because all the above mentioned institutions and the portfolios work under the provisions of the Constitution; and once the Constitution was held the institutions automatically could stand abolished. But in Pakistan every thing is possible and plausible *'in the greater interest of the country.'*

Another situation was widely criticized that despite presence of a platoon of legal advisors present and posted in the President Secretariat; despite availability of a former corrupt judge turned into Attorney General and despite back & call of the Federal Ministry of Law, Gen Musharraf had proclaimed this emergency as the Chief of the Army Staff (COAS) and not as the President of Pakistan. Under the provisions of Sec 243 of the Constitution of Pakistan the COAS was merely a government servant whereas only the President of Pakistan had the prerogative of declaring emergency in the country and that too, mainly on the following two grounds only:

• If there are disturbances in some province beyond control of the provincial government. If it is so then the Federal Government performs administrative functions of that province through the Governor.

• If there is any foreign attack on any part of the country.

On 3rd November 2007, emergency in Pakistan was not declared in any of the contexts narrated above. It was only declared to get rid of certain 'nasty' judges who were going to decide the fate of candidature of a sitting General cum President and Gen Musharraf did not want to take any risk.

Gen Musharraf, giving justification for his illegal step, told the nation that:

'The constitution provides no solution for this situation, there is no way out except through emergent and extraordinary measures,'

But the Pakistanis had increasingly turned against his government, who failed earlier that year [March 2007] to oust the Chief Justice Iftikhar Chaudhry. This time [November 2007], Justice Chaudhry was dethroned along with next senior most judges including Rana BhagwanDas. Next senior judge Javed Iqbal was conveyed an offer to come up and take the oath of Chief Justice under the PCO but he flatly refused to do so. The same offer was floated to the next senior judge named Abdul Hameed Dogar who then sworn in as the new Chief Justice the same evening. He had already promised to be a pliant servant of the military dictatorship when on 9th March 2007 he was called to the Supreme Judicial Council for Chief Justice Iftikhar Chaudhry's trial.

Most of the Supreme Court judges, including the Chief Justice of Pakistan, who was not called to take oath under the new Provisional Constitutional Order (PCO) of November 2007, were held incommunicado. No one, including newsmen and even the judge's own relatives or acquaintances, was allowed to enter the Judges Colony and meet any of those judges. *"Have we committed a robbery? We cannot get out of our residence and find heavy security conducting our surveillance and blocking our way out,"'* one (detainee) judge was quoted as saying, adding that they had been isolated from the outside world.

The security persons who had met the (detained) judges found them in high morale but themselves at a complete loss to understand why they had been detained and treated like criminals. Justice Javed Iqbal, who was offered to take oath as the Chief Justice of Pakistan under the PCO but refused to do so, and being a heart patient, remained all alone in his official residence. *"We were neither allowed to go out nor was anyone permitted to visit us,"* Justice Javed Iqbal told afterwards. These judges did not get the newspapers while they also didn't have any access to the private television channels; thanks to PEMRA (Pakistan Electronic Media Regulatory Authority). The internet connections (DSL) were also removed from the residences of these 'defiant', judges.

New parliamentary elections were due to restore civilian rule by January 2008. Gen Musharraf himself was overwhelmingly re-elected in October 2007 by the then expiring parliament, dominated by his ruling party, but the vote was challenged. The Supreme Court had then emerged as the main check on Gen Musharraf's dominance and was (as it was told by Aitzaz Ahsan earlier and widely imagined by the people) expected to issue a verdict before Gen Musharraf's term expiring on 15th November.

The fact remains that Gen Musharraf was on shaky legal grounds in his re-election by the lawmakers; a vote that was boycotted by most of the opposition; but they still aspired the court to rule in his favour to prevent further destabilizing Pakistan. Some judges, however, had made comments that they would not be swayed by threats from senior officials, repeatedly by the Attorney General Qayyum Malik, that an emergency might be declared if the court ruled against the General.

On the evening of 3rd November 2007, the seven Supreme Court judges, the original ones, rejected the declaration of emergency and ordered top officials, including the prime minister, and military officers not to comply with the 'Emergency Order'. The two-page ruling said that:

> *'There were no grounds for an emergency, particularly for the reasons being published in the newspapers that a high profile case is pending and is not likely to be decided in favour of the military government or Gen Musharraf.'*

On 6th November 2007, an 8 member's bench of the newly framed Supreme Court, headed by the new Chief Justice Abdul Hameed Dogar, reversed the decision given by the 7 members bench headed by former CJ Iftikhar Chaudhry on 3rd November and gave the verdict that the 7 member's bench was not entitled to give any halt to the PCO. Gen Musharraf's PCO allowed courts to function but suspended most of the fundamental rights guaranteed by the constitution, including freedom of speech as has been described in earlier paragraphs. It also allowed authorities to detain people without informing them of the charges.

As stated earlier, the 'Emergency' announcement was followed by arrests of lawyers and other perceived opponents of the government, including all the presidents of bar associations of all High Courts and many more. In the 7 PM news of Channel Four (UK) on 5th November 2007, the newsreader got Mr Muneer Akram, an Ambassador of Pakistan in the UN on line and asked him about the reasons behind this proclamation of emergency. He replied that it had been done because of the growing terrorism activities in Pakistan.

When the newsreader asked him to explain that:

'During 4rth and 5th Nov the Pakistani authorities had picked up, jailed or house-arrested the human rights activists, lawyers, certain political leaders and seven respectable judges of the Supreme Court only, why even a single terrorist, miscreant or religious activist has not been arrested or picked up.'

The Ambassador felt embarrassed having no answer to forward.

One of the reasons forwarded for proclamation of emergency by Gen Musharraf was that the judges of the Supreme Court had allegedly released certain miscreants and *Jihadists* involved in the Red Mosque event of July 2007. The facts would live as an interesting episode of the history that the names of two judges of the Supreme Court who had heard the Red Mosque case were **Justice Nawaz Abbasi and Justice Faqir M Khokhar** and, astonishingly, these two judges were among those five only judges who took oath under the new PCO on 3rd November 2007.

After proclamation of emergency, the main building of the Supreme Court Islamabad was surrounded by the army, Police and Rangers. No body was allowed to go in nor were the judges present inside allowed to come out. In the late night all the seven judges and the Chief Justice were taken out to their official residences and were held in reserve there under house arrest. They were not allowed to come out. During the morning hours of 4th November their houses were locked from outside which was a share humiliation because the inmates were not allowed to come out for other human needs.

Justice Javed Iqbal was a heart patient. His doctor tried to approach him in the hour of pain but was allowed to visit him after a delay of four hours.

In the backdrop of hundreds of persons which were arrested all over the country on the second day of emergency, the lawyers boycotted the courts all over the country and held demonstrations while police were asked to beat them as if they were criminals. Various lawyers were wounded in the police shelling and baton-charge after the lawyers in the Lahore High Court attempted to come at Mall Road. The lawyers of the Karachi Bar Association held demonstrations against the judges taking oath under PCO. The Police arrested 25 lawyers including president Karachi Bar Association Iftikhar Javed Qazi. *Dr Shahid of GEO TV* had forwarded interesting comments on the events then prevailing in Pakistan. According to him:

> *'As if the first u-turn that Pakistani President Pervez Musharraf did on 12th of October 1999 by staging a coup was not bad enough, he has done it again, eight years later, leaving the nation back at square one. Strangely enough this time around it is not a coup against a 'corrupt' civilian government but one against his own army-led regime of which he has been the supreme commander and leader all these years. ...... that is, at its best, an admission of the failure of his own style of governance, the breaking down of the system that he himself created and the collapse of the empire that he built with his own hands.'*

(Referring to *'the News' dated 6th November 2007)*

Gen Musharraf had once vowed in October 1999 to crack down on corruption allegedly done by the former Prime Minister Nawaz Sharif, improve law and order situation and bring real democracy to Pakistan. But not much later, the promises were forgotten and politicians who were booked under the National Accountability Bureau (NAB) were seen enjoying fruits of power. Aftab Sherpao, Faisal Saleh Hayat and Neelofar Bakhtiar were examples.

Fight against extremism and rogue elements were declared as reasons behind the announcement of 'Emergency Order', but he was not willing to concede that there were both fundamental and logistical flaws in the way he handled the issues. Being an army General, continuously supported by a disparaging but willing bunch of politicians, he could not improve the law and order situation. If the writ of the government was not working in the tribal areas, then why was the interior ministry or interior secretary not held accountable? Why didn't Gen Musharraf reshuffle the cabinet and bring a more capable hand to bring things in tribal areas under control? That attitude gave way to critics that the challenges to the writ of his government in Waziristan and Swat probably went un-manageable.

Along with lawyers, it was the media which were singled out for 'special treatment' under emergency proclamation, *'lying bares the paranoia'* that surrounded Gen Musharraf's governance. All the private TV channels were blanked out in Pakistan on the 3rd November 2007 but he should have recalled that the media was not a powerful tool in 1958 when the first martial law was imposed in 1969 when the movement against Gen Ayub Khan took shape and in July 1977 against Bhutto. On all those occasions, media just danced to the tunes of the government machinery. The media was grown up in 2007 and the international tele-lobbies were there to watch and comment upon the true situations taking shapes in Pakistan.

Once again, like many other institutions in Pakistan, the judiciary also went decimated. Honest and credible judges were obliterated from the institution and those who were loyal to the President were seen taking oaths. The press, particularly electronic media, which had been struggling for total freedom for years, was facing yet another crackdown. Mass arrests of lawyers, human rights activists and politicians were carried out across the country. Pakistan was again at a crossroads from where there was little hope in sight.

19th November 2007: In a dramatic development, Pakistan's Supreme Court dismissed all but one of the six petitions challenging Gen Musharraf's re-election in uniform as president and said it would decide the matter later. Gen Musharraf's second term as president hinged on the outcome of the case, which was originally being heard by an 11-members bench of the apex court before the military ruler imposed emergency on 3rd November 2007 and sacked most judges of the superior judiciary.

A 10-judge full court headed by Supreme Court's new Chief Justice Abdul Hameed Dogar, all of whom were sworn in under the Provisional Constitutional Order of 2007 issued by Gen Musharraf, were made members of the new bench to hear this matter. Among the five petitions dismissed that day were those filed by retired judge Wajihuddin Ahmed and Pakistan People's Party leader Makhdoom Amin Fahim, who had unsuccessfully contested the 6th October presidential poll against Gen Musharraf.

SC Validates Presidential Elections, PCO and Emergency:

On 24th November 2007, a seven member's bench of the Supreme Court headed by the then CJ Abdul Hameed Dogar, validated the imposition of emergency and the promulgation of the PCO issued by the Army Chief (COAS) and directed the Chief Election Commissioner of Pakistan to declare Gen Musharraf President for a second term of five years from 1st December 2007, while the later should relinquish the office of the COAS before taking oath as civilian president. The other members were Justice Ejazul Hassan, Justice Muhammad Qaim Jan Khan, Justice Muhammad Moosa K Laghari, Justice Chaudhry Ejaz Yousaf, Justice Muhammad Akhtar Shabbir, and Justice Zia Pervez.

The Supreme Court, while vacating the interim stay of 6th October on the presidential election results, held that Gen Musharraf was qualified to contest the presidential election and did not suffer any disqualification under the constitution and the law.

On 15th February 2008, the Supreme Court issued the full judgement for validation of the Proclamation of Emergency of 3rd November 2007, the PCO No 1 of 2007 and the Oath of Office (Judges) Order 2007, written by the CJP Dogar himself. The Court said that:

> 'In the recent past the whole of Pakistan was afflicted with extremism, terrorism and suicide attacks using bombs, hand grenades, missiles, mines, including similar attacks on the armed forces and law enforcing agencies, which reached climax on 18th of October 2007 when in a similar attack on a public rally, at least 150 people were killed and more than 500 seriously injured.

> The situation which led to the issuance of Proclamation of Emergency of the 3rd day of November 2007 as well as the other two Orders, referred to above, was similar to the situation which prevailed in the country on the 5th of July 1977 and the 12th of October 1999 warranting the extra-constitutional steps, which had been validated by the Supreme Court of Pakistan in Begum Nusrat Bhutto V. Chief of the Army Staff (**PLD 1977 SC 657**) and Syed Zafar Ali Shah V. Pervez

*Musharraf, Chief Executive of Pakistan (**PLD 2000 SC 869**) in the interest of the State and for the welfare of the people, as also the fact that the Constitution was not abrogated, but merely held in abeyance.*

The learned Chief Justices and Judges of the superior courts, who have not been given, and who have not made, oath under the Oath of Office (Judges) Order, 2007 have ceased to hold their respective offices on the 3rd of November 2007. Their cases cannot be re-opened being hit by the doctrine of past and closed transaction.'

Pakistan went through another transformation those days but the dawn was not very far off.

Scenario 51

BENAZIR BHUTTO ASSASSINATED:

{*The topic itself does not come under the scheme and scope of this book but as Benazir Bhutto was assassinated during Gen Musharraf's rule, a military regime, and because the army establishment's role was also identified by the UN; so a brief discussion is here.*}

To start with, a script from the *'TIME' magazine of 3rd November 2007* is reproduced below:

'*Musharraf is deeply unpopular. Hundreds of thousands of people turned out at protests in support of (Justice) Chaudhry earlier this year. Another potential rallying point is former Prime Minister Benazir Bhutto, who returned to Pakistan in October for the first time in eight years as part of a deal with Musharraf that would allow her to run in parliamentary elections early next year. As the leader of the biggest party in Pakistan, it was expected Bhutto would be elected Prime Minister under Musharraf. But the state of emergency [of 3rd November 2007] changes that equation again. A London-based spokesman for Bhutto said the former Prime Minister would lead anti-Musharraf protests.*'

On 27th December 2007, Ms Benazir Bhutto, Chair Person of Pakistan Peoples Party (PPP), was gunned down while she was coming out of Liaqat Bagh Rawalpindi after addressing a public gathering. Just six seconds after, a blast was done through a remote control device which not only caused an instant death of the sniper but also took about 22 innocent lives leaving behind tens of half burnt and mutilated human beings. To keep the investigation agencies away from the clues and clans responsible for doing this act, the local administration of Rawalpindi sent (or was called) a fire brigade lorry who, just after 15 minutes of the crime, swept away all the forensic evidences vital to proceed with investigation. It was a more serious offence committed by the washing staff or the officers who had ordered such blunt activity.

The local police or the investigating team were not given time to gather the samples of blood, type of blast material or gun powders used by the suicide bomber, possible pieces of remote control signal receiving device, pieces of blood stained clothes of victims and possibly of culprits, burnt shoes of victims and possibly of offenders, used cartridges of three bullets fired, some possible identity documents of affected people damaged or half burnt, actual bullet lead pieces, fire-gun with original finger prints of the sniper on it, half burnt mobiles or at least SIMs and so many other things to mention. It was equally heinous offence comparing with the assassination itself.

It has been the history that in Pakistan such investigations are normally assigned to those officers who are experts in twisting the facts according to the wishes and whims of the rulers controlling them. Those officers are not sincere to their truthful cause, neither to the professional demands of their job nor are they loyal to Pakistan. If such would have been the case, we would have definite conclusions of some of the following cases at least:

- Pakistan's first PM Liaqat Ali Khan's murder case of 16th October 1951

- Gen Ziaul Haq's air crash case of 17th August 1988

- Murder of Murtaza Bhutto in September 1996

- Death of Omar Asghar Khan in mysterious circumstances

- Attack on Ms Benazir Bhutto on 18-19th October 2007

The list is not exhaustive. At least one hundred cases of suicidal attacks, bomb blasts and firing by unknown miscreants can be added in which the governments could come out with the contention that those suicidal attacks were carried out by Al-Qaeda or Taliban like people so they were helpless. The careful questioning of Dr Musaddaq of Rawalpindi General Hospital and his associate doctors who had carried out the external post mortem of Ms Benazir Bhutto on 27th December 2007 could lead the investigating teams to the top person who ordered him to play jugglery with actual findings of the post mortem report but the teams were purposefully manoeuvred to keep silent.

Similarly the investigating team could dig out the circumstances (and reach the exact person or group or agency) who had ordered to wash up the scene of crime. A noteworthy development could be achieved by ascertaining that under what circumstances Brig (Rtd) Javed Iqbal Cheema had opted (or forced) to conduct a media conference on 28th December 2007 putting forward a plethora of lies which proved unresolved afterwards. The investigators should have worked out up till now that whether the tape of alleged Baitullah Mehsood voice was real or otherwise. If real, how it had reached [from Waziristan] there in the Interior ministry within hours; so quickly.

The media had genuine doubts that in just 22 hours after the death of Ms Benazir Bhutto, the arrangement of such important conversational gadget for media conference could only be 'arranged' by the agencies in their operational rooms. Might be a job of Intelligence Bureau whose Chief was nominated as one of the three persons in the letters written by Ms Benazir Bhutto to the Foreign Secretary of UK (David Miliband) and Gen Musharraf perhaps days earlier only. Then the uproar for UN team seemed genuine to enquire into the operational record of IB or ISI whatever the case was. Scotland Yard team was there in Pakistan but they were all forensic experts to help the local investigators only and there was no provincial or federal department who was authorised to carry on that investigation then; strange enough.

Before starting their journey for Pakistan, the Scotland Yard team [who were especially called by Gen Musharraf's Government to calm down the roaring voices of the PPP for independent investigations], had rightly indicated that their assistance would not be very helpful in Benazir Bhutto's case because most of the vital forensic evidence had already been destroyed. The most important step in this connection was the protection of crime scene which was washed away instantly.

[*The investigation team should have taken start by taking the driver of that fire brigade's lorry through careful interrogation. The driver was able to lead the team that how the channel of command went upwards. Normally fire brigade engines are not called to wash blood on the roads in police cases.*]

Special circumstances were to be unearthed to reach those masked faces who had become partners in conspiracy of averting justice.

In the first week of January 2008, the Scotland Yard was in Islamabad to investigate the murder case of Benazir Bhutto, a politician of international stature carrying a new hope of democracy for stranded Pakistanis. Till then there was much uproar that basic crime scene evidences required in such important case had been 'purposefully' destroyed by the high criminal hands behind this target killing but there was prevailing a hope to re-gather the scattered pieces of evidence which would put the case on justified correct lines. Consider the following humble submissions:

First step of professional dishonesty was that post-mortem of the dead body was manoeuvred by the hidden hands in a cruel and crude way. The investigators would have ascertained that:

On whose information / briefing the then Federal Interior Minister Gen ® Hamid Nawaz Khan had told the pressmen on the evening of 27th December (the day of occurrence) that the *death of BB has occurred due to a bullet shot wound*.

Dr Musaddaq, the senior member of seven doctor's team to perform the post mortem, then issued a medical report saying that there was only one wound on the right side of BB's head 5x3 cms.

- *Why the doctor had deliberately omitted to mention the second wound, which might be the entrance wound of bullet and was situated near the left ear.*

The various videos footage now available and especially released by Channel 4 [of UK] had shown that the fire was made from the left side of the vehicle then being used by the deceased Ms Bhutto.

On 2nd or 3rd January 2008, Dr Musaddaq told some newsmen that he had a tremendous pressure on his mind about this post-mortem report whereas he had specially been instructed not to speak even a single word on this issue.

- *Who issued him these instructions? Who conveyed these instructions to the doctor and on whose behalf?*

By the way, Dr Musaddaq's life was in danger. In the same talk with newsmen, Dr Musaddaq told them that the *office copy register of the post-mortem report was taken away by the 'higher ups / Administration' immediately* after the moment he signed it.

- *Who were those persons, why they removed the hospital's permanent record from the place [with ulterior intentions]? Where the post-mortem record was kept afterwards and to whom it was shown or read over.*

- *Who ordered Brig ® Javed Iqbal Cheema, a spokesman of Interior Ministry, to hold a press conference in so haste to release the post-mortem report on TV urging that the death occurred due to 'shock wave' felt by the deceased Bhutto and as a result striking with the sun roof's lever / handle.*

• *Who briefed Brig Cheema that the lever could cause a death?*

(The vehicle manufacturing company had later given a written statement to all the newspapers of Pakistan on 29th Dec or around declaring that the handle / lever of that vehicle could not cause death of a person standing there).

• *Why until the evening of 28th Dec the investigation officers could not inspect the vehicle which was the MOST important article of evidence from the scene of crime occurrence. Had they felt its importance, they would have noted that if there was leather / plastic cover over that handle which could make a 'fracture in the skull or not'.*

• *The inspection of BB's vehicle was also vital to ascertain if some blood clots or white fluid was there at the place of or around the roof-handle. If there were blood stains and white material then the possibility of 'death by handle' was there as next day claimed by Brig Cheema. But if there was no blood around then it could indicate that BB had fell down after getting bullet in her head from her left side. Blood clots near handle could have contained BB's hair pieces from her forehead too.*

[However, it could have been more authentic and beneficial if the vehicle could have been inspected at the first sight after it was left over Murree Road when wounded BB was shifted to another private car to take her to the RGH]

On 28th December 2007, the females who had served the last spiritual bath to the deceased body announced immediately that there were two visible wounds on the body of Miss Bhutto [see print media reports]; one was slightly below the left ear (might be the entry wound of bullet) and one big wound on the right upper side of skull (the [may be the exit] wound of the bullet). This finding was also displayed on GEO TV and ARY One-world in the afternoon hours of 28th December but even then Brig Cheema's team did not bother to take care of those announcements.

The persons who gave first account of those wounds seen after the last spiritual bath were (1) Asif Ali Zardari (2) Sherry Rehman (3) Mr Zardari's first sister who herself is a doctor (4) Mr Zardari's second sister. There may be other non-family old but illiterate women who actually touched the deceased's body while serving bath, which were in reality the independent natural witnesses needed to be talked.

Had any investigation officer ever bothered to record their statements to verify the accuracy of the post mortem report?

Under the provisions of (Pakistan) Police Rules 1934 Vol 3, the doctor cannot start post mortem of a dead body unless a police officer of concerned Police Station requests him on a *'Naqsha e Mazroobi'* (wound - details sheet) stating FIR No:, apparent cause of death, statement of (number of) wounds on the dead body and their position with approximate measurements, statement of blood stains, time of removal or custody of body etc and other remarkable appearances, if any. Two witnesses from the crime scene were also needed to sign that diagram / statement of wounds.

- *Who brought the body to the hospital and was the signing officer actually there. Had the Doctor countersigned that 'naqsha Mazroobi Police' and if so then at what time he gave it back to the Police officer?*

- *Was the investigation officer given two copies of the Post - mortem report and at what time?*

- *Where are those copies of 'naqsha Mazroobi Police' and the post mortem report attached?*

The definite cause of death is normally never stated in post mortem report. In Benazir Bhutto's post mortem report then released by authorities had contained that "a **'white brain matter'** is seen in the only wound which was also spread on the deceased's hair around" which clearly proved that the brain matter had been pushed out (might be accompanied by the bullet) while leaving the wound.

- *Who pressurised the doctor to re-write the report [if so] ignoring the most important facts; so fundamental and so evident.*

Brig Cheema's conference told the media that the detailed post mortem was not allowed by deceased's husband Asif Ali Zardari. Under the provision of the Police Rules an application should have been made to the DCO / District Magistrate (DM) Rawalpindi who only was authorised to allow it but the legal course was not adopted in this connection.

- *Who was the person who asked Mr Zardari about this thing and who had conveyed back the doctors about Mr Zardari's consent?*

The point to ascertain was that why a necessity had been felt to ask it from Mr Zardari whereas both the bullet wounds were on head and nothing forbids the doctors to conduct an external examination of neck and head in this situation. As the cause of death was apparent, the doctor did not need to conduct the 'detailed examination' of lower body parts. Thus the question was irrelevant that the legal custodians of the dead [Mr Zardari] did not want the detailed post mortem of the dead body.

Coming back to our main theme, it was the third time that Scotland Yard investigators were requisitioned by the Pakistani governments to launch investigations into Benazir Bhutto's killing. It was January 2008.

The initial demand to call the foreign experts came from high stalwarts of the Pakistan Peoples Party (PPP) at the time of Ms Benazir Bhutto's funeral on 28th December 2007. On the same evening the spokesman of the Government of Pakistan Brig (Rtd) Cheema, in a media conference straightaway ruled out the possibility of calling any kind of foreign assistance for this investigation on the pretext that the foreign investigators do not know our cultural traits, social behaviours and communal characteristics nor would they be able to cope with our legal and procedural requirements. Brig Cheema himself was unaware of our history. Brig Cheema did not know that the Scotland Yard investigation team was first called by us to conduct an inquiry to dig out facts of the assassination of Liaquat Ali Khan, Pakistan's first prime minister, in October 1951. The team stayed here for about three months but then was sent back. The people still don't know about the outcome of results.

Second time the Scotland Yard detectives and Home Office forensic experts were called at Karachi a decade ago to investigate the murder of Ms Benazir's Bhutto's younger brother, Murtaza Bhutto. It was September 1996, when Murtaza Bhutto and seven others were gunned down by policemen outside his family home. The killing triggered riots in Sindh province, and had (later) led to the imprisonment of Ms Benazir's husband Asif Ali Zardari. Within six weeks of the killing, the then president of Pakistan Mr Farooq Leghari sacked the PPP's government on this pretext [amidst other charges of corruption] and the Scotland Yard team, led by Roy Herridge, was ordered to leave the country with their investigation incomplete. Referring to the comments published in a British media on 5th January 2008, a member of that team spoke of their frustrations that:

> "We had a lot of difficulty in accessing material from the local police and other agencies... We did not, I think, establish any direct link which could be used in evidential form with the police in the killing. But we certainly managed to establish that there were discrepancies in the official versions of what happened."

Third time the same situation prevailed. The investigation being conducted by the same Scotland Yard in Benazir Bhutto's assassination was not very different than of his brother's. Pakistani police behaviour, government's misleading statements and their betraying patterns remained un-changed during the past 11 years. There was much hue and cry from the PPP hierarchy that the investigation of Ms Benazir Bhutto's assassination should be done by the United Nations and no less than that. The Scotland Yard team, comprising of five members were all forensic experts. They were not given their scope of work officially known as 'terms of reference' by the Ministry of Interior before departure from UK. They were not told about their limitations but the team was expected to ascertain the 'cause of death, only'.

In Benazir Bhutto's case, the Scotland Yard team remained continuously busy in their job. They visited the scene of crime on the first day, took photographs of the scene from different angle and had prepared a sketch of surrounding dwellings. During the subsequent days the members had examined the vehicles in the police lines which had sustained damages in the attack, had taken blood stains samples from the car and various places, had visited the Rawalpindi General Hospital & District Headquarter Hospital to interview the doctors who had prepared initial medical reports, also examined the post-mortem records and analysed the entries, re-examined the x-rays of Ms Benazir's injured / fractured skull, had also questioned the eye witnesses who were in the said hospital when BB was brought there dead / injured; including one Syed Ishtiaq Shah, Deputy Superintendent of Police on duty with Ms Benazir Bhutto who was also badly injured his front side body due to blast. The team finally went to the *mortuary* in the hospital where some pieces of burnt bodies, some legs, some feet and few deceased / burnt bodies were kept for certain forensic tests.

At the end of 1st week of 2008, the media reports collectively drew the following picture on the basis of day to day news of progress in the investigations:

- The bullet had hit Benazir Bhutto with 50 Newton force [*if the bullet hit her*] thus causing immediate bleeding from and fracture of skull.

- The bullet-lead was recovered from near the scene of crime but no details available if it was blood stained or if it was the same lead which actually hit or touched BB's body.

- The fire was done by a sniper from 8-10 feet distance while Benazir Bhutto's body was about three feet out / above the sunroof.

613

- There was no stain of blood found on the handle of sunroof.

- A bullet hole had been found on Ms Benazir's scarf (*dopatta*) which meant that a bullet had definitely hit her body.

- Ms Benazir immediately fell down in the sunroof after shot fires.

- After 5-6 seconds of shots, there occurred a bomb blast [possibility: *had Ms Benazir Bhutto not fallen in the sunroof, her head would have been chopped off from her body after the blast*].

- The blast occurred at 5.11 PM whereas Ms Benazir Bhutto's body reached the hospital at 5.35 PM. During this time there was a moment when her death occurred due to excessive bleeding. The doctors declared her dead at 6.41 PM.

- The forensic tests of the blasting material had shown that this type of material was also used in 14 other bomb blasts in various 'suicide bomber' attacks in Pakistan before.

- This blast mechanism was called MUV-2 and the material had the same lot number and same code but with different year of manufacture. It can be said that all the 15 suicide bomb blasts had been caused with the material manufactured in the same one factory and (may be) that the same one group / sponsor was responsible for these 15 blasts.

- The first security vehicle ahead of Ms Benazir Bhutto was 2 km away, naturally fully safe during this incident. This vehicle was one of the two armoured / bullet proof cars in which highly responsible figures of PPP [*afterwards identified as Rehman Malik & Babar Awan*] were moving.

- A private car carrying some *Jialas* was being driven by one Tauqir Akram Kaira of Kharian on the immediate back of Ms Benazir's car. Tauqir Akram Kaira died at the spot in the bomb blast.

- The injured Ms Benazir was initially taken to the hospital in the same armoured car whose tyres were burst during blast. After one km it stopped, Ms Benazir was transferred into another private car laying her on the back seat. Makhdoom Amin Fahim and Nahid Khan had to wait for another vehicle at roadside.

- PPP had never come forward with a list of men who were deputed on security job of Ms Benazir; how many of them died if they were actually deployed there.

Parallel to the above investigative points, speculative theories were also on high pitch those days. No one was certain about Benazir Bhutto's real culprits but guesswork and assumptions all around. The Ministry of Interior's spokesman Brig Cheema had tried to convince the nation through his media conference of 28th December 2007 that Al-Qaida was responsible for the blast which had been administered through Baitullah Mehsud. This proposition was right or wrong but Gen Musharraf, after a short while, had to make a public apology before the world media correspondents for the *'irresponsible behaviour'* of Brig Cheema. Gen Mahmood Durrani, Pakistan's Ambassador to the United States, while talking to the *'Washington Post'* termed Brig Cheema's media conference as 'fundamental mistake' while trying to persuade the Pakistani people in connection with Ms Benazir's assassination. Terming this approach as premature he told that:

'You know the government of Pakistan made a fundamental mistake, and that is, on the second day (of Bhutto's killing) they made a big statement. This is what happened. So and so was responsible. I'm not going to make that mistake.'

(Ref: 'the News' International dated 13th January 2008)

According to *'The Times'*, Gen Durrani conceded that government's initial contradictory statements in the aftermath of assassination of Ms Bhutto fed the widespread scepticism. The investigators, both from Pakistan government and Scotland Yard continued to dig out the truth with thriving efforts but could not reach a definite conclusion. Asif Ali Zardari and some stalwarts of the PPP had expressed their dissatisfaction over Scotland Yard's proceedings (because those were called by Gen Musharraf) and raised demand that the investigation should be done by the UN sponsored team. Ultimately, the PPP government had managed to invite UN team but with what results; sheer wastage of poor Pakistani's pocket money.

Ms Shery Rehman of PPP once had given an indication that *'the PPP does not opt to show non-cooperation with the Scotland Yard team but the PPP has not been asked to come forward and join investigation nor they are being consulted.'* Till then PPP's new official stance had surfaced that they had made out a blue print of an application to move the UN awaiting Mr Zardari's final approval. The PPP had also vowed that if Gen Musharraf would not agree to forward it to the UN they would wait till their government in office after elections. Then it would be their first job to make a move in the UN but when they assumed power it took a complete year to approach the UN in February 2009.

Gen Musharraf, while giving an interview to daily *Le-Figaro of France on 12th January 2008* had shunned down the idea of calling any UN sponsored investigator in that respect. For Benazir Bhutto's sad demise, the PPP in distress, misery and agony had sometimes blamed Pakistan Muslim League (Q), sometimes Gen Musharraf, sometimes Brig Ejaz Shah's civil Intelligence Bureau and very sparingly pointed towards other military agencies. PML(Q) came forward with logic that just 11 days before elections no political party would opt to take risk of gunning down rival party's leader because the later would simply attract majority of sympathy votes from borderline or neutral factions / groups. Gen Musharraf was also claiming a little relaxation by arguing that he had already developed a working relationship with the deceased Benazir Bhutto and was hoping to get all American plans implemented through an elected parliament or people's government. No one knew about the whole truth.

Instead of extending cooperation to the investigation teams (whatever their making, affiliations or intentions be), and instead of taking interest in the investigation at least to have a first hand knowledge that what were they doing and what was being (intentionally) omitted, the PPP stalwarts were chasing only one demand that the investigation be done by the United Nations. This demand was raised by Asif Ali Zardari, and then picked up by his close associates like Shery Rehman, Farooq Naik, Rehman Malik and Babar Awan etc.

PPP's Senators Farooq Naik and Babar Awan, both were practicing lawyers in the Supreme Court of Pakistan then. They had prepared a manuscript to move the case to the UN Security Council that an independent investigating commission be framed to investigate this case. For this purpose, the two lawyers had also planned to visit the UN Headquarter during those days. *When the PPP assumed power, they shelved the idea of calling UN teams due to reasons unknown.* Then a moment came that Farooq Naik and Babar Awan were purposefully and intentionally letting the government sponsored teams to sit on the investigation files with zero progress.

Mr Naik and Mr Babar had briefed Mr Zardari giving an example that Ms Benazir's assassination be investigated on the lines of Rafiq Hariri murder case of Lebanon which was otherwise not a true example. Apprehensions were:

• Under the charter, the UN could order an independent investigation if there were claims (and evidence) that the assassination was carried out by some other country. In Rafiq Hariri case it was alleged that the murder was sponsored or funded or managed by the Syrian government.

- In Ms Benazir's case, UN was to investigate the case on the pretext that the assassination had probably been done or sponsored by Al-Qaida group based in Afghanistan and not from its hide-outs in Pakistan.

- In this probability Mr Zardari and his associates actually lost their primary claim that Gen Musharaff or Ms Benazir's four nominated culprits (referring to the letters / e-mails sent by Ms BB to Gen Musharraf & the British Foreign Secretary prior to her departure for Pakistan on 18th October 2007) were responsible for this event.

- During the first week of January 2008, the French Foreign Minister who was on two day's official tour of Pakistan, had expressed their sympathies with Ms Benazir's bereaved family but clearly opined that his government would not stand by them if such request for investigation by the UN came up in the Security Council.

- During the first week of January 2008, the Washington Post had expressed US government's stance that US had all the sympathies with the people of Pakistan at this awful event and was ready to send its investigation team of experts independently if required but they would not consider it appropriate to help any such request brought before the Security Council.

At that moment the situation surfaced that UK had since sent Scotland Yard team thus was not going to allow other country's experts on top of them, China was not approached, US and France had already shown their inability to approve the proposal, and therefore, Gen Musharraf never succumbed to PPP's demand. All they were betraying Mr Zardari at the moment when he needed sincere advice from friends and his party brains.

When one puts various pieces of jigsaw in order, the picture comes up that there were *hidden hands* behind this heinous act of crime. The attack on Ms Benazir Bhutto might have been done by some extremist group but for what benefit to their cause. The inference cropped up that there was a possibility of a faction or wing in some 'agency', which was backing that extremist group for peculiar objectives and, might be, without a formal approval of their seniors.

In the above lines, had the investigators known that the sponsoring *'jehadi'* group had done 14 alike suicidal bomb blasts in Pakistan before launching attack on Ms Benazir Bhutto; and the investigators had also determined that the same detonating material / technique of MUV-2, with the same serial numbers in continuity of lots and marks, made in and supplied by the same one factory with a difference of year of manufacture on them, they should have known until now that:

- Which factory in the world was manufacturing that kind of material?

- How that material was sold or supplied out and through which agent.

- Which was that group which managed to acquire its supply and how this material travelled from factory to the group?

- From where that group got finances to buy it; who was backing.

- From where the group acquired human beings / youngsters to play as suicide bombers and how they were transported to Rawalpindi / Islamabad or other parts of the country.

The general populace did not believe that our intelligence agencies, civil and military, had no answers to the above questions. They knew but did not want to divulge the information due to certain hidden agenda. If the trace out of the above questions [*as had claimed by the Punjab Police later*] escorted the investigators to the [American] camps at Pak-Afghan border then possibly Baitullah Mehsood or his Taliban group might be on the frontline. Had the Pakistan army or the PPP government ever lodged a protest in this respect and framed out their strategies for future.

The US authorities were not apparently happy with Gen Musharraf and worried about wastage of American aid thus wanted to change the horse at this belated stage of 'War on Terror' game. Why the US authorities chose Benazir Bhutto, invested in her, got her prepared to ride democracy and finally managed to send her to Pakistan. Before landing in Pakistan the US arranged their final one to one (Benazir - Musharraf) secret meeting in July 2007 in Abu Dhabi. The US also got two assurances from Gen Musharraf that *firstly: there would be very fair, peaceful and transparent elections and secondly; the life of Ms Benazir Bhutto would not be endangered.*

In this un-declared contract one had backed out; either US or Gen Musharraf. Benazir Bhutto had lost her life, might be at the hands of some *Jehadi* group but surely with backing of the agencies under the sponsorship of either of the two contractual parties.

In January 2008, the team members of the Scotland Yard had gone back after collecting available forensic evidences from various places and after procuring copies of medical reports & doctor's statements from hospital. They were to analyse the evidence in detail at their HQ Laboratory in UK but before leaving they had given an indication, *interalia* that *the audio tape of Brig Cheema,* (then read over and made public before mediamen) *relating Baitullah Mehsud with the murder of Ms Benazir was correct & believable* and thus, in their opinion, the assassination had probably been done by Mehsud's agents.

Consider a report of the American National Intelligence Council, purposefully designed and made-up in 2005 to destabilize Pakistan on the pretext of possession of nuclear arsenal. In this report they had 'predicted' that *'Pakistan would become a failed state within a decade when the religious extremism, slogans of provincial autonomy and linguistic hatreds would be at their peak'. One can see that the political scenario and social conditions of Pakistan are deteriorating rapidly on day to day basis and since then. The Americans, in spite of change in governments, acted on their worked out plan and has brought Pakistan to exactly match the described conditions. Our leaders should feel the heat that how the foreign enemies are going successful in getting opportunity of seeing their malicious designs fulfilled. They are distributing dollars, guns and ammunition to all sects and factions of religious, lingual, sectarian, separatist and terrorist organizations in Pakistan; also directly to the army and certain NGOs.*

The US had made a successful choice in this context to bring their dreams into reality. They had invested a lot in Ms Benazir Bhutto. They had forced Gen Musharraf to accommodate Ms Benazir in all relevant fields where the US had planned to put their footprints. They had given her all policy lines and had continuously instructed Gen Musharraf to take her through success. By the unexpected popularity gained by Ms Benazir Bhutto *on 18th October 2007* when she returned to Pakistan after eight years self exile, the US authorities were really delighted but they wanted to convey a message to her that she should not think herself an unquestioned leader. The US wanted to remind her that she should remain subservient and docile for the real time to come.

For this purpose they got planned a suicide bomb attack on her which (*though took 152 lives and left around 300 wounded but*) exploded only after her going down into the truck body. It was an indicative lesson. The suicide bomber could have exploded him when Ms Benazir was standing open on the truck for nine hours. The moment she went inside the truck body, the bomber exploded him. The message was successfully conveyed to Ms Benazir. He could have done so earlier if he was really after Ms Benazir's life.

Benazir Bhutto, however, in her subsequent behaviour of two months, proved that Pakistan was the only and uncompromised priority for her and Pakistan's national interest was dearer to her. She started ignoring her master's guidance and tried her level best to bring the dissident elements from all the four provinces together which were quite contrary to the doctrine of American designs. To create and keep an atmosphere of harmony among the provinces Ms Benazir had taken very bold steps like:

* Benazir Bhutto had contacted twice with Baitullah Mehsud through her links (through her previous Minister for Interior Late Gen Naseerullah Babar) and conveyed him a message to put forward his demands so that table talks could be arranged.

* Benazir Bhutto had deliberately offered invitation to various religious leaders, political and non political, to come up on negotiation table so that a working relationship was established for a prosperous Pakistan.

* Benazir Bhutto had also contacted Dr A Qadeer Khan, the founder of Atomic Program in Pakistan, to compensate for his dis-respect shown by the military junta during Gen Musharraf's rule. She was successful in dispelling away her questioned image regarding Dr Qadeer's interrogation plans by the US. Ultimately Dr Qadeer was satisfied and delighted to convey her that *'you are just like my daughter and I have no grudge against you'*.

* Benazir Bhutto had categorically announced that the atomic assets of Pakistan would be taken care of by the people of Pakistan and in no case any foreign country (especially referring to America) would be welcome to provide security to our atomic warheads. [*She had repeated this determination even in her last speech at Liaqat Bagh Rawalpindi.*]

* Benazir Bhutto, during her tour to Baluchistan after 18th October 2007, had paid visit to the descendents of Sardar Akbar Bugti who was allegedly killed by the Pakistan army contingent in an encounter in August 2006. She went there to repair the old damaged relationship since her father's premiership. In this move she went successful which also brought a good name to her political wisdom and acumen for unity in provinces.

The above steps of Benazir Bhutto were not at all approved by the controllers of CIA & Pentagon as they could see their plans shattered in connection with Pakistan. These were the *circumstances under which Benazir Bhutto was assassinated* though apparently through Baitullah Mehsood's group but who was feeding them; it is evident from above.

Benazir Bhutto's assassination dilemma was solved but courage to tell the real culprit at his face was needed. The US slogans were definitely pushing our leadership into the sand-grave of Saddam Hussein and Pakistan (despite being an atomic power) was being tipped to meet the fate of Iraq.

Another page of history turns over. PPP takes over reigns of the country.

UN COMMISSION ON BB'S KILLING:

UN Secretary General Ban Ki-moon announced on 5th February 2009 to send a commission to investigate Benazir Bhutto's assassination on Government of Pakistan's request. Armed with a modest mandate and a limited timeframe, a three-member team arrived at Islamabad on 16th July 2009. The unit, headed by the Chilean diplomat Heraldo Muñoz, found themselves plunged into a murky world of conspiracy theories, power politics and conflicting agendas. Muñoz was supported by the Indonesian official Marzuki Darusman and Peter Fitzgerald, a retired Irish police officer who headed the initial inquiry into the assassination of Lebanese Premier Rafik Hariri in 2005. The team had to look into the factor that Gen Musharraf's government initially had blamed the Taliban warlord Baitullah Meshud – an assessment supported by the CIA also, but Bhutto's supporters rejected the official explanation and alleged that Pakistan's most powerful intelligence agency, the ISI, was behind the attack.

After about 18 months of the PPP in power [since February 2008], the UN was asked to send a team to dispel away another conspiracy theory claiming that Zardari himself orchestrated his wife's death; a notion most analysts dismissed because of absence of any concrete evidence. Basically the UN team's mandate was to *"establish the facts and circumstances of the assassination"* and not to undertake a criminal investigation, which remained responsibility of the Pakistani authorities. UN team was apparently committed to assisting Pakistan by doing its utmost to determine the facts and circumstances of her death.

Pakistan kept on waiting for the UN report on Benazir Bhutto's assassination, but on 9th April 2010, the sources revealed that the Punjab police had already told the UN Inquiry Commission that the murderers of Benazir had been traced out and arrested and were being tried. PPP's high stature office bearers did not know it; even Mr Zardari as president was not informed officially. A few low level suspects were arrested and brought for trial just to keep the files alive.

PUNJAB POLICE INV. REPORT:

Furthermore, according to official documents provided to the UN Inquiry Commission by the Special Branch of the Punjab Police, a group of 12 militants was actually sent to Rawalpindi, a day earlier, to physically eliminate the PPP leader. Additional IG Special Branch Punjab Ch Abdul Majeed had supervised the investigation. The documents told that four of the 12 militants tasked to kill Benazir Bhutto belonged to *Darul Uloom Haqqania* in Akora Khattak near Peshawar. The *Madrassa* was being run by Maulana Samiul Haq, the pro-Taliban Ameer of one faction of JUI. Three out of the said 12 TTP militants had already been killed, including the suicide bomber. Of the remaining nine accused, five were arrested by police while the remaining four were missing till the UN team's arrival. It was later held that the assassination inquiry was actually conducted by a Joint Investigation Team (JIT), headed by the above named Addl IG.

In April 2010, the *challan* (final report) of Benazir Bhutto's murder case was submitted in Rawalpindi anti-terrorism court where the trial was on. The three accused shown as already dead included the suicidal bomber Saeed alias Bilal (r/o Waziristan), Nadir alias Qari Ismail and Nasrullah both from *Madrassa Haqqania*, Akora Khattak. The absconder four accused persons were also hailing from the same religious school. The five accused in the custody of the Rawalpindi police were being tried included Rafaqat, Hasnain Gul, Sher Zaman, Rasheed Ali and Aitzaz Shah if their names and identities were true. Allegedly, Baitullah Mehsud had given Rs:400,000 to one Qari Ismail, who subsequently dispatched a group of these 12 suicide bombers and shooters to Rawalpindi to kill Benazir Bhutto.

Going into more details of Punjab Police Report, Aitzaz Shah from Mansehra (only 15 years old) and his co-accomplice Sher Zaman, reportedly trained at Miranshah, were arrested from D I Khan by JIT; two more suspects, Hasnain Gul and Rafaqat, were later arrested from Rawalpindi. As per police report Aitzaz Shah had obtained *Jihadi* training from a well known *Deobandi* religious school in Karachi; *Jamia Binoria*, also referred to as *Jamia Islamia* and known for its pro-Taliban thoughts. After being brain washed and trained to kill, Aitzaz was sent to South Waziristan, travelled back to *Darul Uloom Haqqania* from where he was taken to a *Jihadi* training centre named as *'Wali Mohammad Markaz'* for further assigned activity in Rawalpindi.

Contrarily, the PPP had rejected the confession made by Aitzaz Shah and his accomplices declaring that the said story was fabricated to reduce pressure on the provincial government which had the primary liability of investigating this case because Rawapindi was in Punjab's territorial jurisdiction. The main figure of story was only *'15 years old, a juvenile by law, thus cannot be trusted for such huge task of killing Benazir Bhutto.'*

UN COMMISSION'S INV. REPORT:

During the same month, on 15ᵗʰ April 2010, the United Nations investigation team had submitted their report to the UN Council. It was a report of about 70 pages and in its **Chapter IV under 'Main Findings'**, the conclusion was:

"After nine years in exile, former Prime Minister Ms Benazir Bhutto returned to Pakistan on 18th October 2007, in the context of a tenuous and inconclusive political agreement with Gen Musharraf, as part of a process encouraged and facilitated by the governments of the United Kingdom and the United States. It was an eventual power sharing arrangement but the final terms were never agreed.

Ms Bhutto was murdered on 27th December 2007 when a 15 and a half year-old suicide bomber (as earlier told by the Punjab Police) detonated his explosives near her vehicle as she was leaving the PPP event at Liaquat Bagh Rawalpindi. A range of government officials failed profoundly in their efforts first to protect Ms Bhutto and second to investigate with vigour all those responsible for her murder, not only in the execution of the attack, but also in its conception, planning and financing.

Responsibility for Ms Bhutto's security on the day of her assassination rested with the Federal Government, the government of Punjab and the Rawalpindi District Police. None of these entities took necessary measures to respond to the extraordinary and urgent security risks that they knew she faced.

Gen Musharraf's state machinery remained confined to pass on the threats (to Ms Bhutto's security) to her and provincial authorities and were not proactive in neutralizing them. The federal Government failed in its primary responsibility to provide effective protection to Ms Bhutto on her return to Pakistan. Particularly inexcusable was the Government's failure to direct provincial authorities to provide Ms Bhutto the same stringent and specific security measures it ordered on 22nd October 2007 for two other former PMs who belonged to the main political party supporting Gen Musharraf. The specific threats against her were otherwise being tracked by the ISI.

Ms Bhutto's assassination on 27th December 2007 could have been prevented if the Rawalpindi District Police had taken adequate security measures. The security arrangements for Ms Bhutto done by the Rawalpindi District Police were ineffective and insufficient. The police's security plan, as written, was flawed, containing insufficient focus on Ms Bhutto's protection and focusing instead on the deployment of police for crowd control purposes. In many respects, the security plan was not implemented. Although the plan called for deploying 1371 police officers, the actual deployment did not approach that number.

Among other failings: the police co-ordinated poorly with the PPP's own security; police escort units did not protect Ms Bhutto's vehicle as tasked; parked police vehicles blocked the emergency route; and, the police took grossly inadequate steps to clear the crowd so that Ms Bhutto's vehicle would have safe passage on leaving Liaquat Bagh. The performance of individual police officers and police leadership was poor in areas of forward planning, accountability and command and control.

The additional security arrangements of the PPP lacked leadership and were inadequate and poorly executed. The heroism of individual PPP supporters, many of whom sacrificed themselves to protect Ms Bhutto should have been properly canalised by the Chief of PPP's security [Mr Rehman Malik]. More serious, Ms Bhutto was left vulnerable in a severely damaged vehicle by the irresponsible and hasty departure of the bullet-proof Mercedes-Benz which, as the back-up vehicle, was an essential part of her convoy [perhaps purposefully taken away by Rehman Malik, Babar Awan & Farhatullah Babar].

The Rawalpindi District Police's actions and omissions in the immediate aftermath of the assassination of Ms Bhutto, including the hosing down of the crime scene and failure to collect and preserve evidence, inflicted irreparable damage to the investigation. The collection of 23 pieces of evidence was manifestly inadequate in a case that should have resulted in thousands. The one instance in which the authorities reviewed these actions, the Punjab committee of inquiry into the hosing down of the crime scene was a whitewash.

Hosing down the crime scene so soon after the blast goes beyond mere incompetence and needed fixing criminal responsibility on many. CPO Saud Aziz impeded and obstructed Joint Investigation Team investigators from conducting on-site investigations until two full days after the assassination. The provincial authorities also failed to review effectively the gross failures of the senior police officials on duty.

The deliberate prevention by CPO Saud Aziz of a post mortem examination of Ms Bhutto hindered a definitive determination of the cause of her death. It was patently unrealistic for the CPO to expect that Mr Zardari would allow an autopsy on his arrival in Pakistan while in the meantime her remains had been placed in a coffin and brought to the airport. The autopsy should have been carried out at RGH long before Mr Zardari arrived. The Commission was persuaded that the Rawalpindi police chief, CPO Saud Aziz, did not act independently of higher authorities, either in the decision to hose down the crime scene or to impede the post-mortem examination.

The press conference conducted by Brig Cheema on 28th December 2007 was ordered by Gen Musharraf. The Government's assertion that Ms Bhutto's death was caused when she hit her head on the lever of her vehicle's escape hatch and that Baitullah Mehsud and Al-Qaida were responsible for the suicide bomber were made well before any proper investigation had been initiated. This action pre-empted, prejudiced and hindered the subsequent investigation.

An unequivocal determination as to the cause and means of Ms Bhutto's death was required [through] an autopsy. The Commission could not find any new evidence to suggest a gunshot injury to Ms Bhutto. Instead, a senior PPP official who publicly purported soon after the assassination to have seen indications of a bullet injury admitted to the Commission that she did not have direct knowledge of such an injury.

Ms Bhutto faced serious threats in Pakistan from a number of sources; these included Al-Qaeda, the Taliban and local jihadi groups and potentially from elements in the Pakistani Establishment. Notwithstanding these threats, the investigation into her assassination focused on pursuing lower level operatives allegedly linked to Baitullah Mehsud. The Commission considered it disturbing that little was done

625

to investigate Baitullah Mehsud himself, Al-Qaeda and any individuals or organizations that might have worked on, supported or otherwise been involved directly or indirectly in the planning or execution of the assassination. Investigators also dismissed the possibility of involvement by elements of the Establishment, including the three persons identified by Ms Bhutto as threats to her in her 16th October 2007 letter to Gen Musharraf and the British Authorities.

The Commission identified other significant flaws in the JIT investigation led by the Punjab Additional IG Abdul Majeed. It lacked direction, was ineffective and suffered from a lack of commitment to identify and bring all of the perpetrators to justice. This delay further hampered the gathering of evidence. Despite indications that there were links between the Karachi and Rawalpindi attacks, there had been no communication between the investigators on those two cases.

The investigation was severely hampered by intelligence agencies and other government officials, *which impeded an unfettered search for the truth. They were not having mandate to conduct criminal investigations, intelligence agencies including the ISI were present during key points in the police investigation, including the gathering of evidence at the crime scene and the forensic examination of Ms Bhutto's vehicle, playing a role that the police were reluctant to reveal to the Commission.*

More significantly, the ISI conducted parallel investigations, gathering evidence and detaining suspects. *Evidence gathered from such parallel investigations was selectively shared with the police. What little direction police investigators had was provided to them by the intelligence agencies. However, the bulk of the information was not shared with police investigators. In fact, investigators on both the Karachi and Rawalpindi cases were unaware of information the ISI possessed about terrorist cells targeting Ms Bhutto and were unaware that the ISI had detained four persons in late October 2007 for the Karachi attack.*

More broadly, no aspect of the Commission's inquiry was untouched by credible assertions of politicized and clandestine action by the intelligence services – the ISI, Military Intelligence, and the Intelligence Bureau. On virtually every issue the Commission addressed, intelligence agencies played a pervasive and omnipresent role, including a central involvement in political negotiations regarding Ms Bhutto's return to Pakistan and the conduct of the elections.

The Commission believed that:

'*The failures of the police and other officials to react effectively to Ms Bhutto's assassination were, in most cases, deliberate. In other cases, the failures were driven by uncertainty in the minds of many officials as to the extent of the involvement of intelligence agencies [especially the ISI].*

These officials, in part fearing involvement by the intelligence agencies, were unsure of how vigorously they ought to pursue actions that they knew, as professionals, they should have taken."

The PPP government, with more than three years in absolute power, should have unearthed the perpetrators of this assassination and be brought to justice till now. The FIA teams should have been fully empowered and resourced much earlier to accomplish this important job expeditiously and comprehensively, at all levels, without hindrance. The UN Commission had categorically stated that the performance of the Pakistani police was severely inadequate to the task of investigating the assassination of Ms Bhutto and lacking in independence and the political will to find the truth, wherever it might have lead. The FIA team should have grasped an independent review much earlier to fix responsibilities on individuals for their actions or inactions.

On 22nd August 2009, the AT Court shelved the trial proceedings following a federal government request to transfer the case to the Federal Investigation Agency (FIA). Three days after, the government formed a high-level team to re-investigate Benazir Bhutto's killing. A Special Investigation Group (SIG) of the FIA was assigned the task to fix criminal liability on the assassins and planners behind the murder. This investigation was to be done parallel to the probe being carried out by the United Nations Inquiry Commission. Quite understandable because '*the UN Commission Report can't be presented before any court of law as desired by the UN. The FIA's investigation report would be required for a proper trial against the criminals in the court'*. The United Nations report would have no legal standing for prosecution.

Later, when the media men tried to take version of *Jamia Binoria* Karachi and of *Madrassa Haqqania Akora Khattak*, the responsible administrators simply declined the said accusations levelled against them. It was evident but Pakistan's 'investigative journalists' never bothered to dig out the truth by various available means to apprise the people of facts. On the other hand, the actions of militarized intelligence agencies undermine democratic governance. In addition, the democratic rule of law in the country should have been strengthened by the PPP later.

The assassination of Benazir Bhutto occurred against the backdrop of a history of political violence which was not taken seriously even by the PPP government. The UN team had rightly suggested that to address this issue, Pakistan should consider establishing a transitory, fully independent Truth and Reconciliation Commission to investigate, without fear or favour, all political killings, disappearances and terrorism in recent years.

On 19th April 2010, six senior police officials were made OSD, sidelined and their names were put on the Exit Control List (ECL), for being responsible for lapses in security of Benazir Bhutto on the day of assassination. The government also cancelled the contract of DG Civil Defence Brig Javed Iqbal Cheema, who was then spokesman of Interior Ministry and had claimed that BB's death was due to the hitting of jeep's roof handle and not the bullet. Those officials who were made OSD included former DCO Rawalpindi Irfan Elahi, former Rawalpindi CPO Saud Aziz, SPs Khurram Shahzad, Ishfaq Anwar, Abdul Majeed Marwat and Yaseen Farooqi.

The *challan* (final report) of BB's case was submitted in the AT Court in the first week of February 2011. The police officers Saud Aziz and Khurram Shahzad were arrested in December 2010. Saud Aziz had claimed in his testimony that:

> 'The order to change Benazir's security in-charge had been given by Gen Musharraf himself and the scene of occurrence was also washed immediately on his specific orders.'

Later the court was told by the FIA that Gen Musharraf had been named as an "absconding accused" as he was not cooperating in the investigation. FIA's prosecutor [named Zulfikar Chaudhary] also told the court that:

> 'Both detained police officials were in contact with the former president [Gen Musharraf] and were following his orders. The phone records confirm contact between Gen Musharraf and Saud Aziz.'

On 12th February 2011, Gen Musharraf was declared as a proclaimed offender in the said BB's case. A report of Benazir Bhutto's BlackBerry mobile set was also submitted in the court. No call was sent from or received at her mobile after 3PM that day.

During the first week of November 2011, the Anti Terrorism Court indicted seven people including the former police chief of Rawalpindi named Saud Aziz; Khurram Shahzad, another senior police officer [SP City Rawalpindi] was also charged. In a closed-door hearing at a high-security prison in Rawalpindi, Justice Shahid Rafique charged all the seven men with criminal conspiracy and murder, whereas one Chaudhry Azhar attended the court as a special public prosecutor in the case. The five militants [named in earlier paragraphs], who were believed to be members of the Pakistani Taliban, were arrested four years ago and remained in jail. Two of them had admitted helping in the suicide bombing.

The two police officers were charged for negligence and failure to perform their duties by ordering the crime scene hosed down two hours after the attack, by removing evidence and by reducing Benazir Bhutto's security detail several days before the attack. The two officers were free on bail. All seven suspects denied the charges.

New York Times of 5th November 2011, while commenting on Benazir Bhutto's assassination, had also opined that:

> 'A United Nations investigation reported last year that the failure of Pakistani authorities to effectively investigate the killing was "deliberate" and that the investigation had been "severely hampered" by the country's powerful intelligence agencies.
>
> As per UN's report Mr. Aziz, the police chief, ordered the washing of the scene and impeding the investigation. But it also said that Mr. Aziz gave the order after receiving a call from army headquarters [GHQ], possibly involving Maj Gen Nadeem Ijaz Ahmad, then Director General of Military Intelligence.
>
> Mr. Musharraf, who fled the country in 2008 under threat of impeachment, has also been charged in the case. A Pakistani court issued an arrest warrant for him in February, accusing him of failing to provide Ms. Bhutto with adequate security.'

POST SCENARIO DEVELOPMENT:

The Supreme Court, on 31st January 2012, issued notices to 12 people including Babar Awan, Rehman Malik, Ch Pervez Elahi, Gen Musharraf and eight others in petition, seeking to lodge a new FIR in Benazir Bhutto's assassination case. The petition was moved by the former Chief Protocol Officer of Ms Bhutto named Chaudhry Aslam, an advocate by profession, who was accompanying the entourage on 27th December 2007 and had also sustained injuries during the bomb blast. SC bench headed by the CJP Iftikhar Chaudhry was hearing the petition. The above said 12 respondents including Interior Minister, former law minister, PML(Q) leader and others were asked to file para-wise comments, if they so desire, within a period of two weeks.

Chaudhry Aslam, the petitioner, told the court that he had been trying to get a second FIR registered since 8th July 2009, but in vain. He urged that just after the incident, many leaders disappeared from the crime scene; and that why the *jammers* were not installed at the crime scene.

On 23rd June 2011, Rawalpindi Bench of the LHC had dismissed the plea of Ch Aslam, in which he had requested the court to order putting Babar Awan and Rehman Malik on the Exit Control List (ECL). One of the judges had written an additional note that Ch Aslam was neither an aggrieved party, nor a legal heir of Benazir Bhutto, and thus had no right to seek the registration of an FIR in the BB's murder case.

The CJP J Chaudhry, while heading the 3 judges' bench comprising J Khilji Arif Hussain and J Tariq Pervaiz also ordered the special judge of Anti-Terrorism Court (ATC), seized of the matter of Benazir Bhutto's murder, to submit copies of the proceedings along with order sheets and progress so far made in the case in the next hearing. Ch Aslam had also prayed that the first FIR submitted in the case did not mention the names of the 'real culprits'. In his application, he pleaded to include the names of former Interior Minister Gen Hamid Nawaz, former DG IB Ejaz Shah, former Interior Secretary Kamal Shah, Brig (r) Javed Cheema, former DCO Rawalpindi Irfan Elahi, former CPO Rawalpindi Saud Aziz and SPs Rawal Town Khurram Shahzad and Yaseen Farooq in addition to the earlier mentioned names of Rehman Malik, Babar Awan and Ch Pervez Elahi.

The Chief Justice noted that Mr Zardari was not satisfied with the trial of the case and wanted to know about progress made thus far. *'President Asif Ali Zardari had asked the court - during his address to a public gathering in Garhi Khuda Bakhsh at the death anniversary of the late Benazir Bhutto (27th December 2011) - what it had done in the assassination case of Benazir Bhutto'* [verbatim: **'Chief Sahab! I ask you what had happened to the killers of Benazir Bhutto'**]. Justice Iftikhar recalled. *'Mr Attorney General, how do you see and what weight do you give to the statement of the President?'*

Ch Aslam, the petitioner claimed to be an affected person who received injuries during the fatal assassination attack on the former premier. The CJP observed:

> *'The court's responsibilities had multiplied. The matter of the applicant was of serious nature. According to the appellant, he knows better about the incident because he was there and received injuries.'*

Rashid A Rizvi appeared before the court along with the petitioner. During the hearing, the CJP asked the Attorney General Maulvi Anwarul Haq whether he was satisfied with the progress of the investigation; and commented that a tribunal comprising senior officials from all the provinces could have been formed to probe the BB's murder because the UN Commission's report was civil in nature, not criminal. It was the task of the government to take clues from it and carry out an independent investigation. Affidavits on behalf of the two alleged suspects, Brig Javed Iqbal Cheema and Kamal Shah were placed before the apex court urging that they did not have any involvement in the case.

Let us wait for further developments in the given scenario.

Scenario 52

BB's MURDER: OFF THE RECORD

Referring to *'The News' of 22nd July 2002* : Benazir Bhutto had appointed Rehman Malik as Additional Chief of the Federal Investigation Agency in 1995 which then launched a secret war against the Islamists, which amounted to a direct attack on the ISI. The Pakistani military was equally dismayed by reports of FIA contacts with the Israeli secret service, the MOSSAD, to investigate Islamist terrorists. The FIA leadership under Benazir Bhutto had also angered Islamist elements because they allowed the extradition of Ramzi Yousaf to the US for trial on the New York Trade Centre Bombing in 1993.

> [Details available at another authentic source tells that *'following a tip-off from Istiaque Parker, on February 7, 1995, Inter-Services Intelligence (ISI) and U.S. Diplomatic Security Service Special Agents, including Bill Miller and Jeff Riner, raided room number 16 in the Su-Casa Guest House in Islamabad, Pakistan, and captured Yousef before he could move to Peshawar. Parker was paid $2 million for the information leading to Yousef's capture.'*]

However, one of the first acts of President Farooq Leghari, after dismissing Benazir Bhutto in November 1996, was to imprison Rehman Malik, the then Addl DG FIA on various charges.

As given earlier, after release when Rehman Malik fled to UK and claimed asylum in year 2000, he managed to come much closer to Benazir Bhutto in London. His office at Crown House, North Circular Road used to be a hub of such political and business activities in which Benazir Bhutto's finances were being invested. Numerous local and off-shore companies floated jointly by them for various activities including one named 'Petro-Line'. Its office was also linked or opened in Vienna city of Austria to streamline money laundering from Swiss accounts of Benazir Bhutto. Its brief has been mentioned in previous pages under NRO's head.

Rehman Malik had established good relations with Gen Musharraf, DG MI Ashfaq Kiyani, DG ISI Nadeem Taj and other top brass of Pakistani Army may be through US bosses or under a garb of mediator between Gen Musharraf and PPP since 2006. When Benazir Bhutto mentioned that Ejaz Shah, the DG IB, might be involved in the attack (of 18th

October 2007 at Karachi on her first arrival after exile), Mr Malik was summoned by the DG ISI Nadeem Taj. The security provided to him was unprecedented because Ejaz Shah had accompanied him to the GHQ in order to settle things with DG ISI.

[*Earlier, Rehman Malik was taken aback when he was given extraordinary protocol at the Islamabad airport. He found dozens of top security and protocol officers receiving him inside the plane. A bullet proof car was specially parked close to the plane and he was taken out of the Islamabad airport amid tight security, which was not even available to the federal ministers then.*]

Rehman Malik did not respond to journalists when they came to know about the above referred meeting and asked for his opinion. Talking to the news media, Rehman Malik had only confirmed his meeting with DG ISI but refused to comment on the nature of his talks. On the issue of extraordinary security provided to him by the government, Mr Malik told that they had some concerns about my security and they acted on their own.

Rehman Malik was the chief negotiator of Musharraf - Benazir deal and had established many key connections which he used intelligently after her death. The immediate indicators after BB's death on 27th December 2007 also lead many investigative journalists to float an opinion that if Mr Malik was a part of the whole big game especially keeping in view the above narrated event of protocol by the army. In his first interview, within hours of BB's Death, Mr Malik had claimed that **his car was about forty feet away from BB's car during incident '*but he could not hear gunshots*'**. In fact he was miles away.

Being BB's Chief Security Officer (CSO), he did bother to call anyone in BB's car (Naheed Khan, SP Major Imtiaz, Safdar Abbasi & 'other person') but even then he had presumed that BB was safe and it was what he told the Geo TV after the explosion. Brig Cheema had also confirmed the same on Geo TV but referring it to the verification done by Mr Malik. The CSO did not know that the tyres of BB's car had gone burst after the explosion and Major Imtiaz had moved the BB to Shery Rehman's car after travelling a short distance.

Every sane person understands that what should have been the duties and obligations of a CSO, Chief Security Officer. How Rehman Malik had performed his duty to protect Benazir Bhutto as her old aide and CSO can be judged from the following:

'*On 26th December 2007, at 9.30 PM, Rehman Malik was attending a marriage dinner at Holiday Inn Islamabad where he was invited by one Maqbool Malik, a solicitor from [Malik Law Solicitors & DM Digital TV] Manchester UK. Rehman Malik remained with his friends from abroad till late that night whereas he was supposed to check and supervise his team deployed for the security arrangements at Liaqat Bagh [where BB was going to make a public speech next day at 3 PM] at that time because any miscreant could hide a bomb device near the stage in darkness to be detonated later at an appropriate time.*

On 27th December 2007, Maqbool Malik [from Manchester UK] visited Rehman Malik along with his two brothers in law in Marriot Hotel Islamabad. Their meeting started at 9.30 AM and ended at 1.30 PM when Rehmen Malik departed saying that he was going to Liaqat Bagh. What security checks he had launched at Liaqat Bagh and when; should be a matter of concern for the PPP. He was not bothered at all that who were the persons on duty, how many were they and at what points were they deployed, who was the supervisor of PPP workers, who was keeping liaison with local police, what were the escape routs, who was controlling the routs, who were men to check security of people around stage and hundreds of more questions like that.

Benazir Bhutto was going to address at 3 PM at Rawalpindi and her Chief Security Officer was leaving Marriot Islamabad at 1.30 PM to travel an hour's journey; what was the inside – planning?

*From Liaqat Bagh premises, Rehman Malik was particular to send a call to his guests from abroad asking them categorically that '***Do not come to Liaqat Bagh; note it seriously; don't come here... see you soon***'. What was the background of sending such stern instructions to his guests?*

This event could be analyzed in the backdrop of the cogent fact that the CSO Rehman Malik & Babar Awan were about two miles away from Benazir Bhutto when the explosion took place at Liaqat Bagh.'

The telecast must be available on investigator's record in which Rehman Malik was saying that:

'*They (other person Babar Awan) stopped at the Hospital and found that BB's car was not coming. He took a U turn from there and found that BB's car had already entered hospital and there was a huge crowd over there. Then they left for Islamabad.*'

Mr Malik remained at Bilawal House in Islamabad and confined himself there until Mr Zardari reached Islamabad from Dubai. Babar Awan sitting next to RM had also confirmed that they directly went to Bilawal House in Islamabad assuming that BB was okay and she was directly following their car.

Once Babar Awan found that BB did not reach Islamabad, he immediately rushed back towards Rawalpindi and Mr Malik did not accompany him to Rawalpindi. Babar's statement (who was sitting next to RM) was in complete contradiction to Mr Malik's claiming that:

• They returned to hospital from next U-Turn (as told to Anchor person Mr Iftikhar of Geo).

• They stopped the car when they could not see lights of BB's car anymore.

Later Mr Malik told the newsmen that he was trying his best to get custody of the dead body *As Soon As Possible* from the Hospital. Why he wasn't bothered about the post mortem, the most basic requirement for further investigation when he had been once a Director of FIA.

Last but not the least; the suspicious person with odd looks standing close to BB while she was addressing at Liaqat Bagh, was made to join BB's entourage on special recommendation of Rehman Malik. This person was Khalid Shahinshah who was personal servant of Zardari House, might have known about the explosion in advance which could be the reason he rushed into the armoured car before everyone else.

PPP sources had told that the moment Benazir Bhutto ended her address; this man (Khalid Shahinshah) was the first one to dive into her bullet proof Land Cruiser; an unusual change from his past routine whilst he always boarded the vehicle after Benazir; often hanging by the external pedestals of her Cruiser.

Naheed Khan and Dr Safdar Abbassi got seated in the rear portion of the Cruiser, and when the suicide bomber blew him apart, Khalid was also present in the Cruiser. Afterwards he went over to Zardari House Islamabad where he lived for two days; did not visit Naudero to participate Benazir's funeral, making it there on third day. He disappeared from the Naudero scene too soon after over an excuse of his mother's death.

This person, Khalid Shehanshah, was then mysteriously shot down at his residence in Karachi after six months and none of Bhutto's or Zardari's associate ever bothered to follow the investigation of their old-age domestic servant and Benazir Bhutto's '*jan-nisar*'.

Rehman Malik was a buddy of Tariq Aziz, Secretary and close associate of President Gen Musharraf. Mr Malik then assumed the role of a bridge between Gen Musharraf and Zardari through Tariq Aziz. Fatima Bhutto openly blamed Asif Zardari for assassinating Murtaza Bhutto. Mr Malik was the right hand man of Mr Zardari and hence his role due to his high position in FIA made him even more suspicious.

Rehman Malik desperately tried to stop restoration of CJ Iftikhar Chaudhry's team of judges vis a vis sacking of thoroughly militarized and yes men judges. Mr Malik, allegedly using Farooq Naek's shoulders, was toeing American CIA's dirty lines and policies which were totally anti people. He used to attend all major meetings of Negroponte and US Ambassador in Islamabad Miss Anne Patterson.

'The News' of 8th May 2008 divulged an open secret through Ansar Abbasi and quoted Election Commission's confirmation about Rehman Malik's key role in by-polls delay. The controversy behind the postponement of the by-elections deepened a day earlier when the Election Commission's Secretary Kanwar Dilshad revealed that he had received a phone call from Adviser to the Prime Minister on Interior Rehman Malik, who had asked for a delay. This had confirmed a similar claim by the NWFP government. As Dilshad's statement to 'the News' firmly established that Rehman Malik was the man who had successfully executed the controversial postponement, it was still unclear who, between the Zardari House in F-8/2 Islamabad and the Presidency, actually authored the script of the so-called conspiracy.

Rehman Malik has been known for releasing press statements to create panic in public but just to make the Bhutto's associates believe that he is much concerned about Bhuttos. For instance in mid-2011, he publicly announced that *'the al Qaeda and Tehrik e Taliban Pakistan (TTP) have planned to kidnap and assassinate PPP's Chairman Bilawal Bhutto Zardari as he visits Pakistan next month'*. While saying so he forgot that he had spoken about his own weakness being the Interior Minister.

As per revelations made by *The Express Tribune*:

> *'Some banned outfits have notorious designs against Bilawal Bhutto, quoting the British Security Service (MI5), a UK based intelligent*

agency responsible for national security. The MI5 with coordination of Oxford University is assessing how to provide more security to Bilawal where he is residing. A detailed report on this matter will be handed over to the President by end of this month [September 2011]. Around Rs:136.5 million is being spent on Bilawal's security in Britain'. Poor nation's begged money!

CASES AGAINST MR MALIK CLEARED:

7th May 2010: An accountability court quashed two corruption references against Federal Interior Minister Rehman Malik after the National Accountability Bureau (NAB) opted to withdraw the same. Judge Chaudhry Abdul Haq in his short order said since Bureau did not want to pursue & proceed in the two references filed in 1997, the court absolved the minister and other accused of the charges.

In the first reference, it was alleged that Mr Malik as ADG FIA had sent a team to search the houses of Abbas Raza and Hashim Raza which [the team] allegedly took away Rs:0.7 million and 25 grams gold. In second reference, Mr Malik was accused of receiving two cars worth Rs:1.798 million from Toyota Central Motors in Karachi through Deputy Director Waseem Ahmed as commission for the purchase of vehicles by the FIA worth tens of millions of rupees. When Rehman Malik came in government in 2008 and assumed charge as the Federal Interior Minister, Waseem Ahmed was elevated as IGP Sindh and subsequently was brought as DG FIA after making extension in his service and the Supreme Court had to order for his removal.

The prosecutors told the court that Mr Malik was kept in jail for 11 months in 1997 without obtaining a judicial custody order from a competent court. It may be mentioned here that the Accountability Court Rawalpindi had awarded him sentence in January 2004 in absentia. The competent court had accepted his applications and terminated conviction in both cases on 5th March 2008 when he appeared in the court while being in Pakistan. These convictions were revived again in the light of 16th December 2009's judgment of the Supreme Court, striking down the National Reconciliation Ordinance as void *ab initio*. Mr Malik had to approach the High Court to remove the convictions from his record. His petition for bail and further process was admitted in LHC.

The bench comprising LHC Chief Justice Khwaja Sharif and Justice Manzoor Ahmed Malik admitted the appeals of Rehman Malik [for regular hearing] filed against conviction in two cases and issued notices to the NAB Chairman for 12th January 2010. The minister was also ordered to submit two surety bonds of Rs:100,000 each. He argued; the Supreme Court had held in numerous cases that conviction and sentence awarded under Section 31-A of the NAB Ordinance 1999 in absentia was void; also that there was no proof that he [Rehman Malik] was an absconder and intentionally left the country to avoid trial; and that Section 31-A of the NAB Ordinance was in violation of Article 2-A, 4, 9 of the Constitution.

Rehman Malik moved another application for suspension of his sentence under Section 426 of CrPC, but the court declined to entertain it. The court observed the NAB Ordinance was a special law and suspension of sentence could only be sought through a writ petition under Article 199 of the Constitution. The Court was requested to convert his application into a writ petition, but the court turned down the plea, observing that there was a procedure for it. After a short while, the minister's counsel filed a writ petition and the court passed the suspension order on it. Rehman Malik also sought exemption from personal appearance on the next hearing, saying he was scheduled to proceed abroad next month. The court refused to give him exemption, but adjourned the case to his convenience.

As there was Kh Sharif sitting as Chief Justice and the applicant was from PPP so the appeal had to be rejected. Had there be any person belonging to Nawaz Sharif's PML(N), the acceptance of appeal or acquittal was eminent and immediate. Kh Sharif should have avoided being a part of bench in Rehman Malik's case as Mr Malik's political rivalry with Sharifs and CJ's association with them, were matters of record. Media knew it well.

The PPP had well apprehended that Justice Kh Sharif would go to every extent in pleasing Nawaz Sharif by penalizing a sitting PPP Minister and an ex FIA Officer who had done about a dozen investigations against Sharif's family. As a strategy, just to leave a partisan judge on thorns for ever, President Asif Ali Zardari, exercising his special powers of Article 45 of the Constitution, pardoned Mr Malik and his fellow accused officers. Afterwards, the NAB court also discharged the said cases.

Referring to *'the News' of 23rd December 2009*, Mr Malik, when he was coming out of the LHC, told the newsmen that *'we are not a political party that attacks courts and beats judges to make them flee, leaving their shoes behind. We will never commit a contempt of court. I forgive those who registered fake cases against me.'* But earlier when Rehman

Malik was talking to the US Ambassador in Pakistan, his stance was a bit different. He had told the US Ambassador Anne Patterson during a mutual discussion on 11th November 2009, that:

'The Supreme Court is not likely to revoke presidential immunity of Asif Ali Zardari on corruption charges and if the court does so, then he (Malik) would instruct concerned prosecutors to dismiss these charges before the court. The minister further disclosed that he already had several of his cases disposed off in this manner through dictating prosecutors, who subsequently told the relevant courts that cases against him were baseless.

He [Rehman Malik] also accused Nawaz Sharif for pressurizing Chief Justice Iftikhar M Chaudhry into cancelling the immunity for Zardari. A variety of issues including NRO, growing thickness in MQM & PML-N relations and threats to President Zardari from the DG ISI Lt Gen Shuja Pasha who, he proposed, should be made deputy army chief in March 2010 as a confidence building measure, only to replace Gen Kayani after his retirement in October 2010 suggesting latter's elevation to the post of Joint Chief of Army Staff'.

Rehman Malik had asserted again that *'in one of his own corruption cases, this had been done, and that in another case, the Supreme Court had ruled his imprisonment illegal, and that President Zardari had the ability to pardon anyone'.* Perhaps it was all being done for the President Zardari in focus.

In the same meeting of 11th November 2009, the Interior Minister also told Anne Patterson that MQM had confided in him saying that:

'They [the MQM] had withdrawn support on the NRO when tabled in the National Assembly in 2008 on the instance of the US authorities and that the Army, US, UK and Saudi Arabia were behind this attempt to push the government on the NRO issue.'

Saudi Arabia might be up against Mr Zardari while trying to oust him from the Presidency. Mr Malik had also complained that he and President Zardari, had lost the US blessings at a time when they were direly needed, urging the ambassador to get a statement issued from Washington in support of the PPP government. He also shared his concerns that US Secretary of State Hillary Clinton was not happy with the performance of the present set-up during her visit to Pakistan. He had inquired as to *whether the ambassador was aware that the 'establishment' was involved in working against* NRO *and for President Zardari's removal.* Patterson told Mr Malik that 'we were aware of such allegations'.

The wording of above Wikileaks cable had given an impression that during the meeting, Mr Malik was perhaps nervous and that the US government was distancing itself both from him and President Zardari. The Interior Minister had claimed that the MQM had received 'this message' during the Sindh Governor's trip to the United States in those days and that Altaf Hussain had been approached by the British government in London. Ambassador Ann Patterson strongly denied these allegations, stating that the US Government had not held such discussions with the Sindh Governor.

DR QADEER HELD FOR U.S. PLEASURE:

Earlier in the same year, the important role of Rehman Malik in having relationship with America could be seen through another communication sent by the US Ambassador in Islamabad Ann Patterson on 9th February 2009 to her State Department in Washington. The US Ambassador had held a meeting with President Zardari a day before saying that '........ **Rehman Malik had failed badly this time'**.

The complete text of the cable was as follows:

(S) Summary: President Zardari assured the [US] Ambassador on February 8 (2009) that A.Q. Khan would remain under house arrest and not engage with the media. Minister of interior Rehman Malik also insisted that Khan would be prohibited from talking to the press and politicians, and his movements would be curtailed. Zardari and Malik speculated to the Ambassador that PML(N) leader Nawaz Sharif was about to run A.Q. Khan for the Senate on his party's slate.

The Pakistani government claims that they were trying to establish a legal basis for Khan's detention, as he had been restrained previously by the Ministry of Defence "for his own security." However, the timing of the court decision obviously took Zardari by surprise, reflecting the GOP's persistent lack of coordination and message control. Now the government is trying to catch up. End Summary.

2. (S) President Zardari assured the Ambassador on February 8 that A.Q. Khan would not talk to the press and would remain under strict control. Ambassador conveyed that the release of A.Q. Khan, the world's most serious nuclear proliferators, aggravated by Khan's press conference on his front lawn thanking Zardari and Interior Minister Rehman Malik for his release, was a very unfortunate signal to send to the world. For the United States, it was particularly unsettling coming on the eve of Ambassador Holbrook's visit and as the U.S. Congress considered assistance and trade bills for Pakistan.

The U.S. was seeking a commitment that A.Q. Khan would stay out of the press and his movements would be restricted as before. Zardari argued that referring Khan's detention to the Islamabad High Court was designed to prevent Khan from receiving a Senate ticket from PML(N) leader Nawaz Sharif.

3. (S) Minister of Interior Rehman Malik also reassured the Ambassador and DCM in several phone calls and meetings that A.Q. Khan would be kept under wraps; he would not talk to reporters or politicians, and his movements would be strictly controlled. Malik reported that President Zardari, who heard about the court decision from the Ambassador and then Pakistani Ambassador to the U.S. Haqqani and not his own ministers; had been annoyed about being blindsided; Malik told us that there had been no previous legal basis for Khan's detention.

Note: *This is true. The head of Pakistan's nuclear "Strategic Plans Division" Lt. General Kidwai has often told us that there was no legal basis for Khan's detention except to provide for his own security.*

4. Malik said repeatedly that the press conference had "gotten out of hand" and the press had rushed to Khan's house even before the decision was announced. xxxxx

Media Reaction: (U) Unsurprisingly, Khan's press conference was widely covered by the electronic and print media. All papers ran Dr. Khan's "triumphant" photograph .... Dr. Khan's gratitude toward the government of Pakistan was underscored in a widely reported quote that he is "grateful to the president, the prime minister, and the interior advisor Rehman Malik."

5. (U) F M Qureshi [Shah Mahmood] and the MFA issued the official reaction for the GOP; their remarks were aimed at minimizing foreign reaction .... and that the government maintains the right to appeal the court's decision.

*6. (S) Comment: **The Islamabad High Court is firmly under the control of the government, so it would appear that this was a planned move by*** *some government element, probably Rehman Malik, in a too clever by half move that was not coordinated with Zardari.*

Malik, who has aspirations to become deputy prime minister (or even prime minister), has failed badly this time.

There was not even a hint publicly that Nawaz Sharif ever intended to nominate A.Q. Khan for a Senate seat. Moreover, the new court decision would not make Khan's nomination any less probable. This fiasco demonstrated yet another example of amateur, uncoordinated governance in Islamabad, and Nawaz will waste no time in exploiting this misstep. We will continue to monitor Khan's freedom to determine if the GOP is implementing the restrictions that they promised to continue imposing on Khan.

Patterson

The above communications amongst the US officials explicitly points toward the Pakistani rulers who have been playing in the American hands like puppets. It also reflected about the real intentions of the US policy makers towards Pakistan's nuclear program. They had already got hanged Z A Bhutto for okaying the nuclear program but now through Gen Musharraf, Mr Zardari and Rehman Malik they were able to drag its founder Dr Qadeer through the thorns of arrests and isolation; the process of revenge and punishments was being taken to its end after thirty years. Hats off to the American agents as rulers of Pakistan and still they are holding slogans of 'democracy'. Colonial era has come back perhaps.

Nawaz Sharif should have nominated Dr Qadeer to join PML(N) as Senator of Parliament even he was in custody. There was no bar for contesting election from being in jail or custody. The fact remained that Nawaz Sharif had also agreed with the US stance of keeping Dr Qadeer away; after all, the Sharifs were also old American buddies and still aspire to rule Pakistan through their blessings.

MALIK– WELL PLAYED: NY TIMES

Let us skip over to the affairs a year after.

New York Times of 6th January 2011 had mentioned in an article carrying Salman Taseer's murder story that:

'Government ministers and party officials indicated that they were dropping the campaign to change the blasphemy laws that Mr Taseer had championed. No senior official would be drawn to comment on the religious extremist aspect of the killing at the funeral. Those who did comment indicated a shift in the government position, by suggesting the killing was a political murder and a conspiracy, rather than a religiously motivated attack.

Foreign Minister Shah Mahmood Qureshi avoided to comment and merely expressed his condolences to the family when approached by journalists. The Interior Minister, Rehman Malik, went as far as to say he would shoot any blasphemer himself.

Now, we all know Rehman Malik is a bumbling fool, but this really takes the cake. Well done. Seriously well played'.

What else one could expect from the leadership of the PPP; one should not be surprised that the PPP which despite being in power did not care about bringing to justice the killers of its own leader Benazir BHutto (not carrying out post-mortem, delaying the investigation, not releasing the reports etc). Loss of life in PPP does not carry much significance because everyone knows that death of their members would be an opportunity to garner sympathy votes and a few more seats in the parliament. *'This was a straight forward case of murder of a citizen also what political colour you assign to it. I think what Rehman Malik said was 'brainless' in the given circumstances in Pakistan'*, one reader held.

MALIK'S STATEMENTS – A FIASCO:

Could Rehman Malik be taken serious while issuing such statements on political turmoil in the smaller provinces? He has been issuing hundreds of such speeches on situations in Karachi, around Peshawar and Swat. What happened in the end; nothing but bloodshed. Let us see his actual words since 2009 at least.

The **'Daily Times'** of 3rd May 2009: *'The interior minister asked the Taliban to disarm, saying it was the last warning being handed out to the terrorists.'* [The response came immediately. On 27th May 2009 the Taliban killed at least 35 people and injured 250 by firing on guards and then destroying the 'Emergency Response' building at the City's Police HQ Lahore. Three attackers who died in the attack were unidentified; two of them emerged from a Toyota van used in the attack and fired on security officials. The driver was not able to breach the boundary of security cordon before he detonated the bomb.]

The **'Daily Times'** of **15th July 2009**: *'The Federal Interior Minister Rehman Malik warned that strict action would be taken (against police officers) if any incident of target killing occurs from today onwards'.* [Even then the increase in the number of killings remained appalling. In HRCP's Report, the total number of killings during 2009 was 747, while the number of target killings in Karachi totalled 291. A staggering 218 people were targeted and killed on political grounds and out of them, 61 belonged to the MQM, 40 to the ANP, 39 were activists of the MQM-H and 29 belonged to the PPP. However, in the first 11 months of this year, the total number of killings in the metropolis stands at 1,860 including 711 target killings. Out of the 711 murders, 283 were non-political in nature. The worst months, in which the number of political and non-political target killings was the highest, were July and October.]

The **'Daily Times'** of **2nd January 2010**: *'People involved in violating the law will be brought to justice ... no matter what their political affiliations are.'*

The **Dawn** of **8th January 2010**: *'The government will have a strict no-tolerance policy for target killing incidents.'*

The **GEO TV** of **9th January 2010**: *'The Interior Minister said satellite system is also being used for carrying out monitoring.'*

[During the same period of two weeks, the media was aware that on *1st January 2010* a suicide bombing occured at a volleyball game in Khyber PK province's border town killing at least 95 and injuring over 100.

The PK-politics internet site had also published on *13th January 2010*, the statistics of killings in Karachi to show a mirror to Rehman Malik. The figures were:

Muhajir Qaumi Movement (Amir Group) – 1314
Muhajir Qaumi Movement (Afaaq Group) – 270
Motahida Qaumi Movement (Altaf Group) – 84
Pakistan People's Party (PPP) – 75
Awami National Party (ANP) – 54
Jamaat-e-Islami (JI) – 51
Sunni Tehreek (ST) – 40
Sipah-e-Sahaba Pakistan (SSP) – 14

The **Dawn** of **15th January 2010**: *'Gangsters were present in these localities and action would be taken against them at all cost.'*

[On *30th January 2010*, one of the same like gangster group at Pak-Afghan border caused a suicide bombing at a military checkpoint within the town of *'Khaar'*, in the Bajaur Agency, killing at least 16 people and injuring around 25 others.]

The **Dawn** of **2nd February 2010**: *'Those involved in terrorism and target killings will be dealt with an iron hand.'*

[The miscreants in Pakistan took that statement seriously and immediately responded next day on *3rd February* by causing a suicide bombing within the Lower Dir District area in the North, killing at least 8 people, including 3 American soldiers and injuring around 70 other people. On *5th February*, twin bombings, one of which included a suicide attack, occurred in the city area of Karachi, killing at least 25 people and injuring more than 50 others. *On 10th February*, a suicide bomber targeting a police patrol in the Khyber Agency near Peshawar killed at least 19 people, including 13 local policemen. On *18th February 2010*, a bombing had blasted a local mosque in the Tirah Valley of the same area of Khyber Agency, killing at least 30 people and injuring more than 70 others. What a nice way it was to take notice of government's warning.]

The **Dawn** of **15th March 2010**: *'Interior Minister Rehman Malik directed Inspector General of Rangers Sindh to maintain peace in collaboration with police and deal strictly with those who take the law into their hands'.*

The daily **Nation** of **22nd March 2010**: *'The incidents of target killing have dropped considerably and activities of miscreants are being monitored through satellite'.*

The **Daily Times** of **23rd March 2010**: *'He said that if those involved in target killings think they could escape after committing their crime, they are wrong since they are being watched closely and a satellite watching system is also being maintained for this purpose. I am not just scaring them, but I mean business.'*

[Rehman Malik's above noted statements of March 2010 were replied by the 'interested parties' in a very crude way like that three separate suicide bombings targeting Pakistani security forces occurred from *8th - 12th March 2010*. The media reports told that more than 72 people were killed in these three suicide attacks and more than 190 others were also injured & admitted in various civil & military hospitals of Khyber PK.

On *5th April 2010,* another series of coordinated bombings at the US consulate in Peshawar and at the ANP – PPP party rally in the Khyber PK province occurred killing 50 people and injuring more than 100 others. On *10th April 2010,* another 100 civilian people were killed in an air raid on Waziristan area at Pak-Afghan border through a concerted attack by unknown intruders. Strangely it was not a drone attack. On *17th -18th April 2010,* three more suicide bomb attacks occurred within the town of Kohat of the Khyber Pakhtunkhwa Province. At least 58 people were killed in these three suicide attacks and around 86 others were injured. On *19th April 2010,* a suicide bombing struck a marketplace in the centre of Peshawar city killing at least 25 people and left tens injured.]

The **Dawn of 20th May 2010:** *'No one would be allowed to break the law in Karachi and violators would be dealt with iron hand.'*

The **Dawn of 24th May 2010:** *'The government would not allow anyone to take law in his hand in the city or any part of the country. Those involved in creating a law and order situation would be severely dealt with.'*

[These warnings from the Federal Interior Minister were reciprocated on 28th May 2010 by causing a series of co-ordinated attacks on two Ahmadi mosques in Lahore. The Tehrik e Taliban Pakistan claimed these attacks but it was presumed that some other XE sponsored secret agents had performed that act using TTP's name to create an atmosphere of hatred and enmity between the Ahmediya and Muslim populations of Pakistan. At least 86 people were killed in those terrorist attacks and more than 120 others were injured.]

The **Daily Times of 24th May 2010:** *'Malik vowed that he would not tolerate the elements who were trying to destroy the law and order of Karachi and said that any attempts to harm the peace of the city would be foiled.'*

The **Dawn of 14th June 2010:** *'Peace will be established in Karachi at all costs and no group or faction will be allowed to create any kind of violence and those who do work against the law will face strict action.'*

Referring to the News Agency **PTI dated 15th June 2010:** *'We have decided to take severe action against the culprits and whosoever is involved in target killings will be arrested and taken to task. There is 'zero tolerance' for criminals and anti-social elements.'*

Referring to News Agency **ANI dated 16th June 2010:** *'Peace would be ensured and no one would be allowed to take the law into his hands.'*

[The above state threats of Mr Malik were welcome. On *1st July 2010*, a twin suicide bombing at Data Darbar, shrine of the patron saint of Lahore, killed 50 people while leaving about two hundred wounded and crying in the nearby hospitals. On *9th July 2010,* a suicide bomb attack occurred at a market within the Mohmand Agency of north-western Pakistan. At least 104 people were killed in this suicide attack and more than 120 others were injured. On *15th July 2010,* at least five people were killed and nearly 50 wounded in a suicide bomb attack near a crowded bus stop in Mingora, the main town of the Swat valley. In Swat valley, suicide bombings against and targeted killings of police and the army informants or peace activists had become a commonplace then.]

The **Daily Times of 25th July 2010:** *'The government will take action against the terrorists at any cost, and it does not care whether it remains in power or not'.*

Referring to News Agency **PPI dated 27th July 2010:** *'Target-killing in Karachi has fully ended now* [... but astonishingly 90 persons were killed in Karachi just in one day on 2nd August 2010].'

The **GEO TV of 6th August 2010:** *'Interior Minister Friday reiterated his warning to the elements involved in the terrorist activities in Karachi firstly, to stop violence or be ready for a stern action against them. Secondly, that no criminal who has taken law in his hand will be spared.'*

[Next day the media had managed to dig out the police record showing that as many as 249 targeted killings took place in Karachi from 1st January to 6th August 2010, which were indeed disturbing statistics from an economic perspective as well, given the fact that the city accounts for two-thirds of Pakistan's trade and industry and almost half of its GDP. Conflicting political, sectarian and linguistic affiliations, marked by intense personal rivalries, were the major causes of the blind murders.]

The **Express Tribune of 7th August 2010:** *'The government has officially hired the services of satellite imaging experts to tackle the situation in Karachi... Any house which will be used as a hideout will be demolished and its members will be arrested'.*

The daily **Nation of 7th August 2010:** *'Stern action would be taken against the culprits without taking their political affiliations in consideration.'*

[The government's strategy of 'satellite imaging' was adequately refuted by the fighting factions of Karachi and thus on *3rd August 2010,* MQM's MPA Raza Haider was assassinated in Karachi thereby causing serious threats to the law & order situation. Riots erupted at once and more than hundred people were slaughtered in the city during revengeful reaction of the MQM. The Federal Interior Minister could not bring even a single arrest on record what to speak of trials.

On *14th August 2010,* about 12 suspected militants in North Waziristan were killed by a suspected American attack on a civilian village. On the same day of *14th August,* at least 16 people were killed following an outbreak of violence in Balochistan. No record with police was available for the human rights activists. On *15th August 2010,* condemnations and the promise of a government inquiry followed the lynching of two teenaged brothers, Mughees and Muneeb Butt, by a mob in Sialkot. The killings were allegedly sparked by a mistaken belief that the two brothers were robbers, were caught on film by a Dunya TV reporter and aired on all private media channels.

On *1st September 2010,* at least 35 people were killed and more than 250 injured, following a series of bomb attacks on a Shia Islamic procession in Lahore. The attacks, two of which were said to be from suicide bombers took place at a commemoration of the death of Esteemed Ali bin Abi Talib (RA). Again on *3rd September 2010,* in a similar attack on Shia Muslims at least 50 people were killed in Quetta by a suicide bomber at a Shia rally. Responsibility was claimed by the Taliban who state that the killings were a revenge attack for the killing of a Sunni leader in 2009.

On *16th September 2010,* exiled politician Imran Farooq was found murdered near his home in north London having been stabbed several times. Violence erupted in his hometown Karachi following his murder. Several shops and vehicles were set on fire however no casualties were reported. On *25th September 2010,* four people were killed in Miranshah in an American cum NATO attack. Seven more died in the Datta Khel area of North Waziristan in a similar attack the following day.]

The **Dawn of 17th October 2010**: *'Anyone violating the law must immediately be arrested,'* but on a single day of 20th October 2010, an acute political and ethnic violence suddenly erupted in Karachi resulting in 35 deaths.

The **Dawn of 12th November 2010**: *'Rehman Malik vowed to root out terrorism from the country by taking strict action against the terrorists'.*

[The media immediately placed the statistics till October 2010 for the consumption of the Federal Interior Minister. There were 1,034 deaths in the first ten months of 2010 with the month of August having the highest death toll of the year with 176 people murdered. The month of June saw the second highest death toll of 135 people being killed in various localities of the city. CPLC's records show that this was the highest number of target killings since 1995 {when the figures were 1782; it was again a PPP's regime with Rehman Malik as Additional DG Operations of FIA}.

According to a report in 'The Gulf Today', target killings in Karachi during full year of 2010 had claimed more lives than that of suicide bombings across the country in that year of 2010. Pakistan was struck by 335 incidents of suicide bombings in 2010 that claimed 1,208 people's lives, according to the paper, whereas the number of target killings during the same period was 1,233. The data collected by Gulf Today showed that 122 people were killed in January, 133 in February, 130 in March and April each, 144 in May, 122 in June, 135 in July, 176 in August, 81 in September and 13 people in the first two weeks of October. They said that at least 46 policemen and 2 Rangers' personnel were killed in the city in year 2010 till then.]

Going by individual events, the reports appeared that on *1st November 2010,* a suicide bomber killed two policemen and wounded 10 others as security forces tried to stop him from walking into their local headquarters in Swabi town of Khyber PK province. On *3rd November 2010,* two government schools were destroyed by Taliban militants in an attack in the Mohmand area. On *5th November 2010,* a bomb exploded in a mosque in Darra Adam Khel in North-West Pakistan, killing at least 55 people and injuring over 100. Later that same day a grenade attack on another mosque in the village of Sulemankhel near Peshawar claimed at least two lives. Both attacks occurred during the prayer sessions. On *9th November 2010,* the headquarters of the Pakistan Police's Criminal Investigation Department (CID) in Karachi was attacked by gunner's squad of the militants. After the attack, a lorry load of explosives was detonated; destroying a perimeter wall; 200 deaths and over 100 injuries were reported.

In the ending week of 2010, the people paid their last tribute to Rehman Malik's warnings and statements by causing an armed clash in Khyber PK province on *24th December 2010* in which Taliban militants attacked the security forces killing 11 soldiers but also lost their 24 militant companions as dead. Next day, on *25th December 2010,* a female suicide bomber killed at least 43 people in *'Khaar'* of Mohmand Agency on the way to Swat.

The **Dawn of 15th January 2011**: *'Malik further said that the government would not allow anyone to destroy the [Karachi] city's peace.'*

[But none opted to seek his permission by the way; local police was enough to take care of (& facilitate) them]

The **Express Tribune of 23rd May 2011**: *'The terrorists [who attacked Mehran Air base] were dressed like Star Wars characters.'*

[That was why they were let go Scot free. Also see *'the Express Tribune of 13th March 2011* telling that shooting in Karachi had claimed at least 18 lives in the last 24 hours while police failed to arrest even a single suspect. Six people were killed in the recent incidents of violence across the city two days earlier. An angry mob also set three cars and an office on fire in the Kharadar area against the killing of a political worker. A night before, there were protests claiming more lives taking the 48-hour toll to 22; at least 12 men were shot dead as targeted killings.

Another media report dated *15th June 2011* told that at least eight persons were killed in firing incidents of a day before in Karachi. Firing incidents were reported between armed groups in Orangi, Banaras, Qasba, Ali Garh, Data Nagar and nearby places. The death toll in Karachi violence reached 20 during last 24 hours. About 6 persons were injured in different firing incidents. Two minors were killed in a firing incident in Orangi Town. Fear spread after the incident and shopkeepers closed down their shops. A man was killed in Qasba Colony, while a body was found from Lyari. Another person killed in a firing incident in Water Pump Kashti Chowk.]

The **Indian Express of 14th July 2011**: *'Seventy per cent (70%) [of target killings in Karachi] were by those people who wanted to be rid of their wives and girlfriends or girlfriends who wanted to get rid of their boyfriends.'*

[Rehman Malik could be offered Nobel Prize for so deep research and responsible statement. He was perhaps referring to HRCP report telling that as many as 65 women were killed during first six months of this year; 24 of them were killed by relatives, 26 by unidentified culprits, four were set on fire, three killed on railway tracks, 2 each killed by robbers and Lyari gangsters, three on the pretext of Karo-Kari, while one woman was killed by police. Taking 65 out of 1138 total killings, what was the stance of Mr Malik; needed no comments.

A media columnist wrote that: *'this was strange indeed! Malik was not blaming India or the RAW for this violence in Karachi; unless "wives and girlfriends" were code for India and RAW. Wives against girlfriends or girlfriends against wives; were the women doing the killings and causing the mayhem? Where were the men? This is anarchy, Pakistan-style.'*]

The **Dawn of 28th July 2011**: *'Interior Minister Rehman Malik said that the people of Karachi would soon have a peaceful environment in their city and the government was taking all out measures to achieve the objective.'*

[See also: Statistics compiled by the HRCP Karachi chapter shows that a total of 1138 people have been killed in the city during the first half of 2011, with 490 of them falling prey to targeted killings on different grounds including political, sectarian and ethnic basis. What a peaceful environment it was?

Continuous target killings during July 2011 claimed the lives of over 300 people. The high death toll in July made it one of the deadliest months in almost two decades in the history of Karachi - in fighting linked to ethnic and religious tensions that plague the city. The shooting incidents, starting from 6th July 2011, were perpetrated by unknown gunmen and fired indiscriminately in various neighbourhoods throughout the city. In the third day alone, at least 27 people were shot dead, in what was described as one of the worst days the city was witness to since the PPP-led coalition government came into power.

During the course of the attacks, some three buses were fired upon; some shootings were conducted in Orangi Town, causing many suburban locals to vacate their homes and flee to safer areas. All of the attackers managed to escape immediately after the crime. President Zardari summoned a meeting of top officials to discuss the ongoing violence and find a solution but it was only an eye wash statement like before.

Daily **the News of 2nd August 2011**: *'The interior minister said that any and every action would be taken against the miscreants to restore peace in Karachi and added their masters would not be able to save them... Rahman Malik said that he has ordered for surveillance planes to be brought to Karachi for locating and weeding out the ever-allusive target killers.'*

[To be researched if the US or China wanted to sell such planes to Pakistan and for how much kick-backs]

The **Nation of 12th August 2011**: *'Rehman Malik has said that due to effective measures taken by the government, incidents of target killings have been controlled to a great extent in Karachi'.*

[See also: During the first six months of 2011, out of total of 490 target killing victims 77 belonged to MQM; 26 to PPP; 29 to ANP; 16 to MQM-H; 7 to Sunni Tehreek; 9 to Jamaat Ahl e Sunnat; 2 to JUI; one to PML(N); one to JI; one each to PML(F), Jeay Sindh Qaumi Mahaz, and Punjabi - Pakhtun Ittehad and four to Sipah e Sahaba (SeS) and the rest of the people unknown]

Referring to the News Agency **APP dated 16th August 2011**: *'Rehman Malik said that he had directed the law enforcement agencies to gather information so as to take stern action against "Batha Mafia" as was taken against target killers in Karachi.'*

[Vow...still to gather information! it was just a joke otherwise he knew it well; his IGP, SPs, all Police Stations Incharge and the 'others' concerned always keep ready lists]

Daily **the News of 19th August 2011**: *'Talking to media after visiting police commandos who were injured in an ambush in Korangi, here at Jinnah Hospital, Interior Minister appreciated their courage and vowed to deal miscreants with iron hands.'*

The **'Express Tribune of 20th August 2011**: *'Interior Minister Rehman Malik claimed that more than 100 terrorists have been arrested in Karachi and they will be exposed on television within two days.'* [But astonishingly during the same month of August, 44 more people were killed in non-stop shootings. Most of the victims were members of the Muhajir community, the largest ethnic group in Karachi.]

The above was only a sample of Mr Malik's press statements. One may need a full book for all the divine words he has been uttering to justify the security position in Pakistan viz a viz poor people's tax money. The fact remained that despite the above plethora of statements, Karachi continued to burn from ethno - sectarian violence or target killings. Rehman Malik then announced a new weapon in the government's arsenal to hunt down the culprits: Satellite Imaging. The government had officially hired the services of satellite imaging experts to tackle the situation in Karachi. The Interior Ministry was using this satellite technology for at lease seven months till then. Mr Malik had also added that *'I am not just scaring them, but I mean business.'* Media knew it that Mr Malik had been threatening the criminals since February 2008 at least but without a single apprehension or arrest.

It was the same thing over and over again every few weeks. Political violence used to break out in Karachi; Rehman Malik came to Karachi, held meetings with MQM and ANP; announcements made that those criminals would not be tolerated: Rehman Malik suddenly flew back to Islamabad always on a pretext of urgent meeting at the presidency. It had been the routine since four years at least.

During the third week of October 2011, Mr Malik said that Pakistan would hold peace talks with the Taliban only if the militants lay down their weapons first; minimum agenda for talks was for the insurgents to give up arms. He wished that the Taliban would not *'keep Kalashnikovs and hold talks'*. Both sides indicated they were open to negotiations, but no such condition was set for previous talks, which failed to end violence in which thousands had died. Correspondents held that his comments might not reflect official Pakistani policy. In the past, peace talks with militants in tribal areas near the Afghan border had resulted in short lived accords and accusations that Pakistan was providing the militants with sanctuary.

A senior Pakistani Taliban leader, however, refuted Rehman Malik's wish and told the BBC that talks with Islamabad would not succeed until US forces leave Afghanistan in 2014. Washington continued pressing Islamabad to take further military action against the militants. The same day, Mr Malik, released details of what he said was a plan by militants to kidnap Bilawal Bhutto, to gain cheap popularity amongst the PPP workers and at the same time making grounds for his frequent visits to London causing a high toll on poor national exchequer. He also confirmed that militants were holding Shahbaz Taseer, son of slain Punjab Governor Salman Taseer, but with zero progress in that regard.

A media columnist went angry out of the way by saying that:

> *'On 23rd November 2010: Mr Rehman Malik made another dull foot-in-mouth statement the other day – which can only be explained by recalling the time when he was a little baby and the nanny dropped him on his head twice. His current statement contradicts his last statement which repudiated his comments from the time before. Mr. Malik's latest epiphany refutes dozens of other statements by Mr. Malik, President Zardari, President Musharraf, General Kayani, General Pasha and the CIA.'*

Talking to media reporters at the Karachi airport Mr Malik listed the outfits, commonly labelled as 'terrorist organisations', for creating trouble in Karachi and other parts of Pakistan. How he had come to that categorical conclusion to suggest that RAW, CIA and MOSSAD were engaged in that nefarious mission. Mr Malik is on record having said that his Ministry possessed documentary evidence of Indian involvement. When the media men asked that:

> *'If the ministry knew it then what remedial measures had been taken so far? Secondly; why the problem has not been sorted out yet.'*

The Interior Minister had no answer as his flight was getting late.

The Minister's volte-face could reflect an attempt to distort the factual position under some threatening pressure to divert the attention of law enforcement agencies away from the real culprits. The obvious objective seemed to be to make it too hard to eliminate the menace and let the agonising state of insecurity persist. The other possibility was that the authorities, if they possess enough evidence of outside interference, were unable to deal with these destabilising elements because their hands were tied under outside influences. The situation was a sad and telling indication of Rehman Malik's pitiable subservience for survival; he was actually the main obstacle to dumping the baggage of the so-called war on terror also for which the whole Pakistan was continuously suffering.

Let us wait for dawn.

Scenario 53

A A ZARDARI TURNS BACK (2008):

{NOTE: This chapter does not seem to belong the main theme of this book but considered necessary because the document, marking an alliance between the 'proprietors' of two major but rival political parties of Pakistan, was mutually drafted, agreed and signed to end the military rule established by the 12th October 1999's coup d'état led by Gen Musharraf and to restore civilian democratic rule.}

The PPP's office bearers had forgotten that after so many years of exile when Ms Benazir Bhutto first time visited Islamabad the whole masses welcome her. Everyone appreciated workers courage and their devotions for Bhutto family and the first thing Benazir Bhutto did was to visit the (then defunct) Chief Justice Iftikhar Chaudhry's residence in Justice Colony Islamabad. He along with his other colleague judges was under house arrest and their residences were blocked with heavy barbed wire and the Capital Police was on duty. Benazir Bhutto broke the barbed wire chain, went near the CJ's residence and announced there that *'Justice Iftikhar Ch would be our CJ'* The workers and the media men present there hailed this announcement.

After general elections of 18th February 2008 when Pakistan People's Party (PPP) came up to form the government, there was a series of meetings between Asif Ali Zardari [in the capacity of Co Chairman PPP] and the PML(N). Nawaz Sharif had signed two memorandums with A A Zardari in which the reinstatement of higher judiciary into the position of 2nd November 2007 was the major proposal. Zardari went back at 180 angles to his own agreements. The PML(N) many times reminded him about the Charter of Democracy (COD) but Zardari always declined once saying that *'political agreements are not Qura'an or Hadith'* to be followed sacredly. There was much hue & cry in the media; the PML(N) had withdrawn their eight ministers from the Federal Cabinet in mid 2008 but Zardari did not agree to reinstate the suspended judiciary.

[On 16th March 2009, the people were on the roads and PML(N) were brewing benefits from the Lawyer's Movement and the long march was set towards Islamabad. Then Zardari, Rehman Malik and his ministers cried with full voice urging the PML(N) to solve the judge's issue under the COD but it was too late then.]

Most of the PPP's staff members were not aware of the COD then and not even today. Just to revive their knowledge, a copy of the text of COD is placed below verbatim.

CHARTER OF DEMOCRACY (2006):

Text of the COD signed by former Prime Ministers Benazir Bhutto and Nawaz Sharif in London on 14th May 2006:

We the elected leaders of Pakistan have deliberated on the political crisis in our beloved homeland, the threats to its survival, the erosion of the federation's unity, the military's subordination of all state institutions, the marginalisation of civil society, the mockery of the Constitution and representative institutions, growing poverty, unemployment and inequality, brutalisation of society, breakdown of rule of law and, the unprecedented hardships facing our people under a military dictatorship, which has pushed our beloved country to the brink of a total disaster;

Noting the most devastating and traumatic experiences that our nation experienced under military dictatorships that played havoc with the nation's destiny and created conditions disallowing the progress of our people and the flowering of democracy. Even after removal from office they undermined the people's mandate and the sovereign will of the people;

Drawing history's lesson that the military dictatorship and the nation cannot co-exist – as military involvement adversely affect the economy and the democratic institutions as well as the defence capabilities, and the integrity of the country - the nation needs a new direction different from a militaristic and regimental approach of the *Bonapartist* regimes, as the current one;

Taking serious exception to the vilification campaign against the representatives of the people, in particular, and the civilians, in general, the victimisation of political leaders/workers and their media trials under a Draconian law in the name of accountability, in order to divide and eliminate the representative political parties, to Gerrymander a king's party and concoct legitimacy to prolong the military rule;

Noting our responsibility to our people to set an alternative direction for the country saving it from its present predicaments on an economically sustainable, socially progressive, politically democratic and pluralist, federally cooperative, ideologically tolerant, internationally respectable and regionally peaceful basis in the larger interests of the peoples of

Pakistan to decide once for all that only the people and no one else has the sovereign right to govern through their elected representatives, as conceived by the democrat par excellence, Father of the Nation Quaid e Azam Mohammed Ali Jinnah;

Reaffirming our commitment to undiluted democracy and universally recognised fundamental rights, the rights of a vibrant opposition, internal party democracy, ideological/political tolerance, bipartisan working of the parliament through powerful committee system, a cooperative federation with no discrimination against federating units, the decentralisation and devolution of power, maximum provincial autonomy, the empowerment of the people at the grassroots level, the emancipation of our people from poverty, ignorance, want and disease, the uplift of women and minorities, the elimination of Kalashnikov culture, a free and independent media, an independent judiciary, a neutral civil service, rule of law and merit, the settlement of disputes with the neighbours through peaceful means, honouring international contracts, laws/covenants and sovereign guarantees, so as to achieve a responsible and civilised status in the comity of nations through a foreign policy that suits our national interests;

Calling upon the people of Pakistan to join hands to save our motherland from the clutches of military dictatorship and to defend their fundamental, social, political and economic rights and for a democratic, federal, modern and progressive Pakistan as dreamt by the Founder of the nation; have adopted the following, "Charter of Democracy";

A. CONSTITUTIONAL AMENDMENTS

1. The 1973 Constitution as on 12th October 1999 before the military coup shall be restored with the provisions of joint electorates, minorities, and women reserved seats on closed party list in the Parliament, the lowering of the voting age, and the increase in seats in parliament and the Legal Framework Order, 2000 and the Seventeenth Constitutional Amendment shall be repealed accordingly.

2. The appointment of the governors, three services chiefs and the CJCSC shall be made by the chief executive who is the prime minister, as per the 1973 Constitution.

3. (a) The recommendations for appointment of judges to superior judiciary shall be formulated through a commission, which shall comprise of the following:

i. The chairman shall be a chief justice, who has never previously taken oath under the PCO.

ii. The members of the commission shall be the chief justices of the provincial high courts who have not taken oath under the PCO, failing which the senior most judge of that high court who has not taken oath shall be the member.

iii. Vice-Chairmen of Pakistan and Vice-Chairmen of Provincial Bar Association with respect to the appointment of judges to their concerned province.

iv. President of Supreme Court Bar Association.

v. Presidents of High Court Bar Associations of Karachi, Lahore, Peshawar, and Quetta with respect to the appointment of judges to their concerned province.

vi. Federal Minister for Law and Justice.

vii. Attorney General of Pakistan

(a-i) The commission shall forward a panel of three names for each vacancy to the prime minister, who shall forward one name for confirmation to joint parliamentary committee for confirmation of the nomination through a transparent public hearing process.

(a-ii) The joint parliamentary committee shall comprise of 50 per cent members from the treasury benches and the remaining 50 per cent from opposition parties based on their strength in the parliament nominated by respective parliamentary leaders.

(b) No judge shall take oath under any Provisional Constitutional Order or any other oath that is contradictory to the exact language of the original oath prescribed in the Constitution of 1973.

(c) Administrative mechanism will be instituted for the prevention of misconduct, implementation of code of ethics, and removal of judges on such charges brought to its attention by any citizen through the proposed commission for appointment of Judges. (d) All special courts including anti-terrorism and accountability courts shall be abolished and such cases be tried in ordinary courts. Further to create a set of rules and procedures whereby, the arbitrary powers of the chief justices over the assignment of cases to various judges and the transfer of judges to various benches such powers shall be exercised by the Chief Justice and two senior most judges sitting together.

4. A Federal Constitutional Court will be set up to resolve constitutional issues, giving equal representation to each of the federating units, whose members may be judges or persons qualified to be judges of the Supreme Court, constituted for a six-year period. The Supreme and High Courts will hear regular civil and criminal cases. The appointment of judges shall be made in the same manner as for judges of higher judiciary.

5. The Concurrent List in the Constitution will be abolished. A new NFC award will be announced.

6. The reserved seats for women in the national and provincial assemblies will be allocated to the parties on the basis of the number of votes polled in the general elections by each party.

7. The strength of the Senate of Pakistan shall be increased to give representation to minorities in the Senate.

8. FATA shall be included in the NWFP province in consultation with them.

9. Northern Areas shall be developed by giving it a special status and further empowering the Northern Areas Legislative Council to provide people of Northern Areas access to justice and human rights.

10. Local bodies' election will be held on party basis through provincial election commissions in respective provinces and constitutional protection will be given to the local bodies to make them autonomous and answerable to their respective assemblies as well as to the people through regular courts of law.

B. CODE OF CONDUCT

11. National Security Council will be abolished. Defence Cabinet Committee will be headed by prime minister and will have a permanent secretariat. The prime minister may appoint a federal security adviser to process intelligence reports for the prime minister. The efficacy of the higher defence and security

structure, created two decades ago, will be reviewed. The Joint Services Command structure will be strengthened and made more effective and headed in rotation among the three services by law.

12. The ban on a 'prime minister not being eligible for a third term of office' will be abolished.

13. (a) Truth and Reconciliation Commission be established to acknowledge victims of torture, imprisonment, state-sponsored persecution, targeted legislation, and politically motivated accountability. The commission will also examine and report its findings on military coups and civil removals of governments from 1996.

   (b) A commission shall also examine and identify the causes of and fix responsibility and make recommendations in the light thereof for incidences such as *Kargil*.

   (c) Accountability of NAB and other *Ehtesab* operators to identify and hold accountable abuse of office by NAB operators through purgery and perversion of justice and violation of human rights since its establishment.

   (d) To replace politically motivated NAB with an independent accountability commission, whose chairman shall be nominated by the prime minister in consultation with the leader of opposition and confirmed by a joint parliamentary committee with 50 per cent members from treasury benches and remaining 50 per cent from opposition parties in same manner as appointment of judges through transparent public hearing. The confirmed nominee shall meet the standard of political impartiality, judicial propriety; moderate views expressed through his judgements and would have not dealt.

14. The press and electronic media will be allowed its independence. Access to information will become law after parliamentary debate and public scrutiny.

15. The chairmen of public accounts committee in the national and provincial assemblies will be appointed by the leaders of opposition in the concerned assemblies.

16. An effective Nuclear Command and Control system under the Defence Cabinet Committee will be put in place to avoid any possibility of leakage or proliferation.

17. Peaceful relations with India and Afghanistan will be pursued without prejudice to outstanding disputes.

18. Kashmir dispute should be settled in accordance with the UN Resolutions and the aspirations of the people of Jammu and Kashmir.

19. Governance will be improved to help the common citizen, by giving access to quality social services like education, health, job generation, curbing price hike, combating illegal redundancies, and curbing lavish spending in civil and military establishments as contentious causes great resentment amongst the teeming millions. We pledge to promote and practice simplicity, at all levels.

20. Women, minorities, and the under privileged will be provided equal opportunities in all walks of life.

21. We will respect the electoral mandate of representative governments that accepts the due role of the opposition and declare neither shall undermine each other through extra constitutional ways.

22. We shall not join a military regime or any military sponsored government. No party shall solicit the support of military to come into power or to dislodge a democratic government.

23. To prevent corruption and floor crossing all votes for the Senate and indirect seats will be by open identifiable ballot. Those violating the party discipline in the poll shall stand disqualified by a letter from the parliamentary party leader to the concerned Speaker or the Chairman Senate with a copy to the Election Commission for notification purposes within 14 days of receipt of letter failing which it will be deemed to have been notified on the expiry of that period.

24. All military and judicial officers will be required to file annual assets and income declarations like Parliamentarians to make them accountable to the public.

25. National Democracy Commission shall be established to promote and develop a democratic culture in the country and provide assistance to political parties for capacity building on the basis of their seats in parliament in a transparent manner.

26. Terrorism and militancy are by-products of military dictatorship, negation of democracy, are strongly condemned, and will be vigorously confronted.

C. FREE AND FAIR ELECTIONS

27. There shall be an independent, autonomous, and impartial election commission. The prime minister shall in consultation with leader of opposition forward up to three names for each position of chief election commissioner, members of election commission, and secretary to joint parliamentary committee, constituted on the same pattern as for appointment of judges in superior judiciary, through transparent public hearing process. In case of no consensus, both prime minister and leader of opposition shall forward separate lists to the joint parliamentary committee for consideration. Provincial election commissioner shall be appointed on the same pattern by committees of respective provincial assemblies.

28. All contesting political parties will be ensured a level playing field in the elections by the release of all political prisoners and the unconditional return of all political exiles. Elections shall be open to all political parties and political personalities. The graduation requirement of eligibility which has led to corruption and fake degrees will be repealed.

29. Local bodies' elections will be held within three months of the holding of general elections.

30. The concerned election authority shall suspend and appoint neutral administrators for all local bodies from the date of formation of a caretaker government for holding of general elections till the elections are held.

31. There shall be a neutral caretaker government to hold free, fair, and transparent elections. The members of the said government and their immediate relatives shall not contest elections.

D. CIVIL - MILITARY RELATIONS

32. The ISI, MI and other security agencies shall be accountable to the elected government through Prime Minister Sectt, Ministry of Defence, and Cabinet Division respectively. Their budgets will be approved by DCC after recommendations are prepared by the respective ministry. The political wings of all intelligence agencies will be disbanded. A committee will be formed to cut waste and bloat in the armed forces and security agencies in the interest of the defence and security of the country. All senior postings in these agencies shall be made with the approval of the government through respective ministry.

33. All indemnities and savings introduced by military regimes in the constitution shall be reviewed.

34. Defence budget shall be placed before the parliament for debate and approval.

35. Military land allotment and cantonment jurisdictions will come under the purview of defence ministry. A commission shall be set up to review, scrutinise, and examine the legitimacy of all such land allotment rules, regulations, and policies, along with all cases of state land allotment including those of military urban and agricultural land allotments since 12th October, 1999 to hold those accountable who have indulged in malpractices, profiteering, and favouritism.

36. Rules of business of the federal and provincial governments shall be reviewed to bring them in conformity with parliamentary form of government.

MURREE DECLARATION ON JUDICIARY 2008:

On 9th March 2008, the Pakistan People's Party (PPP) and the Pakistan Muslim League (N) agreed on the framework of a governing coalition at Bhurban, Murree. The agreement represented the move of the two parties to form a coalition government to strengthen democracy. The text of the six-point summit declaration was:

1) Allied parties, the Pakistan People's Party and the Pakistan Muslim League (N) resolve to form a coalition government for giving a

practical shape to the mandate, given to the democratic forces by the people of Pakistan on 18th February 2008.

2) This has been decided in today's summit between the PPP and the PML (N) that the deposed judges would be restored, on the position as they were on 2nd November 2007, within 30 days of the formation of the federal government through a parliamentary resolution.

3) The parties agreed that all allied parties would fully support the candidate for the position of Prime Minister, nominated by the PPP. The PML (N) suggested that the candidate for Prime Minister should be such person who can take ahead the common agenda of the allied parties.

4) The parties agreed that the Speaker and the Deputy Speaker of the National Assembly would be from the PPP while the Speaker and the Deputy Speaker of the Punjab Assembly would be from the PML (N).

5) Both the parties agreed that the PML (N) would be a part of the federal government while the PPP would be a part of the Punjab government.

6) This is the solid opinion of the leaderships of both the parties that the allied parties are ready for forming the governments and the sessions of the national and provincial Assemblies be summoned immediately.

Here the political acumen of the twice Prime Minister of Pakistan Nawaz Sharif could not peep deep inside the shrewd Zardari while signing the declaration wherein: firstly as per clause 2, the judges were to be restored through a parliamentary resolution. Secondly no methodology was given for disposal of the then sitting CJ Abdul Hameed Dogar and his colleague judges.

Both these things back-fired due to incompetence of the PML(N)'s advisors; the parliamentary session was not called within that stipulated period or if called, the resolution for restoration of judges could not be tabled. Nawaz Sharif, in utter disappointment, extended his dead line by some more days, till 12th May 2008, but then he revised his demand saying that the judiciary should be reinstated even through an executive order, if not through Parliamentary resolution. The revised demand was for restoration of the judges not necessarily through the settled resolution in the Parliament because the new date for the session was not perhaps possible.

When the matter got delayed, the PPP's own think tank, Barrister Aitzaz Ahsan and the then president Supreme Court Bar Association (SCBA), while addressing a press conference at Quetta on 1st April 2008 said that conspiracies were being hatched at the presidency against the Murree Declaration. He contended that:

'The Murree accord was signed in the larger interest of the country. It guarantees independence of the judiciary and reinstatement of deposed judges. The legal fraternity did not want confrontation among institutions. Lawyers' Movement stands for strengthening of the institutions which have been weakened by former dictators [Gen Musharraf but still he was in Presidency] just to serve their personal interests. The cases of sitting judges would be decided on merit and that there would be no judicial crisis after the reinstatement of deposed judges.'

Federal Minister for Law and Justice Farooq H Naek on 19th April 2008 had also confirmed that judges would be restored under the Murree Declaration. *"We have said it earlier and say it again that judges would definitely be restored"*, he said while talking to reporters at the Supreme Court premises after attending the Pakistan Bar Council meeting. He urged the people to show patience on the issue and trust in the commitment made by the PPP and its allies. He denied the impression that the government is considering to cut down the tenure of the Chief Justice of Pakistan. He hoped that every thing would be done amicably in the interest of the country. Naek said that the PPP and its allies would uphold the supremacy of Constitution and law at any cost.

However, there were cogent voices contrary to Barrister Ahsan and Farooq Naek's views too. Citing from an article titled *'Nawaz's Murree Declaration is dead now'*, appeared in daily *'The Nation' of 4th May 2008,* written by Humayun Gohar after the lapse of 30 day's mandatory period mentioned in the pact:

'So what's Nawaz really playing at? Is he cornering Zardari or are they together cornering the president [till then Gen Musharraf was occupying the presidency] with a secret methodology and .... Even if the National Assembly is convened urgently, at least two days will be lost, and more while waiting upon the wise old men on the legal committee to devise a roadmap out of the constitutional and legal morass that the Nawaz Declaration is rife with.

It seems that Nawaz and Zardari don't agree on anything anymore.

Zardari loathes the judges. Nawaz wants them restored in his single-minded pursuit of the president. Each, it seems, wants to be rid of the other. But Zardari fears that Nawaz could become a fearsome adversary. Nawaz wants to quit on a high point of grand 'principle' so that he can lionize himself in opposition and wait to win the next election.'

Murree Declaration was announced in a festive mood by both Nawaz Sharif and Asif Zardari. PML(N) announced a joint press conference after his come back from Dubai but Zardari couldn't do like that. It could have been announced when both were together a day earlier in Dubai. Zardari returned to Pakistan only a few hours after Nawaz's press conference so Nawaz could have waited till more hours. Gohar had rightly assumed that:

'Given the unseemly haste and the unrealistically short deadline, the conclusion seems inescapable that Nawaz is steamrollering Zardari, cornering him by confronting him with a fait accompli.'

Thus the talks between the two at Dubai were termed by the PML(N) as **Nawaz Declaration** and it could never be taken as 'Dubai Declaration' because Zardari remained mum on the subject.

Some dissenting notes were secretly extended to the media from Zardari's camp, that the 12th May deadline was never agreed in Dubai. In fact there were arguments between Zardari and Khwaja Asif which forced Nawaz Sharif to settle winding up the whole scenario in the hope of raising more noise before media to befool the masses at large. It was their hard luck that then the two parties could not reach an agreement even in the absence of intelligence agencies for which they had chosen Dubai as their talk-venue. Away from intelligence, Nawaz and Zardari could have come up with an agreement that could pull the rug out from under the Gen Musharraf's feet, just like Murree Declaration but the chance failed.

Leaving aside the sentimental feelings of the general populace, the fact remained that it was not an easy task to restore Chief Justice Iftikhar Chaudhry and others either using leverage of resolution passed by the parliament or through an executive order because anyone could move the Supreme Court for a stay asking it whether it was constitutional. A resolution was not an Act that the Supreme Court could not touch especially where they had already validated the 3rd November 2007's emergency and all actions taken under that umbrella. In any way constitutional and judicial crisis would have been there. The above article analysed:

'The deposed judges made a hurried ruling just before they left that the November 3 emergency was unconstitutional. But the successor court deemed that ruling invalid, as their 'lordships' had already been sacked. So do you think the present judges will allow the former judges back; and in the unlikely event that they do, who will be the chief justice, the present one or the former one?

The constitution says that the Supreme Court will comprise 17 judges. If both sets of judges remain, how will the number be raised, through another resolution cum executive order; only an executive order or a constitutional amendment? If either of the first two options is followed, will the (then) sitting Supreme Court deems it unconstitutional? Will we end up with two Supreme Courts? It's a mess.'

For the sake of academic discussion, some members of Intelligentsia had also considered the above view as erroneous and misconceived, mainly that how could there be two chief justices at the same time and how could the judges given oath on an executive order or an Assembly resolution. Their viewpoint was that answers to these two objections were already available in the Constitution as well as in Zafar Ali Shah case (**PLD 2000 SC 869**).

In the said decision, while validating the takeover by Gen Musharraf in October 1999, the apex court had declared that *'no amendment shall be made in the salient features of the Constitution i.e. independence of judiciary, federalism and parliamentary form of government blended with Islamic provisions'*. The proclamation of 3rd November's emergency and the PCO of November 2007 were a blatant attack on the independence of judiciary in gross violation of not only the Constitution but also of the conditions of validations prescribed by the Supreme Court in the said Zafar Ali Shah case.

Moreover, the said proclamation of 3rd November 2007 was immediately suspended and set aside by the seven judges of the Supreme Court on the same day. Hence, all acts done or purported to have been done, in pursuance of the said proclamation, including the PCO and the fresh oath given to the judges, were in violation of the Constitution and void *ab initio* by prevailing cannons of law.

Further, the famous Judges Case of 1996 (if it did not come in collision with another similar decision of 2002) had prescribed the procedure for the appointment of judges of the superior courts. The oath of office of superior court judges administered by Gen Musharraf or by his governors in November 2007 was clearly in violation of 13 categorical conditions prescribed by the Supreme Court itself.

However, Mr Zardari seemed to be more mature of the two but Nawaz Sharif was actually playing a very clever game to distract the people whereas he was never sincere in calling back the defunct judiciary. He was simply dragging PPP into a sand grave which Zardari had smelt just a moment after signing the Murree accord. That was why Zardari had told US Ambassador Anne Patterson a day after signing the Murree Declaration that:

> 'He and Mr Sharif had agreed that Chief Justice Iftikhar Chaudhry would not be restored and reassured the then Chief Justice Abdul Hameed Dogar that he need not worry about the declaration.'

So in nut shell, Murree Declaration was posed as a big breakthrough for parliamentary cooperation between the two major winners of the February 2008 elections. It was blown up to un-imaginable heights because of its primary clause; to restore all the judges within 30 days who were removed under Gen Musharraf's 3rd November 2007 Emergency proclamation.

The revelations about Mr Zardari's interpretations of the Murree Declaration were mentioned in a confidential diplomatic cable dated 10th March 2008 sent to Washington by the US Ambassador Miss Patterson. She had called on Zardari on the same day to get his version of the 'deal' with Nawaz Sharif. When Patterson asked about the 30 days deadline contained in the Murree Declaration about the restoration of judges, **Mr Zardari laughed and said in politics 30 days could become 90.** He also revealed that he had been in touch with Chief Justice Dogar and assured him he would not be removed.

Mr Zardari was more concerned about the poor image Justice Chaudhry's continuing house-arrest would create for his newly formed government. He had to do something about the judges to save a new civilian government from embarrassment. Mr Zardari was willing to work with Gen Musharraf and his advisor Tariq Aziz, but at the same time, he wanted to work with the PML(Q) without the interference of Chaudhrys. However, later Mr Zardari successfully ousted Gen Musharraf in mid August and assumed the president's office himself.

PML(N)'s Ahsan Iqbal, then Federal Education Minister also, on 4th April 2008 when even 30 day's mandatory period was not over, had given a statement to media that:

'Even before the elections the stance of PPP was not so sure about the reinstatement of the judiciary, and they were never very fond of deposed CJ Iftikhar Chaudhary. When Benazir Bhutto was alive; in her deal with President Musharraf, Justice Iftikhar was nowhere to be seen, and the judiciary was a non-issue, as Benazir always thought it as a Kangaroo Court, and she thought that as Justice Iftikhar was also a PCO-ed judge, so nothing would be changed if he was not reinstated.

PML(N) had always rallied behind the judges and their anti-Musharraf campaign had revolved around this point, and they got their votes from the urban areas on this crunch point.

In August 2008, PML(N) led by Nawaz Sharif had withdrawn its support from the ruling coalition government and the PPP was left to hold onto power with the support of smaller parties. With the resignation of Gen Musharraf under a threat of impeachment by the parliament in the third week of 2008, the people thought that the judiciary would be re-instated taking it that PPP was hesitating to take the step forward because of his presence in the presidency. Weeks passed after the resignation but the issue remained stand still. The faith in the democratic government started fading away and at last the PPP lost PML(N), a key member of the coalition. According to the media reports, Mr Zardari had appealed to Nawaz Sharif to return to the government but there prevailed a wide gulf of mistrust amongst the two.

The *'Washington Times'* in an editorial note *of 27th August 2008* preferred to comment on this issue and said:

'The PPP is headed by Asif Ali Zardari, the widower of the late Benazir Bhutto. He has been reluctant to reinstate Mr. Chaudry because he once refused to grant him bail when he was in jail on corruption charges - charges that could very well be reinstated if the judges are restored. Yet, without an independent judiciary, Pakistan risks sliding into unconstitutional rule once again, with all the impending chaos this might trigger.'

Thinking logically, an independent judiciary does not grow on trees. It has to be built in minds of the people and respected even when it is likely to deliver a judgment unfavourable to one.

Scenario 54

LUTTO TAY PHUTTO {meaning: ROB & RUN}

Defence Forces + Politicians:

The South Asia Tribune - Issue No 54, August 10-16, 2003, published a petition filed, in public interest, by a lawyer before the Lahore High Court. Its contents were so explosive that the Court was unable to touch it. In September 2003, information cell of the PPP had circulated this petition for political training of their workers through their official website. This was regarding an aspect of alleged moral character of some officers in Pakistan defence forces. The petition was filed without any cogent proof or documents and most of the alleged charges seemed to be based on *'lungar gups'* sprayed in the air by officer's closed personnel, might be out of jealousy or resentment.

The Lahore High Court was facing a legal and practical dilemma: *'how to handle the petition, charge sheeting the Pakistan Armed forces and listing details of massive kickbacks and corruption by some of the Generals, Air Marshals and Admirals'*.

The main charges mentioned in the petition included:

- Air Chief Marshal Abbas Khattak (retired) had received Rs:180 million as kickbacks in the purchase of 40 old Mirage fighters.

- Air Chief Marshal, Farooq Feroze Khan was suspected of receiving a five percent commission on the purchase of 40 F-7 planes worth $271 million.

- In 1996, the Army bought 1047 GS-90s jeeps, at a cost of $20,889 per unit against the market value of a jeep then was only $13,000. According to the then National Accountability Bureau (NAB) some senior Army officers made Rs:510 million in the deal.

- One hundred and eleven Army men got 400 plots in Bahawalpur and Rahim Yar Khan districts at throwaway prices, paying Rs:47.50 per kanal (Kanal is about 600 Sq Yards or 1/8th of an acre) as against the actual price of Rs:15,000 to Rs:20,000 (1US $=Rs:56 then). Another 35,000 kanals of lands were distributed among them as gifts.

- Six respondents got 400 kanals in Punjab while former NAB Chairman Lt Gen Mohammad Amjad was allotted a two-kanal plot on Sarwar Road in Lahore Cantt for just Rs:800,000; payable in instalments over 20 years. The market value of this plot was then Rs:20 million.

- Plea bargain of Admiral Mansoorul Haq brought $7.5bn in a General's pockets belonging to the NAB under Gen Musharraf's regime.

- Gen Musharraf acquired a commercial plot worth Rs:20 million at DHA in Lahore for just Rs:100,000 payable in 20 years. Islamabad farm plot should also be added. As mentioned in the report of Director General Defence Services, a loss of Rs:5 billion was incurred due to these allotments.

[*The 'Nation' of 8th September 2001* carries Ikram Sehgal's article titled 'ROADMAPS AND MR FIXITS' which states that:

'Gen Usmani has also much to answer for with respect to Defence Housing Authority (DHA) Karachi, among them the imperial largesse of allotting of an amenity plot to a favourite, who promptly sold it for Rs:14 million (mentioned in my note for Maj Gen HUK Niazi, SJ in the Defence Journal August 2001 issue).

Pervez Musharraf must make the Presidency more powerful, keeping national security and accountability with the President. In the process he has to ensure that the Armed Forces do not get tainted by corruption of any kind, those who have shown any inclination must be retired now. A few black sheep cannot be allowed to tar and feather the entire khaki community on the strength of regimental tie. Those GT Road warriors must be sent home.']

- The Army awarded a contract for the purchase of 1000 Hino trucks at $:40,000 per unit while the local Gandhara Industries (Hino assembling company in Karachi, Pakistan) had offered trucks of the same specification for $:25,000 a piece. In a purchase of 3000 Land Rover jeeps in 1995, Army officials allegedly received around Rs:2 billion as kickbacks.

- The Army management at WAPDA raised the power tariff 13 times in three years besides purchasing electric meters at Rs:1,050 a piece against the open market price of Rs:456, causing a loss of Rs:1.65 billion to the national exchequer.

- Senior officers of the former military regime sold the Pak-Saudi Fertilizers for Rs:7 billion and earned Rs:2 billion commission on the deal.

- In 1996, the Pakistan Navy spent Rs:13 million on installing air-conditioners at the Islamabad Golf Club without any justification.

The petition also contained a mention of some other major scams involving a few serving or ex members of the military junta which were as follows:

- Ex Army Chief, Gen Jahangir Karamat took kickbacks of more than US $20 Million from a Ukrainian tank company for purchase of 300 Ukrainian tanks for Pakistan Army through a middleman named as Col Mahmood, a brother corps officer of Gen Karamat.

Former Prime Minister Nawaz Sharif sent one Maj Gen Zulfiqar, then serving in ISI, to Ukraine and Azerbaijan to get more details of the said deal. Gen Zulfiqar compiled a complete report of the transactions and bribes given. But the Army tried to buy him out by rewarding him with the post of Chairman WAPDA and promoting him to the rank of a three star General.

Allegedly, the then Army Chief, Gen Jahangir Karamat was forced to resign, based on the threat that if he did not, he would be charged for corruption. The Defence circles, however, made it public, just to save honour of the army as an institution, that Gen Jehangir Karamat had himself tendered resignation voluntarily because he had made a controversial speech at National Defence College, floating a demand of 'National Security Council' to be incorporated in the government permanently [which idea was not liked by many politicians].

- Many road contracts were given to a firm Hasnain Construction Company without any public tenders by an ex Railways and Communication Minister Gen Ashraf Qazi. The company, partly owned by a relative of Gen Musharraf's son, was also awarded the lease of a lucrative real estate in Lahore for construction of a Golf Course under the cover of Palm Country Golf Club, Singapore. The relative of Gen Musharraf admitted publicly that he was working for a commission to use his contacts and influence for the company.

- Prime commercial land developed in Defence Housing Authority Karachi was leased at dirt cheap rates to McDonalds (operated through Amin Lakhani) by the then Corps Comdr Karachi Lt Gen Afzal Janjua, allegedly for certain bugs or in friendship.

- The Army's coercive organ NAB struck various under the table deals with various individuals accused of high profile economic crimes in addition to NAB defaulters, forcing them to join Gen Musharraf's government. These include a former Prime Minister and at least one fourth of all elected legislators. Where does the military virtue of a defence outfit stand in these circumstances?

The petition had described that Pakistani military virtue had died, trampled below the treacherous wheels of overpriced military trucks and aircraft and defective planes that crashed in our waters because of dubious maintenance.

'Men who had one green suit to wear', in the words of **Gen Tajammul Hussain**, 'became the tycoons of Pakistan'. It was the beginning of prosperity for few and the beginning of the end of military virtue of a previously frugal and clean military machine, the General maintained. In Gen Tajammul's words, the people of Pakistan have no right to ask that:

- Where does building 90 acres of a welfare colony known as Creek City with the cheapest shack for Rs:6 million fit in? What began as an idealistic journey, ends with the shady deals around creeks in Karachi which the Navy failed to defend in 1971.

- Where does developing 62 acres of prime commercial real estate of Islamabad fit in? Is this the Navy's business that was miserably trapped in a hole in Karachi Port in 1971 War?

- For whose welfare is Navy undertaking a project 1500 km away from the nearest sea?

And in this messy situation, the subservient Lahore High Court was asked to ignore the said petition or shelve it because under the Pakistan Army Act 1952 no court was empowered to take notice of any issue relating with army service or their officers and employees.

The question arises that how it happened so?

The army which was known to the world as first class professional warrior, which was an ideal for students in their youths, which was admired through slogans written and painted on the back panels of every

'Bedford" truck in Pakistan, which was sung through immortal 'milli' melodious voices of top range singers, is being dragged in the Courts to reply the charges of massive corruption levelled against **some of** their high ranking officers.

But this Rome of frustration and disappointment has not been built in a day.

The answer goes back to eighties of the last century when Pakistan's political environment, economy and social structure started devastating. The values were ruined. It was due to the negative effects of 'Afghan Factor'. It was the military rule of Gen Ziaul Haq when the ISI was entrusted a job to help certain militant factions in Afghanistan to fight against pro-Russian military groups. It was the Western powers and mainly United States who were supplying arms and ammunition coupled with attractive packages of financial aid to that military dictator, Gen Ziaul Haq, for onward pass on to the Afghan militants.

OJHARY CAMP FIASCO?

The sequence of events gathered by Tim McGirk and Massimo Calabresi, published in *'World Times' of Canada* under caption *'Is Pakistan a Friend or a Foe'*, explains that how the shrewd Gen Ziaul Haq and Gen Akhtar Abdul Rehman kept all channels of supply under the command of their trusted aides and subordinate Generals. This was the moment when the Pakistan army got engaged and involved in Afghan War though not very openly. These Generals used all possible means to embezzle the most sophisticated weaponry of that time but they were not sincere with Pakistan to save their budget nor were they keen to equip their personnel with modern war heads.

The Afghan cause related Generals remained engaged in selling all kinds of 'saved & embezzled' weapons in black market for cash prices and they remained engaged in this black business till 10th April 1988 when all the record and remaining 'peanuts' of weaponry were set to a deliberate fire in *Ojhari Camp Depot* of Rawalpindi. Gen Akhtar Abdul Rehman of ISI was the chief of this team.

This Ojhari Camp event (caused to be) occurred when six American High Command Officers were on their way to Pakistan to make an audit of weaponry the US had given to Pakistan in the preceding years. On 9th April 1988, the US Army team had stayed in Cairo to break their journey for a night but next day they heard that the camp had been blown up 'accidentally'. The US Army team, in utter disappointment, went back from Cairo.

Perhaps that was the moment when the plan to eliminate Gen Ziaul Haq and his associate Generals was probably worked out (and final scene was displayed on 17th August 1988). After blow up of Gen Ziaul Haq, Gen Akhtar Abdul Rehman and nineteen other high ranking military Generals on in an air crash, the sons of these Generals suddenly appeared as billionaire political barons at national horizon. No court, no agency or organisation was there to ask the origin of their wealth whereas history was the witness to those families and their financial backgrounds.

Many military spokesmen including Gen Hamid Gul had termed [though seldom and in very low tone] the Ojhary Camp stories regarding alleged embezzlement of the American weaponry as baseless. However, the historians and critics simply question:

- That why the inquiry report compiled by the Parliamentary Committee headed by MNA Malik Naeem Khan was not placed on the media record.

- If that report was objectionable, the concerned army officers should have come up with cogent explanations.

- Why, [getting furious over that inquiry report] PM Junejo was sent home on 29th May 1988 using the sword of Art. 58(2)(b) and the parliament was dissolved.

- Ojhary camp was located in the centre of Rawalpindi city and many civilian lives were lost in that fiasco, so some sort of inquiry report, might be an eye wash by some military officer's team, should have been kept on the public record for future reference.

Truth was, that an inquiry report was got drafted by the GHQ but only for the consumption of their American counterparts or to be kept in GHQ's record which ultimately brought discredit for the military rule.

GOLFWAY PROJECT ETC:

South Asia Tribune (SAT), in earlier issues of 26th August 2002 & of 2nd Sep 2002 had broken a scandal of Gen Musharraf's 'Golfway Project', a mix of Rs:25 billion Golf Course in Lahore (Capital of Punjab, Pakistan) and Rs:7 billion Pindi-Peshawar Motorway, in which one Brig (Rtd) Aftab Siddiqui was confirmed to be the major beneficiary. Brig Siddiqui was the father in law of Mr Bilal Musharraf, the Gen Musharraf's son. Gen Musharraf's 'Golfway project' was conceived and launched by an ex- Chief of the ISI.

Earlier, as reported in Pakistan's leading *daily 'Dawn' of 25th September 2002:*

> *'Sheikh Yousaf (Chief of Husnain Construction Company, and the head of Pakistani Firm's Consortium) explained the phases for which his company was passed for converting the M-3 project from the Built, Operate and Transfer (BOT) plan to the government funded project. When asked as to how much his company had been helped by Brig (Retd) Aftab Siddiqui (father in law of Gen Musharraf's son, Bilal Musharraf), he said the gentleman had worked with his company as a consultant.'*

Sh Yousaf had told the media that it was originally agreed that Aftab Siddiqui would get two per cent of the profit from the project for 25 years, but since the project had been converted to a government funded plan, he was paid lump sum for the 'services' which he rendered. Everything was documented and the payments to Mr Siddiqui were made through cheques, the copies of which were provided to a number of government departments including the FIA.

In 2002 for the first time, the elected parliamentarians of Pakistan had picked up courage to bring a former ISI Chief, a retired General, one who was also very close to Gen Musharraf, into the dock for a botched up deal of $100 million with China, in which there were accusations of large scale corruption.

> *'The China Railways deal is already shaping up as the first test case between politicians and Generals with the parliamentarians testing their limits as if they were shadow boxing with Gen Musharraf himself. Former ISI Chief and Pakistan's Railways Minister, Lt Gen (Rtd) Qazi Javed Ashraf faced a probe by the Parliamentary Committee after Railways Ministry officials held him solely responsible for a faulty deal of $100 million with China for importing 69 defective Railway engines against a commercial loan.'*

The PAC members had concluded that Gen Qazi had himself ordered the import of those faulty engines in bulk. Their frames cracked within a year on Pakistani Railway tracks. The probe launched into the deal revealed that Gen Qazi himself took the case to the National Security

Council (NSC) single handedly for approval of the faulty deal with China. The NSC, obviously influenced by Gen Qazi and his closeness with Gen Musharraf, approved the deal.

Then Chairman Railway Board, Shakeel Durrani had also confirmed the above fact. He said on record:

> 'Gen Qazi had actually got the approval of the whole plan from the NSC presided over by Gen Musharraf on 29th December 1999. The recommendations of the Railway's Technical Committee were not implemented and defective locomotives were purchased without fear of accountability because it was the start of tyrannical military rule.'

The case was termed as the first serious confrontation between the elected representatives and the Generals, like Gen Qazi. He was alleged to be a rude military officer who had earlier ordered thrashing of *Information Secretary PML(N), Siddiqul Farooq,* just because the said politician had demanded a probe against the General. The NAB was asked to sort him out. The NAB picked him for interrogation and kept him at an unknown place and when asked by the superior courts it was replied: *'yes! He is with NAB but where he has been dumped cannot be told'.* Gen Qazi also went on air later on the BBC to publicly abuse Mr Siddique.

Further, when the US announced a $240 million grant for development of education in Pakistan, Gen Qazi used his influential relationship with Gen Musharraf to become the Federal Education Minister for reasons known to none. No formal record was kept at Ministry of Education for that foreign aid and its spending.

Now certain innocent questions:

- Why the flag-bearers of NRO scenario were blind towards this aspect of institutionalised corruption in Pakistan.

- Why only politicians and bureaucrats should be punished under NAB ordinance and not the army officials [at least when they work in civil capacity] and judges.

- Why the Parliament never thought of causing an amendment in the Army Act if the Generals cannot be investigated by NAB and cannot be tried in ordinary courts.

- Have any President of Pakistan, being the Supreme Commander of forces, ever bothered to place before the Parliament the statistics of inquiries or Court Martials conducted in connection with corrupt army officers and their organizations.

- Have the Supreme Court of Pakistan ever thought of initiating a *suo moto* action over any financial scam involving army Generals [at least when they work in civil capacity].

- Have any Bar Association ever thought of moving a petition before the SC to bring corrupt Generals in the ambit of 'equal citizenship' given in the Constitution of Pakistan; and for that matter in basic Islamic injunctions.

- Have any prominent anchor of media like Kashif Abbassi, Hamid Mir, Mazhar Abbas or Talat Hussain ever tried to float an opinion inviting discussions and comments of intelligentsia over the issue that if politicians and bureaucrats are being dragged in the streets of public accountability then the Generals and judges should also be treated at par.

The above given charges of corruptions were not apparently proved, nor had the writers given any documents in support of his narrations and allegations. But fact remains that there is no institution or forum where these accusations could be moved for investigation. The media raises questions that if there is any instrument to check the corruption or malpractices of the army high-ups in Pakistan. There should be some mechanism to take account of the wealth accumulated by them to bring them in mainstream after retirement. Kamran Shahid's two *live TV programs over 'Express TV Channel'* during first week of February 2012 are referred.

3 GENERALS CAUSE BILLION'S LOSS TO NLC:

Defying the orders of the then Prime Minister Shaukat Aziz, two Lt Generals and one Major General of the Pakistan Army, being fate makers of the National Logistic Cell (NLC) for five years, had quietly borrowed Rs:2 billion from four banks on commercial rates to make investments in the volatile stock markets and in the process lost Rs:1.8 billion and heaven did not fall.

Army Generals are the sacred cows of Pakistan on whom no law of *Ehtesab* or accountability is applicable, but unfortunately those three got exposed before the Public Accounts Committee (PAC) when an inquiry report revealed that these Generals had been doing those investments despite clear instructions 'not to do so'. A total of Rs:4 billion of the

NLC including the pension fund of its employees, were invested in the stock markets during that miss-conceived adventure.

The PAC was informed through its inquiry report that NLC's Lt Gen Afzal Muzaffar continued to make investments in the stock market till the last day of his retirement in 2008 even though the rest of the government departments and organizations had stopped this exercise in 2006. The NLC would continue to pay the loan instalments of banks for years to come after getting a loss of Rs:1.8 billion in cash. The three Generals were never questioned about their illegal and illogical acts of commission. The PAC members had called the names of brokers and directors of those firms through whom those billions were invested but the matter was dumped somewhere midway. The investments were done despite the orders of PM Shaukat Aziz in 2003 to stop investing in stocks.

Secretary Planning Division Ashraf Hayat had opened the names of five top guns of NLC who, according to inquiry report, were responsible for this massive financial loss. Names were Lt Gen Khalid Munir Khan who served in NLC during 15th January 2004 to 14th June 2005; Lt Gen Afzal Muzaffar (16th June 2005 to 17th October 2008); Major Gen Khalid Zahir Akhtar (25th July 2002 to 27th February 2008); DFA Najeebullah Khan (25th February 2002 to 10th April 2007) and Chief Finance Officer (20th June 2004 to 22nd October 2008).

According to the official inquiry report placed before the PAC, a total loan of Rs:2 billion was borrowed as per details that from Bank Al Falah (Rs:650 million); National Bank of Pakistan (Rs:90 million); UBL (Rs:800 million) and ABL (Rs:500 million) were obtained. Out of this loan, Rs:1.8 billion had already been lost till the enquiry was raised.

The shocked PAC members, however, did not move for recovery of these huge financial losses because top military Generals were involved in the scam. Staff Retirement Benefit Fund of employees was also thrown in the pit and lost for which the PAC was asked to hold for two weeks; but as usual, the whole matter was pushed into the cold room. The PAC Chair person Yasmeen Rehman and members Sardar Bahadur Khan Sihar, Riyaz Fatiyana, Hamid Hiraj, Sardar Ayaz Sadiq, Nadeem Afzal Chann and others, all suddenly went mum because the enquiry was related with Generals.

As a part of its official policy, NLC could invest only 20 percent of the total fund under the management in non government securities, TFCs or shares. However in its 37th meeting of National Logistics Board (NLB) held on 8th September 2003 the chairman NLB approved the investment policy of NLC advising not to invest in the stocks. In its next Board meeting held on 7th January 2005, while viewing the status and results of NLC investments, the PM Shaukat Aziz, in the capacity of Chairman of NLB pointed out that public sector companies should not trade in stocks; the DG NLC continued with the old practice for unknown reasons.

The inquiry report said it analyzed the investment record and reached the conclusion that massive financial irregularities were there. Besides noticing the acts of blatant violations of instructions, procedures and other guidelines, the PAC found other glaring irregularities, but who bothers in Pakistan; never before and not on tomorrow at least.

After the event, Saeedur Rehman has also been working in the Capital Development Authority (CDA) as the Chief Finance Manager while the Generals have retired from service.

The four-member inquiry team recommended the following:

(a) Gross irregularities in investment of stock exchange during the period 2003-2008 have been established as per finding of the report. Names and period of appointment of officers concerned have also been identified who approved Rs:4.1 billion investment in the stocks in defiance of the prime minister's instructions and caused Rs:1.8 billion loss.

(b) The NLC management must implement all those provisions of the investment policy in letter and sprit with immediate effect.

(c) The detailed financial and management audit of all irregular investments be undertaken by a firm of chartered accountant to determine the extent of the financial loss and devise an exit strategy from investment in stocks to minimise losses.

(d) The NLC's current governance and organisational structure is ambiguous and lacks clarity with respect to authority, responsibility and accountability of various tiers of management. It should be reviewed & revamped to ensure clarity and to provide adequate checks and balances as per admissible standards.

Especially to be noted that Gen Kayani would be the last person to ignore such allegations. Such Generals are few who could be placed on that 'corruption list' but the politicians would be very rare to be left over.

Gen Kayani has tried to wash the dirty linen of politicians but there is too much grease in it and bad smell also.

Gen Kayani's jobs included:

Firstly; the restoration of the superior judiciary in March 2009: the issue was politicized and was heading towards an ugly showdown. Just at the right time a quiet word from the GHQ had defused the situation and the judiciary was restored in response to the public demand.

Secondly; a question once arose for Pakistan's 'no first use' policy in respect of nuclear arsenal in South Asian region; here again a timely clarification settled the issue. The wise and well thought announcement had helped much to settle the dust.

Thirdly; in July 2008, again there was a question of placing the ISI under Ministry of Interior [instigated by Rehman Malik]. After four months another similar mis-conceived direction of sending the ISI Chief to India in response to Mumbai attacks, was pushed in. In both cases a correct decision was taken – strategic intelligence is not a single Ministry's concern; the matter was not to be tackled by the England or Dubai based politicians.

Fourthly; Kerry-Lugar-Berman Bill was another grey area where the politicians had tried to push the nation into sand grave of personal interests. GHQ's immediate response in this matter saved the nation from gross humiliation at least.

There was a list of so many other issues which needed special attention in this regard. The US pressure to push Pakistan into North Waziristan was one such situation. The US threat of expanded Drone strikes in FATA & Quetta was another possible situation. The orchestrated unrest in Baluchistan and the engineered killings in Karachi could also be situations requiring decisions in the national interest. In nut shell military was doing the needful what could be possibly done.

Pakistan's army Headquarters (GHQ) had taken note of the above events; a high level inquiry was ordered to look into it.

At the same time one can ponder upon the dubious character of political parties in Pakistan like the PPP & PML [N & Q], that when they are not in power they allege the Pakistan Army for corrupt practices through all media tactics and when they come in power, as in 2008, they provide all shelters to one segment of corrupt army Generals; scandals ignored and charge sheets shelved.

Let us hope that the Supreme Court steps forward to provide justice on the basis of equal basic rights for all and no citizen of Pakistan or institution be declared as 'sacred cow'.

SUB-MARINE KICKBACKS:

The investigations done by various quarters of Pakistan Defence and the French authorities into the Agosta submarine deal after Benazir Bhutto's departure in November 1996, which later led to the removal of the then Chief of Naval Staff (CNS) Admiral Mansurul Haq, was an alleged cover-up move to save many key officials of the Pakistan Navy, besides turning a blind eye to a controversial initial deal of $520 million [but ended up in paying off $950 million]. The deal was actually signed in 1992 during Nawaz Sharif's first tenure. So many facts could have brought to the knowledge of the nation but Senator Saifur Rehman remained only interested in fixing Benazir Bhutto and Asif Zardari doing partial *Ehtesab*. He was otherwise coward enough to speak out the real truth.

The daily *Jang of 11th November 2009* had first time released the news with reference to the French daily *'Liberation Fr.'* that:

> Mr Zardari had pocketed $4.3 million in 1994 while getting green signal from his wife PM Benazir Bhutto for purchasing three Agosta sub-marines from France. The said amount was got transferred into Zardari's accounts during 1994-95 through a Lebanese friendly mediator name Abdul Rehman Al-Assir. The said information was officially communicated by the British government to the NAB in 2001. The CE of French Naval Defence Company had confirmed in person that before signing the contract an instalment of $1.3 million was deposited, through Al-Assir as guarantor & middle man during 15th-30th August 1994 in Zardari's off shore accounts. After a year of contract, in 1995, two instalments of $1.2 m & $1.8 millions were accordingly paid in.

> According to the French Investigations, 10% of the total settled price was to be released as 'commission'; 6% for the Pakistan's Defence personnel equivalent to $49.6 million and 4% for the political heads equivalent to $33 million [some amounts were paid in dollars and some in Euros; then dollar and Euro had almost the same market value]. When in 1995, President Chirac took over France, he ordered

to negate the payments of the remaining amount of commission; as a result 11 French engineers and 3 Pakistani Naval Engg Staff were ambushed in Karachi on 8th May 2002.

Earlier in 2001, the former Naval Chief of Pakistan Adml Mansurul Haq was arrested and pressure from the NAB was built up to pay pack $7.10 million of looted money but, during a hastily arranged 'plea bargain', Mr Haq was released after paying a few thousand bugs only.

Reference is also made to the *'media news' dated 25th January 2010* appeared in all sectors stating about a writ petition placed before the Sindh High Court (SHC) from the official agent of Société française de matériels d'armement (SOFMA) in Pakistan named Ahmed Jameel Ansari. In the petition it was told that Adml Mansurul Haq and Aamir Lodhi were paid commissions & kickbacks from the SOFMA account. The plaintiff told that Aamir Lodhi [then having address of France] was made their partner to give legal cover to those illegal transactions meant for the naval officers. In the whole amount Adml Mansurul Haq got 50% share whereas the Plaintiff (Mr Ansari) and Aamir Lodhi got 25% each. Out of total commission of $7.1 million, Adml Haq got $3.37 million, Aamir lodhi got $1.7 million and plaintiff got $2.0 million.

It was contended in the petition that Saifur Rehman of Ehtesab Bureau had got back all the paid commission from the plaintiff and Aamir Ladhi and an Ehtesab reference was made against all of them. Later Aamir Lodhi got back his entire amount of $1.7 million by orders of the Supreme Court through the CJP Abdul Hameed Dogar [hats off to the PPP's rule after 2008] so plaintiff's amount should also be repatriated.

The NAB was called in the court; the officer placed the record before the court telling that the whole amount taken from Mr Ansari was given back to him when the 'sub-marine kickbacks case' was sent to the NAB's Accountability court because Mr Ansari was not made accused in it and was left Scot free. Moreover, the amount given to the plaintiff from the NAB account was $2.468 million and not $2.0 million.

[*Within the submarine case, another corruption by NAB officials themselves is made out that where the amount of NAB's $2.468 million gone, who had pocketed that big amount taken out in the name of Mr Ansari for giving him relief that he was not named in NAB's challan. Moreover; how the NAB officials had solved the discrepancy of $0.468 million; where the dollars gone?*]

Referring to an interview given by a former Director General Naval Intelligence (DGNI) Adml Javed Iqbal [later remained Pakistan's Ambassador abroad for ten years] to Daily *'the Ummat' Karachi of 21st November 2010,* he had also proved the truthfulness of the kickbacks taken by Pakistan's elite in sub-marine deals. He categorically told that Adml Mansurul Haq's deal was initially caught by him which he handed over to his successor Cdre Shahid Ashraf when he took over as DGNI. He had told Cdre Ashraf about the carrier person of the brief case, place of handing over, date & time of transaction so the later caught him but perhaps had joined hands with him {see details of Rs:1.5 million allegation on Cdre S Ashraf in next paragraphs} under Adml Haq's pressure as Naval Chief. Adml Haq was no doubt involved in the kickbacks, but of some part. Till his tenure, the submarines had reached Pakistan but certain completions were to be made so he got lesser portion of the kickbacks.

The former DGNI Adml Javed Iqbal told that Adml Saeed Khan was the real person to take away big chunk because the deal was implemented in his tenure. Adml Haq got money against that submarine which was being built in Karachi which he halted by raising certain objections. French people then obliged Adml Haq to keep his lips closed.

The Defence forces covered the whole affair due to eye-opening statement of the next DG Naval Intelligence (DGNI), Cdre Shahid Ashraf, who was instantly turned into an example for others when he was recalled from an overseas course, retired prematurely, court martialled and harassed to keep his mouth shut.

[*The Pakistan Navy had charged DGNI Commodore Shahid Ashraf of getting Rs:1.5 million from a naval officer named Cdre Alvi, who was alleged to have accepted illegal gratification and kickbacks from foreign suppliers of naval vessels etc., but made him an approver against the DGNI, for giving a list of naval officers who had allegedly received kickbacks but were never touched and promoted as Rear Admirals instead; through 'connections'. 24 hours surveillance was placed on that DGNI; he was arrested and detained. Several coercive measures were taken against him to force him into pleading guilty.*

Cdre Alvi, in his confessional statement dated 17th October 1998, given under Section 337 of Pakistani Law before the ADC Islamabad, had admitted to have received over Rs:4 million as illegal gratification and kickbacks from foreign suppliers and alleged to have paid some of the amount to DGNI Shahid Ashraf and another officer Cdre Liaquat Malik.]

Referring to various media reports dated 14th January 2011; former Naval Chief Adml Abdul Aziz Mirza had once insisted that the ex-DG Naval Intelligence did receive kickbacks in the Agosta deal as was confirmed by the other two officers, Capt Z U Alvi and Capt Liaqat Ali Malik, who were blamed to have received bribes directly from the French. For the same reason the ex-DGNI was penalized. Capt Z U Alvi and one Col (retd) Ejaz were the two main witnesses with the former having agreed to become approver on the condition of revealing all the details of kickbacks and corruption. Adml Mirza conceded that DGNI Shahid Ashraf was Admiral Mansurul Haq's right-hand man but had received Rs:1.5 million from Capt Alvi, who was the direct recipient of the kickbacks.

The fact remained that the DGNI was silenced because of a letter dated 17th February 1995 issued by SOFMA (the French company that was involved in Agosta deal) had come on record telling about payments of $40,000 to each of four naval officers whose names were mentioned in the same letter. Instead of probing the four officers, each one of them was later elevated as Rear Admiral. The NAB sources had later confirmed it, too. To the Board of Inquiry (BoI), the DGNI Comdr Shahid Ashraf had submitted an explosive statement uncovering many faces including the four officers referred.

The News of 2nd January 2010 had earlier mentioned the details that:

> 'Col Ejaz Ahmad was actively pursuing the interest of the contractors for taking the contract towards completion. Mr Devensay of DCN (French company) had issued instructions through a letter to Col Ejaz stationed in Rawalpindi as agent of DCN to pay $40,000 each to following officers of the Pakistan Navy named a. Cdre Mushtaq Ahmed, b. Cdre Khushnud Ahmed, c. Cdre S V Naqvi, and d. Cdre Naveed Ahmed. All the four officers were members of the committee for evaluation of technical specification of the onboard equipment.
>
> A copy of this letter was shown through R Adm Sarfraz Khan during investigation by Col Zafar in the presence of the Commanding Officer (Cdre Qazi), Cdre Shahid (DGNI) and Cdre Shafiq Ahmed, Registrar Naval Court of Appeals. The copy of this letter was marked to Zafar Iqbal, stationed in Washington as agent of SOFMA, who was arrested by FIA. Mr Devensay had directed him to release an amount of $160,000 out of special fund in favour of Col Ejaz for payment to these (four) officers.'

Former Naval Chief Adml Aziz Mirza (from 1999-2002), in his interview published in media on 14th January 2011, had told that one

Zafar Iqbal, a middle man of the French company, was also interrogated and had admitted to have received $160,000 to be paid to four commodores. He, however, said that both Iqbal and Col Ejaz never paid this amount to anyone of them. The four commodores were never charge sheeted or confronted by a board of inquiry as a fact-finding inquiry had already found them innocent, which led to their promotion as rear admiral.

Participating in an *Express News* programme **Kalamkar** with columnist Abdul Qadir Hasan and Abbas Athar as host, the former DGNI Cdre (retd) Shahid Ashraf said that, in 1992, during Nawaz Sharif's first government, the Navy was given approval to acquire new submarines for $520 million but the agreement of purchase of Agosta class submarines from France was signed on 21st September 1994, during the second tenure of Benazir Bhutto. [Referring to **the Express Tribune dated 5th December 2010**] Replying to a question, the DGNI said that:

> *"I was informed that someone called Niaz was going to pay Captain Alvi a sum of $107,000 as part of kickbacks on the deal. Action could not be taken as the Navy Chief, Admiral Mansurul Haq, was on a visit to France and the US those days.*
>
> *When he returned, I told him the entire story. A meeting was held but remained inconclusive. After the meeting, Rear Admiral Faseeh Bukhari (at present the Chairman NAB) said to me that I should have caught the persons. But I said that my job was to provide information and that he should have got the meeting to decide to arrest the suspects. He got angry and went away.*
>
> *Later, when he learnt that four commodores were 'receiving $40,000 each', the Navy Chief, Mansurul Haque, and Vice-Admiral AU Khan advised me to investigate."*

Now see the story from French side.

The record of the French investigations indicated that the Karachi attack of 8th May 2002 killing 11 French engineers was carried out with complicity of the Pakistan's defence contingent, possibly through Islamist guerrillas, to teach French government a lesson for not paying their settled commissions as promised in the sale of Agosta Submarines. The President Chirac's government had stopped the payment of commissions through an amended legislation. The journalists and anchor persons in Pakistani media were of the view that instead of criticizing the corruption of peanuts of politicians and bureaucracy, they should criticize the *'huge colossal Military corruption of millions of dollars'*, which has brought the country on the brink of collapse. They held that: *'If we want to be objective in our reporting, we should call a spade a spade. It is army which is involved in corruption and is sponsoring corruption.*

[Hats off to the French media; on 18th November 2010, it had noted that: *'now let us see whether they could name Zardari in this case. It is clear – Zardari or no Zardari – that Pakistan Armed Forces has been involved in lots of kickbacks over the years. And this is a serious case involving an EU country. If proven, the case may damage Pakistan's Army / Navy reputation on an unprecedented scale. So watch out former Admirals.'*]

The News of 20th November 2010 had given the details that the deal had led to the removal of the then Chief of Naval Staff (CNS) Adml Mansurul Haq and the framing of a corruption reference against Benazir Bhutto and Asif Ali Zardari but some others mighty and powerful in the navy, who made millions of dollars from the deal, were never held accountable. Across the border, as public pressure in France mounted on President Nicolas Sarkozi to testify over alleged corruption in the sale of French submarines to Pakistan in 1990s, Cdre Shahid Ashraf, the then DGNI, though himself got his share of booty and was punished, had offered help to Islamabad and Paris to book the corrupt and bring back the looted money to Pakistan.

Besides the then DGNI, the former Naval Chief Adml Abdul Aziz Mirza had also given credence to the French investigative report that talked of almost $49 million kickbacks in the Agosta submarines deal allegedly received by Asif Ali Zardari and others, including the naval officers. In an interview with 'the News', Adml Aziz Mirza had disclosed that the then Benazir Bhutto government had urged the Pakistan Navy to go for the French substance. NC Mirza, while quoting the then Naval Chief Adml Saeed Khan, had revealed that Benazir Bhutto's Defence Minister Aftab Sha'baan Mirani had clearly indicated to the Pakistan Navy's high command about the Benazir government's preference for induction of the French submarines.

Despite these clear verbal directions from the Defence Minister, the naval top command had again met and deliberated upon the subject and decided to recommend two options to the PPP government namely the British Upholder and the French Agosta. The government later approved the induction of Agosta. Adml Mirza told that the Navy first formally came to know about the kickbacks in the Agosta deal in 1998 following which it had proceeded against three officials of the ranks of captain and commodore for taking bribes and they were removed from service [*but like civil bureaucracy or politicians no press news, no recovery of ill gotten money, no court martial, no imprisonment and no confiscation of property though the charges were proved; after all they were sacred cows*]. Adml Mirza held that:

> '*My hunch is that besides the politicians, some top ranking naval officers even above the rank of commodore might have also received kickbacks as reflected in the recent French media reports, however, they (the top Naval officials) remained undetected for want of proof or witnesses. Even the condemned former Naval Chief Mansurul Haq was not convicted of Agosta kickbacks but for the bribes that he had pocketed in the other defence deals.*'

It was available on NAB's record that the Agosta deal was never struck by Adml Mansurul Haq but he had actually received some kickbacks after the award of contract for its smooth implementation. Those who had received the lion share of kickbacks for negotiating the contract were never questioned. Amongst them Adml S M Khan, Rear Adml I H Naqvi, Vice Adml A U Khan, Rear Adml A Mujtaba and Rear Adml Jawed Iftikhar were mentionable.

Comdr Shahid Ashraf, in his statement dated 23rd August 1999 disclosed that the Evaluation teams of the Pakistan Navy comprising Rear Adml I H Naqvi, Rear Adml Jawed Iftikhar and Rear Adml S A Mujtaba had visited China, France, England and Sweden. This team recommended Swedish submarine as the first choice. Then another team comprising of Rear Adml A U Khan, Rear Adml S A Mujtaba, Cdre Mushtaq Ahmed, Cdre S V Naqvi and Cdre Naveed Ahmed visited the same countries. Rear Adml Mujtaba was the only officer who went abroad with both the teams but had gone out of way in supporting the inclusion of Cdre Z U Alvi in the team visiting France despite the fact that the later did not qualify the laid down criteria for the project.

It was on record that Col Ejaz Ahmed, agent of SOFMA in Rawalpindi, had been in continuous liaison with the evaluation team and other 'concerned' in Naval HQ and Ministry of Defence (MoD). The whole process acquiring submarines from France took place during the time of Admiral S M Khan, who remained Chief of the Naval Staff from November 1991 to Nov 1994.

The people of Pakistan would like to know that the above mega-corruption cases were never probed either by Senator Saifur Rehman's Ehtesab Bureau, Pakistan Navy or by Gen Musharraf's NAB to dig out the full truth. Why the innocent countrymen were made fools by calling Adml Mansurul Haq in docks and then sending him off under the cover of 'plea bargain' made in haste. It was a cover-up of the dubious submarine deal to save the skin of many in the Navy and on the political horizon of Pakistan. The questions to be answered are:

- The local agents of the DCN International were made part of the NAB investigation or not. If Adml Mansurul Haq was not involved in any 'dishonesty', as it was declared later, why there was a plea bargain and why he came back to Pakistan and received all his merits & perks back.

- Who were actually involved in Agosta Submarine deals of 1990s.

- The French government first offered the said three new Agosta submarines at the cost of $520 million. After some time the price was escalated to $600 million and inflation was given as the main reason. Eventually, Pakistan ended up paying $950 million; why so. Who would dare to punish the culprits and recover the money that was paid in kickbacks?

But who else was the beneficiary besides the Defence personnel. Come along!

Daily **the 'Nation' of 15th January 2011** had published the details of the said rogue submarine deal saying that the sale, and the payment of bribes made to Mr Zardari associated with the deal, officially termed as commissions, were at the core of the 'Karachi event', currently the subject of **two French judicial investigations**. A key allegation in the developing affair was that the cancellation of commissions paid out in the submarine deal was the motive behind a suicide bomb attack in Karachi on 8th May 2002 that left 11 French and three Pakistan Navy's engineers dead. The French engineers were in Pakistan to help build one of the Agosta submarines.

The documents now in possession of Paris based Judge Renaud Van Ruymbeke were 'recovered' during a French police search in June 2010 of the home of Aamir Lodhi, one of the intermediaries involved in securing the Agosta contract. Lodhi held a copy of a report by a Pakistani anti-corruption service, the Ehtesab Cell of Saif ur Rehman.

Mr Lodhi aged 61, the brother of a former Pakistani ambassador to the United States & UK, was a close friend of the President Zardari.

The said raid on Lodhi's home in Paris was carried out by detectives from the French Police National Financial Investigation Division, the DNIF, (Division nationale des investigations financiers). The Ehtesab Cell documents were the object of a formal report by the DNIF, established on 17th June 2010 which revealed that Mr Zardari had received kickbacks worth 6,934,296 euros between August and December 1994.

That report was made a part of evidence collected by Van Ruymbeke in his investigations launched in 2010. Originally written in English, the Pakistani document was translated by the DNIF investigators which provided clear details about the payments made to Mr Zardari, amounting to several million euros, as well as the channels used, including offshore companies, bank accounts and a British tax haven bank transfers to the Virgin Islands. The main document seized by French investigators was dated 9th November 1997, concerning a request by Pakistan to Switzerland for co-operation in a judicial investigation aimed *'to obtain all the necessary information to pursue a criminal investigation and to try the former PM Benazir Bhutto, Asif Ali Zardari, Begum Nusrat Bhutto and other members of the Bhutto government, public servants and certain civilians, too.'*

The Agosta submarine contract was signed between the two countries on 21st September 1994; just weeks after the initial payments were released. At that time, Mr Zardari was also a federal minister in the Pakistani government then led by Benazir Bhutto. Importantly, Mr Zardari was the key figure for all public contracts signed with foreign countries which position earned him the unflattering nickname in Pakistan and abroad as 'Mister 10%'.

The *French Police Report* said the document explicitly referred to the Agosta contract:

> *'This request concerns several cases of malpractice including that of the purchase of French submarines. According to the DNIF investigators, the chronology and the currency of the sums paid suggest that these payments are secret commissions paid by the DCN-I, the commercial arm of the submarine builders DCN, to Monsieur Zardari and Monsieur Lodhi for their considerable services in assuring that DCN-I got the contract.*

> *Huge sums are recorded at the end of 1994 alone, when a company called Marleton Business Inc was set up through a lawyer in the tax*

*haven of the British Virgin Islands for use by Mr Zardari. A payment
of 5.5 million francs (838,000 euros) took place in October 1994 of
which 70% goes to Monsieur Zardari (AAZ) and 30% to Monsieur
Lodhi (AL).*

*A further transfer took place two months later, in December 1994, for
an altogether larger sum of 59.48 million francs, (9.06 million euros)
divided into 41.636 million [francs] for Monsieur Zardari and 17.844
million for Monsieur Lodhi. That represented 6,934,296 euros for the
current president of Pakistan, and 2,971,841 euros for his partner.*

*The official Pakistani documents seized in Lohdi's Paris home also
explain that Messieurs Lodhi and Zardari received their bribes in the
bank accounts of a series of offshore companies all based in the Virgin
Islands and they are identified by the DNIF as: Marvil Associated Inc.,
Penbury Finance, Oxton Trading, Crimities Holding and Dustan
Trading. The banks involved in the payments were also recorded in the
Pakistani documents, as well as the bank accounts used.*

*The commissions paid into the accounts, notably opened by these
companies at the Pasche bank and the bank of Piguet et Cie, in
Switzerland, were probably supplied by transfer from the Banque
française du Commerce extérieur [French Bank of Foreign Trade],
account number 2700 0008358 or IV10000083580.'*

Several high-profile witnesses, questioned in November and December
2010 by Judge Van Ruymbeke, insisted that the bribes paid in 1994 were
approved by France's then Defence Minister, François Leotard, and its
Budget Minister, now France's president, Nicolas Sarkozy.

In a statement given to Van Ruymbeke on 9th November 2010, former
DCN-I Finance Director, Gérard-Philippe Menayas, said *"the total
volume of the commissions was validated, contract by contract, by the
ministers of the budget and defence."*

In a statement given to Judge Van Ruymbeke on 7th December 2010,
Jacques Dewatre, who in 1994 was head of the French foreign
intelligence service, now called the DGSE, testified that *"The approval
for commissions is the responsibility of services which depend upon the
Minister of Defence and the Minister of the Budget."*

Judge Van Ruymbeke's investigation had established that, in order to
convince the Pakistani authorities to choose the French submarines, a
very structured network of corruption was established by a French state

company dedicated to such activities, the SOFMA, which partnered the designers and builders of the submarines, the DCN.

The Judge had enough evidence on record that the SOFMA had set aside the equivalent in francs of 51.6 million euros for bribes to be paid out in the Pakistan deal. Influential agents working with the SOFMA used the money to gain the favours of numerous Pakistani dignitaries, in both military and political spheres. While the practice of commission payments was then legal for France, the reception of bribes was illegal in Pakistan.

Asif Ali Zardari was one of the main benefactors of the paid bribes, according to a former MD of the SOFMA named, Henri Guittet. He evaluated the sum paid to Zardari as being 4% of the total value of the sales contract.

> 'I believe there was one per cent paid upon the signature of the sales contract, which means at the moment when everything can get underway and when notably the deposit and [partial] down payment has been paid, and one per cent later,' he said in a formal statement. 'The remaining two per cent was pro rata with the payment of the clients.'

Another Judge Marc Trévedic, who was heading second set of investigations into the murders of eleven French engineers, collected evidence discarding the theory touted by the Pakistani authorities that the engineers were targeted by al-Qaeda. He focused on suspicions that the bomb attack was directly or indirectly linked to the secret financial arrangements surrounding the Agosta deal. More precisely, that it was in retaliation for the non-payment of commissions promised to Pakistanis after they were all blocked by Balladur's rival Jacques Chirac, after he won the 1995 elections.

The truthfulness of the narration lies in the fact that despite its high trumpeted roars in Pakistan's leading newspapers none of the officers named in had ever approached the editors for clarification nor did any of them ever agitate the court; of course, they were never questioned even.

FALL OUT OF AGOSTA DEAL IN FRANCE:

In ending 2010, families of French engineers killed in 2002 bomb attack in Karachi vowed to lodge a manslaughter suit against former French

President Jacques Chirac, former PM Dominique de Villepin and former executives involved in arms deal linked to the case. The investigations revealed that the bombing event killing 11 French and three Pakistani engineers was revenge for refusing the settled kickbacks for Pakistani officials in the sale of submarines to Pakistan. The deal was to sell three Agosta 90 submarines to Pakistan for an estimated $950 million. The evidence was likely to prove that Paris was aware of a 'risk' to French personnel in Karachi, if the payments were stopped. Also surfaced that the present incumbent President Sarkozy was linked to the kickbacks as Budget Minister in 1994-95, however, he dismissed the allegations.

On 7th October 2010, following the said suit lodged by relatives of the killed French engineers, the France government officially announced to probe into allegations of kickbacks on arms deals with Pakistan though the French investigators were probing into the allegations since 2008.

Investigating Magistrate Renaud van Ruymbeke was deputed to probe allegations that companies [named Heine and Eurolux originally established in Luxembourg] set up with Nicolas Sarkozy's approval had channelled money from arms deal commissions to fund their political activities in France. The then PM Balladur had lost the 1995 presidential election to Jacques Chirac, who promptly cancelled commissions that were allegedly due to be paid to Pakistani officers.

The Express Tribune of 27th November 2010 opined in its editorial that:

> '*An attack of this nature could take place only with the involvement of the military and the agencies. No one else is capable of enacting it. This is all the more true as it took place during the height of power of a military regime. At every turn, the name of the president [Asif Ali Zardari] has been mentioned but .... the military has for too long been exempt from inquiry in wrongdoing of every kind.*'

Most of the people in Pakistan know many such things but nobody would agitate the court nor would the superior courts ever take *suo moto* notice of such high level burglaries by high command defence officers and politicians. It is Pakistan with population of 180 million but only 1%, mostly government servants pay income tax; the rest of them seem to be justified because they know where their tax money would be going.

The French Judge had commented in the last that [in ending 2010] Mr Zardari's **known** assets were worth $1.7 billion; poor guy from a poor country. Let us pray for his long life to enable him to use them.

Scenario 55

Pak Army in Swat (2007-09):

In the beginning of July 2007, the security forces and the police had to face retaliation in Swat. The writ of the government remained under challenge for months. Hundreds of the police and Frontier Constabulary (FC) personnel were taken in custody by the militant groups of Maulana Fazlullah, a local cleric of 32 years and son-in-law of Maulana Sufi Muhammad of *Tehreek e Nifaze Shariat e Muhammadi* (TNSM) fame. It would remain a fact that a series of suicide bombings targeting security forces had followed the Red Mosque Operation of July 2007 in Islamabad. Maulana Sufi was one of the few people who publicly reacted against the said military operation and had announced to wage jihad against the government of Pakistan.

[*It is worth mentioning here that Sufi Muhammad had given a* **Fatwa** *(a religious decree) in which he regarded military training as compulsory for every Muslim. After this decree, hundreds of TNSM workers were reportedly sent in for military training to Afghanistan and other parts of the country. Maulana Masood Azhar, after his release from prison in India, came to Swat and formed a militant organization Jaish e Muhammad (JeM), which later imparted jihadi training to the TNSM activists.*

Interestingly, Maulana Sufi Muhammad had expelled both Maulana Fazlullah and Maulana Faqir Muhammad, the militant commanders in Swat & Bajaur, from TNSM on charges of turning his peaceful movement into a violent one.]

During Gen Musharraf's rule, first time in the history of the Swat valley, the gruesome public beheadings of army soldiers were witnessed, and military gunship helicopters and artilleries seen blitzing the suspected hideouts of what the government regarded as miscreants. The people in the turbulent valley of Swat and around were openly accusing the clergy-led MMA government and military regime of showing criminal negligence.

A script of the facts given in 'Swat Analysis' by *Mushtaq Yusufzai* appeared in '*the News International*' dated 4th November 2007:

'*It was for the first time in Pakistan's major tourist centre that private properties, audio & video shops and barbers shops were blown up in*

694

the district by hidden forces. Threats were issued to women's educational institutions and nursing schools, asking the girls to stay back indoors and pushing the administration to close the institutions.

The government — in the name of restoring the writ — launched an operation through police and paramilitary security forces. Though, this led to another episode of violence in the valley, killing more than 150 people over the past one week. The militants, besides killing scores of security forces in one suicidal blast and numerous clashes, also beheaded 10 security forces personnel, policemen and government officials.'

Next day, a truck carrying the Frontier Constabulary (FC) personnel was blown up in Mingora town killing 34 people including 30 soldiers and four civilians whereas 25 FC men and ten civilians had sustained injuries. During the same days an attack on the Senior Superintendent of Police (SSP) Mazharul Haq left him badly injured and four of his cops dead. A large number of junior officers were also killed or injured in different incidents of bomb blasts and suicide attacks.

Interestingly the Inspector General of Police (IGP) Sharif Virk could not face the media due to his known spinelessness nor had he the acumen and capacity to lead his force in such turmoil. The force had felt that the Police suffered due to cowardice, lack of courage and cold attitude of their IGP who had hardly visited Swat Police offices during those days of chaos and confusion; even he didn't take phone calls.

Swat has a population of 1.5 million. As per statistics provided by the Home Secretary [in July 2007], most of the 45 people who were killed and 106 others who were injured in 43 different terrorist attacks in Swat since January 2007 were law enforcing personnel. Another 20 people, including 17 FC personnel, were killed and 31 others injured on the day when the forces took positions in the valley. The Home Secretary NWFP had himself told that:

'Maulana Fazlullah has a fighting strength of 4600, with an added 400-member Shaheen Commando Force that patrol the streets of Swat with guns placed on their vehicles. The Maulana's stronghold reins the 59 villages of Matta sub division'.

Another extract from an article 'Inside Fazlullah's HQ' by *Rahimullah Yusufzai* appeared in *'The News' dated 4th November 2007* is placed here:

'The people laughed whenever the young Maulana made fun of the 'corrupt and inefficient' police or lambasted the government for its inability to provide security to the Swatis. He drew applause when he explained how he was forced to send his Shaheen Commando Force to fight crime, patrol villages and towns and bring killers, criminals and car-snatchers to book in the absence of the police and other law-enforcing agencies. The Maulana claimed that the crime graph had come down since the cops gave up their duty after coming under attacks by unknown people.'

It may not be out of place to mention that the dependence of more than 60 per cent of the region's inhabitants rest upon the tourism industry which, sadly enough, had come to a complete halt in the wake of the then clashes between the militants and the security forces, leaving thousands of innocent people without their only source of income. The subsistence of more than 15 per cent of the locals rested with the business of hotels alone. There were more than 1200 hotels and resorts in the valley that were functional in serving their guests. However, in 2007 alone, they suffered a huge financial setback as the tourists avoided Swat and preferred to go somewhere else.

WAR WITHIN STATE? NO:

The world media tried to label the situation in Swat as *'khana jangi'* (war within the state) as per eastern vocabulary but it was not. The death toll had not even reached hundreds in Swat whereas:

[Referring to the daily 'Jang' of 27th May 2009, about 213 global territories were reportedly dragged into such deadly internal friction between years 1816 to 1997; out of which 90 events could be counted after the World War II. In Algezire about 0.2 million people were killed during 1991-2002. In Rwanda, one million people were killed in just three months of 1994 during an armed scuffle between the central government and rebels which had actually taken start in 1990. In Sri Lanka, about 80,000 human beings were killed during 25 years' brawl between the government and Tamal Tigers. In Somalia, about 0.4 million people had been killed since 1991 and in Darfur the death toll was touching 0.5 million figure during the internal friction in the last six years. During the Iraq War the death figure since America's first attack in 2003 {as per ORB Polls of the UK} had reached 1.1 million till August 2007 {including 4296 American soldiers}. Still there is no guarantee of peace in any of the said areas despite best efforts by many global agencies.]

TALIBANIZATION OF SWAT? NO

Like the earlier mentioned episodes of Swat, the whole Pakistan had suffered a lot during the last ten years on this account. The western media called it *'Talibanization process'* whereas there in Swat it was altogether a different phenomenon. One could differentiate between the two; see the details.

Pondering upon the history of Taliban's making, it may be note worthy that Mullah Omer had started his Taliban movement with less than 50 *madressah* (religious school) students after the fall of *Kandahar* in November 1994. Then thousands from Pakistani *madressahs* had rushed to join the new force and by December 1994, just within one month of seizing control, he had a force of 12000 youth with him. A new phenomenon developed in Pashtun society; that of *madressah* students and mullahs with guns in their hands, ruling the Pashtun tribes and all others around in minority.

These Afghani and Pakistani mixed *Taliban* ruled over Afghanistan till 9/11 when the Americans ousted them from government and Gen Musharraf helped America in doing so. The *Taliban* were forced to leave Kabul first, then many major cities and finally pushed towards mountains of Southern Afghanistan. Soon the Pakistani *madressah* students started coming back to Pakistan and joined back their schools. In Pakistan these students developed their own religious groups and factions and started their armed activities which were alleged by the West as more criminal and less religious.

Killings, bombings and coercions became order of the day and attacks on each other's mosques and gatherings created another wave of terror in Pakistan. Tall and known religious leaders came on their back and then the dollars pipeline from various countries kept them active till today so that the nuclear country should go weaker. The process is still on. The fact remains that certain criminal gangs joined some Pakistani religious sects to take shelter and protection for their criminal activities and started using the name and banners of Pakistani *Taliban*.

The geography played a pivotal role in the scenario. The Durand line between Pakistan and Afghanistan had divided many tribes and the situation prevails as after sixty years; out of the seven tribal agencies, six have tribes on either side of the Durand line. In the words of Asad Munir (ref: *'the News' dated 17th February 2009*):

697

'....... the religious leaders (in tribal belt) wanted a greater role for themselves in decision-making and that is why the area often saw uprisings led by religious personalities. The later had hold of the leadership as long as the war and jihad were on but once the conflict was over, it reverted to the Maliks and Khans.

The present Talibanisation is not just a movement for Shariah and its enforcement; the mullahs want power, authority and a defined role in decision making in the social system of Pashtun society.'

The Americans have been raising alarms since a decade that Osama Bin Laden was hiding in border areas inside Pakistan. Sometimes, their secret service announced that he had moved in the Quetta's settled areas where he also held regular meetings of his 'Shoora'. No concrete proof. No solid evidence in this context [and subsequent claims of 2nd May 2011 also proved these estimations wrong]. America's whole philosophy was relying upon working of a research team led by a geographer Thomas Gillespie of the University of California, Los Angeles who used to develop geographic analytical tools that had been successful in locating urban criminals and endangered species.

Relying on their night-time satellite images and other techniques, their scientists had once suggested that Osama was in Parachinar, a town 12 miles from the Pak-Afghan border and hiding there since his escape from the Tora Bora region of Afghanistan in 2001.

But at the same time Gillespie did not believe in 'sitting in a cave theory'. All US military techniques had apparently failed to locate Osama. They forgot the fact that these Taliban, were once part and focus of the US policies, on US dictates, who were driven into quagmire after the Russians had left Afghanistan and then they were at the point where they had to fight back and negotiate their terms. As a result the Afghan and Pakistani agencies went helpless.

Some people seriously thought that there was no way out except to go for 'negotiations'. Quoting instance from contemporary history, the British had negotiated with the IRA in Ireland in the 1990s taking shelter of a ceasefire. They had to give in to some of their demands on give-and-take principle to earn peace and development which is still there.

Taliban leadership had once decided to send their fighters to Islamabad as a reaction of Army operation in Swat valley. Some of their underground associates had already started wall-chalking in Islamabad and kept the Capital administration busy in quickly white washing the chalking in different sectors of the Capital city. Many religious scholars in Islamabad were sent messages from Taliban that they must support Taliban or leave the Capital otherwise they would be considered partners of the 'Pro-American Zardari government'; not very different from the military regime of Gen Musharraf.

Astonishingly the Taliban of Swat & Bajaur had included the names of some *Jehadi* leaders in their hit lists who were not willing to fight inside Pakistan against their own countrymen. Their hit lists had incorporated some leaders of banned *Lashkar e Tayyaba* (LeT), *Harkatul Mujahideen* and *Hizbul Mujahideen* which were trying to stop youngsters to fight against Pakistani forces. Taliban had declared all these 'Pro-Pakistan' *Jehadis* as their enemies.

As per report of '*the Daily Star*' dated 12th February 2009:

'Names of Maulvi Nazir from South Wazirastan, Hafiz Gul Buhadar from North Wazirastan, Hafiz Muhammad Saeed, Maulana Farooq Kashmiri and Syed Salahudin were also included in the hit list of Taliban.

Another Taliban leader in Mohmand agency Maulvi Omar Khalid had threatened student force of LeT to leave the tribal agency otherwise they would be killed. It was accused that these boys were only interested in fighting against foreign troops in Afghanistan meaning thereby that they did not want Islamic government in Pakistan'.

Another development surfaced those days that the Taliban had killed a Polish engineer as a reaction of big army operation in the Northern Areas. Initially Pakistan was ready to release some arrested Taliban fighters in exchange for Polish and another Chinese engineers but due to objections raised by the US Command the deal between Taliban and Pakistani authorities could not be finalized. Pakistan had successfully negotiated the release of kidnapped Pakistani diplomat Tariq Azizudin in those days and got free the kidnapped Army personnel in 2007 by liberating some Taliban fighters. This time US pressure complicated the situation.

Pakistan Army was facing another East Pakistan like situation after 38 years from Darra Ademkhel to the mountains of Swat. Negotiations could not take place so the kidnapped Polish engineer Piotr Stannczak was killed by Taliban. For another kidnapped Chinese engineer, one

Afghan Ambassador in Islamabad Abdul Khaliq Farahi, one Iranian diplomat Heshmatollah Attarzadeh and one kidnapped UN diplomat in Quetta, the civilian and Army leadership had decided not to negotiate any exchange. For each kidnapped envoy the Taliban had normally demanded the release of their two dozen arrested fighters.

The Army intensified its operation in Swat as half a million people out of the estimated population of 1.5 million had left Swat in one month. The ground reality of Swat was different from of 1971's East Bengal because this time army was fighting with Taliban who were apparently demanding the enforcement of Islamic law in Swat and the local political leaders were supporting this demand under public pressure.

ANP's Chief Minister of Khyber PK province Ameer Haider Hoti, Governor Awais Ghani and Army high command had once recommended to enforce long pending *Sharaia* regulation; called *'Nafaz e Adal Regulations'* but then the army was finally asked to restore peace first. Ultimately, Taliban had to quit Swat and the inhabitants repatriated to their homes at last.

During the army operation in Swat, Maulana Sufi Muhammad of *Tehrik e Nafaze Shariat Muhammadi* (TNSM) had assured the ANP leadership [once *Nizam e Adl Regulations* promulgated] to launch a long march from Dir to Swat valley after the imposition of *Sharia* law and would also appeal his son in law Maulana Fazalullah and other Taliban leaders to surrender arms. Assurance was also given that he would try his best to open all girls' schools in Swat.

> [*It may not be out of place to mention that Lt Gen Masood Alam was the Commander of Swat Operation, though was sent by Gen Musharraf but was subsequently retained by Gen Ashfaq Kayani to complete the Operation. He (Lt Gen Masood Alam) was going to retire on 18th October 2009 but asked to continue his service; was afterwards sent to the Waziristan Agency to handle the FATA Operation there as the Corps Commander.*]

The government had not made an immediate commitment at that moment but there were negotiations between Government and Maulana Soofi Mohammad's team and it brought some success though army had to control that area afterwards. Taliban had virtually occupied about 80% of the Swat valley during the previous two years. That demand of the reinstatement of their old *Nizam e Adl* in Swat was appealing as it has been successfully running with them since 1849 till 1969. When Swat was made a part of Pakistan in 1969, the general laws of courts and justice were implemented there like in other parts of Pakistan.

Swat is neither a tribal area nor does it borders with Afghanistan then why has it become a stronghold of extremists. Since 1926, Swat had developed its own central administrative system with two types of courts functioning in the State. Courts headed by the religious scholars, known as Qazi courts, and judicial courts headed by the 'Area Tehsildars'. The Qazi courts dealt with cases of divorce, inheritance and some other minor cases involving Shariah while all other disputes were referred to the Tehsildar's court. The appellate forum was that of a 'Haakim', and a final appeal could be made to the 'Waali'. The whole process of complaint till decision used to take only one month at the maximum so the people accepted the system.

In 1975, ZA Bhutto declared Dir, Chitral and Swat as normal administrative units like other districts of NWFP. In the initial years of implementation of Pakistani Laws in Swat, the people did not retaliate because it was a new set of laws for them considering that the western system would be better. With the passage of time their illusions got clear and they started murmuring to bring back their old system of justice based on Islamic Sharia. During the two regimes of Benazir Bhutto their joint voices went on a high pitch which had originally emerged as a 'Tehreek' in 1988 demanding Shariah system of Justice again. Soofi Mohammad was the founder leader of that Tehreek then and remained so in all subsequent activities.

In 1992, on collective suggestions of lawyers, the PATA (Provincially Administered Tribal Areas) Regulations were abolished by the courts. However, surprisingly no alternative system was advised and this created a judicial vacuum creating unrest amongst the general populace. It was this vacuum that provided fertility to the seeds for November 1994 uprising by the TNSM. This led to violence and the TNSM took control of six districts and there was a law and order situation all around. An MPA of the PPP, the then ruling party, was also killed. The situation was controlled by the Police after a month's hectic efforts.

When Nawaz Sharif came into power in 1997 he had felt the heat of the local demand. The then Chief Minister Mehtab Abbasi opened negotiations with Soofi Mohammad and Islami Shariah was implemented in Swat again after a suspension of 29 years. When Gen Musharraf came into power in 1999 he once more ordered to remove that Islami Shariah system of justice from record and forced the people to pass through grinding of Pakistan Penal Code and Pakistan Criminal Procedure Code, both acts coming from since 1868 with no major change. The *Tehreek* again went alive and TNSM members declared themselves as Swati Taliban.

The Talibanization process in Swat continued throughout Gen Musharraf's rule in the garb of demands for Islami Shariah system. The incumbent PPP government of 2008 remained ignorant of the people's unrest in Swat and our so-called intelligence agencies could not brief the new government on this aspect. So much so that the political governments in the province and Federation both ordered their security forces and then army to confront and open fire on the general populace just in the name of 'writ of the state' trumpeted high by the Federal Interior Ministry.

Contrarily, instead of consulting their departments and trying to look into the route causes of Taliban's increasing influence coupled with expanding occupancy, all the federal and provincial ministers remained busy in displaying photo sessions on TVs and media pronouncing almost daily that 'writ of the government' would be maintained at all cost.

What happened then! About four hundred thousand inhabitants lost their homes and businesses and migrated in their own country. Refugee Camps were erected mostly in Mardan district. The fact remains that the ministers raising writ slogans were actually the residents of Karachi or London who had never visited Swat. In that uprising for Islami Shariah Justice System the lawyer's community, who were the most affected class in the absence of Pakistani routine rotten system of justice, also stood for *Shariah* in Swat.

Ultimately when negotiations started, except *Jamaat e Islami* (JI), all other political and religious parties and public representatives from Malakand Division participated in the consultative meeting (*jirga*) held at Chief Minister's House to re-implement *Nizam e Adl* Regulations and appreciated the move as a step towards peace in the volatile Swat valley.

Local leaders and representatives of JUI(F), PML(N), JUI(S), PPP (Sherpao Group), *Pakhtunkhwa Milli Awami* Party, Pakistan *Tehrik e Insaf* (PTI) and PML(Q) attended the hours-long consultative meeting, in which the ANP-led provincial coalition government announced implementation of *Nizam e Adl* Regulations with certain amendments for the erstwhile Malakand Division after receiving a go-ahead signal from the supreme leader of defunct *Tanzim Nifaz Shariat e Muhammadi* (TNSM). A 29-member TNSM delegation, led by Maulana Muhammad

Alam, had attended this meeting. This agreed *Nizam e Adl* regulation was the same or similar to TNSM's earlier code of November 1994.

The JI did not attend the *jirga* saying that the ANP-led government was responsible for all the bloodshed and destruction in Swat and elsewhere in the province. Elaborating their stand the JI maintained that:

> 'The ANP *wants to save its skin by involving all political parties for the wrongdoing it committed in the province.*'

JUI(S)'s Senator Maulana Samiul Haq, who also addressed the *Jirga* meeting, said that:

> 'The implementation of Nizam e Adl Regulation was neither a violation of the constitution nor against the country's judicial system, and warned that if the move was sabotaged, then it would not only be harmful for Swat but also for the entire country.'

PPP (Sherpao)'s Chief Aftab Sherpao was one of the participant of that *jirga* meeting but it may be noted here with interest that the same Sherpao was the Federal Interior Minister in Gen Musharraf's cabinet (and remained on seat for more than five years) when the unrest in Swat started raising head in his militarized regime but he never advised his military boss that the Islamic *Nizam e Adl* be reinstated in Malakand division nor he ever bothered to keep this unrest on record.

It may be cited as an acute 'professional dishonesty' and speaks adverse of our leadership's patriotism for Pakistan that the job which he could do at the initial stage without loss of lives and property, he kept it for next government to do causing it too late.

In those days there were demonstrations by the women and girls in various parts of the country with placards carrying picture of a girl with a line saying, **"Save me, save Swat, Save Pakistan"** because their schools were being burnt. If TNSM were after Islami Shariah system, which they got then who were burning schools particularly of girls in all areas which come under their control including Swat. If they were true Muslims then they should not impose any restriction on women getting education.

There was no one to tell the Taliban that Hazrat Ayesha (RA) got education; they should have known that the Holy Prophet (PBUH), after conquering Makkah, did not close down schools of the Jews and the Christians but here in Pakistan, these girls' schools were being burnt by Taliban or by 'someone or some group' in the name of Taliban.

For this reason majority of Pakistanis considered Talibanization as a conspiracy against Muslims and especially Pakistan. That is why over the last decade, the image of Pakistan as a safe and civilized country has tumbled dramatically. It is now ranked as one of the most dangerous places on earth. This has affected investment, tourism, mutual cooperation among neighbouring states and our foreign policies to a great extent.

In early months of 2009, the Federal Interior Minister, Rehman Malik, announced in the Senate that the schools in Swat would be re-opened within seven days and the Pakistani people would see complete eradication of militants in the area. *Immediate confirmation was seen by the media because the Pakistani Taliban insurgents had destroyed four schools [two for boys and two for girls] on the very next day to pay an honourable tribute to the Federal Minister's hollow statement.*

It has been the normal way of working for Taliban; to terrorize the residents they always preferred to attack government buildings showing their power and strength. Thank God, had the schools been not closed, big casualties would have been there. They used to see police stations and schools as symbols of government authority and they believed that army camps were based there. Till the end of first quarter of 2009, the militants had destroyed 170 schools in the valley where about 55,000 girls and boys were enrolled therein.

The then Federal Information Minister Miss Sherry Rehman had also announced that schools in Swat would reopen on 1st March [2009] after the winter break but most of the population had fled to the nearby cities of Peshawar and Mardan while many police officers had either deserted or simply refused to serve. The teachers had also refused to work because the government was unable to provide them protection. Thus even if the authorities had announced for reopening of schools, nobody was there to mark their presence.

The PPP government, after holding reigns of power in 2008, believed that many of the militants in Swat had infiltrated from Al-Qaeda and Taliban hideouts in ethnic Pashtun areas on the Afghan border. They had fled from there in late 2007 when the military launched a big offensive to clear them out. Despite stern efforts, the government was not able to trace out that FM radio, or if traced they could not block its transmissions, on which the names of the persons beheaded on the main squares of Mingora city that day were read over and the Swat Taliban used to announce their policies. The state intelligence infrastructure had totally failed. The ISI and IB had completely stumbled down.

ARMY'S OPERATION RAH E HAQ:

Brutal attacks on schools in Swat, destroying the structures of buildings, beating up the teaching staff, the action against those opposing the Taliban and the expanding control of the militants was hardly a secret then. Gen Kayani, the COAS visited Mingora and announced his decision to retaliate the militants with full power. In this respect, the military's declaration of a new resolve was welcome. Big operation was launched to gain back the control of Swat and it succeeded.

Referring to the **BBC News dated 6-8th December 2007**, the Pak army started 'Operation Rah-e-Haq' against the extremists in the valley on 25th October 2007 with the following details:

'*On 24th October 2007, about 3,000 infantry troops of the Pakistan Army were sent to Swat and deployed to the hill-tops of the rugged terrain to confront Taliban forces. Next day, heavy fighting started with a suicide bomber attacking a paramilitary truck and killing 17 soldiers and 13 civilians. Fighting erupted in the hills with Taliban forces attacking military posts and the military attacking Taliban's mountain hideouts. By 31st October, reportedly 130 militant fighters were killed. However the next day about 700 militants overran a military position on a hill in Khwazakhela and 48 military men were captured and paraded through the streets. Also, police forces in Matta were completely surrounded by the end of the day.*

On 3rd November 2007, 120 police and paramilitary troops in Matta surrendered and then the Taliban also overran the nearby town of Khwazakhela, thus taking two police stations and took a large arsenal of weapons that was in them. There was no major fighting until 7th November 2007, when the Taliban continued their advance and took the town of Madyan. The police there also gave up their weapons, vehicles and control of local police stations. In short, the insurgents had occupied the floodplain side of Swat River while the army troops held the road alongside the river and surrounding forested hills. This left the Taliban in control of most of the Swat district and by then they had already set up their own local 'governors' in Tehsil Kabal, Matta and Khawazkhela.

On 12th November 2007, soldiers belonging to 12th Regular Army were deployed to Swat to reinforce the already 15000 men from military and police and mounted a number of operations to counter the militants. However, on 15th November, the militants advanced from Swat, which was now under their control, into the next district named Shangla and Alpuri [the district HQ of Shangla] fell to the Taliban insurgents. An alarming situation it was and the army had to strike back with force which they did.

By 17th November 2007, about 100 militants were killed in the fighting and ultimately on 25th November, Taliban forces decided to leave Alpuri to avoid further loss of their men. The Taliban evacuated Alpuri and took up positions on the mountaintops around the town.

On 26th November 2007, in Swat, Pakistan artillery resulted in the death of two top Taliban commanders. With artillery fire and ground forces, the Pakistani Army recaptured many strategic hilltops from the Taliban and managed to drive the Taliban back to the Swat district.

By 27th November 2007, the army troops had retaken the Swat & Shangla back but certain pockets of Swat like Matta, Khwazakhela, Charbagh were still held by the insurgents. The security forces concentrated on Imam Dehri, the native village of Maulana Fazlullah, and nearby Kuza Banda, Bara Banda and Nigwalai. Once fighting commenced, most insurgents retreated to nearby areas and the highest peak in Kabal district was retaken.

On 28th November 2007, after suffering colossal losses, the militants in Swat vacated all seized police stations and other government buildings suddenly and decided to go underground after closing down their famous FM radio channel. On the same day, the Pakistan Army had cleared Imam Dehri, Maulana Fazlullah's seminary & HQ; police resumed their normal duty in Alpuri and around in Shangla. Till then about 50 more militants were killed in four days of fighting and they vacated Matta, Khwazakhela, Charbagh and Madyan police stations also.

Till 5th December 2007, the Pakistan army had got full control of Swat valley again and the Operation Rah e Haq was declared successfully concluded.'

The Operation was wrapped up in mid-January 2008; Pakistan's army confirmed that they had taken control of the Swat Valley after a three month operation against pro-Taliban Islamic fighters. '*The Pakistan Army's troops have pushed out the miscreants from the Swat Valley to an adjoining isolated area in the mountains*', Major Gen Ahmed Shuja Pasha, the DG Military Operations wing of the GHQ had told the media.

As per GHQ report, thirty-six (36) soldiers and nine civilians were killed during the offensives [during Dec 2007-January 2008] without saying how many militants died. More than 615 people were arrested, 100 of whom were detained for further interrogations. The Swat operation continued targeting supporters of Maulana Fazlullah till late. At least 10 of Fazlullah's close allies were killed but Fazlullah himself fled to Afghanistan. As many as 230 militants were killed in a two-week operation, the army told in another media briefing.

However, the army had to come back again with Operation Rah e Haq II which was launched in July 2008. This time the military operation was led by both Air Force and Army because the militants, who had gone underground six months back, had surfaced again with the same old agenda of killings and harassment.

After elections of 18th February 2008, the ANP assumed government in Peshawar, and one of their key electoral planks was to talk peace with Swat's militants. However, this otherwise sensible approach was not responded in kind by the Swat's local Taliban who in fact opted targeting the local ANP leadership soon after the party had assumed power in that northern province.

Gen Pasha had urged that any possible resurgence of the militants would be prevented if people withdraw their support and stop donating money to the fighters. At the same time it was noted that the US government, which was otherwise declaring the Taliban as their first enemy, started raising cries at the world forum accusing the Pakistan Army for their alleged brutalities and killing of 'innocent citizens' in the name of humanity and declaring the problem as a big human rights issue. The British government, however, had a contrary viewpoint.

The above scenario proved only one phase of the Swat Operation. The poor and comparatively untrained 'miscreants' were killed and the supervisors fled to the Pak Afghan border areas. They came back again after six months with more training and better weapons to attack the army troops again. Despite the victory by the Pakistani army, Taliban militants slowly re-entered Swat over the following months and started engaging security forces in battles that lasted throughout 2008. By early 2009, the Taliban had managed to regain control of most of the Swat and at least 80 percent of the district was under their control.

Then the Pakistan Army had to launch Operation Rah e Haq III in January & February 2009 to secure the main supply lines and consolidate Swat District. Frontier Corps infantry troops provided help to four army infantry brigades. The forces regained Mingora and were poised to push the Taliban out when Sufi Muhammad was released and Shariah Law was introduced in Swat and Malakand. The provincial government was confident of the outcome of the peace deal. However, the TTP betrayed the government again by regrouping and capturing Swat, Buner, Mingora, Shangla and its surrounding areas.

[*On 16th February 2009, the Pakistani government announced that it would allow the Shariah law under the government's supervision with shariah courts setup by the Government of Pakistan under the Shariat appellate bench of the Supreme Court in the Malakand region. In return, Fazlullah's followers agreed to observe a ceasefire negotiated by Sufi Muhammad.*]

Tracing out the root causes; in 2001, when the conflict between Al Qaeda and the US began in earnest, the Pakistani *jihadi* organisations started targeting the state in well-planned moves. Swat was chosen as one of the core areas [along with Waziristan and Bajaur] by them for this purpose due to the presence of a large youth pool. An analysis proved that 75% people believed that unemployment forced the youth to join the militants.

With failing public finances the education system almost collapsed; the poor started sending their offspring to *madressahs* due to unemployment and rising inflation. After graduating from such schools these youth wanted employment but unfortunately such opportunities were few, except when the militants offered them jobs for fighting the state in the name of religion and all of them were paid from 'clandestine aids' in dollars.

An examination of the factors in Swat shows a close link between poverty and militancy. Poverty in Swat is attributable mainly to lack of assets and skills. The district development indicators showed [in early 2011] a decline when Swat dropped in its ranking from 15th to 17th position out of 24 Khyber Pakhtunkhwa (PK) districts.

Referring to the *'Dawn' dated 18th March 2011* wherein Khalid Aziz, Chairman of the Regional Institute of Policy Research in Peshawar had opined that:

'Swat has a population growth rate of 2.6% a year, a little above the rest of the country. In Pakistan, there were 51 million employable youth in 2006 but projected to increase to 90 million in 2017. Pakistan *otherwise would be unable to meet this challenge and Swat like places would thus be confronted with more risky situations.*

[Thus] a nexus between lack of resources, inequality and militancy was visibly seen; almost overnight increases in the wealth of some jihadi leaders like Nek Muhammad and Baitullah Mehsud from Waziristan, Faqir Muhammad from Bajaur and Mullah Fazlullah from Swat were living examples.'

Reportedly, Maulana Fazlullah was once summoned to North Waziristan to participate in coordination amongst the different groups. The chief of those operations was one Ibn-i-Amin who had been placed in Mohmand Agency areas to direct operations in Mohmand, Bajaur and the Swat Valley. Then new recruits were sent to Tirah in Khyber Agency for training to undertake terrorist strikes in the urban areas which ultimately brought humiliation for the security forces.

To conclude: **on 12th May 2009,** the last phase of Swat Operation was launched and till the ending June 2009, the military action in Swat and adjoining districts like Dir & Boner was 'complete'. Various areas of Malakand Division were taken back from the Taliban, but the army stayed on in the valley to conduct 'search and destroy' operations, as per briefing by Major Gen Athar Abbas in the first week of July 2009 at a press conference. The same operation was reassigned the priority of creating conditions for safe return of the dislocated population of Malakand Division including Swat. The Taliban's command & control structures, logistics and training infrastructure were destroyed and a large number of Taliban leaders were either killed or arrested.

UN Refugee Agency had told that over two million people were displaced as the result of fighting between the Taliban militants and the security forces in and around districts of Swat {only Swat has population of 1.5 million}; only 10% of them could be accommodated in camps by the UN and state departments collectively. The media had witnessed the disastrous living conditions of those forced to crouch in the roadside makeshift camps in all areas around till late June. The World Health Organization (WHO) remained the most concerned about the increased risk of those IDPs (Internally Displaced People / Persons).

The IDPs lying in open were more disturbed from possible assaults from the Pakistani Taliban and from American Drone attacks at the same time. A day earlier then, two separate drone attacks had killed 48 persons in Waziristan tribal agency and were the fifth US drone strikes there in less than one month.

The world media told that about 1600 terrorists were killed and another 700 apprehended since Pak Army launched the said military operation against Taliban in late April [2009] after militants [in early April] had entered the Buner district from the adjacent Swat and refused to vacate the area despite their pledge to do so.

The statistics available from the **GHQ *in November 2011*** told that during Army's eight years' stay in Swat valley against extremism, 1900 Pakistani army troops were martyred and 5000 injured whereas 4000 miscreants were killed and 3000 arrested. While during the Swat / Malakand operation of 2007-09 only, 340 Pakistani army troops including officers had been martyred; 1800 miscreants were killed and 2000 were arrested.

Let the world hope that the American drama of intrigue and bloodshed comes to an end earlier.

(Part of this essay was published at www.criticalppp.com on 14th May 2011)

Scenario 56

GEN MUSHARRAF QUITS (2008):

During every military rule the graph of army image initially moves up but then starts declining sharply. As that rule is prolonged the institution comes under attack from all corners and the media takes lead in educating the general populace regarding the ineptness and corruption grooming in the ranks & files of all departments and state organizations. In Pakistan, the army image distorted so badly after each military rule that the next coming chief had to wash away their dirty linens with much labour, efforts and hard work.

When Gen Yahya Khan had left his mischievous rule in 1971, Gen Gul Hassan had to work hard for restoration of image of his disheartened and shocked army. When Gen Ziaul Haq got crashed in 1988, the public had mixed feelings of hatred, disappointment and dismay about the Pakistan Army for which Gen Aslam Beg was there to take up this Himalayan task.

Most of the intelligentsia think that Gen Aslam Beg was on the right track especially while he tried utmost to drag out the Pakistan Army from the sand grave of misused false notions of Islamic-phobia pushed in by Gen Ziaul Haq but Shafqat Mahmood keeps altogether a different view about him. Referring to his opinion appeared in *'the News'* dated *4th September 2009*:

> *'In my reading of post-Zia history, there is no greater sinner than Aslam Beg. By his actions after Zia's death and indeed throughout his tenure of office, he caused great harm to this nation. He did not let democracy settle, manipulated parties and politicians and corrupted them, brought governments down.... It is easy to blame Ghulam Ishaq Khan (GIK) because he had his share of sins but without Aslam Beg goading him on, much of what GIK did would not have happened. It was Beg who asked Hameed Gul to form the Islami Jamhoori Ittehad (IJI) and stop Benazir and the Pakistan People's Party (PPP) from coming to power. When he could not stop it, it was he who led the media and dirty-tricks campaign to undermine it and bring it down.'*

> *They [Gen Beg & his military friends] launched operation midnight jackal, engineered a no-confidence move against her [Benazir Bhutto], got the MQM to take on the PPP in the streets of Karachi, thwarted*

the Pucca Qilla operation, which was leading to the capture of a huge cache arms stored by terrorists in Hyderabad, and then prevailed upon GIK to dismiss her government; it not only hurt Pakistan but derailed democracy.

After the Benazir government had been dismissed in 1990, he distributed money and did everything to make an IJI government come into power. Nawaz Sharif had taken over in perhaps October and by December; officers of military intelligence (MI) were making contact with the PPP to instigate it against the government. Not only that, Beg deliberately started to undermine Nawaz by taking a position different from that of the government during the First Gulf War.

His [Gen Beg's] serving military officers started provoking the PPP to take on the Nawaz Sharif government through street power. Fortunately, for us, his time ran out and GIK trumped him by appointing a new army chief, two months before his term of office was to end. This was unprecedented and the only reason it was done was to make him a lame duck and thwart his ambition for power. Beg left with much regret but a legacy of bitterness was created that tainted the entire decade of the 90s. Democracy could not settle after that.'

Coming back; the same type of image-laundry job was taken up and handled by Gen Ashfaq Kayani because Gen Musharraf's performance during his eight years as Army Chief cum Chief Executive cum President had continuously been pushing his institution (of Pakistan Army) into a sand grave of public repugnance, revulsion and disgust.

In Gen Musharraf era, the army started loosing its credibility at very early stage when the sitting judges of the Supreme Court of Pakistan and the High Courts of respective provinces were asked to take a fresh oath of office swearing allegiance to military rule and to state that they would make no decisions against the military. After 12th October 1999's coup, many people had filed petitions in the Supreme Court of Pakistan challenging the said unconstitutional act. Under The Oath of Judges Order 2000 the Chief Justice of Pakistan Mr Justice Saeeduzzaman Siddiqui refused to become a part of the new hierarchy and so did many other judges. Some of them, which were not in the good books of Gen Musharraf, were not asked to take oath.

The people felt a bad taste in their mouths when Gen Musharraf, immediately after taking over the reigns of the government, had replaced nearly all the controlling slots of National Accountability Bureau (NAB) after appointing a serving Lt Gen as its head. All the provincial NAB offices were given under the command of serving Brigadiers or Major Generals and were given a special agenda. A year after the NAB Ordinance was 'suitably' amended as per future needs of the military governance and the politicians were coerced to join his master's voice through hook or crook.

A PPP member Aftab Sherpao was called from London; his old NAB file was sent to cold room and was given the most important slot in cabinet, the Federal Interior Minister. Same like honours were given to Rao Sikandar of Okara, Faisal Saleh Hayat of Jhang and one Miss Neelofar Bakhtiar, politicians of the PPP who were offered key offices in the Federal Cabinet too. They were directed to form a new faction of PPP adding another P, making PPPP, for public consumption.

Similar deal was negotiated with ousted Prime Minister Nawaz Sharif and his family members to send them to Saudi Arabia and former Chairman Ehtesab Bureau Saif ur Rehman through secret negotiations and the same have now become public stories. The tenures of Lt Gen M Amjad and Lt Gen Khalid Maqbool are a case study in this regard. The tales of those times are quoted as examples of arm-twisting techniques coupled with sweet pills of compromises on public expense and undermining the rule of law. All was fair to strengthen Gen Musharraf's military rule. In NAB most of the registered cases were either finished or shelved after applying 'plea-bargain' clauses of the amended NAB Laws.

After Lt Gen M Amjad, another serving Lt Gen Khalid Maqbool was pushed into the Chairman's office of the NAB. True or false, the stories of corruptions involved in dubious 'releases' during those days are still spoken in secretariat offices of Islamabad. The people still quote the ruling patterns of some serving Army Generals who were called as NAB's Chiefs to eradicate high profile corruption from state departments but ended their tenures with opening of enquiries against their own persons on same like charges of corruption or compromises in plea-bargains during their stay in NAB. The tenures of Lt Gen Khalid Maqbool and Lt Gen Shahid Aziz each may be compared going in two opposite directions under this head.

The army's image cannot be considered as positive when the people would not be able to find, see or hear even a single case of corruption opened against any army officer serving in civil capacity during eight years of Gen Musharraf's rule with an iron rod of NAB in hand. Illegal use of authority and loss of Rs:1.82 billion to the NLC by two serving Lt

Generals and one Major General can be found on the other pages as a reference. One case of Admiral ® Mansoorul Haq can also be cited (penalized because he was from Pakistan Navy not Army) in which he was freed after accepting equivalent to two million Dollars in plea-bargain negotiations as against corruption charges of 95 million dollars.

The Pakistani people, after having an access to the world media, do not seem to be astray if they think that why an army officer is not answerable to the higher courts under the charges of corruption done by him in civil capacity. Army housing schemes can be quoted as an example. The uniformed establishments have been minting money since 20 years in the name of Army / Navy / PAF welfare housing schemes, doing purely private business but using military funds coupled with influence of respective forces, benefiting from the personnel and technical resources and frequent military deployments and allotting plots to their officers on special reserved prices but when some discrepancy occurs, the matter can only be referred to the Army Act 1952 where it becomes a secret disciplinary action.

A GENERAL BETRAYED THE NATION:

The serious blow to the legitimacy of army institution came after 2002 elections. The National Assembly could not start work for more than a year till December 2003, until Gen Musharraf made a deal with *Muttahida Majlis e Amal* (MMA), a six-member coalition of Islamic parties, agreeing to leave the army by 31st December 2004. With their politico-religious support, pro-Musharraf legislators were able to muster the two-third majority required to pass the 17th Amendment, which retroactively legalized Gen Musharraf's 1999 coup and many of his decrees.

The people nearly started cursing army when in late 2004, Gen Musharraf, quite contrary to the grace of Army Chief's uniform, went back on his agreement with the MMA and got a bill passed in Parliament through his stooge legislators allowing a president to keep the office of the Army Chief, too.

[*What benefits MMA got out of that deal, is another interesting story.*]

It can be traced out from newspapers that how Gen Musharraf had allegedly purchased certain Islamic minded politicians headed by Maulana Fazlur Rehman, the then leader of opposition in the National Assembly; and Mr Akram Durrani, the then Chief Minister of NWFP.

The price was allegedly paid in the shape of 1200 *Kanals* military land near the city boundaries of Dera Ismail Khan, the original constituency and hometown of JUI's Chief. The lands were belonging to the Military Lands & Cantonment Department and were meant for awards to the families of retiring or dying soldiers. On behalf of Maulana Fazlur Rehman and the then CM Durrani, the pieces of 200 *Kanals* each were leased out to their brothers and other family members.

The full investigative stories were once published in the print media. Maulana Fazlur Rehman got angry, termed it as scandalous and threatened the newspapers for dire consequences in the court. The media welcomed Maulana's initiative and published copies of all related documents like orders of Military Office, mutation from the Revenue Department, possession letters duly signed and undertaken, statements of farmers etc who were ploughing the lands on behalf of these 'bigs'. This price was paid to the Leader of Opposition to calm down during that parliamentary session where the 17th Amendment in the constitution was debated; how cheap. That is why Gen Musharraf did not bother to do away his uniform on 31st December 2004 as per his original promise. He was sure of silence in the house and media for the price he had paid to the Maulanas.

Three years after, an enemy of the three; the army, PPP and PML(N) circulated a joke on internet; an application form for aspirants to the post of Prime Minister of Pakistan. The form asked applicants to choose from a list of reasons for applying: '**to escape court trial; to make more money; to grossly misuse power; to serve the people** [*if you choose the last, attach certificate of sanity from a recognized psychiatrist*].'

After implementation of the 17th Amendment, Gen Musharraf started inducting serving and retired army officers into the civil service structure. Naturally this exercise was being done at the cost of aspiring civil servants who were blocked in promotions and other benefits. Most of the army personnel were awarded key posts in lucrative departments. To cite an example, to fill in 19 slots of ambassadors to represent Pakistan abroad, 17 were recruited from the army whereas the Foreign Office Cadre could occupy only two slots. Further, these 17 army officers were given the best choice of countries in America, Western European countries, Middle East and Saudi Arabia.

Final drop scene of Gen Musharraf's drama started on 9th March 2007 when the Chief Justice of Pakistan had refused to bow his head before the military dictator. [*In some other chapter, the whole episode has been given in detail.*] By-passing those troublesome weeks of judicial paralysis in the country, a day came when decorum was abandoned as accusations roared in Pakistan's National Assembly in last week of July 2007 sessions pointing towards the episode of Red Mosque killings of about two weeks earlier then. The government was labelled as *'Murderers! Murderers of innocent people!'* The speaker kept on shouting at the members to maintain order.

Declan Walsh, representing *'the Guardian (UK)'* in Islamabad, writes in his paper on *2nd August 2007*:

> President Pervez Musharraf's rule has been *'catastrophic'* but his regime could yet "turn really nasty" said Stephen Cohen of the Brookings Institution in Washington and author of The Idea of Pakistan. "The country hasn't had a crisis of this magnitude since the 1970s when East Pakistan split off and became Bangladesh". But in this case it's an Islamist movement that wants to transform the country from within'.

Secretive meeting between Gen Musharraf and the exiled opposition leader Benazir Bhutto in Abu Dhabi in mid 2007 had triggered speculation of a power-sharing deal. Neither side had confirmed the details but the supporters could understand that switch over was ahead in the name of 'controlled democracy'; in which Benazir Bhutto would take over as the Prime Minister and Gen Musharraf as President. Modalities were also worked out that how Gen Musharraf would manage to do away an important clause of 17th Amendment allowing 3rd time premiership for her. The final meeting in Dubai was welcome by a bad news that a government spokesman was assassinated in Baluchistan.

That sharp game was managed through Rehman Malik and Tariq Aziz of the President's Secretariat because of their time old acquaintance. Nawaz Sharif was also setting their billions worth property business in the central London those days [subsequently handed over to his younger son when the former left for Pakistan in 2007]; he had known all those developments between the military regime and the PPP but purposefully kept quite in the hope of getting the same fruit by default. Rather, he was going one step ahead by negotiating *'Meesaq e Jamhooriat'* with Benazir Bhutto [already successfully signed by the two in 2006].

In the fall-out of Red Mosque episode of Islamabad in July 2007, the stern reaction from the tribal belt crippled the upper part of the country. During the same month [of July 2007] alone, the suicide bombers had killed about 200 people, mostly tribal militia, FC *jawans* and some of regular members of the army. The fighting went most intense in

Waziristan's tribal belt where the pro-government leaders were beheaded and their homes blasted, barbers threatened and music shops were set on fires.

The general defiance triggered by Chief Justice Iftikhar Chaudhry's refusal, caught momentum amongst the civilians at large which ultimately swelled into a powerful movement against Gen Musharraf's army rule. Since March 2007, the lawyer's community had been out on the streets and roads hurling insults at Gen Musharraf and the kindest word used to call him was 'dog'; as per 'the Guardian's narration' mentioned above. During the same era private television channels played their role to revolutionize Pakistani politics. Live debates had taken place even on road sides against state sponsored censorships.

43 deaths and dozens wounded in Karachi on 12th May 2007 had already shaken people's will to support Gen Musharraf; the July's episode of Red Mosque gave them a lead towards change in government by all means. The civilian revolt reached its climax when, against all expectations, the Supreme Court's full bench threw out Gen Musharraf's case against the deposed Chief Justice Mr Chaudhry and brought him back into his seat on 20th July 2007. The dents in military rule continued.

In the month of landing Benazir Bhutto in Pakistan after eight years exile, October 2007, during which our rubber-stamp parliament was also going to complete its natural tenure of five years, Gen Musharraf brought forward his last desire of extending his rule. He wanted that dying and chaotic national assembly - the product of a rigged vote in 2002 - to prefer him as president for another five years. For this he needed a serious deal with Ms Bhutto, and had promised to lift long-standing corruption charges against her and his husband Mr Zardari. The US and Britain had manoeuvred that deal by presenting themselves as the main guarantors in between because both the super powers had successfully given an impression that Gen Musharraf was still their best bet. From inside, both powers wanted to get rid of Gen Musharraf, in fact.

WINDS AGAINST GEN MUSHARRAF:

In post-election scenario; *on 10th June 2008,* while talking to Dr Shahid Masood in a *Geo News program,* Lt Gen (Rtd) Moinuddin Haider, said that:

> *'After becoming an American ally in 2002, Gen Musharraf had ignored the cabinet, the GHQ and the army's high command. Gen*

717

Musharraf should resign (then Gen Musharraf was sitting President of Pakistan) before impeachment proceedings are initiated against him.'

He categorically pointed out that massive rigging was committed in the elections of 2002 and military agencies & Rangers played a vital role in this regard. Gen Musharraf completely trusted Shaukat Aziz and never rejected anything said by the later. He, interalia, also told that in his view, Nawaz Sharif was not taken into confidence on the Kargil episode.

Besides, Federal Interior Minister Gen Moinuddin Haider had also served as Governor Sindh and Corps Commander Lahore. In Pakistan Army, he was considered as senior and a very close colleague of Gen Musharraf. He had been with Gen Musharraf since 1961 but:

'.... after joining hands with American allies we began to know about many things later. We believed that there was no US base in Pakistan and Gen Musharraf had also assured us about the same. However, the US Central Command revealed that their 64,000 army personnel were on the soil of Pakistan. I was the interior minister but I was kept in the dark about such a big reality and it hurt me'.

Gen Haider told that the whereabouts of those picked or arrested by the agencies were not ever known. He stated without any fear or shame that:

'We held and handed over to the US around 600 persons from all over Pakistan. The ISI played a major role in this regard. The personnel of the FBI were present in Pakistan and those picked up by the agencies were never produced before the courts but taken to the Bagram airbase in Afghanistan straightaway.'

To a question, the former interior minister said that large-scale rigging was carried out in the 2002 general elections in which the agencies played an important role. He, however, said that he did not know as to where and how these (rigging) plans were prepared.

Those were bad days for Gen Musharraf. The wind had started blowing against him. Earlier, during February to May 2008, another odd situation had cropped up for him when top brass retired Generals and influential officers of Pakistan Army started convening meetings and criticized pro-Musharraf policies in open. It was a big loss for Gen Musharraf who remained in Army Chief's uniform for nine years though allegedly on bogus footings.

Some influential retired Generals and officers, under the banner of their association, assembled in Rawalpindi in 2008 basically to condemn the most unfortunate calamity which had struck their Army's image in the second week of June when the American war planes hit the tribal areas in Pakistan killing about 26 persons including one major and 13 security forces men. The retired officers warned that the military regime must review its post 9/11 US dictated policy of 'war against terror' to avoid confrontation between the country's army and its civilian population.

The forum of the retired officers had especially discussed in detail that during 2006-07, a suicide bomber had attacked a Pak-Army recruitment and training centre in Dargai (of Malakand Division), and had killed at least 42 soldiers and injured dozens. It was the first ever major offensive against Pakistan Army within the Pakistani territory and believed to be the reaction to the Bajaur missile attack during the previous month killing more than 80 civilians.

Like ordinary minds even these retired Generals, including those who headed the ISI in the past, felt that *'discredit of all the losses goes to Gen Musharraf'*. Former ISI Chief Hamid Gul demanded that Gen Musharraf must stop serving the American interests as Washington's 'hired hand'. Another ex-ISI Chief Lt Gen (retd) Asad Durrani had also passed similar remarks. Lt Gen (retd) Jamshed Gulzar, the former Corps Commander Rawalpindi lamented *'that the military regime has exceeded all limits to attain America's objectives'*. In Lt Gen (retd) Talat Masud's view the attacks on Bajaur and Dargai was an extremely dangerous sign so the government must focus on the political solutions.

In short, Gen Musharraf could not foresee that he was running out of options. Going back, a poll by the Washington-based International Republican Institute announced on 1ˢᵗ August 2007 that Gen Musharraf's popularity was at 34%; down 20 points since February that year. The International Crisis Group had rightly pointed out then:

' .... *If politics fails, he (Gen Musharraf) could impose a state of emergency. But that would accelerate the slide towards a **military-led**, **failing state status** prone to domestic unrest and export of Islamic radicalism domestically, regionally and beyond'.*

The subsequent events proved it was true.

AFTER GENERAL ELECTIONS OF 2008:

After February 2008's general elections, Gen Musharraf had gone mad for desperately trying to cling on to the Presidency because his King's party PML(Q) could not win majority seats. Meanwhile the new PPP coalition had manoeuvred to immediately convey a clear message that the military dictator should move out of the presidential palace. [*BBC's program "Have Your Say" dated 23rd February 2008* is referred]

The intelligentsia held that Gen Musharraf should have quit himself then honourably instead of going through the ugly drama of impeachment by the newly elected parliament but he was perhaps waiting for green signal from the White House recalling the settled clauses of the NRO negotiated with late Benazir Bhutto [*to accept his continuity as president*]. The PPP and Mr Zardari were not willing to give him that relaxation because [firstly] Gen Musharraf had not agreed for BB's third time prime minister-ship till his presidential elections on 6th October 2007 at least; being proud of his uniform. Secondly, Benazir Bhutto was no more in the world to honour the said deal.

However, it remained a fact that Mr Bush & his associates were pleading, not pressurizing, the new PPP government to allow Gen Musharraf to stay on but was declined. [*The US is always known for promoting democracies in the world but also having likings for fighting dictators: albeit Gen Musharraf was neither a fighter then nor dictator any more.*]

'*The Washington Post*' *of 23rd February 2008* said that:

> "*After six years of relying on President Pervez Musharraf to combat extremism in Pakistan, the Bush administration has begun a slow and awkward separation from its ally, reaching out to disparate new political and military leaders to ensure future cooperation with the United States. 'No one wants us to be involved in giving Musharraf the bum's rush, pushing him out the door,' a senior State Department official said. 'We're quite clear that we're going to work with him, but in a new role, as we'll work with new leaders in the parties, the army and civil society'.*
>
> *While waiting for the new opposition coalition to form a government, the Bush administration is exploring a range of ideas, including a proposal by Sen. Joseph R. Biden Jr. (D-Del.), to triple non-military aid, sustain it for 10 years, and focus on schools, roads and health care; U.S. officials said.*"

Inside the US, the media and the public were still talking of Gen Musharraf as the best bet against war on terrorism. Ironically, it was Gen Musharraf who had opted to be backed by Muslim hardliners, whereas the political parties which had won in the general elections were liberal and progressive. The lack of information about the ground realities was playing havoc all around. Like today, in 2008 too, the newly elected PPP leadership had repeatedly told the world that fears about the nuclear arms falling into the hands of terrorists were highly exaggerated: a notion to allow Gen Musharraf to continue. The PPP reiterated that the same were '200 *per cent safe with the army*' headed by Gen Kayani and not by Musharraf. Once a soldier removes his uniform, he is gone and the troops do not obey him.

'*So why is the US administration so hell-bent in supporting Musharraf?* A cogent question was being discussed every where in America.

The daily '*Dawn*' *of 24th February 2008* had stated that:

'*US Secretary of State Condoleezza Rice has backed President Pervez Musharraf in the strongest possible term, calling him the man the United States has been dealing with as the president and wants to continue to do so. Her endorsement comes three days after President Bush telephoned his Pakistani counterpart, apparently to assure him that his administration still recognises Mr Musharraf as the president of Pakistan despite the changes that followed the elections.*'

However, the world media had openly discussed that Gen Musharraf was going to resign soon to avoid being pushed out by the new coalition of the PML(N) and the PPP which would be assuming power shortly. '*The Hindustan Times*' (HT) of the same day (*24th February 2008*) had given a detailed analysis saying that:

'*A senior political analyst close to the establishment also confirmed to HT that Musharraf's departure was very much a possibility. Asif Zardari and Nawaz Sharif agreed on Saturday to work together to oust the President, so chances are that he will go voluntarily instead of risking impeachment. The analyst even named Aitzaz Ahsan, who led the lawyers' campaign against Musharraf's dismissal of the former CJ Iftikhar Chaudhry as the likely nominee for the next President. Ahsan is currently under house arrest. Other names doing the rounds as possible contenders for the post of President are those of Asif Zardari himself and Yusuf Raza Gilliani, who was the speaker of the national assembly during Benazir Bhutto's second term.*'

Pakistan's 'Daily Times' of 25th February 2008 opined that:

'*The fourth major player (apart from Zardari, Sharif and Musharraf) is the Chief of Army Staff, General Ashfaq Kayani. General Kayani seems to have put the integrity and reputation of the institution he commands above the political interests of the former COAS (Musharraf). As the new chief, General Kayani has so far fulfilled John Milton's prayer that: 'They also serve who only stand and wait.' How long and what he is willing to wait for is the question that only he can answer.'*

In an article titled *'Time Over to Quit Honourably'* written by *Dr Ijaz Shafi Gilani*, then available with media told that many observers had counselled Gen Musharraf to quit honourably after he made the fatal mistake of imposing Emergency rule on 3rd November 2007 but he had gone too late afterwards. Mr Gilani held that:

'Seven months later he has been publicly disgraced more than any sitting ruler in Pakistan's history. But he has persisted stubbornly, apparently without much remorse for the repercussions to the nation as well as his own person. Both have bled profusely. According to the latest survey findings [done in May 2008 before his quit in August] 61% of the Pakistanis believe that Musharraf should be punished for violating the Constitution of the country, only 21 % are in favour of the "forgive and forget" option, while the remaining 18 % did not give any answer.

In a question over imposing 3rd November's Emergency, only 11% believed it was not a mistake, the remaining were split between the "forgive and forget option", favoured by 23%, and the impeachment and dismissal option favoured by 64% and only 2% in this case did not give an answer.'

'The Wall Street Journal' of 15th August 2008 had later mentioned that *'ordinary Pakistanis have been growing more dissatisfied with their president. A recent opinion survey found that 75% of Pakistanis disapproved of his performance, according to the poll, by the International Republican Institute, based in Washington. Two years ago, the president's approval rating was 60%, the survey indicated.'*

When Gen Musharraf imposed his first Martial Law in October 1999, around 70% had favoured his unlawful act according to survey findings of Gallup Pakistan. Till ending 2007 there was a dramatic shift in popular mood since then.

Notwithstanding whom the general populace of Pakistan had voted for in February 2008, the popularity rating was decisively influenced by the divide on the issue of independent judiciary. On the unfavourable ladder

(Bad Rating) Gen Musharraf was on the top at 59 % followed closely by Maulana Fazlur Rehman and Altaf Hussian both at 53 %. It can be assumed that perhaps Gen Musharraf wanted to quit honourably, but his so called companions had misled him with false hopes and encouraged him to remain in tact with the power game without merit. Against another question about the General's perceived source of strength, the 47 % of the sample [of the people] opted for 'the United States', 26 % opted for 'the Armed Forces', 8 % opted for 'the people of Pakistan', 14 % opted to choose *'He has no power any longer'* and the remaining 5% did not answer.

It was an irony of fate that Pakistan's army dictator had no acumen to read the message [of the public opinion] though it was clearly written on the front wall.

Referring to *'Thaindian News' dated 28th May 2008*, Gen Musharraf was seen under pressure to quit from almost all quarters including his former aides in the army. Former Gen Jamshed G Kiani and Gen Majid appearing on TV debates had blatantly criticised Musharraf's policies as president and chief of the army staff and demanded his resignation. Till then 26 former Generals in various meetings had issued the same like demands. The same week Asif Ali Zardari had openly said that *'it would be better if Musharraf quits himself otherwise he may be impeached.'*

In November 2007, Gen Musharraf had taken oath as the 'civilian president' but declared the Army House Rawalpindi as his Camp Office. During May 2008, a petition was filed by one Farooq Hassan under Article 184 A in the Supreme Court urging to get vacated the Army House. *'He has illegally occupied the Army House,'* the petitioner urged. The Defence ministry had already moved the PM Office to get it vacated. The only hope for Gen Musharraf was from the US admin to persuade the PPP, the then ruling party, to allow him to continue as president and for this purpose Deputy Secretary of State John Negroponte and two US Senators were also called in Pakistan but Mr Zardari had told the US team quite openly that *'given the opinion of the Pakistani people, there is no room to allow Gen Musharraf to stay on.'*

Gen Musharraf had to quit anyway.

Wikileaks disclosed in the first week of *December 2010* that Mr Zardari and the Army Chief Gen Kayani had worked separately for the 'honourable exit' of Gen Musharraf and ultimately had agreed to give at least Guard of Honour for the later on his departure. However, both Mr Zardari and Gen Kayani had started distancing themselves from Gen

Musharraf in a very calculated way. During the US Admiral Mike Mullen's visit to Pakistan in early 2008, the US Ambassador Anne Patterson had briefed him that:

> '..... As expected, Gen Kayani is taking slow but deliberate steps to distance the Army from now civilian President Musharraf. The army Generals would need his permission to meet the President [a move apparently aimed at denying the beleaguered former military ruler from lobbying for his further extension as head of state].
>
> ..... Zardari blamed President Musharraf for not taking enough responsibility for the war on terrorism in Pakistan which resulted in a marked increase in anti-American sentiments in the country. Anti-US feeling will go away when the old faces go away adding that the US government should no longer rely on just Musharraf in fighting terrorism.'

Detailed reading of some of these [Wikileaks] cables had suggested that by that time all three major players, Mr Zardari, Gen Kayani and the US Ambassador, had made up their minds that 'the time was up for the former military ruler'. The cables also hinted that Gen Kayani had been drawing benefits from Gen Musharraf's mistakes while dealing with the Parliament and PPP's government on issues pertaining to the Tribal areas and Pak-Afghan borders.

DROP SCENE OF A GENERAL'S DRAMA:

'The Economic Times' of 29th May 2008 had also brought the facts to the lime light that Gen Musharraf had made up his mind to quit Presidency in few days in order to avail a safe passage and to avoid pre-empted moves from the PPP government to impeach him. Even his close aides were expecting an announcement in that regard any time. They were of the view that after losing all hopes of survival in power, the President had made up his mind to lead a retired life. One of the closest officers told that:

> 'There is no question of any extra-constitutional step by him or on his behalf. The President has lost the capacity to invoke constitutional provisions like 58(2)(b), dissolving the assembly and the government. The question of introducing an impeachment motion would not come as the President will leave office and get a safe passage. The drop scene of the drama that started on 9th March 2007 is bound to appear any time soon. Gen Musharraf has consented to leave the Army House immediately [when the petition of Barrister Farooq Hasan was

accepted by the Supreme Court] and he may move to the President House within 48 hours before calling it a day.'

In ending May 2008, Gen Musharraf held a marathon meeting with the Army Chief Gen Kayani in urgency; described as an 'extremely important', at the Army House Rawalpindi which continued till after midnight lasting for about four hours. This was their longest 'one on one' encounter, and it assumed significance in view of the then political and security situation in the country. Gen Musharraf was left with no option but to quit. He had already been briefed by 'important officials' not to think about any step that may further aggravate the fragile political situation in the country.

Meanwhile, Brig Aasim Salim Bajwa [*who had served Gen Musharraf as his military secretary in his initial days and was made commander of the Triple-One Brigade by the General himself before relinquishing the office of the Army Chief*] had been ordered to 'take care' of the presidency and its occupant. 111 Brigade of 10 Corps is responsible for the security of the president, federal capital and Rawalpindi. This Brigade has always played a main role in staging coups in the past including that of 12th October 1999.

'The Wall Street Journal' of 15th August 2008 had finally broken the news that Gen Musharraf, a close US ally, was likely to resign [soon] following secret talks aimed at easing his departure. Pakistan's Parliament was expected to take up impeachment proceedings against him. Gen Musharraf continued to tell his supporters that he would fight the impeachment charges but, broken within himself, he had decided to depart. He was waiting for the final signal: guarantee of safe passage and immunity from prosecution. There were only 48 hours in between.

The US was only concerned that how Pakistan would behave in post-Musharraf era. The changing activities of the ISI had increased the American's worries. They were not much anxious about Gen Musharraf who was undergoing intensifying political pressure to leave his Presidential office. Pakistan's coalition government, led by his political opponents, was preparing a list of impeachment charges, mainly based on his declaration of 3rd November 2007's Emergency. Before that he was re-elected to a five-year term as president in a controversial vote by an electoral college.

Federal Information Minister Sherry Rehman had admitted that the coalition had finalised the charge sheet against Gen Musharraf and handed over to the Law Ministry for preparation as a legal document. The President could exercise his 'constitutional right' to resign and ultimately he used that option to save his skin and to avoid embarrassment.

Under Gen Musharraf's leadership, strong economic growth helped create a broad and politically demanding middle class; a plus point. His relaxation of government controls over television media was also appreciated but it created political dissent in the people who wanted democracy. His failure to deal decisively with Muslim extremists had undermined his authority with many voters. All negative aspects were ignored because of good economic achievements but a fatal mistake, cracking down on Pakistan's judicial system, took him to horns and ultimately he lost the whole game. *'The leaders of this country will have to realize that something has changed in the country, if they don't perform, the people will agitate. The old ways are no longer appropriate,'* a parliamentary watchdog group had commented.

Gen Musharraf's supporters like PML(Q) openly and the MQM secretly continued to suggest him that he should resist being driven out. He had told a group of about 40 officials to *'fight back the impeachment'* believing that he still had the votes to prevail. *'No, he's not going to quit'*, the former Railways Minister Sh Rashid Ahmed had told after meeting the General. *'He's not going to give in to this pressure; he has the ability to resist.'* Sh Rashid pressed, however, Gen Musharraf's resistance went weakened. Perhaps he got more disappointed when many of his former supporters had joined a series of resolutions in provincial assemblies calling on him to hold a no confidence vote in the Parliament, or to resign. Gen Musharraf's narrowing corner was apparent when the Balochistan Assembly adopted a unanimous resolution similar to the country's other three provincial Assemblies, asking him to quit or face a vote of confidence.

India's leading newspaper *'The Hindu'* had reported *on 16th August 2008* that Pakistan's ruling coalition kept up the pressure on Gen Musharraf to resign before it moved an impeachment motion against him while a senior prince of the Saudi royal family had also visited Pakistan to negotiate Gen Musharraf's safe exit otherwise he would have been kept there for accountability and prosecution by the PPP & PML(N) jointly.

According to TV reports, Prince Muqrin bin Abdul Aziz, the head of Saudi intelligence, who had played a lead role in preventing PML(N) leader Nawaz Sharif's return in September 2007, was back in Pakistan this time to negotiate a safe exit for Gen Musharraf. He met the President during his one-day visit and also Mr Sharif in Lahore to convince the PML(N) leader to give the embattled Gen Musharraf a "safe exit." Nawaz Sharif had agreed but on condition that Gen Musharraf would not speak to the media for four months. Major Gen Rashid Qureshi, however like a good subordinate, kept on denying Gen Musharraf's meeting with the Saudi Prince and at the same time urging that *'he was guilty of nothing so why quit'*.

Pakistan's army also remained aloof. The Army Chief Gen Kayani had taken the military out of politics although he had made it clear to the government that they would not see their former chief humiliated or disgraced.

Finally, *on 18th August 2008,* Gen Musharraf had to resign from the office of the President to avoid his impeachment which was on cards then.